THE COW IN THE ELEVATOR

TULASI SRINIVAS

THE COW IN THE ELEVATOR   An Anthropology of Wonder

Duke University Press · Durham and London · 2018

Printed and bound by CPI Group (UK) Ltd, Croydon, CR0 4YY
Text designed by Courtney Leigh Baker
Cover designed by Julienne Alexander
Typeset in Minion Pro by Westchester Publishing Services

Library of Congress Cataloging-in-Publication Data
Names: Srinivas, Tulasi, author.
Title: The cow in the elevator : an anthropology of wonder / Tulasi
    Srinivas.
Description: Durham : Duke University Press, 2018. | Includes
    bibliographical references and index.
Identifiers: LCCN 2017049281 (print) | LCCN 2017055278 (ebook)
ISBN 9780822371922 (ebook)
ISBN 9780822370642 (hardcover : alk. paper)
ISBN 9780822370796 (pbk. : alk. paper)
Subjects: LCSH: Ritual. | Religious life—Hinduism. | Hinduism and
    culture—India—Bangalore. | Bangalore (India)—Religious life
    and customs. | Globalization—Religious aspects.
Classification: LCC BL1226.2 (ebook) | LCC BL1226.2 .S698 2018
    (print) | DDC 294.5/4—dc23
LC record available at https://lccn.loc.gov/2017049281

Cover art: The Hindu goddess Durga during rush hour traffic.
    Bangalore, India, 2013. FotoFlirt / Alamy.

For my wonderful mother,
Rukmini Srinivas

CONTENTS

My own efforts to describe practices and processes of wonder in temples in the Malleshwaram neighborhood of Bangalore are dense with a multilingual sociality that is the background of all social interaction in Bangalore. There was constant and endless talk in many different languages—Tamil, Kannada, Hindi, and English—combined with the ethnopoetics of gesture. This linguistic and cultural diversity is not easy to represent. It needs to be tracked through its moves, its imagination, its sites of encounters, and its permeability and vulnerabilities. I have tried different ways that I can imagine to make the reader aware of this rich linguistic and cultural field including dense descriptive interludes, reproduced stories, and explanations.

I have used ethnopoetic notations in an effort to evoke the intensely elaborate linguistic and imaginative poetics of the area. I use italicized lettering at the first use of an Indian-language word, ellipses to indicate pauses, and occasional speech patterns to evoke the dialectical difference from Standard English.

Usually, when quoting a devotee, priest, or ritual practitioner, I give the source language in text, and then for clarity, I translate the non-English words and indicate the source language within parentheses; so, often, the Kannada, Tamil, Hindi, or Sanskrit words appear within the body of the text followed by the English translation with the source language within parentheses, such as *ammelai* (Kannada: afterward). In some cases, for easy reading I use the English translation within the text in which case the original language will occur within parentheses. Brackets are reserved for glosses in translated materials.

Occasionally, I use a Sanskrit word that is known to specialist scholars, so I merely translate in parentheses without references to language of origin. In yet other cases where the word has filtered into English-language usage, such as the word *karma*, I do not translate after the first usage, nor do I italicize, except when it is used as word qua word, as done here. All words spoken in English in quotations are marked within secondary quotations, so they appear as "Original-language quotation 'Super! Okay.'"

In contrast to standard academic transliteration of Indian-language terms, I have usually elected not to use diacritics, on the assumption that this is an ethnographic text and those who do know Indian languages will not need diacritics to correctly pronounce the word. Rather, I render transliterations as close as possible to what will result in correct English pronunciation. Thus, I render both ś and ṣ as *sh*; for example, *shakti* (spiritual power) rather than *śakti*. Further, I have indicated aspirated consonants with an *h*—for example, *chaturthi* (the fourth day), such as Ganesha Chaturthi—rather than rendering the word according to the standard academic transliteration of *caturthi*. In direct quotations from authors who have used diacritics, the diacritics will be indicated as in the original; in these cases, the reader will notice, for example, spellings of Shiva as Siva, or Vishnu as Visnu. I have indicated Indian-language terms (except for proper nouns) with italics.

Many terms in this book are shared across Indian languages with slightly different pronunciations, and thus transliterations. For example, in Sanskrit, the name of the god Rama is pronounced with the final *-a*, but in Hindi it is pronounced as Ram, without the final *-a*. Other terms have greater variations; for example, the festival of lights may be called Divali or Dipavali (lit., row of lights). Throughout this text, I will use the Sanskrit transliteration for proper names (Rama, Ganesha) and will add a Sanskrit ending for other nouns (such as *prasadam*) though I will use the more common *darshan* instead of *darshanam*, since these are closer to the vernacular pronunciations used by my collaborators in Bangalore. I also retain the Sanskrit transliteration for *dharma*, both because I draw on and employ definitions of dharma that are outlined in Sanskritic texts and because my collaborators used Sanskrit terms.

Lastly, I retain the name *Bangalore* for continuity throughout the text since that was the city's name when I began fieldwork, though in keeping with many place names in India, it has since reverted to its precolonial name of Bengaluru.

ACKNOWLEDGMENTS

I did not originally set out to write on wonder. This study began life almost twenty years ago as a fragile and unwieldy text on ritual life. My purpose at that time was quite clear to me. It was to write about changes in ritual life in Bangalore as a local case of globalization. But as I looked at my notes, I began to notice how frequently descriptions of the inexplicable and the wondrous lurked. My overstuffed and nervous notes were rife with people describing the conditions of wonder. Some might say I got distracted from discussing religion and globalization. But I learned that the true nature of wonder was to turn the strange and the unexpected into a force of redemption, to use wonder to think about globalization from a different perspective.

Over the years, my original advisors been very supportive of this transformed endeavor. Nur Yalman and Robert P. Weller have been amazing, and Michael M. J. Fischer took the trouble to visit me in Bangalore.

This study would not have been possible without the care of my parents, Rukmini and M. N. Srinivas. They welcomed me back home in 1998. They were generous with their time, ideas, and friends, and they made the return to Bangalore a real pleasure. My mother's warmth and intelligence, her faith and love, and the wonderful meals and conversations she offered made my life easy. My father's amusement at my gaffes in the field, and his delight at sharing the experience of fieldwork, his gentle counsel, and generous offer of reading lists, stay with me.

My in-laws, Mr. Venkatachar and Vanalakshmi, provided me an alternate home closer to Malleshwaram, filled with warmth and good food. To them and to their extended families I owe a great deal. While doing fieldwork, my husband's young cousin Sharath Srinivasan was invaluable help. In the twenty years since, he has become one of the neoliberal elite of the city, a tribute to his hard work and dedication. Thanks to my friends Surabhi and Ravi Parthasarathy, Manisha Karekar and Seshadri Vasan, Suri Hosakoppal and Sadhana, Subhashini and Vasanth, Sudarshan Holla, Ravina and Sunder Belani, Aditya Sondhi, and Krishna and Aruna Chidambi, who have been unceasingly hospitable to me in Bangalore.

At the National Institute of Advanced Study in Bangalore, my home institution during the period of original fieldwork in 1998–99, I would like to thank the then director, Dr. Roddam Narasimha, for his support; the late Dr. Ravinder Kapur and his wife, Mala Kapur, for their friendship; the late Dr. Raja Ramanna; Professor Sundar Sarukkai and Dhanu Nayak; Hamsa Kalyani, the wonderful librarian, and Manjunath, her scientist-spouse; and Mr. Srinivas Aithal, an indefatigable problem solver. Other colleagues in Bangalore have followed my research and helped in innumerable ways, small and large. Thank you to Professor G. K. Karanth of the Institute of Social and Economic Change, who encouraged my first publication on this material, and to Dr. Kanthi Krishnamurthy for arranging an invitation to speak at Azim Premji University in 2015, thanks to Dr. Carol Upadhya for an invitation to speak at NIAS, the National Institute of Advanced Studies.

But despite the joy of friends, the writing of an inquiry into wonder has been an exercise in sustained suffering, over many continents, for which I was utterly unprepared. Some generous scholars have made this long journey worthwhile. A part of the writing took place in the delightful German town of Bochum. I am indebted to the director of the Kate Hamburger Kolleg at Ruhr-Universitat Bochum, Professor Dr. Volkhard Krech, and Dr. Sven Bretfeld, who invited me to Bochum in 2013 and made my stay there wonderful. During this fellowship year in Germany, I gave a talk in Goettingen, at the Center for Modern Indian Studies, which helped shape my thinking on ritual creativity. I thank Rupa Viswanath, Nate Roberts, Srirupa Roy, Peter Van der Veer, Tam Ngo, and Patrick Eisenlohr. Particular thanks to my research partner in Germany, Dr. Andrew McDowell, now of L'École des Hautes études en Sciences Sociales, Paris, without whose support and intellectual help this book would not have progressed much beyond its first incarnation.

The road of writing about wonder was incalculable to its end in the sense that the process always extends beyond maps employed to negotiate its confusing intersections, switchbacks, and very *longue durée*. The initial research was supported in part by the Pew Charitable Trust and the Lily Endowment and by postdoctoral fellowships at the Center for the Study of World Religions, Harvard University, and the Institute on Culture, Religion and World Affairs, Boston University. I thank my advisor and friend Peter L. Berger, then director, Institute on Culture, Religion and World Affairs. I am grateful to Charles and Cherry Lindholm and Merry White for their warm friendship, to Michael Herzfeld for his hospitality and mind-numbing puns, and to Michael Puett for his generosity in sharing his work on ancient Chinese ritual thought.

My women friends and colleagues—Sarah Pinto, Antoinette DeNapoli, Namita Dharia, Arthi Devarajan, Jenn Ortegren, and Hanna Kim—read various sections of the text and were generous and timely with valuable comments and suggestions. Hayden Kantor patiently helped me track down several stubborn citations, and Andrew Hutcheson took such incredible photographs that they gave me fuel for thought on wonder. I am grateful to my colleagues at Emerson College, who have been very supportive of making time for me to continue with my research. Deans Jan Andersen and Amy Ansell, and colleagues Samuel Binkley, Elizabeth Baeten, John Anderson, and Pablo Muchnick deserve special mention for their warmth and support. I would also like to thank Dr. Wolf for his resolute belief in this project.

This book owes its genesis and completion to Harvard University, where my cohort mates in the Theory of Anthropology core class—Nicole Newendorp, Vanessa Fong, Sisa Dejesus, Sonja Plesset, and Erica James—helped me conceptualize this study. More recently, it was completed at the Radcliffe Institute for Advanced Study, where Dean Liz Cohen, the director of the fellows program, Judy Vichniac, and her incredible team help create an academic idyll that fostered my thinking. I thank my research partners at the Radcliffe, Julia Fine and Apoorva Rangan, for their help in editing this manuscript.

I began speaking about ritual and emotion initially in 2012 at Cornell and Syracuse universities. Thanks to Dan Gold of Cornell and Ann Gold, Susan Wadley, Joanna Waghorne, and Tula Goenka at Syracuse University. Portions of this work have been presented at the American Association of Religion meetings in 2011; the South Asia meetings at Madison, Wisconsin, in 2011; the American Academy of Arts and Sciences; and the Department of Religious Studies at the University of Kent at Canterbury in 2011. I am grateful to my friend Jeremy Carrette of the University of Kent, who first invited me to speak on wonder at the fiftieth anniversary of the British Association of Studies of Religion. Jennifer Ratner-Rosenhagen and her spouse, Ulrich Rosenhagen, of Madison, Wisconsin, both scholars of religion, gave me a venue to work through my thoughts on wonder at their conference on Rudolph Otto. Thanks to Ulrich and his sister, Anna, I got a tour of the fleshpots of Hamburg just before I began the fieldwork, which put the ethical lives and moral concerns of the Malleshwaram priests into perspective, and thanks to Jennifer, who so generously shared thoughts and readings with me. Francis X. Clooney and Anne Monius of the Center for the Study of World Religions were kind to invite me to speak at their colloquium as I worked through some of the material. Levi McLaughlin invited me to North Carolina State University and was so generous with his time, and Lauren Levy arranged for my talk at UNC Chapel Hill, where I met the amazing Leela Prasad, who, with one or two insights, elevated my interest in ritual and ethics in Karnataka. I am grateful too to James Bielo and his colleagues at Miami University at Oxford, Ohio, for inviting me to give a keynote lecture at their conference on Religion and Creativity, and for booking me to stay in an amazing nineteenth-century midwestern farmhouse. Lindsay Harlan gave me a lovely evening at her beautiful home during a visit to speak at Connecticut College, and Richard Sosis's invitation to the University of Connecticut came at an opportune moment as I was wrapping up this book.

In New Zealand, my thanks go to Will Sweetman, Ben Schoenthol, and the members of the Australian and New Zealand Association of Religious Studies not only for an invitation to speak at their national meetings but for the wonder of being able to see the endangered Kea parrot in its cloud forest. While watching the parrots, their innate curiosity and sense of playful mischief, it only takes a bit of insight to see how creative and improvisational enterprises might lead us back to enrich and enliven our original intentions.

I am particularly grateful to Kirin Narayan, a wonderful friend, who after a long flight from Australia listened to my endless stories of the field and stopped me in midsentence to ask incredulously, "A cow in an elevator?" and to add with conviction, "That's the title of the book." My gratitude to her not only for the gift of the title but for her generosity in sharing writing tips and references, and for remembering the perfect epigraph for this volume from her school Sanskrit recitations.

But the *longue durée* of writing and thinking does not mean that we are fated to be perpetually and thoroughly lost, only that our plans and explanations will remain partial and provisional to be joyfully overturned by the uncanny swerves of contingency where expected plans take a creative detour. The serendipity of running into Ken Wissoker on the street in Denver is a moment of wonder. His patience as I stumbled through a description of this work and his wise counsel during the process of getting it to publication make me forever grateful. He, Elizabeth Ault, Susan Albury, and their team have been all that an author could desire. Additionally, I would like to thank the anonymous reviewers who read and commented on the manuscript with such precision and insight.

But centrally, thanks are due to the two priests Krishna Bhattar and Dandu Shastri, and the localites of Malleshwaram. They bore my presence and my frequently annoying and nosy questions with good grace and saw to the task of educating me with kindness. They have given me so much material that this work is the beginning of a two-part book series on Bangalore—a bi-logy, as it were. They saw the pursuit of wonder as a joyful opportunity and in doing so they attuned me to the dawning truth of the importance of the imagination seen beyond disciplinary horizons. It is their devotion, instruction, and creativity that I acknowledge in this work. It is their friendship that I cherish.

Most importantly, my gratitude is to my family. They understood better than did I that through acts of the imagination, we can make a meaningful home. Thanks to my mother, Rukmini Srinivas, to whom I owe such a profound debt that the contours of it are indistinguishable. She is generous with her time and her emotions, and has made so many sacrifices to make my world tenable for me.

Thanks also to my wonderful sister and colleague, Lakshmi Srinivas of the University of Massachusetts, Boston, for her pertinent analytical comments, her storytelling ability, and her sense of humor. When I was down, she would always pick me back up, despite her own writing concerns. Our continuous and wide-ranging discussions about contemporary India, preferably over cups of tea and some cake, have formed the foreground and the background of this book.

And finally, thanks to my spouse, Popsi Narasimhan, who cheerfully packed up our house in Boston and moved "back home" to Bangalore for my fieldwork. In the past twenty years, he has tirelessly dealt with the daily mundanities of our everyday life in Boston, of getting our pet parrots fed and the bills paid, while I mentally inhabited a world in far-off Bangalore. Writing can be a selfish act, and he has been unceasingly supportive of my selfishness in this regard. I am full of gratitude to him for making this, and other explorations of wonder in our lives together, possible.

Tulasi Srinivas
Cambridge, Massachusetts

O Wonderful!

Haavu! Haavu! Haavu!
Aham-annam Aham-annam Aham-annam
Aham-annaado Aham-annaado Aham-annaaadah
Aham-asmi Prathamajaa Ritaasya Poorvam Devebhyo-amritasya Naabhaayi!
Bhuvanamabhyabhavaam
Suvarna Jyotih
Ya Evam Veda Ity'upanishat
Aum Shanti Shanti Shanti!!

O Wonderful! O Wonderful! O Wonderful!
I am food, I am food, I am the food
I am the eater, I am the eater, I am the eater
I am the poet, the scholar, the saint
First born
Earlier than the gods, in the center of immortality.
I have overcome the whole world
I am effulgent!
He who knows this, such is the secret doctrine.
Aum peace, peace, peace!!

—From the *Taittreya Upanishad*

WONDER, CREATIVITY, AND ETHICAL LIFE IN BANGALORE

Anthropology demands the open-mindedness with which one must look and listen, record in astonishment and wonder that which one would not have been able to guess.
—Margaret Mead, *Sex and Temperament in Three Primitive Societies*

You tell stories. Our stories. Telling stories and doing this *kainkaryam* [ritual] is the "same." They both help us dream of a better place.
—Krishna Bhattar, chief priest, Krishna Temple

Cranes in the Sky

August 28th, 1998. Ganesh Visarjana Festival, Malleshwaram, Bangalore city.

On the fourth day in the second half of the lunar month of Bhadrapaada, as happened annually, Hindus were celebrating the festival of Ganesha Chathurthi.[1] In Hindu mythology, the elephant-headed god Ganesha is a protectionary deity with a gargantuan appetite who removes obstacles in the lives of humans. According to custom, a ten-foot-high, brightly colored clay image of the deity was installed in a makeshift pavilion at the popular Ganesha Temple in the neighborhood of Malleshwaram in the city of Bangalore.

Ten days later, on the fourteenth day of the waxing moon known as Ananda Chaturdashi—day of ecstasy—the deity was ceremonially immersed in a local body of water, an annual rite of propitiation and leave-taking, or *visarjana*.

On the day of the visarjana, under dreary gray skies, I, along with several hundred devotees, waited at the temple. Consummate ritual participants knew where they could sit comfortably and wait, and they hung about in small groups under the trees and on the temple steps, chatting desultorily about family, food, and friends.

Suddenly, an enormous, blinding-yellow lorry arrived at the temple gate, honking its loud "heehaw" klaxon horn. On the flatbed was a gilded, crystal-covered, peacock-shaped palette illuminated by rotating lighting chains that spun in a whirling dial behind the lorry's cab. A huge klieg light mounted to the cab sent a single ray deep into the night sky. It was bedazzled and dazzling. The assembled crowd shouted, "*Ayyoo! Nodu, nodu!* [Kannada: Amazing! Look, look!]," nudging one another to take notice.

As the lorry lurched into the temple courtyard, temple-goers scattered and leapt aside. Dandu Shastri, the *pradhan archakar*—chief priest of the temple—took charge. He quickly organized the crowd of neophyte priests, devotees, and hangers-on and had them load the heavy clay deity onto the palette, which held a wooden *mantap*—pavilion—decorated with flower chandeliers. Once the deity was loaded, the driver pressed a switch, and the sound of "Ganesha Sharam, Sharanam Ganesha!," coordinated with flashing lights, blasted into the wet evening air.[2] The delighted devotees exclaimed, "*Bombhat! Su-per! First class!*" They crowded closer, pressing me against the dented green fender of the lorry. Seated on the cab, the priest Dandu Shastri noticed me and asked, clearly expecting a delighted reply, "*Yeppidi irruku?* [Tamil: How is it?]." As we began our procession to the nearby Sankey tank, a local man-made lake, I assured him I had seen nothing like it.[3]

The procession wound through Malleshwaram, rerouting frequently to avoid construction rubble, evidence of the endless building of the city. Cranes and scaffolding rose into the dark sky, a lacy network drawing solid gray boxlike apartment buildings out of the earth. Despite a rolling blackout and the dangerous pits in the street where the government had been inefficiently laying power lines for months, residents poured out of the buildings, drawn first by the ray of the klieg light piercing the sky and then the lights of the procession as it got closer. They prayed in the streets, bowing in submission, thrilled at the serendipitous *darshan*, or sacred sighting. Delighted with this audience, Dandu Shastri stood beaming on top of the truck's cab.

An hour and a half later, we arrived at the edge of Sankey tank just as the sun, low in the sky, emerged from behind the clouds. At the water's edge, new luxury apartment buildings gleamed, while in the distance the ghostly outlines of more tall cranes were visible, marking where a brand new skyline was slated to emerge.

Several other processions had arrived before us. Near the shore, all the activity had churned the water into a deep coffee-brown polluted by the scum and detritus of worship: overripe fruit, sodden flower garlands, torn plastic bags, cups, and dripping clay oil lamps floating in the water. The bands of devotees struggled to plow into water deep enough to successfully immerse their deities. Many gave up and deposited their deities too close to shore, only to have them sink partially, a portent of misfortune in the coming year.

From the cab of the truck, blocked from sight by the blinding glare of the klieg lights, I heard Dandu Shastri exhort the young priests, "*Time bandbit-tide! Bega, bega!* [Kannada: Time has come! Hurry up!]." The crowd parted, expecting—as did I—that a crowd of youth would swarm onto the lorry to carry the deity into the lake and submerge it.

Instead, the lorry itself seemed to respond to Dandu's call. Growling and whining, an enormous mechanical crane emerged from its base and towered over the cab. The tracks of blue spotlights outlining its frame lent it a surreal, unearthly glow as it slowly unfurled to a huge metal hook at its end, from which dangled the palette, the deity—and Dandu Shastri. The hook had painted omniscient, heavy-lidded eyes in the style of popular calendar art depictions of the god Shiva. The crowd gasped at the unexpected sight and rocked back on its collective heels, pressing me further against the cab.

The crane lifted the palette and the deity swung slowly out over the water. The devotees, now joined by several hundred bystanders, craned their necks for a better view as Dandu Shastri performed the leave-taking *puja* (worship) on the swinging palette high above the water. He garlanded the deity and the crane, hook and all, and offered the one techno-divinity, wondrous in its fusion and terrifying in its monstrosity, the sacred camphor flame. The crowd roared their approval, chanting their hopes for the god's return the next year, "*Ganesha banda! Kai kadubu thinda, Chikkerenall bidda, Doddkerelle yed-dha!* [Kannada: Ganesha came! He ate all the sweets, he fell in the small lake and then rose in the big one!]."

The crane extended further out over the water, casting its kaleidoscopic reflections over the waves, thousands of blue-lit fractal images of the deity. Devotees around me clapped and exclaimed, "*Ashcharya vagi idde!* [Kannada: It's amazing!]." Others clicked their tongues in surprise; young men

FIGURE I.1. Flatbed truck holding Ganeshas for immersion.
Photo by Sharath Srinivasan.

emitted piercing whistles and lighting fireworks. Amid the chanting, whooping, whistling, clapping, and the sounding of the lorry's klaxon horn, the deity was released into the deep water, where it sank quickly and completely. Mrs. Shankar Gowda, a local temple-goer and connoisseur of ritual, turned to me and gave a succinct and emphatic summation of the evening's events, *"Adbhutha vagi itthu!* [Kannada: It was wondrous!]."

Beaming as he was swung back over our heads and deposited on solid ground, Dandu was clearly delighted by the success of the new technology of immersion. He stayed for the next hour, accepting the crowd's congratulations and speaking to every single person.

AS EVIDENCED BY the events just described, this work offers an ethnography of amazement, of wonder as a sublime yet everyday experience that emerges and evolves in the performance of ritual in the temples of Bangalore city in South India.[4] My thesis on wonder is simple. I propose that wonder is apparent in everyday ritual in Bangalore, and that practices of wonder align with moments of ritual creativity or improvisation that occur sporadically but then sediment and become instituted as part and parcel of the ritual. Wonder is both a symptom and a mode of challenge to existing ontological assumptions about being and becoming, a tiny space of resistance that stands within the brokenness and precarity of everyday life in the city.

Victor Turner, *the* student of ritual life, suggests that ritual is a liminal mode of being, a threshold state that is momentary and delimited. In that threshold state, ritualists are encouraged in a collective bonding, which in turn allows resistance to the larger society in limited, carefully circumscribed moments that can quickly be domesticated. He terms this bounded space "anti-structure" and the statis that precedes and follows it "structure" (1969a; 1969b). The key of anti-structure is its ephemerality—that when the ritual ends, or soon thereafter, practitioners fall back into the familiarity and solidity—the durability of structure. For Turner, the statis of structure is eternal and normative. "Disturbances of the normal and regular," he writes, such as conflict and ritual, "merely give us greater insight into the everyday and the normal" (1974, 34). While that is certainly true, Turner's privileging of the fixity of structure as the valid metric of society makes the anti-structure of ritual valuable only as its counterpoint. Anthropologists have largely understood ritual as a sacred process for domestication of dangerous forces both within us and without, to lend stability to structure. So most studies of ritual have focused on the efficacy of the process (Seligman et al. 2008, 368–70; Puett 2013).[5] This is understandable, for after all, durability is the desired state for the society at large, and efficacy of process is valuable. But the notion of fixity has long been overvalued; in contrast, we must also look at the changes and creativity in rituals (Michaels 2016). After witnessing the truck procession and hundreds of other examples like it where wonder and amazement broke through in Bangalore, I wondered, what if the desired state is not stability but fracture? What if today the pursuit of wonder is the point of ritual rather than the quick return to the solidity of structure?

The conversations and exclamations overheard during that visionary immersion convinced me that for ritual practitioners, the moment of fracture contained within the extraordinariness of ritual is the space in which they want to linger.[6] For the practitioners at Sankey tank, the moment that wonder struck was *the* transformative moment, a fracture of the ordinary not merely for the individual, or even for the society, but for the world at large.[7] Jonathan Z. Smith, a scholar of religion, suggests that ritual is "a mode of paying attention" (1987, 104), of attending more closely to the habitus, the *doing* of religion in Hinduism. This book is an invitation to pay attention to this particular mode of paying attention and thus attain a new understanding of contemporary Hindu ritual process that orients toward this fracture— toward wonder.

Indeed, in turning to wonder, what is made apparent is that the processes of ritual interact with new capitalist economies in Malleshwaram and conscript a capitalist bewitchment to a ritual wonder. I explore how priests and ritual practitioners in Malleshwaram co-create wondrous experiences through creative temple rituals that resist, appropriate, replace, and recast modern capitalism—the mechanism of their precariousness.[8] Through the use of creative ritual, they grant themselves agency (*adhikara*) to express and build their own futures through their practices and theologies.[9] A consideration of wonder shifts our focus from textual treatises and tradition to discourses and practices of emotion, expression, and creativity.[10] This allows for the *process* of making,[11] crafting, and manufacturing worlds, possibilities, and dispositions, in its embryonic and collaborative stages. I argue that the changes in ritual—ritual creativity—are the pursuit of the transformative moment of wonder, the impractical and magical, in which religious identity shifts to be located in the emergence and poetics of praxis rather than in the fixed constructions of doctrinal orthodoxy. I document this world-making work of the wondrous (Ramberg 2014) toward a new understanding of ritual process (Durkheim [1915] 1995; Turner 1968, 1969b; Orsi 2005) in which ritual is creative, built through iterative miniscule improvisations for a world in which wonder comes alive.[12]

Ritual process is composed of miniscule iterative small shifts. These small shifts in process, the micro process of ritual, appear dialectical—by which I mean they both rupture and capture elements of ritual life and theology and forms of neoliberal life and ideology simultaneously—but they are dialogic in that they converse and build on one another. This rupture-capture process is what allows for the endemic creativity within the space of fracture that ritual produces despite the overarching precariousness of everyday life in Malleshwaram (Bateson 1936).

Wondering about Wonder

What exactly *is* wonder?[13] The *Oxford English Dictionary* defines wonder as "the emotion excited by the perception of something novel and unexpected," and extending to an "astonishment mingled with perplexity or bewildered curiosity." As an essential definition, it brings to the forefront the little that we know about wonder: its extraordinariness, suddenness, and seemingly divine-like rupturing of the mundane (Vasalou 2015). Descriptions of the experience of wonder are even less concrete: a sudden gasp of surprise; childlike amazement. Wonder is experienced as elusive and ineffable. In an attempt to grasp this slipperiness, Philip Fisher has defined wonder as "a sudden experience of an extraordinary object that produces delight" (1998, 55), which turns us toward the material otherness of the wonderful in an attempt to illuminate an accompanying primary passion that manifests as creativity (Descartes [1649] 1989, 52).[14]

The Western intellectual history of wonder recognizes it as difference that locates sublimity. Beginning with the Greek philosophers Plato and Aristotle, wonder was seen as the internal state of enlightenment, possibly cohabiting with a Socratic *aporia*, a disorientation of passion (Bynum 1997). Platonic and Aristotelian notions of wonder were significantly different: where Aristotle seeks to dissipate wonder and move toward reason and knowledge, Plato attempted to open us to the passions, to vulnerability and joy, to a different kind of knowing (Rubenstein 2008). Both understood that difference provokes wonder. Critical thinkers who wish to link wonder and alterity in their cultural histories or ethics begin in this shared focus on otherness (Greenblatt 1991; Irigaray 2004).[15] This curiosity about the other manifested in the nineteenth century, in the age of exploration and inquiry.[16] Early scientists and doctors understood wonder as that which clung to the mysterious, fueled curiosity, and edged the curious toward experimental knowledge (Cox and Cohen 2011). Wonder, to them, suggested new realities and new possibilities—a mood that can be created and sustained as a way of contesting the received knowledge of the limits to living, as well as a way to transform the ontological possibilities of life itself (Scott 2016, 474–75).

In the twentieth century, the religion scholar Rudolph Otto wrote *Das Hielige* (*The Idea of the Holy*), a treatise on the unknowability and ineffability of wonder. He argued that wonder returned one to a feeling of the "numinous" ([1923] 1958, 15–17), which encompassed, in alphabetical order, awe, bewilderment, curiosity, confusion, dread, ecstasy, excitement, fear, marvel, mystery, perplexity, reverence, supplication, and surprise. It is also a return to passion, as something not to be discredited as lacking reason, as in the Cartesian view, but to be embraced as an interaction with the inexplicable divine. Within Otto's physiognomic context, wonder included not only "the psychological process of affect, but in turn also its object, the holy," a knowable attribute of the "*mysterium tremendum*," the divine ([1923] 1958, 22).

The enduring history of wonder suggests a human need for it. "Deep inside," as Lorraine Daston and Katharine Park suggest, "beneath tasteful and respectable exteriors, we still crave wonders. . . . We wait for the rare and extraordinary to surprise our souls" (2001, 368).

I found the spaces of the temple and the people in them—who referred to themselves as "localites"—to be that surprise to my soul. Like Dandu Shastri, they were joyful, radiant, and full of a radical hope in the possibilities of the future, despite the everyday precarity of their existence on the margins of the global marketplace. They were anxious as they were buffeted by winds of economic and cultural change entirely beyond their control, and it would be all too understandable if they allowed their humanity to be drowned in the resultant sea of dread. But instead, they seemed to be linked at a level of wondrous and joyful knowing. They joked and laughed together as they adored the gods every day. They sang and worshipped in the hope of a new tomorrow.

Their joyful attitude put me in mind of a poem from the *Taittreya Upanishad*, which I include as an epigraph to this work. Written to be sung in a Sama Vedic musical meter, it is estimated to be some 2,500 years old.[17] Toward the end of the text is a section called the "Bhrigu Valli," which tells the story of a seer who suddenly realizes his interconnectedness with the universe of creation, as both the consumer and the consumed, the eater and the eaten, part of the circle of eternal life. The poem is filled with long drawn-out "aaahs," termed *dirgahs* in Sanskrit poetic meter, evidence of the seer's surprised appreciation and his wonder at the connectivity of life. "*Haavu! Haavu! Haavu!*" he breathes, "O Wonderful! O Wonderful! O Wonderful!"

Feeling wonder, as this Upanishadic seer understood, is a practice and a pursuit that forces us back on our intellectual haunches, as it points both beyond itself and into itself, crossing and recrossing, gathering and dissipating, forcing us into new ways of thinking and recording. An experimental regime of ritual in the pursuit of wonder fuels a sense of creativity and of radical hope that I felt localites inhabit in Malleshwaram. But it is important to note that this radical hope does not merely arise in individuals; it is social, a wider net of tough-minded yet ecstatic inspiration to action to create the world of one's imagination.

This radical social hope was unexpected to me, another wondrous surprise. As I watched the shining truck and the deity at the lakeside and heard the crowd's ecstatic response, I understood that social hope is a necessity in neoliberal reality, for neoliberalism argues for a corrosive individuality—biographical solutions for systemic problems—that creates both alienation and constant dread. The hope I found in Malleshwaram created spaces of resistance to this corrosion of neoliberalism, while allowing for a pragmatic capturing of what might work in the moment. This radical social hope is key to anti-alienation, to a sense of feeling and being "at home" in the modern world.

And while hope created action, it is also true that action creates hope. I saw the ways that localites understood that in the everyday lay the opportunity for a resistance to neoliberalism's deadening effects, as well as its joyful reconstruction into something bearable. Here was the everyday building of a resilience in the face of sudden and shattering economic and social change.

And so I argue that we need an *anthropology* of wonder, not only as a counterpoint to wonder's rarified existence in Western philosophical and literary texts but also in order to think about wonder as grounded, as birthed, and as stoked by human beings, and which allows for a social hope to grow in communities despite and against the losses that living in the neoliberal moment bequeaths to us.

Modern Fractures

During the immersion, while everyone was delightedly wonderstruck, I watched the gilt crown of the deity slide quietly into the lake with a feeling of sadness at the loss. After everyone had left, and a handful of the temple habitués were getting ready to return to the temple, Dandu Shastri asked me with concern: " 'Why were you sad? No, No!' *Poyatan but thierripi varavaan! Yedir-pudirru . . . Idde yedirkalam ode pirappu* [Tamil: He left but he will come back! The continuity of the past and the future. This is the birthing of a future!]." His words seemed to offer a "twofold vision of an opaque past and an uncertain future" (de Certeau 1984, 159). Ritual practitioners like Dandu Shastri and Krishna Bhattar, the chief priest of the Krishna Temple, recognize these adjacencies, the space between the lost past and envisioned future, as *the* sites for a necessary genesis of wonder.

Indeed, while writing on ethics in South Asia, Anand Pandian and Daud Ali gesture to these double-faced, Janus-like adjacencies between lost past and envisioned future: "Modernity in South Asia has always been two-faced, looking forward to the challenges of contemporary existence only from the standpoint of the inherited traditions that lend meaning and direction to its futures" (2010, 13). I will argue that through the pursuit of wonder—in which wonder is a rhetorical and aspirational catalyst to create rituals that not only rupture and resist but also embrace and extend modernity's enduring and seductive paradigm—ritual practitioners explore, interrogate, and slyly resist the dominant model of a Western-derived neoliberal modernity to which

FIGURE I.2. Ganesha images on crane floating above the lake. Photo by Sharath Srinivasan.

they are subject,[18] and that these discourses and practices are potentially transformative of contemporary modernity, capturing, yet also rupturing, both past and future conditions. These explorations and resistances are small ethical acts in themselves, and when accumulated, they lead to an interrogation of what constitutes a moral knowing in the contemporary world.

To me the loss of the deity into the lake was weighted with the losses I saw around me in the city that I knew and loved. Bangalore's unchecked development had led to and exacerbated several urban problems: the lack of adequate middle-income housing, water shortages, power cuts, endless traffic jams and attendant pollution, chronic waves of epidemics, breakdown of services, and a complete degradation of the environment (Gadgil and Guha 1995).[19] Under earth movers and power saws, urban sprawl expanded until the city planning authority of Bangalore, the Bruhat Bengaluru Mahanagara

Palike (BBMP), was declared the largest municipal corporation in the country. It was small wonder that land prices rose by 300 percent in about ten years. The horrors of neoliberal development were unleashed on an unprepared city.[20]

Krishna Bhattar, the chief priest of the Krishna Temple in the neighborhood, often spoke with bewilderment and wounded sadness of the contemporary everyday. Following the etymology of the word *wonder* in German, *wunder*, we find an indication of a wound, gash, or fracture, small or large, prolonged or rapid, as well as a response to this fracture. Krishna Bhattar spoke of climbing over piles of rubble in the street, of getting lost in neighborhoods he had visited his entire life because all the landmarks he remembered had changed in six short months, of "catching water" that came in a thin trickle despite the overflowing monsoon rains, of the loss of petrol and time following incomprehensible traffic routes and driving in the opposite direction to our destination to avoid yet more roadwork. This vertiginous disorientation was Nietzschean in its cosmic loss.[21] In my own nostalgia for a city lost, I could relate to Krishna Bhattar's sense of fracture and fragmentation, and it brought us closer.

Neoliberal modernity, a phrase I use frequently in this text and by which I mean the current era of global capitalism that began in the mid-1990s, enlarges this sense of fracture and loss: the continuous loss of good jobs, loss of health, loss of equanimity, the loss of eco-habitat toward endless development, lack of resources evidenced in drought and blackouts, and loss of a sense of community and shared culture. All suggest a "being on the edge," an existential threat that is sudden and life changing yet somehow always present. A billboard in Malleshwaram brought this gestalt to a focus. It seemed to be advertising a heart attack though in reality it was a public awareness campaign of the symptoms of a stroke. It seemed to encapsulate the vulnerability of living in a growing megacity like Bangalore.

Out of my sense of loss at the submersion of the deity in the lake and a subsequent leap of faith into the scene of that loss grew an attempt to record my interlocutors' relationships to both faith as it is understood in practice in non-Christian religious worlds and loss in a contemporary neoliberal moment. Taking that moment as a point of departure, I have sought a willing engagement with the loss and incompleteness of modern life. The work of describing ritual practitioners—priests, devotees, ritualists, witnesses, and storytellers—has brought into view the fruitful acts of doing and undoing, formed through relationships between loss of presence and presence of a deep devotion enacted in practice of ritual acts.

FIGURE I.3. Billboards advertising care for stress-related heart attacks.
Photo by the author.

In the classical literature on ritual and ritual acts, ritual has been understood as embedding itself in routine life but not becoming routinized (Durkheim [1915] 1995; Mauss [1923] 1967; Hertz 2006; Levi-Strauss 1963, 1966). Rituals are a part of everyday ordinary life, yet they allow practitioners to enter another extraordinary state, characterized by an internal, often magical logic. When practitioners step back into the everyday world, they and it are transformed. Anthropologists have understood that ritual as a structure allowed different temporalities to manifest themselves, always, in "another" time while having a narrative continuity with the routine world from which they emerged and returned (Biardeau 1976). For Levi-Strauss, what was surprising was that even though the outcome of ritual was known, yet it enabled a refraction of the world for participants (1966). How this refraction occurred for individuals within the society, and what happened to the structure of the ritual and the society as a result, was the concern of classical ritual studies. More recent schools of thought have rejected this focus on structure, the structure of ritual, or the enduring structure of society, pivoting toward a focus on ritual's efficacy and functionality, its ability to do what it sets out as its objective, what Seligman et al. term its "sincerity" (2008). But what if we are less concerned with structure or function, and more with the processes of ritual refraction?

A reoriented exploration of ritual process toward dynamism suggests that an understanding borne of what ritualists *say* they do and *what* they do over a period of time will move us beyond the pragmatic limitations of what ritual *does* in order to think through what ritual *is*. Or, to put it another way, a focus on what ritual practitioners say they do and what they do moves us from a consideration of efficacy to considerations of imagination, from the depredations of the present to the possibilities in the future. And, if we allow that the ritual practitioners—the Dandu Shastris of this world—have a *philosophy of ritual*, rather than explaining their mores away through philosophy, we require, at the very least, a re-placement of philosophy in anthropological theorizing.

Of Bangalore's Boomtown Bourgeoisie

As my fieldwork continued into the new millennium, luxurious, high-rise gated apartment buildings with gyms, pools, and concierge services became the ideal housing stock of Malleshwaram. Long lines of "foreign" cars such as BMWs and Hondas jockeyed for space in front of the glass walls of Namdari and other organic grocery stores. From being a genteel, elite, upper-caste community of spacious bungalows and gardens for large families, all of whom knew one another, incestuously marrying, feuding, eating, and gossiping, Malleshwaram became a heterogeneous, largely anomic, multiethnic, fast-paced bedroom community of apartment blocks inhabited by career professionals in the information technology (IT) industry. Some were upper caste, but many were dominant or lower-caste educated youth, drawn to Bangalore from all over India. Real estate values in Malleshwaram "hit the roof" while I was doing fieldwork, creating a neighborhood of instant millionaires, land and building rich yet often cash poor, a space of middle-class aspirational dreaming.[22]

It is no accident that this project is set in the megacity of Bangalore at the end of the twentieth and the beginning of the twenty-first centuries, for Bangalore is the home of experimental technology and of "instant" Internet millionaires (Belliappa 2013). The city is the singular home of experimental innovation and creativity in India, the "belly button" of the global IT industry. In the Indian national imagination, Bangalore's "exceptionalism" as a high-tech urban development model made it iconic and emulatable for other Indian cities (L. Srinivas 2016, 2).[23] Its roster of smokeless factories, crucibles of experimentation in the new knowledgeware economy, include many in the global Fortune 500: AT&T, Hewlett Packard (HP), Digital Equipment Corporation (DEC), IBM, Samsung, Texas Instruments, Apple, and Motorola. Recognized as a specialty technology hub linked to circuits of neoliberal capital that span the world, Bangalore has earned the sobriquet "the Silicon Valley of Asia." It is a city on the cutting edge of innovative scientific, biomedical, genetic, and engineering expertise (Harriss 2007, 4). The urban gestalt of Bangalore is one of experimentation and creativity, largely oriented to an entrepreneurial culture but amorphous enough to include varieties of imaginaries and practices.

In 2005–6 the Indian IT industry generated earnings of US$17.8 billion, an enormous amount of foreign exchange for a poor country.[24] The direct employment figures were roughly 1.3 million, which translated into several million other, indirect jobs in a phenomenon that A. Aneesh has referred to as the "liquefaction of labor" (2006, 9), wherein legions of "flexible" labor grew (Beck 1992; Ong 1999). Bangalore's rapid growth was seen as prophetic for wider-spread economic expansion and soon received the dubious distinction of being the "fastest growing city in Asia" (Kripalani and Engardio 2003), marked by the sudden growth of a bourgeois, consumer-hungry, global elite who style themselves as India's "new middle class" (cf. Waghorne 2004; Derné 2008; Brosius 2010; Dickey 2012).[25] In 2016 the estimated population was a staggering 9.8 million, a true boomtown. I was told that the city grows by approximately eight thousand undocumented in-migrants every day.

Yet despite these statistics of a booming growth, Bangalore remains a middle-class city, not a "maximum city" like Suketu Mehta's (2005) Mumbai. It is a medium, middling city—medium originally as scaled to a provincial metric and a small-scale metropolitan imaginary. It is described in Indian government categories as a "second tier" city.[26] Localites are the middle class that populate Bangalore and who see themselves as ambassadors of a new Indian dream of meritocracy and power. Entering Bangalore's middle class is less about income or land or even consumption habits, though they all play a part (Appadurai and Breckenridge 1995; Liechty 2003; Srivastava 2012). It is about learning to act, look, and sound middle class through status-based practices; it is "not merely a question of money but of linguistic and aesthetic knowledge and respectability" (Fernandes 2006, 34). The boomtown bourgeoisie of this thriving city show a muscular "capacity to aspire," a key metric by which the middle class can be defined (Appadurai 2004), allowing as it does for widening sets of possibilities for upward mobility.

IN MALLESHWARAM, A neighborhood to the north of Bangalore, temple ritual is part of the quotidian lives of people, intertwining their devotional life and aspirational mobility. During the time of my study, localites often arrived at the temple to greet the deity as one would an old friend, after an evening stroll, or on their way to or from marketing. They would invite the priests home to perform house blessing and prosperity rituals. Young professionals would sometimes stop on their way to or from work, or dressed up while on their way to a pub or party to pray for a promotion or to bless a newly bought car. Still younger devotees, often in gender-specific bands of four or five, would stop off on their way to school or college, particularly if it was a public examination day. Temple publics were not restricted to within the bounded walls of the temple.[27] Processions and festivals elastically stretched into the neighborhood: physically, materially, and visually through the processions; sensually through temporary wooden gateways decorated with flowers for special pujas; through the scents of cooking *prasadam* (consecrated food) which one staunch scientist pronounced "a heavenly smell"; aurally through the sounds of temple bells and music (which neighbors seemed to enjoy); and through the mythic imagination, the *yedir-puddirru* (Tamil: this and that) of daily life.

Against expectations of growing secularism, India has seen a remarkable and visible growth in ritual acts largely due to the growth of the boomtown bourgeoisie. Funds from the market economy have enabled temples to be built and restored, allowed forgotten pujas to take place, revived ancient ancestor sacrificial ceremonies, and resurrected many deities. Popular spending has reinvigorated the traditional festival calendar, and life-cycle rituals such as weddings, funerals, births, birthdays, house-building, and car-buying celebrations have all been energized and made larger than ever before. Ritual life is full, competitive, and intense, not only because it "makes creation again" but also because it seemingly allows people hope to survive and flourish in times of extreme uncertainty and change (Eliade [1957] 1961, 99–100).[28]

Wonder, and its pursuit, both as discourse and practice, through creative rituals expands imaginaries of the possible, destabilizing the statis of both ritual life and social structure. Shot through with improvisation and ingenious variation, ritual creativity forms an experimental habitus of ritual in which ritual practitioners' iterative ritual creativity sediments into an "experimental Hinduism" set in a precarious urban regime where complex, threatening, and uncertain conditions of the contemporary world feed into the quotidian experience (DeNapoli 2017). Experimental Hinduism here describes a whole world of iterative, strategic, and creative improvisations within and around Hindu rituals as they interact with modernity. Hindus in Malleshwaram link the immediate social, economic, and political tissues of their lives with creative ritual and demonstrate the ongoing relevancy of core Hindu values for dealing with contemporary situations and problems, inspiring people to confront what it means to be Hindu, Indian, moral, and modern as categories of being that are permeable and negotiable (DeNapoli and Srinivas 2016). As these practices help to shape changeable views of power, practice, pluralism, and the problem of how to live with otherness, they sediment into an ongoing interrogation of ethical life.

Krishna Bhattar, Dandu Shastri, and the localites encouraged me to consider the larger question of how these emergent Hindu ritual worlds, defined in the context of Christianity and the colonial definition of religion, resisted and reformed post-Enlightenment European political theology in counterintuitive ways (Asad 1993, 5–15; Sweetman 2003, 15).[29] They gestured toward the building of an indigenous theory of religion through the complex vocabularies for multiple activities that are rather casually grouped under the category of religion, wherein both the contemporary and the comparative are at stake. Studying wonder, as Dandu Shastri and Krishna Bhattar do, makes an anthropology of Hinduism possible whereby the singular Abrahamic model is interrogatable. The question therefore is no longer whether Hinduism qualifies as a religion but rather what it can offer us by way of critical analysis for the category *of* religion. It gets us beyond the frayed questions of the embedded longevity of colonial power differentials, toward a consideration of a renewed agency of the periphery to illuminate the center.

My Guides into Wonder

In my wondering about wonder, three people were my crucial guides: my father, the anthropologist M. N. Srinivas; Dandu Shastri, the pradhan archakar (Sanskrit: chief priest) of the Ganesha Temple; and Krishna Bhattar, the pradhan archakar of the Krishna Temple. Each of them raised three themes regarding my interrogation of wonder: positionality, creativity, and ethics.

ETHNOGRAPHIC POSITIONALITY

In their 2010 article in *Current Anthropology*, João Biehl and Peter Locke call for a Deleuzian anthropology of "becoming"—ethnographic projects that hone in on the messiness and unpredictability of individual lives and that allow us to focus on acts of becoming. They propose that anthropology can learn from literature and process theology and its ability to unpack the inner complexities of the human experience: "Continually adjusting itself to the reality of contemporary lives and worlds, [this] anthropological venture has the potential of art: to invoke neglected human potentials and to expand the limits of understanding and imagination" (2010, 317–51). Stretching the limits of understanding through continuous adjustment was an immersive, artful endeavor that appealed to me because of its sympathetic relationship to the other.

In August 1993 I was in Bangalore over my summer vacation from graduate school in Boston. I was looking rather vaguely for a topic of study for my research when my family and I happened to visit the Ganesha Temple, something we did not do often. We sat on the granite-paved *katte*, or platform, under the peepul tree and watched with fascination as Dandu Shastri, feet planted apart and hands folded on his stomach, stood, loudly discussing the possibility of installing "*komputer vellake*" (Tamil: computerized lighting chains) for the upcoming festival surrounded by a group of neophyte priests, assorted temple vendors, and supplicants.

After his conversation with the bank manager, Dandu Shastri came to greet us, wiping his brow on his white *angavastram*, or ceremonial shawl. My father told him that we were watching his dispatching of the many tasks, sacred and quotidian, with admiration. Dandu Shastri smiled and said, "*Ayyoo! Yenna pannarde saar? Idde numba 'business' illiya?* [Tamil: What to do sir? This is our 'business,' is it not?]." He spun his wrist, elevating his hand in a series of wavelike upward motions used to indicate both change and progress, and elaborated, almost as though he had read our minds, "Everything is changing so fast. Everything! Everything is new. So we must 'keep up.'" Then he added self-deprecatingly, with a broad smile, "All this is play [Tamil: *valayate*]," indicating how easy his job was despite what we had witnessed. My father watched him intently and then observed, almost casually, "Someone should study this place and these fellows!"

On the car ride home, Dandu Shastri's skillful negotiation of these changing life worlds rattled around in my brain. It lingered in my memory for the whole holiday, along with my father's observation that someone should study the ritual practitioners and priests. Was I that someone? My inexperience and lack of confidence surfaced: I was concerned that it would be thought that my father, a renowned social anthropologist, had picked my topic and field site.

But my initial fascination with watching Dandu Shastri—in Emmanuel Levinas's terms, the moment of rupture—refused to subside. I thought I was simply engaging in "opportunistic research," given that Bangalore was my hometown (L. Srinivas 2016, 1–5) and I had access to these temples, but in point of fact it was ultimately, as many of our studies are, a way of learning to know and understand myself.

Before I entered the temples, I was simply unaware of my caste. To say that I was "unaware" automatically suggests I am upper caste, for how else could I ignore the acts of power and social practices that accompany caste evocations in India? But I was not alone. In the post-Independence generation of Indians, there was a generalized amnesia about caste as applied to self (Krishna 2011, 7–14). In my case, this amnesia was made more complicated by the fact that my parents, both academic idealists, had come of age in the interwar years and had collegiate secular educations. They did not practice caste-based purity rituals at home. My parents were humanists and their friends of different caste and religious backgrounds were invited to, frequently visited, and dined in our home. We never visited temples in Delhi where I grew up, and we had no close family like grandparents who lived with us to maintain our caste boundaries.[30] Our puja room was a small nook, never more, and rituals were minimal in the household, if not largely absent. My parents performed no annual funerary rituals, a rite that most Hindu households undertook, and there were no garlanded photographs of bygone elders to whom we offered ancestor worship. We were Hindu, I knew, but that was about it.

So I read about caste in graduate school in the United States, thirsty to understand my own society and myself. Broadly a system of labor relations in the *jajmani* system (Bayly 2001), it also expressed hierarchies in social and political brokerage practices of the dominant castes (M. N. Srinivas 1956, 1959). But I saw the system from the viewpoint of an urban Indian educated in the West who enthusiastically embraced a global discourse of equality (Béteille 1991; Fuller 1997, 13). Caste, to me, was a system of radical injustice, and one of social interdependence peculiar to India (Hutton 1963; Ghurye 1969).[31] While clear evidence of exploitation *and* governmental efforts to right caste prejudice through affirmative action or caste-based "reservations" existed all around me in India, I knew that in practice, caste, in opposition to the rigid system described in Hindu religious texts, functioned as a flexible system wherein the scriptural norms were routinely interpreted to suit contingent circumstances both making the system more generous and more violent toward individuals and caste groups (M. N. Srinivas 1962a). In service to acknowledging the inhumanity and violence of the caste system toward all lower castes, and in a civil-rights-style push toward building a more egalitarian society that recognizes a need for reparations, both valuable and necessary initiatives, recent scholarship has glossed over this contingent flexibility, making our understandings of the system more rigid still.[32] In the work of my father, M. N. Srinivas, on the Sanskritization and Westernization of castes, I understood not only the intersections with status and power but the resilient plasticity of the caste system as a whole, and its adaptive capacity to withstand the stresses of change. While unpalatable to many in its brokerage of power, it also gestured to the innate dynamism of Hinduism in transforming itself according to changing circumstances (M. N. Srinivas 1973).

However, this academic quest to understand caste was set against who I was in the society in which I had arrived for my education. I was an Indian student with little money and no means in President Bush's America. In that part of my life, I understood how the obverse of privilege worked on the ground, a worm's view of the world, lost in the dirt (Parry 2000, 27–29). I was invisible at best, and on some, mercifully few, occasions, visible only as an embodied target for racial and ethnic slurs. Ever-alert and ever-fearful, I felt ground down in this ground. I learned to live on the edge of unbeing and to slink around in spaces not made for me. At the same time, the privilege of education made me appreciative, if not yet understanding, of lives lived in dread and the need for radical social hope.

When I began my fieldwork in early 1998, I was unprepared and largely unaware of my own problematic positionality in Bangalorean publics, in which the expectations of my behavior as an upper-caste South Indian woman would run afoul of other identities I had: as a graduate student, a feminist, a child of a well-known Indian anthropologist, and a daughter who was raised in a secular household. I knew that the temples I was studying were largely, though not exclusively, Tamil Brahmin (known colloquially among the Westernized middle classes of south India as "Tam-Brahm") strongholds. But it was in these temples that I was educated into what it meant to be a Brahmin middle-class woman.

In my upstart foolishness, I began fieldwork wearing loose jeans with a cotton *kurta* (tunic). The first few days I was an oddity and generously smiled at by localites. But as I stayed on and people began to know me, I faced criticism. I was told I needed to comb my hair, that I was not *najuka* (Kannada: refined) enough. Why didn't I wear a little jewelry? Was I married? Why didn't I wear *kumkum* on my forehead? Or my *mangalyam*?[33] Who was I? I was befuddled, and then depressed, by the barrage of criticism even while I understood it to be evidence that I was being absorbed by the field and that my interlocutors had come to feel an attachment to me.

My bewilderment was also an embodied one. My Western education, which entailed being seated at tables and chairs, came back to haunt me. As

I sat for long periods of time taking notes on the stone floor of the temple cross-legged in the lotus pose, my thighs hurt and my legs fell sleep. I would fidget, moving my feet around, trying to get comfortable, on one occasion being rebuked by the male devotees for allowing my feet to point toward the *sanctum sanctorum*, a cardinal sign of disrespect. When I moved to correct this, I thoughtlessly stood in the men's queue and was pushed back, admonished firmly that I was in the wrong place. I was upset for I could never see the deity, blocked by a phalanx of men.

The temple became an everyday space of endless bewilderment and irritation for me. Sam Keen notes that this everydayness is key to a "mature sense of wonder" and "most often called forth by a confrontation with the mysterious depths of meaning at the heart of the quotidian" (1969, 23). And with regard to my near constant bewilderment, James Siegel terms it an "invitation" (where "to invite" is synonymous with to invoke), rather than an introduction. He saw that bewilderment should serve as an active, and therefore positive, tool in the work—a kind of gateway—rather than as just a passive, neutral reaction: "When I began my first work as an anthropologist, I was lost but I did not know it. . . . [But] I had not made enough of my bewilderment; I had merely let it resolve itself. . . . I wanted to become actively confused rather than passively so . . . in order to wander away from what I had been taught. . . . Here, I thought, was the way to find bewilderment" (2011, 1–2). I too was "actively confused," but unlike Siegel I saw no agency there. Rather, I saw it as a failure in myself, a failure not only to "see" properly but to be seen properly as well.

So I retreated to sit on a pavilion threshold away from the temple, yet within its grounds. The pavilion allowed me to see and not be seen. Sitting on the threshold of the pavilion, I turned to Victor Turner, who wrote of thresholds of *rites de passage*, of living "betwixt and between," for I felt he would understand this slow, reluctant self-transformation. Another Turner, Frederick Turner, speaks of the anthropologist, a person "who alters the system studied and is reciprocally altered by it, whose truths are what works best, and who penetrates the hermeneutic circle by a process of successive approximations and corrections" (F. Turner 1986, 89). There on the temple pavilion threshold, I viscerally felt my native nonnativeness.

I had, unbeknownst to myself, followed André Green's proposal to cultivate self-estrangement, but in my case it was doubled, for I was not stepping out of a familiar lifeworld and then reentering it as a stranger, as Green advocates; rather, I was stepping out of a lifeworld from which I was already estranged through my parents' choices to move away from caste-based occupations, and into secular academic worlds (Green 1999). I had reentered the lifeworlds of the Malleshwaram temples as a trifold stranger, who looked both familiar and not, confusing localites and myself in equal measure. I was an un-Brahmin-Brahmin and an unwomanly woman.

I felt a sense of inquietude—gaps, silences, limits, and opacities—familiar in its promise of intimacy concomitant with refusal. This sense left me on a permanent threshold "betwixt and between" that neither ethnography nor biography could heal or make whole at once. The temple pulled me beyond my taken-for-granted world, yet I never found a home in that beyond. It made fieldwork for me both a normalizing and an exclusivizing endeavor, a political site where the decolonizing of the ethnographic imagination seemed to be the politically correct thing to try to achieve, but one that was far away from my ethnographic self who was trying to "fit in" (Appadurai 1990; Clifford 1988; Gupta and Ferguson 1992, 1997).

In dismay and fear, I began avoiding the temples. I could not look my interlocutors in the eye and feel comfortable in my skin at the same time. After a month of this, my mother, having noticed my avoidance, asked me to break a coconut on her behalf in the Ganesha Temple the next time I was there. So I took the coconut to the temple, determined to perform my errand quickly and leave. Dandu Shastri caught sight of me from where he stood in the lower courtyard of the temple with his big feet spread apart, a stance that made him seem to grow from the very earth he stood on. He hailed me jovially and inquired where I had been. "*Kathe polle poyatte!* [Tamil: You left like the wind]," he exclaimed. The metaphor, that I had come and gone like an untrustworthy breeze, was not lost on me. He reminded me that I had missed the monthly ritual of Sankasth Chathurthi, the fourth day of the new moon when Ganesha cleared the path of all troubles. He had saved me some prasadam from the puja, and he sent a young boy to get a bag that he handed to me. Vishwanatha, Dandu Shastri's son, watched me accept the small bag and said, "Father missed you." I was moved.

Ironically, that very day, Jean-Paul Sartre's *Search for a Method*, in which he elaborates on the theme of relationships, had come to my attention. "Research is a relationship," Sartre writes. "Research is a living relation between men. . . . The sociologist and his 'object' form a couple, each one of which is to be interpreted by the other; the relationship between them must be itself interpreted as a moment of history" ([1960] 1963, 72).[34] My own father's relationship with the other surfaces in his writings about the olfactory and visual charms of Bandikere, a Kuruba shepherd's colony a few hundred feet from his childhood Brahmin neighborhood of College Road.

As an over-protected Brahmin . . . boy growing up on College Road, I experienced my first culture shocks not more than fifty yards from the back wall of our house. . . . The entire culture of Bandikeri (the area behind our house where lived a colony of Shepherds, immigrants from their village, located a few miles from Mysore) was visibly and olfactorily different from that of College Road. Bandikeri was my Trobriand Islands, my Nuerland, my Navaho country and what have you. In retrospect it is not surprising that I became an anthropologist, all of whose fieldwork was in his own country. (M. N. Srinivas 1992, 141)

My father's published and well-known exhortations to study one's "own" society encouraged me to return to the temple.[35] I paid attention to the words he had written more than thirty years earlier on the importance of considering methodological issues "particularly when the society is undergoing rapid transformation" (M. N. Srinivas 1966, 149). Yet questions of ownership of the society continued to trouble me, leaving me to wonder about my own and others' behavior, my self formation, and giving me classic anxiety dreams that haunt me even today.[36]

I reentered the temples. Krishna Bhattar, the chief priest of the Krishna Temple, noticed that I was being ignored. He asked me, "Are you having difficulty [Tamil: *sankocham*]? Why don't you wear a sari? People will talk to you." I was ambivalent about his advice. "Why should I? God never says anything about saris!" I shot back, inflexible in my righteousness. Krishna Bhattar smiled and said, "Well, God might not, but women do!" The next week, I arrived at the temple wearing my mother's silk sari and an ill-fitting blouse. Immediately, the women of the temple moved toward me, clicking their tongues in delight, "How nice you look!" They discussed their tailors and the problems of getting blouses stitched. They were empathetic and kind. I stood there in the women's queue, dressed in my borrowed sari and talking to my friends, my critique of the literature on caste made real to me: there were no feminist readings of caste to leaven the analysis with generosity.[37] Even the emergent, exciting Dalit literature, a new reading of caste, was focused on maleness.[38] None of the literature illuminated my positionality as a Brahmin *woman* and an anthropologist going back to the unfamiliar familiar.[39]

But as my sari and my self-consciousness tripped me up and made me feel fragile, I asked myself despairingly, "*Why* ethnography?" Kirin Narayan's beautiful words came to rescue me: "For the discipline of paying attention; for becoming more responsibly aware of inequalities; for better understanding of the social forces causing suffering and how people might somehow find hope; and most generally, for being perpetually pulled beyond the limits of one's own taken-for-granted world" (Narayan qtd. in McGranahan 2014).

I had thought I could enter and remain "myself," but the field changed me. Slowly, I became more observant. I neatly plastered my hair with oil and adorned my forehead with kumkum. I found my place in the "women only" queue rather than remaining with the mix of strangers at the rear. Caste and gender slowly imprinted themselves on me. I had become pliant (Gold 2016, 13). I see now that I made a virtue of necessity, but it made me part of temple life in a way that my plain white kurta could not. I grew used to sitting on the rough stone, and protective cal"ouses formed where previously there were none.

Ethnographic subjectivity is an evolving state that emerges in participant observation (Chawla 2006). I began to discover a deep aesthetic pleasure in my world. I enjoyed picking out the jewel-toned silks from my mother's closet and seeing myself in the mirror. I bought more saris, accompanying my female interlocutors on sari-buying trips that lasted long afternoons and yielded reams of data. My pliancy became more than just survival; from strategy, it shifted to method, and then to an identity. On those trips, I found another part of my feminine self, a joyful self, that stayed with me even after I left the field. But I also found points of confluence with other women of all castes and classes. I found that other women did not like the gender separation in queues at the temple; they did not like that only men were allowed to recite the Vedic scriptures or view the deity up close; they did not like being told who they should be, or what they should do. My appreciation of these women grew as time passed and I was privy to the multiplicity of roles and subjectivities they inhabited. I came to understand from them that all hierarchies, including caste and gender, were capable of being upturned, or "adjusted." I began to see my pliancy anew, not merely as capitulation but as a method and identity that enabled receptivity, openness, compromise, survival, and even resistance—an *active and deliberate* giving-in to wonder, if you will.

I also came to understand that even for my upper-caste and male interlocutors at the temple, all was not easy sailing. Precarity can be part of what seems to be a world of privilege. The creative improvisation of Krishna Bhattar and Dandu Shastri, with its celebration of making do, was for localites a way to find resilience in dread-filled times. In such moments of clarity, I saw the localites as heroic figures, battling a sometimes grim everyday reality

FIGURE I.4. Dandu Shastri, chief priest of the Ganesha Temple. Photo by the author.

with incredible bravery, joy, and creativity. My obsession with myself and what I was doing ceased as I turned to shared passions.

RITUAL CREATIVITY

Dandu Shastri, the chief priest of the Ganesha Temple, was in his midsixties in 1998. He had been a priest since childhood. A rotund man with elephantine dentition and a thin *rudumi*, or topknot, he had a bellowing laugh, a gargantuan appetite, and a childlike delight in his world. He wore an enormous gold *mala* (necklace) made with rare Rudrakshi beads from the Himalayas.

He told me sotto voce at our first meeting that he was "not from Bangalore" but was a Smartha Brahmin from Andhra Pradesh. He seemed to be suggesting he was an outsider. His mind was always spinning with new ideas, and he would greet localites in midthought, spewing out ideas without preamble, as though his listeners were privy to his thoughts.

Dandu Shastri began our meetings in 1998 by talking about the sheer joy of his job as a priest. He identified with his temple's deity. His flashy rings all bore carved images of Ganesha, and his gold imitation Rolex watch sported a gold Ganesha face. He ascribed all his abilities as a priest to the deity whom he unconditionally adored.

The story Dandu Shastri told me of his call to service was magical. Some eighty-five years earlier, Dandu's father, a poor priest in arid Andhra Pradesh, was given a bus ticket to Bangalore by a friend. It happened that the year before, an image of the deity was found by a group of young men at the top of a rock outcrop in Malleshwaram. Dandu's father arrived in Bangalore and immediately became the head priest of the newly constructed shrine to the deity. He then brought his extended family to Malleshwaram, and his brother became the chief priest of the Kannika Parmeshwari Devi Temple on Eighth Cross Road. Dandu Shastri, trained by his father, inherited the job of chief priest upon his father's death in 1978.

Dandu Shastri lived in a modern home with a Ganesha statue embedded in the wall, close to the Ganesha Temple. He lived with his wife, Mrs. Dandu; his son, Vishwanatha Shastri, who was training to be a priest; and his two grandsons, Ganesh and Subramanya; as well as assorted hangers-on, priestly cousins, and nephews looking for work in Bangalore. An autodidact, Dandu Shastri displayed his credentials prominently; one entire wall of his living room, or "hall" as it was known in Bangalore, was covered with professional certificates and photographs of him with important politicians and celebrities.

I quickly learned that Dandu Shastri was a visionary and a technocrat; he understood the epiphanic power of images to shift our vision of the world. He constantly thought about the change he saw around him, considering how to navigate it and to help others do so through creative rituals.[40] He confessed that he wanted to transform the way we think about ritual—by which he meant puja, *utsava* festivals, and the life-cycle rituals in which he was most involved—in order to make it "modern," and to find a new way to an as yet unimagined future.

In 1991 Dandu Shastri told me tearfully of the government "takeover" of his temple that had occurred a decade prior. According to his telling, his own probity had made him many enemies in the Temple Trust and among the officials of the Government Charitable Endowment Department, known colloquially as the "Muzrai department."[41] The state, through the legal armature of the Karnataka Act no. 33 in 2001—the Hindu Religious Charitable Endowments Act, which answered "a long-standing public demand to bring about a uniform law" for all religious institutions—devolved upon itself the power to abolish occupancy on lands defined as "religious or charitable inam" if illegal usage of money or "mismanagement of temple funds" was alleged.[42] Indeed, the usage of the word *misman-agement* is telling as it draws together neoliberal understandings of the governance of the sacred polis and the economy into the sacred confines of the temple.[43]

The wording of the act specifically named the priests as the parties respon-sible for "rendering religious service in or maintaining the institution as a *pujari* (priest) *archak* (ritual priest) or the holder of a similar office by what-ever name called." By 1998 the state of Karnataka had forty-three thousand temples, matts (sacred seats), monasteries, *dargahs* (mausoleums), mosques, and other sacred institutions under its fiduciary care, inviting fairly widespread charges of priestly mismanagement. To some, the enormity of the number of institutions in state care pointed not only to the larger cultural distrust of the priesthood, but also to the strategic manipulation of this distrust to render the lands and treasures of religious institutions unto the state.

Dandu Shastri said it was a "*rhomba* 'shock'" (Tamil: too much shock) when his temple was annexed by the Muzrai department. To redeem his reputa-tion, he spent long hours every day burying himself in the work of ritual. To him, the deity was the imaginative resource that enabled his transformation and engendered his respectability. He would frequently gesture to the deity and speak of wonder, in particular his wonder at the kindliness of the deity toward him and his family and the obligation to create a situation in which wonder could exist in the temple for all devotees.

As early as 1966, in a plenary address to the American Anthropological Association, Fredrik Barth suggested that the study of change was urgent and central to the anthropological endeavor. As he said, "We need new concepts that allow us to observe and describe events of change" (1967, 661). The most famous anthropological essay on ritual change is "Ritual and Social Change: A Javanese Example", Clifford Geertz's study of the stalled funeral of a young boy in Java. First published in the winter of 1957, the essay begins with the problem of "dynamic functionalism" and the shifting of Javanese social and cultural worlds. For Geertz, the failure by anthropologists to treat cultural and social processes on equal terms, either an "omnibus concept of culture" or a "comprehensive concept of social structure," does not allow for the "dy-namic elements in social change," born when social structure and culture are misaligned, to be properly formulated or understood (1957, 33). Geertz's example of tracing these "dynamic elements" begins with the unfortunate death of a young Javanese boy. The boy's funeral is halted because of a con-tentious debate between the pro-Islamic radical reform Masjumi group, or Santri, and the anti-Muslim animist cult of Permai, or Abhagans, over how the funeral ritual is to be performed. The Muslim priest refuses to perform the funeral since the boy's uncle is Abhangan and therefore automatically suspect. The funeral grinds to a halt for a few hours, leaving the body of the young boy simmering in the sunshine while family members, local politicos, priests, and functionaries engage in a complicated moral drama of warring allegiances and beliefs. Geertz notes that funerals in Java are meant to be a "languid letting-go," but in this case the residents show a froth of "unusual" emotion. They scream, cry, shout, argue, sulk, and storm away. But at the end of the day, the parents of the boy arrive. The priest and the family find a way to perform a suitable funeral for the young boy and the funeral feast is held for the kampong (village).

Geertz suggests that the breakdown in ritual is, both implicitly and explicitly, a result of political and cultural change, where social structure and cultural change are at odds with one another. But what if we engage in a thought experiment? What if, rather than a breakdown of social and ritual relations, this is a story of ritual improvisation?[44] Geertz associates the fluidity of the participants' emotions with disruption. But what if we consider that they might have more to do with the passions of creativity? Indeed, Geertz himself comes to this very conclusion in a later text suggesting that ritual is a site of dynamism for the birth of new cultural orders (1980b). Catherine Bell summarizes this debate as follows: "Ritual as a performative medium for social change emphasizes human creativity and physicality: ritual does not mold people; people fashion rituals that mold their world" (1997, 73).

Linda Penkower and Tracy Pintchman articulate insights that suggest that ritual can be, and usually is, creative. "Appropriating or modifying rituals when convenient or desirable," they suggest, is "the norm" (2014, 17). They highlight an interpretive shift in ritual where the new normal of endless shifts is understood by practitioners as the regenerative power of ritual, where "ritual enables people to experience the ontologically real and meaningful, to regenerate cyclical notions of time, and to renew the prosperity and fecundity of the community" (Bell 1997, 11).[45]

CREATIVE ETHICS

Krishna Bhattar was the charismatic pradhan archakar of the Krishna Temple, two blocks east of the Ganesha Temple. When I began fieldwork, he was in his midthirties, a handsome, slim man with dark, glistening skin and fine, chiseled features. He looked like a movie star artlessly playing a priest. He dressed in white silk, with twelve brilliant red and white *namam* (Tamil: a

FIGURE I.5. Krishna Bhattar and his father. Photo by the author.

caste mark) of Vaishnavite devotion on his face and body. Like Dandu Shastri, he too wore his hair in a priestly *rudumi*, but his was thick, jet black,
and neatly knotted, the envy of many of the female devotees. He gave an
impression of being dignified, serious, and in control, inducing the unspoken
assumption of distance. As I got to know him, I found him to be thoughtful, well spoken, scholarly, philosophical, confident, and generous. He was a
wonderful guide, and I often turned to him with my many questions.

Krishna Bhattar woke every day at 3:45 a.m., bathed in the darkness before
dawn as his ritual purity demanded, wore *madi* (Tamil: ritually pure) silk
clothing, and then prayed, offering his personal supplication to the deity at
dawn (*acamanam*) in private, threading the wicks of the oil lamp by himself.
He read and meditated for an hour before heading to the temple. Only on his
return did he eat a spare breakfast.

Like his meal, his house and puja room were austere, except for a few
beautifully wrought ancient silver idols of Krishna, Rama and other Vaishnavite deities, silver vessels, and a few silver lamps. Krishna Bhattar had one
certificate on the wall of his living room—the state-based award of *Agama
Ratna* (Sanskrit: jewel of the liturgical texts), designating him a special priest,
learned in the scholarship of liturgy.

Krishna Bhattar told me about how he got his job, a story of patronage and divine intervention. After the neighborhood of Malleshwaram was built in 1889, the upper-caste Vaishnavite residents requested of the government a suitable site for a Vishnu temple. After securing the land, they hunted for an appropriate Vaishnavite image to be consecrated in the temple and found a Krishna idol in the Mysore Palace treasury.[46] The consecration of the main shrine and the deity within was celebrated on August 22, 1902. Krishna Bhattar's ancestor became the priest for this new temple.

About a year after I got to know him, Krishna Bhattar confessed that his father was not his biological father but his biological uncle and that he was "gifted" (*datte*) to his uncle in order to inherit his Brahmanical calling of priesthood. He added: "I never thought I'd be a priest. But one day there was *Jeeyar* [Tamil: His Holiness] doing a *homa* [Sanskrit: Vedic fire sacrifice] in the temple. I tried to join and he said, 'No, you cannot because you have a crop'—a modern hair cut without the priestly tuft. I had doubts about whether I should do this job, but I thought God will help me so I am to do it. But I vowed on that day to look like what people think of as a priest." I respected the self-awareness evidenced by his acknowledgment that his traditional garb was a performance and that he had doubts about his belief. His resolution came from critical reflexivity and questioning.

Krishna was the only priest who was cosmopolitan enough to introduce me to his wife, Valù. He referred to her as his "missus." Valù was the daughter of a powerful priestly family in Bangalore. I asked Krishna Bhattar whether it was an "arranged marriage" or had he fallen in love? Krishna Bhattar was amused by my question and said "half and half." Then he added, "To love someone else one should know oneself first, is it not? Mind must be 'mature,'" he said. Then he explained: "Marriage is our *svadharma* [Sanskrit: our dharma]. Our *achara* [Sanskrit: custom]. Our *samskriti* [culture]. Here in our India everything is 'moment.' Love is moment. Life is moment. Everything happens in moment. *Appadi* [Tamil: just like that], we 'adjust'!"

Krishna Bhattar's answer was typical of him. He was a natural philosopher, interrogating the everyday and the normative in crucial, thoughtful ways, crafting an ethics in the everyday. He peppered his conversations with words that demonstrated his ethical leanings: dharma, loosely translated in Sanskrit as duty or moral code; and achara, translated as custom or practice, which he linked implicitly to samskriti, culture.[47] In Hinduism, dharma was initially mostly related to ritual before it also encompassed the morality of actions (Olivelle 2009, xxxviii). Unlike some of my anthropological contemporaries, whose important thinking on ethical formations in

South Asia informs my own thought, Krishna Bhattar's inquiry was less focused on the broad cultural and political implications of "South Asian ethics" or "ethics in South Asia" than on the boundary condition of the ethical in and for itself. Talking with him led me to think about dharma anew in terms of the achara of contemporary creativity.

In the Krishna Temple, I often found liturgical hymnals of mantras strewn about, here collectively called *pratishta* (Sanskrit: textual references). Localites often referenced the hymnals to recite the correct set of Vedic mantras at the proper time. Krishna Bhattar never referenced them at all, having collected the necessary mantras in his memory as part of the Vedic training he underwent to become a *purohit* (temple chaplain). He had learned all the mantras "by heart," he said, employing an expression as popular in India as in the English-speaking world. He distinguished the liturgical texts as dharmic, as prescriptive, to be learned by rote, but what he did liturgically, as achara, as descriptive, and as a space for creativity.[48] Achara, therefore, was "dharma in practice, the practical, 'real' life of dharma that acts as a normative precedent for future action" allowing for a fluidity of dharma in everyday life (Davis 2004, 814). This distinction allowed Krishna Bhattar permission to improvise hacks in the everyday to deal with continuous and life-altering changes—a "creative ethics." Collectively these hacks and creative moments built to an aesthetic poetics of an "experimental Hinduism" (DeNapoli 2017), an ethos and ethics of religious experimentation.[49]

Localites, priests and devotees together, recast the idea of dharma, which operates predominantly as a descriptive category in the scholarship on Hindu traditions and South Asian religions, into an analytical concept for imagining the indeterminacy of the moral (cf. Jain 2011). As we will see in the following pages, dharma becomes fused with achara to create a fluid ethical analytic—a creative ethic—not merely an individual moral code that operates in the everyday as an imagined text (DeNapoli and Srinivas 2016).[50] The idea of a *creative ethic* is a modest one. It is both a creative ethos as well as a process of iterative, poetic, and inspired actions that systematically transform the ordinary into the visionary. The achara of creative ethics suggests, as does Krishna Bhattar, the responsibility to offer other possibilities. On occasion, creative ethics are so nascent as to involve a chaotic improvisational rendering in the moment, in which a range of ethical behaviors that includes the unethical and the morally ambiguous and "what really matters" (Kleinman 1995) are birthed.[51]

Creative ethics involves an anthropological imagining of doing rather than philosophical thinking; it is less a textual discursive model and more an act of "loosely constructed actions, enunciations, embodiments and articulations" creating an unpredictable trajectory as a sediment of repeated actions that are special to localites themselves (Pinto 2019). Through creative ethics, localites get beyond the tedium of habit, the "uncanny of everyday life" (Das 2015a), where a broader understanding of "new regimes of living" inheres in the category of experience (Collier and Lakoff 2004). There is constant experimentation and constant evolution of the ethical form, not as a singular critical form but as a series of adjacent adjustments and improvisations that are emergent. This is not to say creative ethics cannot come from a position of disempowerment but rather that it emerges from and occupies a reciprocal relationship and mutual recognition between the powerful and powerless, the devotee and god, between priest, devotee, and deity.[52] Creative ethical practices do more than simply engage, highlight limitations, and demand alternatives; they open up the world to creative formations and re-formations of resistance allowing for experiences that are alive, creative, life-affirming, radical, and freeing; an anti-alienation strategy to combat the stresses of modern living.

Going Forward

For some, creative ethics as described above might unmoor the certitude of life. For me, it expands boundaries. In keeping with creative ethics, I write what I know, while also, more importantly, I attempt to *write into* what I do not yet know.[53] Given the essential otherness of wonder, I have gradually come to feel that the best way to experience this work is as an experimental folio: notes and scribbles written over a period of time and to some extent mirroring the creative play, open-endedness, and interrogation of its subject rather than as a conventional textual treatise displaying mastery and closure.

The fragments within this folio, a series of notes collected over sixteen years, are brought together by a commitment to "thickness" rather than through a parsimony of material, a layering of experience that leads naturally to an anticipation of the unexpected.[54] Rather than presuming endings and completeness, this text invites the unfurling of wonder and creativity, an opening of its joints.

In keeping with that objective, this ethnography seeks to be part of the ongoing critical discussion in religious studies of the place of "non-Western" "religion" (Carrette and King 2005). Religion in South Asia has had a contradictory history. On the one hand, it has been a trademark of scholarship in the region, a symbol of textual "great" traditions and lived "little" ones.

On the other hand, religion in South Asia, particularly Hinduism and Buddhism, have long troubled the definition of religion itself, being a place where polytropic ambiguities challenge the singular certainties of interpretive categories—an understanding that Western scholarship with its legacy of colonialism and Orientalism brings discourses of power to interpretations of non-Western canonical texts, practices, and indigenous philosophies (Embree 1990; King 1999; McCutcheon 2001, 2007; Pennington 2005; Sweetman and Malik 2016).

If we accept that our conceptual apparatus of religion is haunted by post-Enlightenment European Protestant political theology (Asad 1993; Masuzawa 2005), which still structures our understanding of ritual's efficacy (Seligman et al. 2008, 368–70; Puett 2013), we understand how the problems of universalization create a new set of challenges for a possible "Indian way of thinking" about religion and its study (Ramanujan 1989, 41).

A consideration of what ritualists do, along with serious consideration of what they *say* they do, moves us beyond a consideration of practices of piety and sly resistances to dominant modes of religious being to a nuanced, serendipitous yet strategic rendering of the agentive, joyful, and curious religious being in a neoliberal world. It gifts to us a way of getting beyond the horizon of religious studies while allowing us to ask what is this "beyond"?

The organization of this book charts the significant forces that fashion neoliberal modernity—space, mobility, emotion, money, technology, and time—and the ways in which ritual life in Malleshwaram engages them. Chapter 1 explores the spatial changes in Bangalore and in Malleshwaram, and the rituals that accompany the building of this bewildering landscape, arguing that dwelling in a modern landscape is precarious and requires ritual "permissions" from the gods. It speaks to the nature of the transformation of land from a gift of the gods to a capitalist system of value. Chapter 2 charts the passions of ritual life and the shift from aesthetics to ethics. It is the tracing of a deep emotional journey through the performance of a gender-based quarrel between the gods in which new ways of being and belonging are unexpectedly birthed toward an aesthetic rendering of the emotions of ritual life. Chapter 3 deals with the (im)mobility of global capital within the context of creative rituals. Through an interrogation of the seeming "frictionless surface" of money, I build a political economy of religion. I explore how accumulations of wealth and the depredations of poverty (and perceptions of both) are tied to the enactment of a good and virtuous ritual life in contemporary Bangalore. Chapter 4 focuses on technology and how technological novelty extends the boundaries of the possible, forcing the boundaries of the real to expand as well. In chapter 5, considerations of ritual time and neoliberal time provoke an interrogation of creativity and novelty and the tedium of work, against the background of fraught salvage of a disused temple and the repurposing of divinity for the contemporary world. It speaks to the nature of sustainability of life, both human and beyond human.

In this work, the anthropology of wonder acknowledges not only the wonder of different worlds but also our own wonder as anthropologists encountering those worlds. Wonder must be shared, for even as it revels in the special or the singular, it contains within it the desire for collaboration or intimacy with others. Krishna Bhattar emphasized this nature of wonderment, drawing a parallel between the "storytelling" of the anthropologist and the creative ritual of the priest: the work of priesthood in storytelling that he compared to the crafting of creative rituals, which I quoted in the epigraph to this chapter: "You tell stories. Our stories [Tamil: *Namblode kathai*]. Telling stories and doing this ritual is the 'same.' They both help us dream [Tamil: *kanavu*] of a better place."

CHAPTER ONE

ADVENTURES IN MODERN DWELLING

We are the children of our landscape; it dictates behavior and even
thought in the measure to which we are responsive to it.
—Lawrence Durrell, *Justine*

Everyone is building a house, apartment, *veedu-vaashal*
[Tamil: houses and thresholds]. They call me and I go!
—Dandu Shastri, chief priest, Ganesha Temple

The Cow in the Elevator

In January 2009 I found myself trying to help lure a reluctant cow named
Kamadhenu into a mirrored elevator. Her handler pushed her rear end
while I held a tempting sheaf of ripe bananas in front of her. Kamadhenu was
spooked at seeing her reflection in the surrounding mirrors of the elevator.
She lowed miserably, uncertain of this claustrophobic mode of transport.

I had been invited by Dandu Shastri to a *grihapravesham* (Sanskrit: lit. house
entering, a house-blessing ceremony) at a high-rise luxury apartment complex.
The apartment complex, called "Golden Orchards," was dominated by a midcentury modern aesthetic. It sat like a giant white tower with its mirrored dark
windows and steel railings in a pristine landscape of lush green bamboo foliage.

A central part of the grihapravesham, derived from ancient Hindu agrarian customs, required a sacred cow to walk through the new house. The house to be blessed in this case was a penthouse on the eighth floor. The young priests and the doorman, charged with getting the materials for the grihapravesham ready, were trying to coax the unwilling Kamadhenu into the elevator when I met them.

After an hour of sweet talking, bribes in the form of bananas, and some hefty shoves to her rear end, we were successful. Kamadhenu rode in the elevator, her eyes brimming with fear. Once off the elevator, though, she quickly regained her composure, chewing her cud in a bored manner as she was led down the fancy mirrored corridors. There was little evidence of Hindu ritual celebration anywhere—no mango *tornana* (Sanskrit: garland for a doorway), no oil lamps, and few flowers. The place seemed silent and forlorn.

The marketing manager for the building joined us. Wrongly believing I might be an investor, he attempted to sell me an apartment by listing its many wonders: "This is best complex, Madame! Full amenities." He proudly informed me that the apartment complex had expensive, tumbled Carrarra marble bathrooms and luxury Scandinavian faucets. I was unimpressed, but he continued: "We have *purohits* [Hindu chaplains] to do all rituals, Madame. You are Hindu, no? If it has to be done 'in absentia,' then we will get your details—*gotra* [Sanskrit: lineage descent], *nakshatra* [Sanskrit: astrological details of birth], and all—and we can perform it for you. Many people buy here, Madame! These are 'super' apartments!" In response to my question about sales, he referred to his easy sales of luxury apartments and his enormous commissions as "*majatime!* [Kannada: fun time!]."

The view from the penthouse was truly commanding; the whole of Malleshwaram lay at our feet, green treetops swaying in the breeze. We could see a few tiny bungalows with their tiled roofs, the remaining holdouts in a rapidly rising city. The newly built high-rises surrounded us, punctuated by the maws of open excavations with their ubiquitous scaffolding.

Despite the luxury, all of us felt the loneliness of the anomic surroundings. Dandu Shastri was unusually quiet as he issued orders to his assistants. No one joked or laughed. Once the *homa kunda* (Vedic fire pit) was prepared, he lit it with little enthusiasm and performed the invocations in a mechanical manner. "These houses are all the same. No one ever lives in them. They are bank accounts," he said to me sotto voce. He asked the manager for "details," as he put it. The manager took out his phone where he had stored them, and recited the nakshatra and gotra of the absent owner.

When it was her turn to participate, Kamadhenu obediently followed directions. She wandered through the million-dollar home, climbing a short flight of stairs to the enormous bedrooms and lifting her hoofs to cross the thresholds of the walk-in baths, she stoically left a heap of dung on the marble floor of the kitchen, much to the delight of the participants for whom the cow-pat was an added blessing.

ARNOLD VAN GENNEP, in his pioneering work on ritual ([1909] 1960), focused on limens, or thresholds, as significant stopping spaces within rites of passage. He wrote that ritual subjects were liminal for the duration of the ritual, lodged "betwixt and between" positions assigned and arrayed by law, custom, convention, and ceremony (Turner 1967, 93–103; 1969a, 95, 1969b, 94–96, 102–6). For Van Gennep limens were not only dangerous and difficult spaces but also magical. He differentiated three phases to ritual space based on their relationship to the limen: preliminal (separation or isolation, during which individuals are separated from their group), liminal (in between or transitional), and postliminal (reintegration into the social group). Half a century later, Victor Turner's focus on the continuity of social structure led him to argue that liminality was limited both temporally and spatially, and was essentially a space of anti-structure, but he acknowledged that the limen was a profoundly creative and indeed transformative space for individuals partaking in ritual, stating, "Liminality . . . [is] a realm of pure possibility whence novel configurations of ideas and relations may arise" (1967, 97).

Consideration of a space of liminality thus provides the ground for a strategic consideration of the possibility of creativity and wonder. Ritual process is transformatory, creative, and generative, for it allows its participants to remain in the dangerous and productive space in between—the liminal space—constantly. Shifts in the discourse of wonder create and sustain a way of contesting received limits while simultaneously reconfiguring and reimagining ontological possibilities[1]—what we might term a simultaneous "rupture-capture." I argue that this engages a dual process of rupture-capture that allows ritual participants to occupy and engage two seemingly contradictory forces at the same time. Michael Puett insightfully theorizes that ritual allows for subjunctive spaces—wishful emotive spaces oriented to the future—that encourage both the appreciation of perspective and the imagination of horizons (2008, 18). This recognition of the space between what is now and what is possible is but a condition of subjunction, which simultaneously allows for "recovering the moments of wonder that make the ordinary extraordinary; for seeding new initiatives that cultivate fresh vocabularies and trajectories" (Mathur and da Cunha 2006, 7).

In Malleshwaram, the rituals of space and dwelling such as the griha-pravesham work in three primary ways: to organize and categorize space as sacred and nonsacred, the ecological to the built; to sanctify and domesticate space by purifying it to be occupied; and to remedy mistakes made in the material articulation of the space itself. Rituals are not limited to temple publics but flow unchecked into the spaces of the city. The actions of loss and change ensured that the city was no longer merely fixed and material but was instead *in a process of world making*. When seen thus—as world-crafting events—the city's rituals basically devolved into two types—the prophylactic and the remedial. Through the recording of these ritual acts, I explore the architecture of this wonderment.[2]

Grounded Wonder

When I began fieldwork in 1998, elderly residents of Malleshwaram, many of whom had lived there for their entire lives, spoke fondly of the tutelary deity of the neighborhood: Kadu Malleshwara—Shiva of the Forest—in the form of the lingam or priapus with a third eye.[3] Shivanna, eponymously named after the deity, and a devotee of the Kadu Malleshwara Temple, called the deity "Kannappa," an etymological reference to the Tamil word for eye. The panopticon of the Lingam's eye—*kanne*—is a significant source of wonder to localites.[4] Shivanna insisted that the deity's third eye was all-seeing and that this clairvoyant insight inhabited the space of the temple, its environs, and even the localites, affording them a moral insight that others did not possess. In Malleshwaram, as elsewhere in India, the Hindu sociocosmic order is expressed as an aggregate of territorially specific, interdependent, mutually constituting and sustaining myths reflecting a parallel spatio-temporal cosmological order.

But according to geologists in the Bangalore region, the Kadu Malleshwara deity was an outcrop of ancient gneiss rock, part of the rock that formed much of the peninsular Deccan plateau. Devotees to the temple spoke of the rocky outcrop on which Malleshwaram was built, "*gaare kallu*" in Kannada, as undergirding the durability of all life.

In opposition to the hard longevity of the rock was the fluid persistence of water; its liquid capacity to bring fertility was part of Bangalorean folklore. Riparian pleasure abounds in *Sthala Purana* (Sanskrit: the myths of place) of the great temples of the region. Tanks—man-made lakes—and streams in and around Malleshwaram dominated the imagination as *jeevananadi* (Kannada: the river of life), symbols of fertility, prosperity, and plenitude.[5] Rama, the watchman at the Ganesha Temple, who had grown up in a small house where the hills of Malleshwaram met the flat land of Swimming Pool Extension,[6] poetically described the neighborhood of his youth as "*thumba 'mood' itthu* [Kannada: it had mood]," implying that it was emotionally connected and evoked different modes of feeling. To the older localites, this topos of Malleshwaram, of rocks, trees, and lakes, was a singular evocation of the much-beloved sacred geography of India. For inhabitants, the landscape of the city was grounding—locational, emotional, dreamy, discursive, self-framing, protective, and prognosticatory.[7] For them, the landscape and its connections with ecological and local divinity were real—sensual and visceral.

But in the early 1990s when Malleshwaram became *the* experimental site for building, Bangalore developers Kaytee Developments, Purvankara Builders, and Brigade Developments, along with Bombay developers Prestige, Raheja, and Embassy groups, in cahoots with corrupt city government, bulldozed and dynamited the rocks and drained the tanks to make way for more building lots. A series of exogenous factors, including the liberalization of the Indian economy in the early 1990s followed by the global market for labor, washed over Malleshwaram—what economists bleakly call "human capital externalities" (Glaeser 2011, 316–42)—making Bangalore a hotspot of growth. During the twenty or so years of my study, land value in Malleshwaram rose at a rate of over 300 percent per decade. The neighborhood changed from low-lying, middle-class, and upper-caste small bungalows of local "old money" families to vertical upper-middle-class luxury apartment complexes, largely occupied by a new, boomtown bourgeoisie, a global software workforce, to whom locality and ecology seemed unimportant. The neighborhood became more diverse, anomic, and unsustainable, resulting in public service issues such as water shortages and rolling blackouts.

The shifting visual field of the neighborhood, with the cutting of trees and the eruption of giant billboards and towering edifices in a few short years, led to a state of dizzying disorientation.[8] Bungalows were knocked down to make way for midsized apartment buildings, and in turn midsized apartment building were bulldozed to make way for luxury complexes.[9] Rapid and widespread automobilization compounded the disorientation.[10] As the ecology became precarious against the onslaught of the rapidly growing and changing city, its precarity encouraged an emergent understanding of the city as an archive of lost wonder,[11] a space where mystery nourishes discourse and where practice and emotion intersect to create a growing disorientation. The ghostly presence of the lost topos of Malleshwaram is one of the causes of a pervading sense of the uncanny, in which the unhomelike feeling of the uncanny[12]—the strangely, uncomfortably familiar—is embedded in change. This enduring disorientation transformed nostalgia itself into an endless condition of loss. I was sensitive to the evocation of loss in its material built form, for this was the city in which I had grown up and become an architect. I knew most of its streets and byways, its peculiarities and delights. My own nostalgia echoed in the anger of citizenry who felt their city was being slowly destroyed by the triple forces of a kleptocracy—rule-bending developers, pay-to-play bureaucrats, and corrupt politicians. Dwelling in these vacuous yet comfortable spaces made residents recondition and organize their experience of the fractured city as the experimental parts of a subjunctive condition, in which the imagined utopia could be made real.

But I realized quickly that for some, this nostalgia was read as a loss of a socially homogenous city and a Hindu identity. The loss of a landscape that was familiar and accepted was easily attributed to Western-style capitalism, allowing for political and politicized arguments for a retrieval of a "Hindu" past and arguments for a "return" to a lost mythic landscape that was not local but national.[13] At the time I began my fieldwork, these arguments were being forcefully made by means of the nationalist project of the building of a temple at Ram Janam Bhoomi complex in Ayodhya, a radical reconstruction of a muscular—and modern—Hindu identity.[14] But when a group of young men went around with sacred bricks for donations that would be used to build this iconic Ram temple, localites met them with polite disinterest.[15] The nostalgic condition foreclosed the possibility of passing from the domain of the possible to the realm of the actual. In this case, nostalgia operated as an agentive state of resistance opposing the quick amnesiac forces of development.

And Ungrounded Wonder

By 2002 Malleshwaram was on the cusp of a second wave of development fueled by large investments, legal and otherwise, from Mumbai and Dubai.[16] Illegal land grabs became commonplace in the first few years of the twenty-first century. Elderly residents like Mr. Krishnan and Chellappa, both of whom had inherited large homes, told me that they were frightened to live alone because developers' *goondas* (Hindi: thugs) threatened elderly residents with injury or even death if they refused to sell. In such instances, wonder

FIGURE 1.1. Billboards for new luxury apartments. Photo by the author.

assumed its original meaning, as a wound. The smaller apartment complexes were destroyed to make way for architect-designed and -planned "estates"— high-rise, luxurious, gated communities replete with amenities and a global modernist aesthetic that became the norm for dwelling in the city.[17] These estates protruded aggressively into the Malleshwaram sky and dwarfed the earlier generation of apartment buildings.

With names like "Palm Beach," "Golden Thresholds," "The Gold Coast," and "Golden Orchards," these mansions-in-the-sky advertised the new, if generic, wonder of a globally understood "good life" combined with the urban Indian understanding of nature as a utopian retreat from the ills of urbanity. The moral morphology of the city was always suspect and its spaces were risky as Western-educated Indians accepted imperfect Western metropolitical imaginings. This sanitizing of the cityscape toward the bourgeois ideal of comfort and safety led to different vernacular understandings of the city that have become embedded in the everyday fabric of the built form of the city as well as affective subjective engagements with it (Dharia 2015).

The wonder previously located in the local landscape now was imagined as a foreign land or dreamed-of place. The closed, vertical, exclusionary, and securitized spaces of the complexes were an unsurprising outcome of the growing in-migration of the city and the rapid building speculation that had begun in 1992. The residents of the new estates spoke with awe of the marvels of these vertical cities, using phrases like "*bombhat* [Kannada: excellent]," "*thumba channa gidde* [Kannada: very nice]," "super," and "*adischiyama* [Tamil: amazing]." They dwelt meticulously on the details: how the building had tall trees within the atrium; how the developer had taken care to provide water through innumerable underground sources with pumps running 24/7 so the residents need not worry about water shortages; how the smooth lifts were imported from Germany to provide gentle, speedy rides.

The shifting of discourse from the wonder of nature to the wonder of the built form was symptomatic of the broader ontological premises of changing life circumstances. But while the topography had changed, the discourse of wonder remained. Michael Scott has termed the collection of phrases and magical stories describing a place as "wonder discourses." He suggests that they imbue the place with a "heightened interest in or mood of wonder in a given context" and encourages this discursive practice "as a way of cultivating wonder" (2016, 475).

But this wonder was only accessible to the very rich. Entry to these luxury complexes involved running the gauntlet of Gurkha *darwans* (doormen), armed with *lathis* (truncheons) and ancient rifles and dressed in khaki uniforms, who were tasked with keeping undesirable people out. The changing wonder discourses of Malleshwaram are at odds with the original sociocosmological order of the city, but the very fact of their continuation suggests the possibility of a way of life, and aspirations to this way of life, existing in a continuous discontinuity, temporally, spatially, and socially.

Back to Earth

I frequently walked through the neighborhood smelling the scents of the flowers and fruit of the vendors, and listening to the sounds of the traffic. I thought about de Certeau's essay of walking in the city and how the sensual mapping of the city was inscribed on the walker.[18] Walking in Malleshwaram, along a spine of hills, allowed for both the view from above, where the city appeared as neat and ordered geometries set on a terrain, and the other, the view from within, where the disorderly intersections of locality and beingness emerged. But in walking through Malleshwaram repeatedly, I noticed that in some areas there were triangular areas of "leftover" land that often were used as parks or for electric substations and other civic infrastructure, while in other places streets simply ended against a hillside.

Since its construction in the later part of the nineteenth century, Malleshwaram, unlike other parts of the city, has been distinguished by its unique city grid.[19] Ten wide, tree-lined avenues with eponymous names such as Sampige Road and Margosa Road are intersected by eighteen east-west streets called "crosses," which are numbered Eighth Cross, Tenth Cross, and so on.[20] In a peculiarity of colonial planning, the grid completely ignored the undulating topography of Malleshwaram, resulting in the "leftover" spaces and the dead-end streets.[21] As the city grew and the neighborhood became more clogged with traffic, the city authorities designated many of the streets as one way. This led to repeated and growing disorientation.[22] One found oneself in an *Alice in Wonderland*–like scenario in which one encountered the same clogged traffic over and over again at different intersections. Such disorientation often led to creative solutions. Temple processions on foot would resort to shortcuts when traffic clogged the main streets or simply when a particular route was perceived as more efficient. These so-called shortcuts were always assumed to be superior for their efficiency, even when they led through challenging terrains of open sites, hillsides, walls, boulders, and garbage-strewn conservancy lanes. Where actual shortcuts did not exist or city planners had obstructed them, localites would find or invent new ones. For example, city officials annoyed residents by barricading the railway line with barbed wire, thus forcing localites on foot and two-wheelers to cross only at the bridges rather than over the rail lines. When I accompanied a temple procession, I saw that localites not only had cut back the barbed wire in places to create gaping openings but had also marked the shortcut by stringing blue-colored lights on the barbed wire itself. The shortcut was the ever-present seduction of the improvised, of life itself, a resistance to the limitations of the city, allowing localites a permanent liminality.

Anthropologists like myself, when we mistake the map for the territory, mistake a philosophical system for the world. The map then overdetermines the inquiry. In this view, the philosophical ideas become an end in themselves, not linked to raising further ethnographic questions or elucidating other social and cultural phenomena. But the shortcut was a diagnosis that in Malleshwaram the notion of public controlled space was transformed creatively into a space of aspirational mobility through the shortcut, suggesting a different understanding of publics from the Habermasian one of shared imaginations of private readings of texts.[23] In Malleshwaram, public memory is linked in an indexical relationship to the space and provides a stable memory. But new meanings interweave into the space with new usage. This shortcut mapping of the localites requires a new kind of cartography.

Memorialized Cartography

In 1998 Hemalatha, a middle-aged female devotee of the Ganesha Temple whom I had bumped into at the Eighth Cross vegetable market, gave me directions to the temple as "next door to the park." When I arrived at the location she described, however, I found not a park but rather a concrete slide shaped like a kneeling elephant in a fenced area. Upon inquiry, I learned that the park had been eaten into by shops and that the unusable fragment with the decrepit slide was all that remained. When I went back and asked Hemalatha about the missing park, she said calmly, "Yes, yes, there is no park there now. We call it Park, that's all! Everyone knows the park. . . . The road there is West Park Road because of the park." By locating the absent in the present and thus destabilizing the text of landscape, localites are able to remember a lost topos and a forgotten city.

A decade later, I asked Mr. Ramanuja, a trustee of the Krishna Temple, for directions to the home of a fellow patron of the temple. He waved his hand vaguely and confusingly to the north, saying, "If you have gone to Raja Mills, that's too far." Raja Mills, a local textile mill built in the late nineteenth century, was located west of Malleshwaram and had been a significant landmark in the neighborhood, marking the boundary between Malleshwaram and the city.[24] But the mill had been demolished in 1997, some ten years prior to our conversation. In 2012 it was home to the huge and ostentatious Mantri Mall, a series of shiny glass towers touted as "the biggest mall in Asia." When I returned to Malleshwaram a year later, Hemalatha was happy to direct me to the new mall: "Mantri Mall! That's where Raja Mills was."

Residents frequently referred to lost signs of a neighborhood: "the corner where the cobbler used to sit," or "the *Hurigalu angadi* [Kannada: snack shop] where we used to wait for the bus. How much snacks the shopkeepers used to give us." Such references emphasize the use of locality as a form of address and therefore of perspective and situation.[25] The spirit of Guy Debord's *dérive* as a "delirious subjective association" and "interpretive method" toward a transformation of the external world is revitalized with this Malleshwaram context.

But just when I thought I understood Hemalatha's memorial mapping, she added, "Now in Mantri Mall, they say they will have Taco Bell *and* Krispy Kreme! Children are waiting for next year when they will come!" The margins of the neoliberal world had become the aspirational center. Paradoxically, while residents talked about lost spaces, they located themselves easily in both past and future conditions and skated comfortably between the two, much to my confusion. For localites, the Mantri Mall is *both* a mall—a place for new consumables—and the lost Raja Mill. The relation of experience to memory offers a setting for life remembered, and the lost landmark provides a sense of stability even though it no longer exists.

These maps of the imagination recover the moments of wonder that make the ordinary extraordinary and seed new initiatives that cultivate fresh vocabularies and trajectories (Mathur and da Cunha 2006, 7). The memory of the missing circle, the absent mill, and the lost *maidan* all allow for navigation through a landscape that remains alive in the imagination of residents; evocation of the lost mill enriches the present. Most localites gladly go to Mantri Mall, so rather than a nostalgic return to a pristine past, remembrance of the Raja Mill represents an ability to exist in a past selfhood, a reiteration of the present, as well as the actual present. Within this affection lies the possibility of an uncharted future.

So residents not only accepted older axes within the city, recovering peripheral spaces postrupture, they used and extolled emergent spaces in new ways. Such memorialized and futuristic cartography seamed together suggests that there are other possibilities of urban worlds—possibilities connected to the affective, the inner, and the religious lives of metropolitan subjects. The imagination of the topos and the adjacency of the future creates a potential for different thresholds of meaning, in which the postponement to a more providential time of a solution to the precarity of the world is validated. The imprint of these lost spaces indicates a complex relationship to time in which the past, the present, and the future are linked not in linear progression but in a porous and plastic way in which temporality is able to be manipulated and which allows for an enrichment of the new through the residue of what was (Sloterdijk 2014). The legacies of past imperfections act as resources for casting the imagination of both present and future. The pleasures of retrospection are multiple, for they allow the inhabitants of Malleshwaram to "rise above" even while enmeshed within the temporal flux (Niebuhr 1951, 19).

The sense of transcendence provided by such absent landmarks as the Raja Mill allows for an "elevation of memory" (de Certeau 1984, 92; Harvey 1989, 1), but such illusions of existence—the places that inhabit the memory, the lost or repressed—have a way of returning and recasting the present. They can easily become decontextualized, since they only reside in the imagination, but through them locality—the temporal—is reconstituted and recalibrated. Malleshwaram is a palimpsest, where traces of what came before reemerge cyclically to foretell and undergird the new while also allowing for the regenerative spirit.[26] This state encompasses an imagined condition of possibility existing interstitially within the spaces of the built city. The spaces of openness and wonder are fused together in the city, creating an affective urban form that lingers in the imagination of its residents. The adjacency of past and future signal other adjacencies as well. This mental mapping was a thread of continuity, allowing nostalgia and futurity to live together in the imagination of the residents.

"Dead-Endu" Ganesha

On my way to the Ganesha Temple in 1998, I would routinely pass a triangular plot of land owned by the Bangalore city municipality. It housed a huge electrical panel, fenced in and marked by a weathered concrete panel with the universal sign for danger, the skull and crossbones. The panel butted up against a large tree. Some thoughtful individual had painted a sign that read, in misspelled English, "Do not commt noisance here. Violatrs will be prosecuted"—a polite Bangalorean colloquialism discouraging public urination. Despite the sign, the space stank, for men regularly used it as an open-air toilet, urinating against the fence and spitting defiantly onto the sign.

But by the end of the year, I noticed that a shrine had sprung up under the tree, made of ceramic tiles and holding a small Ganesha statue. A plate of kumkum, or red turmeric powder, and a small offering box were wired to the shrine doors, indicating a sort of self-help shrine. A local general practitioner, my friend Dr. Swamy, gestured to the deity one day when we walked by together. He explained: "As long as this Ganesha is here, no one will do nuisance here. They cannot. A crowd will cut their throat. You see how many there are now in Malleshwaram like this. My friend Dr. Ratnam, he put a Ganesha [statue] outside his gate. He lives on a dead end near Eighteenth Cross, and people would come to his compound wall and throw their rubbish. Now see how nice and clean it is. They are thinking of getting a priest."

Although these spaces were often owned by the municipality, they were frequently neglected and garbage piled up around them. Localites spoke openly about the municipality's corruption and the decay of public areas. They alleged that the prolonged neglect led directly and calculatedly to the illegal acquisition of such spaces through a crypto-capitalist network wherein developers bribed municipal officials. Thus, land dedicated to the common good was "repurposed" for private profit. After prolonged neglect, the spaces were perceived as unused and ownerless, and were therefore violable without censure. Small sanctums, such as the one dedicated to Ganesha described above, repurposed the spaces as sacred and Hindu and protected them from violation.

A few months later, in early 1999, Dandu Shastri and I were on our way to yet another early morning ceremony and passed the "electrical shrine," as I had tagged it in my mind. Since my last visit, it had sprouted a flagpole and a red-and-yellow flag, the sign of the "sons of the soil" linguistic Kannada Cheluvaliga, a local Kannada-pride movement.[27] The raising of the flag was a spatial cultural claim, as the linguistic pride movement was largely anti-migrant, fearing the loss of Kannadiga culture and the Kannada language (Nair 2007, 240–52).[28] This local culture war occasionally erupted into violence when bands of lumpen young men would wander about frightening and threatening perceived outsiders and sometimes defacing public and private property that was deemed anti-Kannada. Hence, the red-and-yellow flag was a double-edged sign, of violence to outsiders and protection for Kannadigas—a sign of Kannadiga pride.

Dandu Shastri pointed out the flagpole and the shrine to me. Someone had lit a lamp and the shrine had been decorated with fresh leaf *torana*. Dandu said, "You remember how dirty it was, with men committing nuisance there?" He insisted that we offer worship to the "dead-endu" Ganesha, as he termed the little shrine in the cul-de-sac.

Ten years later, I found that any oddly shaped open lot of land owned by the municipality had either a small do-it-yourself Ganesha or Hanuman shrine or the red-and-yellow flag. Ganesha shrines, Hanuman temples, and shrines to other such popular gods cropped up regularly and without notice in open pieces of land that had been civic spaces, thus preventing their illegal acquisition for private purposes—a prophylactic measure of ensuring land tenure through divine occupancy.

The blurring of the boundaries between sacred and municipal, between vestigial and valuable, is a symptom of a recalibration of the space. By placing a Ganesha in the leftover space, residents shifted the illicit acts of throwing garbage or of building an unlawful building from a simple act of antisocial behavior to an act of antireligious violence. Despite the occasional aggression of bands of young men—"hooligans," as Chellappa called them—seemingly for the protection of Kannada culture, localites largely saw these actions as senseless mayhem, markedly unlike the gentility of Kannada culture. With its sense of civic propriety and communitarian civility, what they called *najuka*.

FIGURE 1.2. The newly built gateway to the "dead-endu" Ganesha shrine decorated with flags of Kannadiga pride. Photo by the author.

In its active religio-civic life, Malleshwaram invested upper-caste Kannadiga preoccupations with najuka. Najuka was used in multiple ways in the temples. Most directly it was used to describe fineness (as in "this grade of cotton or silk cloth is not fine enough to offer the deity") and finesse, a sense of rightness that was not authoritarian, but refined, thought to be a reflection of one's inner being. "Sari neatly folded, hair tightly tied down, earrings in place, being soft spoken, and gentle" were all signs of an adult female aesthetic of najuka. Anyone without these attributes was found wanting. My windblown hair, quick speech patterns, and uncontainable *sari pallu* were commented on by men and women alike as wanting in najuka. But najuka was more than an embodied ontology. It was used in a broader metaphorical sense to denote civic responsibility (as in "so-and-so is *thumba najuka* [Kannada: very refined] because he or she gave money for a new water fountain"). Being thumba najuka was a trace of patronage, of an early civic life bound by caste and gender, of a sort of *noblesse oblige*, where the well-heeled created civic institutions, a core value on which the community was founded. So not only was najuka the measure of a man or woman in a given society, but it was also the measure of the community itself. In short, najuka was how localites thought of and measured their moral value.

The discourse of najuka as public civility endured in civic institutions and was written into the spaces of the neighborhood. Religious and secular institutions that dot the Malleshwaram landscape today—the Raghavendra Swami Matha (a caste-based association), the Yedugiri Yethiraja Matha (another caste-based ritual group), the Malleshwaram Ladies Club, the Shri Chamundi Scout group, the Malleshwaram Association (a residents' association), the ASC study circle (coaching school for students)—all were civic places for shared public enjoyment and use. These institutions of civic life were seen as bulwarks against the moral decay in the city.

But in contemporary Malleshwaram the shrines at homes and civic institutions had taken on new and strange meanings more aligned with protection of property rights through divine occupancy rather than civic service to the community. Ganesha's presence marked places such as the "dead-end" as sacred, and therefore inalienable as government or private property.

Earthen Prayers and Black Money

Field notes, Malleshwaram, Bangalore, March 3, 1999, 8:00 a.m.

I accompanied Dandu Shastri for a Bhoomi puja (Sanskrit: invocation to the earth before building). These pujas were done at construction sites before placing the burden of the building on it, their purpose a beginning, a point of embarkation for the journey of building. It was one of the many pujas deemed necessary by all developers, Hindu and Muslim alike; no construction worker would work on a site where the puja had not been performed, for it was considered an invitation to bad luck. "Who knew what lurked in the earth?" said Rajesh, one of the construction workers at the site. Bhootha (Kannada: unhappy ghosts) were said to haunt unconsecrated sites, causing accidents: scaffolding might cave in, or water rise in pits; machines could run amok, slicing off limbs—all these and more were hazards that workers attributed to an unhappy ghost or to the earth if it was not placated. The migrant construction workers, most of whom were from impoverished areas of the northern states of Haryana and Madhya Pradesh, worked without hard hats and shoes. The Bhoomi puja, for them, was a ritual insurance that Mother Earth would not unleash any terrible force on them.

I realized, as we arrived at the site, that I knew the family who had lived in the bungalow that had occupied the building site. When I had first met them, their house seemed to be falling apart. The overhanging eaves leaked water and the steps to the home were broken. The family was cash poor but land rich. They reported that developers had come knocking on their door repeatedly, offering what seemed to be unbelievable sums of money. Most of it was "black" money—money that was unaccounted for, and therefore untaxable, and delivered to them in a suitcase. Within a week, the main part of the home was pulverized to dust with some well-placed illegal sticks of dynamite. Within a fortnight, the site was cleared of rubble and a tall green metal fence bore a sign with a vision of an Edenic idyll and writing in a flowery font: "Welcome to Golden Orchards—the home of the future."

Dandu Shastri's assistants carried what he laughingly referred to as his "briefcase" holding the contents of what he called "office work"; in actuality the thick cloth bag contained the implements required for the puja: a silver bell, a silver salver, a kooja (jug) and silver lota (glass), a silver lamp with cotton wicks, a little camphor, a matchbox, two Vedic-style wooden spoons, some arshana (turmeric powder), and kumkum. We were met at the construction site by the site contractor, who was called "Contractor Sayabru" (Kannada: Contractor Sir); his assistant, the chief builder known as "Mestri"; and the clerk of the development office known on the site as "Writer."[29]

We stood near a patch of bare earth that had been cleaned, watered, and made ready for the puja. A line gang of female construction workers scurried to and fro carrying piles of cement from a huge yellow cement mixer that growled hungrily as gravel was fed into it. Dandu Shastri's assistants spread out a cloth and on it placed nine packets of legumes that represented the nine Hindu Vedic astrological forces—Mercury, Venus, Earth, Mars, Jupiter, the sun, the moon, Saturn— and the twin fragmented dragon, Rahu and Ketu, the astrological forces of the cosmos. Dandu Shastri recited the Bhoo sukta, a mantra for the placation of the earth, as the contractor built a small Vedic fire altar out of bricks. The smoke from the fire billowed and was directed in the eight compass directions as a purificatory measure. Dandu Shastri then used the traditional Vedic twinned wooden spoons, one representing the male half of the universe and one the female half, to pour ghee into the fire, offering a worship to Lakshmi and Bhoomidevi (the Earth).[30] *Each piece of land and the building on it were worlds that had to receive the right mix of potent mantras to make them fit for habitation.*[31]

Under Dandu Shastri's instructions, the Mestri brought a short-handled hoe and a long-handled iron crowbar and dug into the earth to place small offerings: a silver amulet, a copper yantra (plate with magical cosmological design etched on it) with the design that signified the planet Saturn, a brass yantra with the Cosmic Purusha etched on it, and a small gold piece with an image of Lakshmi.[32] *The rupture of the Earth was necessary, I was told, in order for Bhoomidevi to accept the offerings. A little of the Earth was mixed with turmeric, and the writer, the contractor, the Mestri, and the workers all applied it to their foreheads in a gesture of supplication and protection.*[33] *Dandu Shastri applied kumkum to a brick that the Mestri brought, garlanded it, and the entire group worshipped it, offering it the sacred flame, water, milk, and the nine lentils of the universe. Thereafter it was carefully set aside for later use in building.*

IN 1999, "BLACK" money, as untraceable and unaccounted-for money was known in the city, comprised about 30 percent of every transaction. By 2006, it was up to 70 percent of every transaction as localites attempted to hide their wealth in land holdings. Black money supported *benaami* (Hindi: unlawful) transactions and made the land market in the city porous and inflated.[34] Only the measurements of cartography could acknowledge that the city was twice the size it was thought to be (Nair 2007, 177), but the mapping of the neighborhood became hazardous as land regularly "went missing" from record books. Evaluators and city officials were threatened and harassed, and turf wars among crime bosses, corrupt politicians, and development syndicates erupted over land grabbing (188–89). The laws of development became the laws of the concrete jungle. Security of life became secondary as land grabs and criminal unruliness connected with the building industry swept through the city.

A "ghost market" in land emerged in Malleshwaram, and city authorities were known to "traffic in illegalities," ensuring that a "complex economy developed in the interstices of the state apparatus" (Shipton 2009, 148). When I began fieldwork in Malleshwaram, land transactions were becoming increasingly opaque, leading to inquiries, commissions, reports, and other task force paperwork by the government. Cheating over land became a parallel economy. Fake transactions were recorded on counterfeit government-issued stamp-paper readily available for sale outside the offices of the City Corporation. The local and national newspapers, in both English and Kannada, were full of stories of crime waves, murder and mayhem, and the toppling of politicians and corrupt corporators over land (Nair 2007, 188–89).

Black money flowed through the city's real estate holdings, useful in veiled transactions that were too ephemeral for government inspection to "catch." The black money market rendered the government a passive accessory to public defrauding and reduced the collection of taxes needed for infrastructural growth. The Bangalore Development Authority (BDA), attempting to acquire land for parks and lower-income housing, was stalled by illegal occupation, litigation, and other strong-arm tactics deployed by crooked developers who were abetted by a tired and cynical citizenry. Many of the apartments were cold and dark—concrete bank accounts for excess money. Buildings became active frames of negotiation where temporalities were transformed into intensities of cash.

The sacred brick as center of the home ensured that the house was built on a "good foundation." "Good," Dandu explained to me, meant not only strong in terms of building but also a strong moral foundation that kept the dangerous forces of ill health, penury, fear, and ill-wishing away from the family that would occupy the house. "Doing puja to that brick is important," Dandu Shastri told me, "because it becomes the pillar supporting the family." I pointed out that many of the homes he saw built had streams of unethical black money financing their building, and so protecting their moral center seemed odd to me. He smiled and said, "The whole world is like that, Tulasi. Nowadays dharma is achara! Black money is so much that we don't know if it's black even [sic]," implying that the unethical nature of the market was its accepted customary functioning.[35]

Recent ethnographic descriptions from India show how the mobility of global capital has affected India as a moral universe. Venal consumption habits, corruption and graft, radicalization of religious identities, rupture of family bonds, and gender and caste violence all flow into the public debate to construct a picture of Indian society that "lacks values" or has adopted values alien to "Indian culture." When faced with ethical problems, localites often identified the contemporary age as *Kali Yuga* or the age of evil, and a moral darkness before the apocalypse.[36] The threat of widespread societal vacuity appears to have a particular impact in the changing social landscape of contemporary India, resulting in growing popular interest in religion over the past decades. The wound in the social landscape, paralleling that of the overbuilt city, allows for a space where wonder can emerge.

Moving Marble

In 2006, when I returned to Malleshwaram, I found myself back at the Golden Orchards apartment complex where I had witnessed the Bhoomi puja. In the seven years since I had last been there, the apartments had all been completed and bought by wealthy IT entrepreneurs. When I arrived midmorning, the apartment complex was a hive of activity. Chauffeurs waited for their clients beside idling fancy cars, chubby youngsters supervised by elderly nannies played near the pool, middle-class ladies in spiky high heels drifted in and out of the marbled lobby, and maids carrying pails of water rattled through the "servants' entrance." Through the everyday din I could discern the unmistakable sounds of demolition, of hammers hitting concrete.

As I wandered in, two female construction workers passed me carrying piles of marble tiles on their heads, followed by the Mestri. The Mestri commented that there was something worryingly wrong in the complex: anyone who stayed on the south and west sides of the building invariably had money problems. Ramesh, the wealthy young resident of the penthouse, told me that his business of making large instruments to cut paper had made him a millionaire many times over, but that he had suddenly "lost all the business" after he moved to a west-facing apartment. Others were experiencing financial difficulties so unusual that, at a residents' meeting in 2005, they decided to call in a *Vaastu* consultant—a Hindu ritual specialist on the science of *Vaastu shilpa shastra* (lit. the code of beautiful building, an ancient Hindu prescriptive code of building rather like feng shui).

This return to a premodern harmoniousness proved highly attractive to the middle classes of urban India, who were plagued by guilt, doubt, fear, and greed. The cosmological origins of the building code were supposed to lie in the divine *Vaastu Purusha Mandala*, the magical imagery of the Hindu cosmos that imbued everything built in its image with divine balance (Shukla 1993; A. Kumar 2005). The divine architect Vishwakarma made the tools and crafted these balanced cosmic worlds; his acknowledgment and placation were imperative. *Vaastu Shastra* delineates remedial measures for health, wealth, harmony, and happiness through correction of faulty buildings.

The Vaastu consultant's job was to remedy "bad" vibrations of construction and to give advice for remedies based on the shastras. At the Golden Orchards complex, the Vaastu consultant had come by and done a "thorough job," according to Ramesh's delighted report. The consultant had found that all the west- and south-facing apartments had a "problem." He told Ramesh that the designated "servants' entrance" of his apartment was the profitable one, unlike the entrance he was using, which was the entrance of loss, and that to solve his fiduciary problem, Ramesh needed to switch the two entrances. Ramesh was stunned: "See, all our money was flowing away because we were coming by the wrong door! So I quickly got my contractor, you know, and now we are changing it."

When I arrived, the huge panels of expensive Italian marble that had graced the main entry were being carefully removed from the hallway and transported down the corridor toward the servants' entryway. There was much shouting as a gang of sweaty workmen tried to remove the marble without breaking the individual panels. Ramesh and the Mestri were giving contradictory instructions on how to do this, resulting in confusion and raised voices.

Ramesh was delighted to see me. He explained that the guest toilet, with its elegant commode and gold-flocked wallpaper, was also to be remodeled into a servants' bathroom and an Indian-style toilet was being installed. Ramesh's wife, Lata, bemoaned the loss of her fancy wallpaper: "Now I'll have to order it from that showroom again! That fellow will make such a *hulla-gulla* [ruckus] and say it's out of stock and we will have to wait for months, and make hundreds of calls! If Ramesh goes to London next week, I'll get him to pick up some good wallpaper for the new toilet." Then she added to me, "It's really bad that these architects don't check on all this. Such a problem!"

Nilanjan Babu, a Vaastu consultant, educated me when he stopped by for a consultation after Ramesh's bathroom was complete: "Vaastu is a science. There are three forces, *Vayu*, *Jala*, and *Agni* [Sanskrit: wind, water, and fire], and these must be kept in their right place. If something goes wrong in life, it is because these elements are out of place. When they are balanced, we can be happy, prosperous, and live a good life." He listed a few remedies that Vaastu facilitated: how a mirrored wall placed in the right direction helped ensure fairness in the division of family property, how a "small change" like moving a bedroom enabled a couple to have children, and so on.

Meera, a Golden Orchards resident, told me that she would "never" build a house without Nilanjan Babu's consultation: "I did my previous house and got it fully done up. Interiors, curtains, all antique furnishings, modern bathrooms, everything! And after we moved in, so many worries—illness, my dad died, Sanju, my son, got sick, he got into bad company at school—all that started to happen. We thought the house must have some bad things and we did so many *shanthis* [Sanskrit: remedial worship] for it. We finally called Nilanjan Babu. He said the ground was not good. So just like that we just sold it off! Finally, I had peace of mind." Vaastu was a remedial and reworlding exercise in which, as Nilanjan Babu claimed, "feeling at home" was the core concern.

With the parallel increases of precarity and aspiration brought about by neoliberalism, Vaastu consultants have become all the rage in Malleshwaram to counteract the disharmony and rupture of modern urban spaces. Nilanjan Babu's cell phone number was being circulated among the female devotees in the Krishna Temple as a "good" Vaastu consultant.

I spoke to Nilanjan Babu as he was performing a Vaastu "checkup," a diagnostic visit to a home. He likened the flow of space to the flow of blood: "See, if the blood [Hindi: *rakt*] is bad, if it is blocked, then the person cannot be well. Like if the house is wrong or the space is blocked, then the family cannot be happy and well. Something will go wrong." He walked all over the apartment muttering to himself, then he took out a book in which he did some brief calculations. Finally, he told the clients that their house was very bad for their health. They looked perturbed. He soothed them, saying there was a quick and inexpensive fix. First he recommended that they build an extra wall before the front door "to act as a block for the energy flowing out of the house." Then he suggested moving the kitchen from its current placement in the north to the southwest corner, which he claimed was the corner of *agni*, the fire god, and therefore the rightful place for the kitchen where healthy food could be consumed, thereby creating healthy bodies. Staring into the bedroom which the family saw no problem with, Nilanjan Babu told them to move all their beds so that they would sleep with their heads toward the east. He then added that to lead a "comfortable" life, they needed to move all the cupboards and closets, make the puja room bigger, and reposition the master bedroom and the en suite toilet.

By the end of the visit, the family was in a complete flap, desperate to do whatever was needed to domesticate the many bad energies of their home. Nilanjan Babu indicated the problems lay between between materials, spaces and forces.[37] The task therefore, as he saw it, was to unfold the built spaces, to examine how they had been enfolded and what materials they were made of and enfolded, and what was to be done to rectify them, to keep them in harmony with the designs of the Cosmic Purusha. With this in mind, the larger argument involved a bringing together of that which has always been perceived as separate—form and life—through endless cycles of building and improvisation.

Here, space and topography become tissue-like substances that form the body of the Cosmic Purusha, or eternal spirit.[38] Space itself is fluid. The Vaastu consultant acts as a space doctor, diagnosing the illness of the space by such effects on the residents as ill health, debt, and fear. The Vaastu consultant is expected to suggest remedies for the "condition." Tellingly, one Vaastu expert called himself "Doctor" Raviraj.[39] He said, by way of explanation, "You see, houses have *doshas*[v] [Sanskrit: bioelement], just like bodies have illness. So what I do is to rid them of all the doshas. Nowadays Vaastu remedy can be done without demolition or breaking of construction. It is important to understand the Vaastu for main door, Vaastu for kitchen, Vaastu for toilet, Vaastu for bedroom, and all. Incorrect Vaastu affects the money, health in the house. House will be better place after Vaastu. No bad things will happen."

Rukmini, a devotee of the Krishna Temple, said that Vaastu was very "popular" even as "far back as the 1950s": "My aunt had a house in Poonamalli, outside Madras [now Chennai], and she said that the well had gone dry because the house had not been built *Vaastu prakaram* [Tamil: according to the Vaastu codes]. So they got a Vaastu expert and he said that the cowshed was in the wrong place, and that the main door faced south when it should face east or north. . . . So when they changed it, it's true. The well filled up again." For Rukmini, Vaastu was the management and domestication of unharmonious forces in the universe that were unleashed by bad building—bad energies left in the building, overusage of precious space, and irregular building processes—that created spaces that were not in line with the harmonious nature of the universe and did not therefore give residents peace of mind. Rather, these ruptured spaces were active in creating unhappiness and disharmony in their lives.[40] Vaastu is an indigenous critique of contemporary capitalism, rupturing it as a major force and positing an alternative local cultural understanding of space while simultaneously allowing as legitimate the modern, neoliberal ideal of a prosperous life. I was told by Nivedita, a young architect who had worked on Golden Orchards,

> This Vaastu has become super popular with the middle class. It became popular about ten years ago after that book came out called *Maha Vaastu Shastra* [Sanskrit: The Great Vaastu Reader]. These Vaastu guys give the impression that if your flat is built according to those standards, then everyone will be perfect, you know. Everyone is on the search for this perfect *Gomukh* [Sanskrit: shaped like the face of a cow] site.[41] One of our clients paid two crores extra for a site because the site was Gomukh. All these rich guys were all bidding for it and it went up by two crores![42]

For Nivedita and others, *Vaastu Shastra* was a way to manage the uncertainty and precarity of life. To build according to Vaastu, Nivedita said trenchantly, was to "build in the face of fear" of loss. She was annoyed by the changes demanded by the Golden Orchards residents: "This Golden Orchards became such a pain! Finally, we said we can't do any more. But now in my office I have a Vaastu consultant. We call him our Vaastu guru. All clients expect their houses and apartments, even factories, to be Vaastu checked. Better to do it in the beginning. Then we can say that all the plans have gone through a Vaastu consultant rather than have it become a problem later."

The Vaastu norms and codes of space accept rupture as an inevitable aspect of life and utilize ritual as that which makes the rupture whole again in imitation of the cosmic ideal. In a strange and uncanny turn, Malleshwaram has returned to its purified roots within this ritual frame.

But when does the need for remedy end? Nilanjan Babu was clear, saying, "There is no end. Life keeps changing. Too many troubles." Modern spaces are inherently unharmonious, unhomelike, and, therefore, uncanny. They do not fit with the perfection of the cosmos and so are continuously haunted and haunting, although not specifically in the Freudian sense of internal, psychological familiarity. Here, the uncanny is not seen as an internal psychical disturbance but rather as a true external and material disturbance of landscape and building. Vaastu allows for a material agency whereby changes in the form of the buildings and its materials allow for remedy and realignment of forces that are askew. The enacted ritual plays a central role in the navigations of these cosmological flows to align them with this-worldly aspiration. Proper performance of rituals domesticates and gives direction and access to the flow of money, health, power, and resources. As Dandu Shastri said, performing rituals is "like turning on a tap that is closed. Everything begins to flow!"

Building Wonder

In dealing analytically with multiple aspects of building—the ruptures of emergent process, multiple subjectivities, a subjunctive aspirational city culture, and serendipitous growth—the city, both in the abstract sense and as a space that is felt, walked through, and interacted with, represents the construction of an intimate moral and vital experience, a sensing of wonder. As "new information and life technologies enable new types of networks and allow people to imagine and articulate different destinies," changes in the world we inhabit "remake our most intimate inner processes; emotion, cognitive style, memory and our deepest sense of self" (Biehl, Good, and Kleinman 2007, 10, 55).

Wonder becomes a key component, engaging the imagination to posit a different landscape. Retrieving wonder through the memory of a divine and beautiful landscape or engaging wonder through the imagining of a viable and improved future is strategic as it allows, in its consideration of broad horizons of possibility, the building of a "better" moral self and space. In doing so it renders a sense of freedom of possibilities for the residents trapped in the unendurable and broken world of Malleshwaram. This fecund context of the present includes insights into the future. The repetitive focus on rupture, followed by articulations of possibility in the city, should be understood not as a mere memorialization of a lost world but rather as an expressed hope to fix it, to establish something durable and wonderful that does not constantly fray or break down—a creative practice of being vulnerable and open to the prophetic condition of the city.

In this landscape of possibility, wonder is a generative force that allows for a rupture-capture of the techniques, tools, and strategies of capitalism: an anti-alienation mechanism, while there is a simultaneous resistance and reconstruction of the modernist project. Ritual as technique of the wondrous, crafted through religio-technological imaginaries, can be an internally located antidote to the neoliberal promise. This paradox is enabled by a philosophy that allows for expansion and inclusivity alongside control and containment.

Bangalore, November 1999

Toward the end of my fieldwork, I felt the true force of *unheimlich*, the uncanny existential unhoming, a feeling of being unmoored. For the two years of my first bout of intensive fieldwork, I lived between my parents' home and Malleshwaram. I would stop by their home to talk, eat, think, and blow off steam. It had been several years since I had lived at home, and I enjoyed spending time with my parents and my sister, Lakshmi, when she was there, busy with her own fieldwork on cinema audiences in Bangalore.

I would tell my parents about what I encountered in the temples. My father enjoyed my tales, laced as they were with my bewilderment. He was moved to empathy but also, I confess, to amusement. I, in turn, enjoyed his obvious fascination with the priests, the rituals, and outlandish creative trials that I bore witness to.

He listened, stalwartly offering reading lists and tips to make my fieldwork go more smoothly. He would read my field notes, his illuminating marginalia in tiny-yet-firm script, etched in potent green ink. He had his own editorial style: double underlining some ideas, adding question marks to others.

Nearly two years later, as I finished fieldwork and started planning to return to college life in Boston, my father fell ill. Less than a week later, he passed away.

Time became stilled. Wonder and bewilderment may be the place where thinking begins, but for me it became the place where it ended: an abyss. I found myself drowning in grief and loss. *Just* as I had begun to talk to my father about things that mattered to him, loss and wonder in a city that he had known since birth, and was learning the meaning of this mattering, the reason for my finding my voice was taken abruptly away. My bewilderment grew, encompassing me whole, silencing me. I found that I could not bear to look at my field notes with the thoughtful marginalia, for they only conjured up my loss and distilled its green potent poison.

In the following thirteen years, in a vain attempt to return to my previously unbroken life, I forced myself to return repeatedly to Malleshwaram and to the temples. In my mind I was unmoored and yet unmoving at once. But wondering about ritual in Malleshwaram required me to stand within my unexpected vulnerability. As my life changed, reoriented, I saw it mirrored in the changing worlds of the ritual practitioners of Malleshwaram.

But unlike me, focused on loss and retrieval, the ritual practitioners seemed to have a prescription for the durability of life, to be able to see a boundless possibility to repair and heal, to imagine differently, to create, through repeated invitations to, and evocations of, wonder. I was bewildered by their positivity, their good cheer, and their abundant hope in a city and a world where, it seemed to me, life was becoming increasingly uncertain and precarious, but almost unknowingly, I traced the microscopic new changes in this world, watching them mount, sedimenting into a different way of being.

I returned to my notes to make sense of the trajectories I found in Malleshwaram and suddenly noticed that not only did the word *adbhutha* occur repeatedly, but that I had translated it variously as "oddity," "strangeness," "alien," "astonishment," and in one case as "divine." My father had placed a bright green question mark next to the last translation, and at other points where I had struggled, he had added his distinctive smiley face, not the generic emoticon that had emerged as a global icon of joy but *his* emoticon of interest, a smiley face *with eyebrows*.

As I looked at my notes, I bewilderedly started counting how many times adbhutha appeared, and I found myself wondering about the accuracy of my translation. As I wondered, I found my self searching for a composite word that would encompass the different ways localites used adbhutha. In doing so I stumbled my way to wonder. And simultaneously I realized, sitting and looking at the vignettes in my notes, that through the pursuit of wonder, Krishna Bhattar and Dandu Shastri were constructing a way for us to contend with the loss of the familiar, and the terror and amazement of the new and strange, to create and to share a world that we could bear to live in.

CHAPTER TWO

PASSIONATE JOURNEYS: FROM AESTHETICS TO ETHICS

Feeling can create its own reality.
—Warren Buffet to journalist Charlie Rose, August 17, 2011

Simply, only, they adjust! Otherwise *full* tension!
—Krishna Bhattar

The Wandering Gods

Field notes, Krishna Temple, Malleshwaram, January 13, 2013

It was nearly midnight. The streets around the Krishna Temple were silent and dark, lit only by an errant streetlight. Krishna Bhattar, with Shreyas, a young priest who was his assistant and perpetual shadow, sat on the threshold of the pavilion where I was waiting patiently for a festival procession to return to the temple. A small handful of devotees waited inside the lit temple, their bodies casting long shadows in the lamplight. A chilly wind sprang up, and Krishna Bhattar wrapped himself tighter in his red wool shawl. He asked somewhat impatiently, "When will Thayaar [Tamil: mother deities] return? Are they lost? Where are they?"

Shreyas immediately whipped an iPhone out of the folds of his veshti (Tamil: sarong) and touched its blue-lit surface. I looked over his shoulder. He had

FIGURE 2.1. A typical evening procession in the Krishna Temple, with Perumal and Thayaar riding on the palanquin. Photo by the author.

pulled up Google Maps and was following a pulsing blue dot on the map of Malleshwaram. Near the main boulevards some of the streets were marked an ominous red, indicating a bottleneck. Shreyas switched to text mode, tapped on the keyboard, and waited. When the signature "bing" of a received text sounded, he looked up and announced, "They will be here in ten minutes, they say. They got stuck up near the railway line. Traffic jam! But it might be longer. . . . Sampige Road is fully blocked." Krishna Bhattar roused himself. I overheard one of the devotees grumble, "How much longer will they take?" Another laughed and said, "God only can find his way through Bangalore traffic nowadays!

THE PROCESSION WE waited for was part of the Kanu Pandige festival that in turn was part of the Tamil agrarian harvest festival of Pongal, which takes place at the end of the Hindu lunar month of Dhanurmasa (December/January).[1] Pongal is celebrated among Tamil diasporic groups in Bangalore who trace their cultural origins (whether real or fictive) to Tamil country on the eastern coast of the subcontinent. Astrologically coinciding with the star conjunct of Makara Sankranthi, a day dedicated to the sun god Surya, the festival marks the advent of the northward journey of the sun after the winter solstice, a movement traditionally referred to as *uttarayana*.[2]

Kanu Pandige is understood to be a ceremony of the home and farm—of domesticity, women, thresholds to the house and hearth, and calf and cow. It is the postharvest lean time in the agricultural cycle. Cattle are feted for their labor and women are allowed a break from the endless hard work of food production and child rearing. Married women return to visit their natal families and celebrate the harvest. Many just enjoy the time to relax and be cosseted by their natal families. Although localites told me it was about the celebration of prosperity of the marital home, a festival of conjugality, it seemed that Kanu Pandige was a festival of *anticonjugality*, a recognition, though in small part, of the stresses and estrangement that women feel in their marital homes.

In the Krishna Temple, the ritual involved the female consorts of the main deity—Rukmini and Satyabhama—together called Thayaar, or the mothers. The festival enacted a moment of separation in the married life of the deities, where the female deities, Thayaar, left the male deity, Perumal, to play truant.[3] Play acting by the ritual participants involved the deities' joyous "return" to their natal home, the home of the Brahmin patron founder of the temple, Sri Iyengar, and his descendants.

The ritual bleeds out of the temple and into the home, the streets, and the neighborhood at large. In the sense of its urban staging, it was typical of the 103 other processions, small and large, that I witnessed in Malleshwaram over the years. By focusing on a single ritual, the Kanu Pandige procession, over a twenty-year timespan, I show how the ritual itself is stopped yet mobile, morphing and changing through time and within the space of the neighborhood; and how urban (im)mobility assumes a progressive narrative of capitalist expansion, a rendition of the neoliberal ethos in Bangalore. The emotions that accompany such life stoppages evoke the precariousness of neoliberal life, the aspired-for yet often thwarted social mobility. The procession in its totality speaks to mobility, both physical and through aspiration of moving up in class and education.

This theatrical journey of the gods, their mobility through the neighborhood, is overwritten by ethical narratives of virtue, hospitality, and care. Civility and community are the implicit goals of the procession. But the entire Kanu Pandige procession is also seen as charting the movements between the affective poles of the god and goddesses; between Perumal's illuminating anger (*raudram*), Thayaar's sad longing (*viraha*), and the final reassuring peace (*shanti*) of their transformative reunification.

I had been told by Krishna Bhattar explicitly that the Kanu Pandige procession was an affective pageant, and that the performative journey full of joy and the pleasure of homecoming were its medium. He said, "Where feelings become central to what we know, as opposed to what we think, a wisdom rooted in our emotions emerges. Our entire being, mind, and body are moved and moving in wonderment, even if we are rooted to the spot in utter amazement. This state is difficult to reach." When tightly bound by capitalistic, modern demands to conform to the clock of the workplace or institution as localites are, emotions are both on the surface and difficult to validate at the same time.[4] Through the Kanu Pandige procession the streets of Malleshwaram become the stage for an enactment of familiar and expected emotions of loss and homecoming, which neighbors can relate to in their gendered and social dimensions, and these familiar emotions are expanded to include the disorienting and often violent losses that neoliberal modernity brings to the localites' lives.

Indeed, through watching the Kanu Pandige procession numerous times, I learned that Krishna Bhattar's categorization of it as a moral, passion-filled, explicitly normative public drama about conjugal life was accurate. A composite processional journey (Sanskrit: *utsavam*) known as the Kotara Utsavam, it brings together four different established emotive circuits: the procession of the joyous Thayaar to their mother's house, Thayaar's journey to their father's house in the Brahmin patron's home, the angry circuit of Perumal searching for his truant wives, and the reluctant return travel of Thayaar to their conjugal life in the temple. The established emotion of the many circuits is woven through with eruptions of unexpected emotion: the sensuous pleasure of devotees as they host Thayaar, the ambivalence of patrons over the tardiness of the procession's arrival, and the anxiety of the priests and devotees. Passion is the tissue that links the normativity of piety and the imperative for wonder into a tightly knitted skein. The wandering gods of Malleshwaram allow us to evoke the street as a participatory theater of emotions—an intersubjective, shared, and transcendent city space.

Krishna Bhattar said that the patron's family waited with anticipation for Thayaar's arrival and treated them as married daughters, celebrating, gifting, and feasting before their return to the temple and their married life with the deity. Thayaar's reluctance to return was echoed by the devotees, who refused to let go, stopping their progress in the street. Thayaar played truant to the point where the waiting Perumal—in this instance Krishna in his warrior-kingly mode—felt angry at the separation and frustrated at being kept waiting. In the play acting of the ritual, Perumal rode out to look for Thayaar, galloping around the neighborhood on a steed. As Perumal searched for them, the procession of Thayaar sneaked back into the temple. The affective matrix of the happiness of the women, the agentive longing of the family, and the waiting frustration and anger of the male deity as he attempted to, quite literally, domesticate his truant wives were the source of much joking commentary and reflection on gender relationships among localites.

As do the gods, so also the localites. Gods waited in traffic jams and so did localites. They experienced the frustrations of waiting for that which they could not immediately command. This immobility came to rest quite literally in the neighborhood. Movement around the neighborhood and in the city at large was rarely fluid (Caldeira 2000; Tsing 2005), and the gridlock, with its consequent starting and waiting, generated a range of emotions in the participants, from anger and frustration to gratitude and joy; the emotions attendant to neoliberal life: the tension of precarious work, the loss of separation and change, the anxiety of waiting for access and services, and the anger of inequality and denial.

I begin with waiting as a function of both the Kanu Pandige procession and neoliberal living: Thayaar waits to go "home," Perumal waits for them to return, and localites wait to get jobs, houses, and families and to engage the various processes and attributes of living a full life. Waiting comes to be seen as a stoppage, an immobility. Whereas the anxiety of domicile is emphasized in the first chapter of this volume, this chapter explores—through the procession—the fractured emotions attendant to mobility and its concordant separation. Viraha—the pain of cleaving—that Thayaar feels in which patience, or *porumai*, is valued by localites as a way to survive the seemingly endless spaces of waiting translates to the patience and endurance required to flourish in modern neoliberal work environments. Through an imitation of the god's emotions localites find power to deal with the delays that they find in daily life. I argue that the Bangalorean rubric allows localites to survive and even to find hope and joy in neoliberal modernity through a process of "adjustment."

Adjusting thus becomes the Bangalorean path to resilience. This adjustment is pragmatic, instrumental, ad hoc, and experimental. Forged out of necessity, such creative experiments force us to consider religion not as text or in relation to the text but as lived, experienced, and practiced toward pragmatic ends—a "practical piety" embedded in local networks of relationships and values (Reader and Tanabe 1998; Herzfeld 2015). The common understanding of wonder as a goal to be pursued through improvisations and adjustments in ritual allows the ritual participant to contemplate the previously unknown and unseen, where the serendipity of improvising is an essential part of the process of finding the form of an idea that has not yet arrived (Solnit 2005, 5).

Waiting

Field notes, Krishna Temple, Malleshwaram, January 14, 1998

It was my first week in Bangalore, and I was watching the Kanu Pandige pro-cession. Malleshwaram was suffering one of its periodic unpredictable rolling blackouts, and the pneumatic sound of hundreds of kerosene generators filled the night. The procession was a necklace of spectacular glowing orbs of light, and a wall of sound; the torches formed a halo around the thick knot of priests, temple musicians, and devotees.

At 11:00 p.m., we arrived at the patron's home, which was lit entirely by silver oil lamps softly incandescent.[5] The heady smell of jasmine garlands that hung from the ancient mango trees in the forecourt of the home perfumed the night air. "You are late!" was repeated to us several times by several people as we en-tered the forecourt of the house.

The gathered friends of the family were devout but hungry and irritated: "This Krishna Bhattar, always he is late! I don't know why they cannot be on time once at least. Why can't you tell us the proper time?" Another said, "We are kept waiting for hours for you. The young people have to be at work the next day, and so they have left." I was puzzled by what seemed to me to be inappro-priate expressions of welcome, but everyone around me seemed used to these chastisements. I noticed that many of the younger priests made excuses for the delayed arrival and pleaded with everyone to "adjust."

I knew some distant members of the family, and so female members of the family graciously took me into the beautifully decorated home and proudly showed us all the gifts for Thayaar. Arranged on seven wooden steps in the cen-tral hall of the home, the gifts filled 108 sterling silver trays. There were silk saris with gold lace, gold and gemstone jewelry, newly harvested rice and coconuts, beautiful garlands thick with jasmine and lotus, and trays of nuts and sweets. As one guest proudly told me, "Mrs. Iyengar, she decorates the house beautifully for this angamani utsavam [procession of Thayaar]. Nowhere will you find it like this!" Mrs. Iyengar, the lady of the house, generously invited me to stay for the ritual dinner that had been cooked by specialty caterers, and I did. I joined the last group for dinner and waited along with the friends of the family for our turn after the procession had moved on.

As I did so, I realized that gods are always waiting. They wait in Hindu myths for a variety of acts and accidents to occur. For the gods, waiting is an agentive act, for unlike humans, they do not wait in ignorance. They are fully aware of what or whom they are waiting for and what will eventually happen. Yet they wait for the proper time for things to happen.

FIGURE 2.2. Thayaar seated on a swing, receiving offerings at the patron's home. Photo by the author.

As the friends of the family noted, localites were, like the gods, constantly waiting: waiting in traffic jams, in queues, for services, for mobility (Bissell 2007, 277–80). Waiting, and the patience it requires, form the central narrative of the Kanu Pandige procession: Perumal waits for his wives, the family waits for their daughters, Thayaar waits so they do not inadvertently run into Perumal, and the priests and devotees wait for blessings.

Poornima Shastry, a friend of the family, said, "You see, once again we are waiting. Waiting for the procession to arrive. Nowadays life is all about waiting. I wait in traffic jam. I wait for the *mali* [Hindi: gardener], the *dhobi* [Hindi: laundryman], the *istriwallah* [Hindi: ironing man], the maidservant, Mythili the cook, the water . . . everything I wait. Even my son who is a software CEO; he is always waiting for calls from the U.S. or UK! Simply tension. Just full tension!"[6]

Underscoring Poornima's experience, Henri Lefebvre notes that in contrast to our thinking that modernity is a time of instant gratification, it has become a time of endless waiting (Butler 2012). Jean-François Bayart's (2007) powerful political critique of global capitalism rests on the proposition that waiting is crucial to the modern experience. Waiting forces as-

FIGURE 2.3. Trays of offerings for Thayaar. Photo by the author.

piration, the building upon certain hopes, when basic social goods are elusive; and so Craig Jeffrey argues that modern subjects "define themselves as people in wait" (2010, 177).[7] As Noelle Molé points out in her seminal work on job precarity in Italy, workers in the neoliberal economy are expected to bear their own risks in exchange for the benefits of participation (2010, 40). This precariousness of existential vulnerability leads to dread when facing the material realities and moral orders of neoliberalism (40–41). Not only is precariousness of existential significance but it also underlines the radical replaceability of every life and of everyday life—the grievability of life. So this fear, this dread—an anticipatory interpellation of neoliberal practices— creates a "neurotic participant" who "governs himself through responses to anxieties and uncertainties" (Isin 2004, 223). Waiting is part of modern subjectivity and therefore of identity—a "semi-permanent condition of limbo" (2008, 177).

After watching the procession, I was left with many questions. Is waiting a necessary precursor to wonder? Does one need the build-up of waiting in order to fully and properly prepare to move into wonder? SriValli, another devotee, whose house Perumal visited on Pongal day, smiled and said exactly that: "When Perumal comes, we must be ready. Who are we to dictate his time? He comes to us when *he* is ready. We must just wait. He comes fully dressed, decorated and ready . . . he is after all *alankara priyam* [Tamil: lover of aesthetics]. *Nambleke sevichaa kodukarar!* [Tamil: He gives us the opportunity for supplication!]" Human waiting is a microcosm of the deity's divine waiting, the understanding that acts take time and come to full fruition only in their own time.

The act of waiting emerges as a powerful discourse in the procession, one that threads through it, underscoring frustrations and the longing arising from separation called viraha. The procession forms the ground on which the emotions of longing, frustration, anger, and pain are played out. Waiting for both the gods and localites is a kind of immobility, a stoppage in the flow of economic forces and the physical flow of mobility. In waiting, the work of ritual is to provide a stabilizing and hopeful force, not discounting the feelings that waiting arouses but allowing them to manifest in domesticated ways. The moral texture of waiting within this context is that of uncertainty of outcomes and precarity of conditions.

Waiting requires patience (Tamil: *porumai*), and patience was construed by the localites as a gendered attribute—a virtue—particularly befitting women and girls. Madhavi, the six-year-old grandchild of Mrs. Iyengar's niece Jayashree, was getting very angry and impatient at the long wait for the procession. She wanted to eat the snacks and was repeatedly told that she had to wait. She threw a tantrum, screaming and flailing her arms. Finally, in exasperation, Jayshree said, "*Konchom porumai venum!* [Tamil: You need to have some patience!]." The notions of tolerance for waiting and that waiting is a struggle emerged repeatedly through such virtuous exhortations as "*Porumai venum*" (be tolerant) or "*Koncham porumai*" (find patience). That porumai is a feminine attribute seems to suggest that women, or devotees who love god with a devotion that is attributed to the feminine, or those who are in marginal positions, are more capable of moving to wonder through waiting. How is the present of waiting construed? Is it merely "full tension" as requiring porumai, or is it seen as a form of expectation?

Clara Han, in her study of medical caregivers for mentally ill relatives among the poor in Santiago, Chile, echoes the idea that the process of waiting is a struggle involving neither "a series of possibilities that are given in advance nor . . . the adjustment of aspirations or expectations to objective chances" but is an "indeterminacy of lived relations within the present" (Han 2011, 8–9; see also Bourdieu 1998, 208–45). This waiting for life, the indeterminacy of lived life in the present, makes the procession a performance true to the anger of neoliberal disenfranchisement (Sassen 2000, 2003; Tsing 2005).

As a critique of modern life, waiting gestures toward a need to take stock of the continuity, discontinuity, and simultaneity inherent in human society. The many and varied narratives of waiting serve as a corrective to the expectant immediacy of abundance and innovation: the instant gratification of modernity. They allow for renewal and durability while demanding patience and a tolerance for uncertainty. The act of waiting underscores the indeterminacy of the present but also reorients us toward the possible future.

Moral Mobility

On any auspicious (Sanskrit: *muhurtha*) festival day, several processions took to the roads of Malleshwaram. Whereas the capitalist spaces of "circulation, consumption and communication" (Augé 2008, 98) focus on "spaces of flow" (Castells 2000), roads and public spaces are central arenas where much of the work of mobility is done. As with the Ganesha immersion procession described in the introduction, most of the processions had to find alternative routes through the neighborhood to circumvent the construction rubble, the pits for road construction, or any arbitrary stop along the road due to traffic jams. The circumnavigation required by ritual was subordinated to the practical aspects of road building and construction in the city.

Unlike scholarship on the street as infrastructure, where roadways are seen as post-Enlightenment, emancipatory modernity, here the processions become ways to disrupt mobilities and immobilities, aspects both seen and unseen of the spatial, aspirational, imaginative, and social world created by neoliberal Bangalore. Subordinating the work of ritual means promulgating a teleology of ever-expanding capitalism while ignoring emerging subversive practices and generative social mobilizations that have the capacity to transform from within. So focusing on the stops and starts of the gods allows us to ask how these rituals shift the subject to the power of neoliberal politico-economics, as well as how they shape and act on social and moral subjectivity. In Malleshwaram the mobility of the gods becomes a prism through which the understanding of comtemporary mobility as a whole is shaped.

In Bangalore conversations frequently centered on mobilities or lack thereof, both large and small—plane schedules to the U.S. and the UK, travel insurance, holidays to distant destinations, travel through the choked city, phone connectivity to children in different parts of the world, the borders of the internet, the village poor coming to the city were some of the everyday examples I heard repeatedly. In these stories, mobility is triumphal, focusing on new modes of transportation and communication that have improved mobility among middle-class populations and have tended to celebrate speed, flexibility, and creativity. A decrease in the importance of Fordist modes of production in favor of more flexible economic practices, centered on exchange and the mobility of capital (Amin 1994; Hardt and Negri 2000), and free markets, smooth communication, and fluid movement occupy the public imagination. But markets often are exclusionary, borders often are closed, communication often is interrupted, and movement, both physical and social, often is blocked, particularly for the poor, but even for the aspirational middle class (Massey 1993, 59; Ferguson 1999; Sheller and Urry 2006; Manderscheid 2009, 28; Ghannam 2011, 791).

In this mobile-yet-stopped-world, morality shifts as well. It is nuanced, including within it both the aspirational moral as well as a codified set of ethical regulations. Defined as "a kind of habitus or unreflective and unreflexive disposition of everyday social life," morality is not thought out or codified into an ethical set of rules beforehand but is improvised in the moment (Zigon 2008, 8).[8] This flexibility is not a stepping away from the moral discourse or habitus, nor is it a revolt against or criticism of existent dharma. Rather, it is seen as mitigatory and necessary, a practical means, achara, by which to keep the flow of life circulating, a creative ethics of life. This form of ethics is about "acting morally in the collective self interest," (Durkheim [1898] 1973, 163; Lambek 2010, 12), not only fitting our definition of what constitutes ethical life, but also gesturing to new regimes of living and the experiments in moral reasoning and practice that emerge when there is "much to lose, much to gain and much to preserve" (Kleinman 1995, 362). Such ethical experiments extend our understanding of what questions are deemed ethical and how ethics is made operational.

Gliding Swans and Bucking Horses

Field notes, Krishna Bhattar's house, Malleshwaram, January 13, 2002

Krishna Bhattar gathered the priests in his living room and did a quick runthrough of the events of coming days, his expectations for the various processions and their routes, and additional points about the processions. There was much joking among the younger priests as they ate and drank, swirling their hot coffee around in the steel tumblers. Krishna Bhattar told Raghu, one of the younger priests, to "make sure everything is tied tightly" on Perumal's horse vahanam (vehicle). He added as an aside to me, "They buck around a lot, you know, on the horse vahanam, to show the god's power, his bhaga [Sanskrit: glory, power, fame], and his raudram, his rage, when he is looking for Thayaar."

Krishna Bhattar then exhorted the priests to enact, through embodied performance, the rasa, or essential emotion, of the procession: "The Thaayar procession must be like a hamsa [Sanskrit: swan] gliding along, swaying back and forth."⁹ Adding that swans are symbols of the reincarnated soul in Hindu mytho-poetics, he demonstrated the swanlike hamsa walk by gently swaying his body to and fro and rocking the palanquin. For Krishna Bhattar perfecting the swaying hamsa gait popularized in Bharatanatyam dance, gestured to the need to produce wonderment through embodied action; a practical injunction to the other priests.

Krishna Bhattar continued, "And the Perumal procession must gallop, gallop, like a virya ashva [Sanskrit: heroic horse or hero on a horse]." One of the teenage priests behind him broke into a gallop. Krishna Bhattar looked at him smiling and said, "Exactly!" The types of walks that he demonstrated indicated a familiarity with the performance genres and the regimes of emotion he wished to create in the interaction between seer and performer. Here, walking is not, as de Certeau would suggest, a way to make legible a plan (1984, 109, 159) but is instead an emotive performative genre or rhetorical device through which to generate a mood of wonderment.

Krishna Bhattar's imitation of the walks that palanquin bearers were to follow was not mere pedagogic instruction of "rehearsing" but an opening to wonderment where the hoped-for transcendence of that state of beingness "is a further resonance—glimpse, touching, and knowing of the state of bliss itself [ananda]"—a moral philosophy of transcendence elucidated through embodied and mobile performative aesthetics (Zarrilli 1987, 214).¹⁰

After the priests had left, Krishna Bhattar said that his training of the younger priests in the dressing of the deity, the emotive walk, and the ways to shift emotion in the receptive audience was all about the creation of wonder and ascaryam (Tamil: surprise). He became poetic: "Ascharyam kannadi [Tamil: the mirror of wonder] allows for the reflection of the presence of the Lord." The idea therefore is to create astonishment as a stage for the wonderment within which new sacred spaces emerge. Krishna Bhattar stopped and asked rhetorically, "Why is this procession or any procession or puja important?" He answered, "Bhakti bhava yethanam [Tamil: We must raise the emotion of bhakti]."[11] In Krishna Bhattar's understanding, raising bhakti is the imperative and it is therefore his moral duty to create a situation where wonder is felt, since wonder leads to devotion.

He added: "People must feel the viraha *through* the rasa [Sanskrit: emotion, literally 'the juice']. They must feel the longing that families feel for their daughters. They must feel Thayaar's *sukham* [Sanskrit: happiness, contentment], their *shantam* [Sanskrit: peace], and their *hasyam* [joy] at going to their father's house. Then they must feel Perumal's *krodham* [anger], his *raudram* [rage], and his *bhibahatsam* [disgust] at the women's lateness to come back home. *Ide mukhyam! Illena yengerende adbutha varum?* [Tamil: This is important! Otherwise where will wonderment come from?]."

Krishna Bhattar noted that the rasa of the ritual performance was the key symptom in locating the "rightness" of any ritual creativity. The presence of the wandering gods in the dark streets brings to light for devotees the presence of love, grace, beauty, and even inspiration through the creation of a "mood of wonderment" that is articulated and understood through rasa.

In Krishna Bhattar's analysis, rasa and its dialogic counterpart, *bhava*, audience reception, are the animating dyads of emotion in performance, through which generation and reception are linked and resonant (Lutz and White 1986). The emotive walk as a way to perform emotion is central to the ideas of circulation, mobility, and rasic enjoyment. Rasic enjoyment is "at once an inner and outer quality as the object of taste, the capacity of the taster to taste that taste and enjoy it, the enjoyment and the tasting of the taste" (Schwartz 2004, 8–9).[12]

The understanding of aesthetics as capable of shifting registers of meaning and awareness toward the creation of wonderment in and for the beholder is central to an underpinning of contemporary popular discourses on emotion that priests such as Krishna Bhattar allude to.[13] The key premise is that inhabiting the sensual through gesture and being enables feeling to flow toward wonderment. In his study of divine wonder, Rudolph Otto states that the "numinous," which is his word for ineffable wonder, is achieved through feeling. It is recognized rather than understood analytically. The unexpected gasp torn from the devotee when experiencing the numinous is a symptom of this feeling. This focus on the need for feeling wonderment echoes Krishna Bhattar's concern in the Kanu Pandige that devotees need to "feel" the rasas because the "feeling" of pleasure recognition, awe, dread, and delight all rolled into one is central to experiences of the godly, the sacred, the divine,[14] an experience that he said many seemed to think was "lost" in the contemporary mundane world of cell phones, jobs and cars.[15]

For Rudolf Otto ([1923] 1958), wonder is not only an object of analysis, it acts as a mechanism by which to differentiate the ineffable from the mundane. In his attempt to describe the ineffable, sensuousness and feelings of wonder becomes a mechanism of analysis. In following the procession, I felt a sense of being thrilled, which the rich theatrical texture and subtle rhythms of the performance brought home to me. Ananda Coomaraswamy's translation of the classical performance treatise *Abhinayadarpanam*, in which he charts the shift from embodied action to mood and helps us get a sense of how ineffability can be evoked, helped me understand this thrilling feeling I had. "For wherever the hand moves, there the glances follow; where the glances go, the mind follows; where the mind goes, the mood follows; where the mood goes, there is the flavour" (Coomaraswamy 1977, 17).[16] For Krishna Bhattar the training in the swan walk was part of understating the modality of gestures, which in turn allowed for the possibility of training in feeling a rasic pleasure, in getting at the "flavor" of the ritual (Pollock 2016, 74, 110, 120). But it was also more than that. For Krishna Bhattar feeling and understanding rasic connoisseurship is a strategy that allows for the possibility of uncharted wonder to break through and disrupt the ordinary.

In watching Krishna Bhattar sway and teach the young priests to sway and walk I was made curious about the estrangement of the ordinary. Classical understandings of ritual see its performance as allowing participants to lift out of the ordinary and into an extraordinary state. Sloughing away the mundane is seen as a necessity to shift gears into wonderment and bewilderment, so much so that the usage of stimulants to change perception is often accepted and encouraged in ritual.

But Krishna Bhattar's training in processional walks, the epitome of granular ordinariness and embodied pedagogy, did two things simultaneously; it valorized a perception of the world as ordinary, yet it allowed and privileged the possibility that through this routinized walking participants would break through to the other side, and see and feel the wonderful. He suggested explicitly that the possibility of the extraordinary would coalesce in the ordinary everyday. Krishna Bhattar routinized the ritual and its performance, but he also hoped for and strategically pivoted toward wonder; the possibility of disruption; a worlding, which is a generative living in the world and a creation of and in it. It is the worlding that need not have taken place, but does so as an improvised maneuver to hold the extraordinary in the everyday of modernity. Acts of worlding are ordinary yet deeply disruptive of ordinariness, negating automatic perceptions, enforcing a re-cognition—a renewed vision of the everyday—as a valuable foil for creativity in which the divine might emerge.[17]

Krishna Bhattar understood that he was creating a didactic possibility of a moral philosophy of transcendence

Parsing this new notion of wonderment as a pedagogic and moral experience, Krishna Bhattar and other priests find the problem to be simple: how does one construct the context of ritual so that the possibility of wonder can take effect?

The emphasis on context as the condition for an affective worlding is, as the scholar A. K. Ramanujan suggests, a problem peculiar to Hinduism's obsessive attention to categorization.

Such a pervasive emphasis on context is, I think, related to the Hindu concern with *jati*—the logic of classes, of genre and of species, of which human jati are only an instance.[18] Various taxonomies of season, actors, emotions, essences (rasa), etc. are all basic to the thought work of Hindu medicine and poetry, cooking and religion, erotics and magic. Each jati or class defines a context, a structure of relevance and a role of permissible combination, a frame of reference, a meta communication of what is right and what can be done (Ramanujan 1989, 53).

Ramanujan demonstrates that various seemingly disconnected moods, motivations, diets, medicines, sexualities, temporalities, landscapes, and ontologies are all linked through a taxonomic system. So for participants in the Kanu Pandige procession when the procession moves physically it shifts the context spatially, but when it changes form, it shifts contexts emotionally, ontologically, motivationally, and morally, allowing for new possibilities to swing into view. So for me, the repeated viewings of the Kanu Pandige procession revealed that movement, description, and theory are capable of being one.

The Pain of Cleaving

Field notes, Krishna Temple, Malleshwaram, January 14, 2002

Five years after I watched Krishna Bhattar train the priests, Padma, a middle-aged devotee in the Krishna Temple, who had become my friend and sari-buying companion, asked me if I had been with the procession to Thayaar's mother's house in the Golla Colony. Noticing my puzzlement, she said, "You know Thayaar first goes to 'mothers' house,' no? In the Golla Colony." I shook my head as I experienced a sinking feeling and wondered . . . what more did I not know?

That year I followed the procession from the patron's home to that of Thayaar's mother in the Golla Colony. On maps of Bangalore it is charted as "Milk Colony" in reference to the hereditary Golla caste occupations of shepherding

and milk selling.[19] The informal settlement sat across the railway lines to the north of Malleshwaram now squashed between the Orion Mall and Brigade Towers, a gigantic apartment complex, its former grazing land now engulfed within a sports complex. The shrine there, a Raja Rajeshwari Temple, was almost a womb-like space, dark and intimate. It held a folk form of Parvati, a Shaivite evocation of the feminine power of the goddess, supposedly the "mother" of the markedly Vaishnavite Thayaar. This conflation of Shaivite and Vaishnavite divine kinship was a delightful cross-pollination of the Hindu sects that could seem so separate from one another in textual renditions of Hinduism and in the minds of many Hindus.

As we entered the colony, I found groups of women waiting outside their decorated homes with lights, flowers, and fruit offerings. They sang, smiled, and walked briskly alongside the procession carrying their offerings and reprimanding their children who were with them. They laughed as they walked along, and I listened to their excited conversation: "They have come! Come quickly!" they shouted to one another. They chatted happily in the leaf mantapa (pavilion) outside while Thayaar reviewed their trays of gifts in the temple. Chandrika, one of the women, announced, "See the murrukku [savory fried treats]? My mother and I made them yesterday with pure ghee! We made different shapes to celebrate Thayaar's festival!" Another younger woman, Deepa, said she had bought the gold and pink bangles to wear for the festival and matched them to the blouse piece she had been given for the festival. There was excitement and happiness in the air.

Shantha, a middle-aged woman who worked as a clerk in a local bank, remembered the Thayaar procession from her childhood: "It has not changed much. Some of what we give is different but many things are same. We are just happy when Thayaar come to us." Then she added,

Thayaar are just like us. They also want to be with their family. When I came here my husband and his parents lived together. They stayed with us until they "went" [died]. At that time, I didn't have job. I used to do everything in the house. Cook, clean, take care of them. I used to wait for the time when I could go to Tumkur to my family. Every time I had a child for the pregnancy I would go. That's why I had my third child! [She smiled.]

At the Golla Colony, the entire community had gathered gifts for the deities within the temple and laid them out on plastic and stainless steel trays. Doddi Gowda, one of the men there, directed my attention: "Look at the saris!" The saris offered were bright red and bright green "art silk" with tinsel lace.[20]

Padma smiled at me and whispered "chamak-dhamak" (shiny), in reference to the flashy "Bollywood style" of the saris worn by stars of the film industry. Other gifts included wicker plates of beautiful woodland and native fruits such as jackfruit, mangoes, and bananas, and coiled, variegated garlands of flowers.

As Thayaar was wrapped in their new saris, another younger woman, Sarita, spoke to a woman next to her: "Such pretty saris, no? I like the purple color. So nice! Next time we go shopping for Namu's wedding, we should go to India Sari house. That's where they got these saris!" They stood around me laughing and, at the priest's exhortation, singing songs. They watched carefully as he dressed the deities and offered the trays of sweets, fruits and gifts. After the gifting, they formed a disorderly queue to go into the temple and receive the prasadam, which was two kinds of rice, sweet and savory, given on new paper plates and a cold drink in a plastic disposable cup. Suddenly, piped music blared over two megaphones. The lights and music created an atmosphere of fair-like jollity as people took their paper plates, found places to eat, and chivvied the children. The women were tired but at peace: "It was so nice! I feel like I have gone to my native place, my home!"

After the gifting concluded, the Thayaar procession reassembled to go to the father's house. The musicians picked up their instruments, palanquin bearers lifted the gods, and the priests fell in line. They walked in the Oyayal style, the lilting cradle walk that Krishna Bhattar had taught them, carrying Thayaar to the official gate of the Golla Colony, their steps slowing as they came closer and closer to the gate, performing Thayaar's reluctance to leave their mother's home. In turn the emotion bled forth and the community performed their reluctance to let Thayaar go. They burst firecrackers in front of the procession, and the palanquin bearers swung back and forth three times to indicate the reluctance to leave. The viraha of parting for another year was severe. Shantha and I were walking together, and she said, "Who wants to leave their mother? Nobody!"

We finally left the Golla Colony and arrived at the Brahmin patron Mrs. Iyengar's home at 11:00 p.m., where we were chastised yet again for our lateness. "No time-sense," I heard some friends of the family say. Others echoed this sense of delay: "Children have to go to school. It gets too late!"

But despite their untimely arrival, the deities were seated in the outer courtyard and the decorations offered by the Golla community were quickly stripped off and replaced with the gifts of the Brahmin patron's family. The family brought out the 108 sterling silver trays of offerings with dramatic precision. Krishna Bhattar did a wonderfully quick job of re-dressing the deities. He attached the

FIGURE 2.4. The Palm-Leaf Pavilion at the Golla Colony. Photo by the author.

FIGURE 2.5. Golla women with offerings for Thayaar. Photo by the author.

new garlands, affixed the new ornaments, and draped the new, mutely colored, heavy silk saris.

FOR FAMILIES WITH daughters, the emotion of the festival is significant and enduring—the conjoined emotions of longing, desire, affection, happiness, and loss—the marked emotion of the state of viraha. These complex emotions are experienced as evidence of their *prema* (love) for their daughters. The sense of loss centered around the women's departure to their marital homes, a direct link between mobility and emotion. Even today, the popular manifestation of the loss of daughters upon marriage is enacted in music, film, and theater.

The expression of this particular thread of emotion of loss and longing for women is allowed by patriarchal Hindu society. The festival is redolent with emotions of separation and cleavage. It speaks to women's emotions: of mourning the loss of their birth families while at the same time feeling the trepidation and joy of joining their families of marriage, of the frailty of human bonds, and of the dual homes that women inhabit and create.[21] It speaks to the emotions of hospitality, and of the work of caring.

The elderly doyenne of the Brahmin patron's home, Mrs. Iyengar, was very familiar with waiting and separation, having left her own family and married as a teenager as most women of her generation did. The feelings of angst-ridden separation were domesticated by the promise of annual return to the natal family. She explained, "My father took me on his knee when I was just ten years old and told me, 'Soon you will leave me.' I was his favorite. He used to call me '*Chinna*' [Kannada: his golden one]. Though my married life was always happy, I missed him and my old life so much so when I went back to Mysore, it was a big treat for me to spend time with him. But I had my family here also—my husband, his parents, my children, nieces, and friends."

I spoke to Shubha, a young woman who was praying with hands folded and eyes closed, at Mrs. Iyengar's home. She said she liked the procession very much.

Look how beautifully it is decorated. It makes me peaceful just to see. Today there is too much tension in life! Simply tension! The gods are like all of us. They too have tension. . . . See these Thayaar. They are going to their father's house. It's been so long since I could go to my native place to visit my family. My job is here; my husband's family is here. Tension!

See, my mother-in-law . . . she gives full tension to me. She'll say things to my husband. He'll get angry. Like that life goes [sic].

Her face was sad as she said this. Then she added thoughtfully, "*Namblode karma ide . . . yeppame virahath le iruukanam* [Tamil: It is our karma to live in a separated state]." I made a joke about difficult mothers-in-law, and she brightened, responding, "Must be that Thayaar also had tension with Perumal's mother!"

Viraha (Sanskrit: separation angst)—and the longing borne of it—is a perennial theme in the philosophy, art, theater, literature, poetry, and music of the subcontinent. It is an erotic, emotional, and aesthetic understanding of love as a relationship between two divided and separate selves—the deity and devotee, two lovers, mother and child, self and other, guru and disciple, *prakriti* (Sanskrit: nature) and *purusha* (Sanskrit: consciousness), *atman* (Sanskrit: soul) and *Brahman* (Sanskrit: god). Indeed, any yearning borne of separation between self and other that aspires for transformative union, whether possible or not, is to be understood within the trope of viraha.[22]

Mrs. Ramanuja also alerted me to the understanding of viraha[23] as an enduring condition that accompanies modernity: "My son in Delhi only gets leave once in six months to come home. Even when children live next door there is no time to be together. Everyone is so busy. All this is the sadness of viraha." The procession is understood to speak to the drama and pathos of separation, the beauty and pain of unfulfilled and unfulfillable longing, the irrevocability of loss and cleavage, and the yearning for melding into a whole in which the devotee relates to the deity as a lost lover evoking feelings of desire and pain for reunification (Hardy 1983).[24]

But localites make a broader case for a sympathetic widening of the loss and longing from the natal family to the conditions of modernity: "It is about aspiring to the world, a sense of there being a wider array of paths, possibilities, styles and aims 'out there,' about the aspiration to make global modernity one's own" in the sense evoked by globalization (Schielke 2012, 29). In this sense, viraha is a powerful recognition of the inherent sadness and loneliness of the modern condition (Larkin 1997; Piot 1999).

I asked Krishna Bhattar about his thoughts on viraha, the longing for a lost time and place that women expressed as the central and abiding emotion of the Thayaar procession. He nodded and asked if I had read the *Mukunda Mala Stotra*, a popular sacred text of parables. I confessed that I had not, so he told me a parable from the text, of a king named Kulusekhara who praised Vishnu as the font of wonder, as Varada, the bestower of benedictions.

Kulusekhara understood that in the midst of want and scarcity, Varada had the power to endow a devotee entry into eternal bliss (Sanskrit: *ananda*). According to Krishna Bhattar, the gateway to this bliss was viraha for it was a pietic pedagogy, one that trained the devotee into longing for the Lord.

Longing for a lost time or place implies the possibility of finding it again. One longs to return, but returning is painful, because the flow of time always presents something different. When I joined the devotees and spoke of the loss I felt in seeing the trees of Bangalore cut to widen roadways, or a beautiful old building leveled, Krishna Bhattar responded: "For you, each tree is a loss. But that is because you are not in Bangalore every day. When we return to a place in our past and we see it has changed, we feel loss. Yes. Because we are trying to return to ourselves before the loss." Experiences followed one another inexorably and returning seemed impossible. Krishna Bhattar explained that experience, or *anubhava*, is the basis, the hinge, of existence. Its root word *bhu* means *to be*, and it signals experience as both existential and epistemological in one. He said that viraha was therefore a condition of life and of living.[25]

But a wondrous event such as the Kanu Pandige procession yielded a kind of gripping at the center of emotions that dissolved the inexorable passage of time, if only for a little while. The inner experience of wonder is not merely limited to the external and the real but is also an intermediate state of knowing, a crucial leap of the imagination, in which the imaginative experience has its own reality, its own time. While priests focused on subjective experiences of wonder as transformative of the individual, the greater preoccupation of devotees sharing the experience with each other is creating an intersubjective web of pleasure and delight, a community-based experience. Within this context, wonder becomes feeling and resonance between individuals, building to a greater strength.

And the Angry God

In 2006 I returned with the procession from the Brahmin patron's house to the temple at midnight, to find the Perumal awaiting the return of his truant wives. Dressed in bright pink and red, with a blue Mysore turban, the deity was seated on a horse palanquin. Krishna Bhattar explained the rasa of the moment to me. "He [*indicating the deity on the horse*] does not like waiting," Krishna Bhattar said. "He is angry."

As we waited, eight energetic young Golla men swooped down on the deity, whooping the popular name of Krishna, "Govinda! Govinda!" They

FIGURE 2.6. The waiting, kingly Perumal at the Krishna Temple. Photo by the author.

lifted the palanquin, and, in a bucking horselike gait, rushed out of the temple precincts. Krishna Bhatter had instructed the young priests sternly, "On no account must the Perumal fall!" So three of the young priests had climbed up onto the palanquin and were holding onto the deity for dear life as the men bucked and pranced. They smiled and laughed, clutching their dhotis and scarves as though they were riding mechanical bulls. The young Golla men bearing Perumal got quite a workout, lifting the heavy palanquin to shoulder height and shaking it vigorously to indicate Perumal's wrath. They trotted with it up and down the hills of Malleshwaram bucking the palanquin as they ran.

Krishna Bhattar was coordinating the Perumal and Thayaar processions, directing the fine timing needed to pull off the performance. The Thayaar procession was a few minutes late. Krishna looked at me and said, "Full tension!" in English, indicating his anxiety about coordinating the two processions. Then he smiled and said, indicating his affinity with the deity, "Perumal has 'tension.' I also have 'tension'!"

The Thayaar procession finally arrived, entering quietly and stealthily by the side gate. Krishna Bhattar ran to help untie the deities and to exhort the priests to unpack the garlands quickly, "*Shuruka, shuruka!* [Tamil: Fast,

fast!]," he said, occasionally berating them for their leisurely pace with a disgusted expression, "*Innike na parungo, ivva yellmain slow* [Tamil: Look today, all of them are slow]." The sense of time rushing past was not lost on him or anyone watching him, for he kept consulting a large watch on his wrist and looking anxious.

The Perumal procession reentered the temple some half hour later, bucking in anger. Krishna Bhattar had arranged Thayaar in the pavilion and music was playing. We then witnessed the playacting of the enraged Perumal greeting his truant wives and Thayaar placating his rage.

LOCALITES CONSTANTLY REVEALED their sense of "tension," of a gnawing anxiety, expressed largely in terms of a fear of loss: loss of jobs, loss of homes, loss of their children to "bad habits"—evidence of the notion that life is always becoming, that simply *being* puts one in a state of unease.[26]

But devotees of the Kanu Pandige procession explained to me that watching the god act in "tension" and anger freed them to act as well. Suresh, a young devotee, said, "When I see Perumal getting so fed up with waiting, I feel like I can say I am fed up also!" Devotees gain tremendous enjoyment both out of the enactment of the deity's frustration, and from affiliating with Perumal's rasa of anger. When they saw the deity riding angrily along, devotees would mimic the "horse's" gait and prance alongside, laughing in recognition, clapping, whistling in glee, or walking alongside the procession. Interestingly, though Perumal enacts his frustration at the delay of his wives' return, few of the male devotees I questioned seem to focus on the gendered angle of the problem. When I asked some of them if their wives were late coming home, they laughed sheepishly. Then one of them gathered up the courage and said, "She is always late when she goes to her mother's house. Always! But I am not like Perumal. I don't go chasing after her." I asked another Westernized couple and the woman replied, "We both come home late from work!"

Perumal's anxiety and anger is an ideal emotive model. It is a male gendered virtue, in opposition to porumai, the female attribute of waiting with patience. Raudram is the righteous anger of the male god, one who should not be kept waiting. After all, waiting for anything implies subjugation and not dominance.[27] Channeling this raudram allows devotees to feel agency, exactly what neoliberalism would expect them to suppress in the construction of their modern subjectivity; this anxiety also allows the devotees a shift in their perspective from anxiety and reproach to justifiable anger. Here, the anger of the god does not make him evil but rather *justifies anger as a legitimate emotion.*

Krishna Bhattar instructed the palanquin bearers, when carrying the desperate Perumal on his horse, to gallop with forcefulness. It was necessary, he said, for the "horse" to buck and rear with Perumal's fury, as it increased the bhava. Engaging anger, frustration, and staged awe at the sudden unfamiliarity of what should be mundane allows for agency and the deployment of emotion toward a rupture of the neoliberal paradigm and its inability to quash the affective dimension of human becoming. What we see here is a mobile displacement of anxiety and aspiration through a seeming virtuosity of worship. Rituals confront with wonder and affiliation the tedium and anomie of capitalist life.

Just as the relationship between the self and the social order is nuanced and complex in modern India, so anger and suffering are not perceived simply as bad or wrong. Rather, they are necessary as foils for goodness and rightness and just to maintain the social and moral order of the world (Dissanayake 2005, 190). Anger, an unwholesome force, cannot exist in God, as God is dharmic, or, simply put, "right." Therefore, his anger too is justified. Conversely, adharma, or (again simplistically) wrongness, accumulates among men and demons (Doniger 1976, 49). But it is only through the existence of the contrast—dharma to adharma, rightness to wrongness—that the universe exists and with it balance and a true sense of plenitude and possibility. Thus, even seemingly random anger, suffering, and frustration have their places in the universe and are justifiable.

As Wimal Dissanayake notes in his study of the mythopoetics of Indian cinema, adharma is not a negative condition but is the antithesis of goodness. Dharma needs adharma to distinguish itself and so also divinity needs evil to define itself. As Wendy Doniger notes, "On this view God is powerful and good; he chooses to place evil and suffering in the universe, not because he is forced to do so by Karma, nor that he is so evil that he enjoys seeing others suffer, but if he wishes to create a universe at all, it is by definition necessary for that universe to contain good as well as evil" (1976, 49). So we might say that a universe of feeling that has porumai must have tension as well.

Suresh, a young IT engineer who wore Nike T-shirts all the time exhorting us to "just do it," recounted a story in which he had been waiting for the bank man to come with a festival offer to open a savings account, but the man had repeatedly called and broken the appointment: "The day after this festival I was really fed up! So much tension he had given me! I called him up and I said, 'What man? When are you coming? I cannot keep waiting for you. . . . Otherwise I'll simply go to another bank!' Next day he came!" Padma told a similar tale of waiting for a tailor to sew clothing she had ordered and repeatedly going to the shop only to find the tailor absent. Watching Thayaar, she decided on a sneak attack. Arriving at his shop at an unexpected time, she found him there drinking tea: "I told him, 'See here, what you are doing is not good. If you cannot do the blouses just say that. But don't keep making me come here every day.'"

The procession, within its theatrical milieu, captures these feelings of frustration, anxiety, and reproach, and grants the middle classes a sense of heroic power in their triumphs over daily challenges. They are thus empowered, through the transference of divine potency to the devotee, to feel what they are expected to suppress, rupturing and capturing neoliberal standards and confines. Perumal's *viryam*, his courage and heroic emotion, allows devotees the pleasure of agency in dealing with the frustrations and failure of the mundane intimate.

Watching the anxious god act in anger is a cathartic experience for participants who feel stunned, helpless, and powerless in the face of the anxieties of everyday life. They act, mimicking the gods. So participants and spectators are not expected either to perform or to receive the performance as is, hermetically sealed, or to resign themselves to be taught to feel appropriate responses (Pandian 2009). Rather, they are enabled and, indeed, entitled to rupture performances productively to conform to their own needs and expectations, to mimic the feelings and enactments of the gods. It is through such participation—which may seem disconcerting to some—that ancient rituals are modified to allow for disruption and wonderment and to fit the needs of the moment.

But just as the emotion of the mobile performance bleeds into and legitimizes the everyday spaces of neoliberalism while resisting it simultaneously, so too the emotions of neoliberalism bleed back into the ritual, restructuring its liturgy and making it contemporaneous. The combined sense of heroic triumph over daily challenges and of aid against anxiety is the cornerstone of the angry god's appeal, and anger creates change.

Full Tension!

The central anxiety, the abiding tension, of neoliberal life in Bangalore was made manifest for me the day after the Kanu Pandige festival, when I arrived in the morning to find Krishna Bhattar leaning against the door of the sanctum. Unusually, he did not greet me but gestured to me to fall back and wait. I obeyed and saw that he was silently watching an older, soft-spoken female devotee whom I knew by sight. She came alone every day to stand in the corner and sing all through the morning service—in a liltingly beautiful voice—to the Perumal deity. Krishna Bhattar always gave her prasadam with great respect, whereupon she would quietly leave. Today, however, her face was flushed and her normally tightly plaited hair in disarray. She shouted at the top of her voice: "How dare you do this? Here I come and sing your praises everyday . . . is this what you do to me? [*Here she gestured disrespectfully to the deity.*] You just stand there like the lump of stone that you are!" She burst into loud sobs. Krishna Bhattar looked at me and said by way of explanation at his noninterference "Full tension!" Then he added admiringly, "*Adde nindasthuthi* [Tamil: This is true devotion]. Only a true devotee can reproach God like that. She is so angry because her son Prasad lost his job and is now very sad. She is worried that he won't be able to get married now. *Yenna panamudiyoon?* [Tamil: What can anyone do?]."

As Krishna Bhattar and I watched her cry, keening and swaying back and forth at her son's loss, he explained that *nindasthuthi*—irreverence, reproach, or satirical praise—was only possible by those who felt very close to God, those who loved him like a family member.[28] Within this context of intimacy, the devotees' anger and sorrow also exemplify not only the necessary balance discussed earlier, of dharma to adharma, but also the relationship of dharma as a code of ethics to achara (practice), by which the code of ethics is made flexible through practice.

In human terms, to act on this model requires one to be in tension: to be upset, enraged, angry, sad, and to see this as part and parcel of the whole, creating a dissolution of the line between "modern" and "nonmodern." The ability to reproach in a critical insouciant or angry tone is symptomatic of love and connection and the suffering that accrues from intimate and living connections. It is authorized by a direct relationship with the divine and informed by a sense that the priority and omnipresence of the divine undercuts all distinctions and hierarchies.

Since 2006 anxiety and anger have played through the publics of India. In 2012 and 2013 metropolitan India saw a rise in middle-class public protests: violent *bandhs* (Hindi: closures), rioting, arson, as well as nationwide peaceful protests over incidents of rape, control of women's sexuality, and other indicators of middle-class anger. Many economic pundits saw these protests as linked to frustrated aspirations to a good life, as the GDP slowed to 6.5 percent in the 2011–12 fiscal year, the lowest since 2003–4.[29] Savings rates plummeted from 25 percent approximately 22 percent, and the

Finance Ministry of the Government of India estimated that 89 percent of tax payers earned between 0 and 5 lakh rupees per year. The growing groups earn between 3 lakh rupees and 17 lakh rupees per year (Nayar 2012). The lack of avenues for upward mobility and economic stagnation led to political mobilizations. Anger, reproach, and the need to hold people accountable were common and seen as justified, resulting in the social and political Aam Aadmi (Ordinary Man) movement.[30]

The widespread use of the word *tension* was a diagnostic of these stresses and the accompanying anxiety, the counterpoint to dreaming and aspiration for the good life. "Why keeping tension?" or "Don't keep tension!" was a frequently uttered question or injunction in Kannada when I was anxious or fraught. "Tension" is a dominant emotion in newly neoliberal India and evidence of the frustrations of everyday life, of precarity, of the inability to predict most events, of a stark lack of access and a fear of being left behind. As many blogs and newspapers note, the Indian middle classes are angry about everything and anything that puts them on edge—a slow economy, increasing costs, unpredictability of every aspect of life, and stagnating salaries. In fact, urban life in general is thought of as anxious. Residents of Malleshwaram were acting as folk sociologists theorizing on the tensions of urban modernity (Berger and Luckmann 1966).

After watching the female devotee wail for a while longer, Krishna Bhattar said to me, "*Yellame, life oru periya tension, illya?* [Tamil: Life is one big tension?] But Perumal understands all emotion. Even anxiety. *Perumali than nileyaan. Swami than unnmai!* [Tamil: Everything in life is an illusion and transitory. Only God is stable. Only God is reality!]."[31]

Adjustments and . . .

Field notes, Krishna Temple, Malleshwaram, January 14, 2014

Fifteen years had passed since I first witnessed the Kanu Pandige procession. Today, I arrived at the temple at 6:20 p.m. and found it empty. The security man at the gate handed me a printed timetable for the evening. I realized to my surprise that not only was the timetable printed in English instead of the local languages of Tamil or Kannada, indicating a different audience, but also that the printed time of departure for the procession was 6:00 p.m. Unusually, the procession had already left, keeping to the scheduled time.

I hastily got into the car to drive to the Raja Rajeshwari Temple in the Golla Colony, hoping to catch the procession on the way, but I arrived there to find the temple decorated with no procession in sight.[32] I drove to the Brahmin family's home and called a friend, who explained, "We are at Mr. Iyengar's house. Come quickly, otherwise you will miss everything!" I had arrived breathless, puzzled by the change of order and wondering why the procession had stopped at the Brahmin house first.

The gifting was already in full swing. The Brahmin family had significantly expanded as many non-Indian young men and women seemed to have joined it. By their accents I knew that they were from the United States, Australia, and England. Two of the young men, in North Indian–style kurta pajama, were brought forward and introduced to Krishna Bhattar by a member of the family: "This is Dan, Arthi's husband, and this is Robert, Lakshmi's fiancée. The marriage is next year." Krishna Bhattar garlanded them as the yajamana (male performers of the sacrifice).[33]

The procession left the house at 8:30 p.m., and I followed, attempting to decline gracefully the invitations of the family to stay. The family returned indoors; no one but me seemed perturbed by the changes in ritual practice.

I had last witnessed the procession a few years earlier, so along the way I asked Krishna Bhattar about the changes. He said simply, "It was switched [Tamil: maathi] around. They did not like it to be so late when we went to their house. You know that. So they asked if the Golla Temple could be later. So now we go there after." When I asked if this did not affect the ritual, he smiled at me and rotated his hands from the wrist in a typical "Well, I don't know" gesture. So I decided to ask Mr. Raju, the head of the Golla processional committee, and a local politician: "Yes, Madame, they [the Brahmin family] came to us and said, 'It gets very late for us by the time you all finish there so can we have it first?' We said, 'No problem.' It is better for us like that. See, here so many people come. They like to get darshan of the Thayaar so we must give them time." I asked him what the outcome of the change was. He smiled and said, "We get more time, Madame! No need for rushing." He, like Krishna Bhattar and the Brahmin patrons, cited efficiency as the reason for the change.

The procession, which included stray dogs and the boys who carried the lights, crossed the railway tracks through an illegal break in the fence to which had been added strings of lights to improvise an archway through and under the broken fence poles. This improvisation allowed us to squeeze into spaces previously forbidden. The crossing at the interstitial space spoke of other barriers being broken. The boys kept an eye out for a late-night train on the tracks while everyone crossed and shouted when they saw oncoming lights. Everyone managed to cross safely before the "night mail" train whooshed past.

We arrived at the Golla Colony at 9:30 p.m. There, Mr. Raju's anticipated huge crowds greeted us with delight. Krishna Bhattar seated the deities and briskly stripped off the jasmine garlands and muted kanjeevaram saris given by the Brahmin family. He then re-dressed Thayaar in matching pink "chamak-dhamak" style saris with beautiful purple and red rose garlands. The waiting devotees were vocal in their admiration of the deities' finery. I wondered, would the deities now go back to the temple in the gifts of the Golla Colony, Thayaar's mother's family?

It seemed that it was so but nobody, other than myself, seemed to question that Thayaar, who would have previously returned to the temple, their supposed marital home, in their patrimonial gifted clothing, was returning in a matrimonial clothing, denoting a different caste and sectarian affiliation. It took me time to understand the shift and its consequences. Rather than stripping off the Golla decorations and replacing them with Brahmin ones, the reverse had occurred. The deities were returning to the temple in the finery that the mothers' family, the Golla community, had gifted them. The switch also metaphorically overturned the patriarchal premise of the whole procession. The female deities were supposed to go to their fathers' home and return with gifts, yet here the father's gifts were replaced by the mother's gifts. No one seemed to notice or to care about the profound difference in character, power, aesthetic, and value. Rather, they viewed it pragmatically, citing the saving of time.

I was secretly delighted at this untoward and undocumented subversion of patriarchy and Brahmanism in one fell swoop. Krishna Bhattar seemed delighted as well, but for other reasons. He saw me watching him and said, "See, Tulasi, see! These people are happy to see Thayaar. They don't want to let them go. Such joy they show. Full community feeling." He said the last phrase in English to emphasize his point of feeling welcomed.

At around midnight, after the gifting and feasting, the Thayaar procession began the slow trip back to the temple, walking the classic eight-step called ooyayal (Tamil: cradle) and cradling the deities as they went. As usual the procession moved slowly and stopped frequently, to walk forward and then retreat backward three times performing their reluctance to let Thayaar go. They progressed only a few hundred feet in an hour, allowing time for expressions of joy, dancing, singing, parading, and picture taking. Shreyas was taking many photographs and videos on his new iPhone, "for the new temple Facebook page." Krishna Bhattar began to get anxious about the timing of the next circuit and said, "Come, let us go back. The Perumal procession must begin."

FIGURE 2.7. Perumal and Thayaar reunited at the Krishna Temple. Photo by the author.

Thus I found myself with Shreyas and Krishna Bhattar seated in the temple courtyard in the stone pavilion at midnight waiting for Thayaar to come home.

IN 1999 MY FATHER, the Indian social anthropologist M. N. Srinivas, gave a talk titled "An Obituary on Caste as a System," which was published posthumously as an article of the same title in the *Economic and Political Weekly* in 2003. In it, he argued that caste was changing and was perhaps even dead as a system. In order to understand how such a culturally entrenched system of hierarchy could "die," he explored a historical example of a concerted effort to root out caste. This was the twelfth-century bhakti movement, a religio-cultural movement that had unsuccessfully attempted to undo the tight grip of the caste system. The moral to be drawn from the bhakti movement's failure, Srinivas argued, is that "an ideological attack on caste which is not backed up or underpinned by a mode of social production ignoring or violating caste-based division of labor is totally inadequate" (2003, 454). In order to deal a death blow to the caste system, "a combination of wholly new technologies, institutions based on new principles and a new ideology which includes democracy, equality and the idea of human dignity and self-respect has to be in operation for a considerable time system," and it was those very circumstances that Malleshwaram and indeed other parts of India were experiencing (454).

The supposed ancient roots of caste in Hindu religious myth are the evocations of the body of Brahma in the four *varnas* or caste groupings (Hiltebeitel 2011, 592; Gould 1987). Paradoxically, the Hindu canonical texts on social life and morality, the *Dharmashastras*, give no indications concerning ritual pollution or the purity–impurity premise (Olivelle 2008, 240). Under British rule, "caste" became "a single term capable of expressing, organising, and above all 'systematising' India's diverse forms of social identity, community, and organisation" (Dirks 2001, 5); the cruel establishment of some castes as "criminal" in colonial India (Rawat 2011, 27) and the bureaucratic system of categorization in modern India (M. N. Srinivas 1962a; Leach and Mukherjee 1970) rigidified social systems that were previously fluid.

My father took the view that while the caste system as a whole was dying, individual castes like the Golla who are urban, educated, and politically mobilized were flourishing, resulting in a "horizontal stretch" rather than the traditional vertical hierarchy of caste (M. N. Srinivas 2003). This life cycle model of caste stood in opposition to its previous status as an enduring religio-social system of stratification (Sinha 1967; Berreman 1968; Leach and Mukherjee 1970; Appadurai 1986a; Gould 1987; Raheja 1993). It also suggests, unlike Dumontian understandings of caste, that caste becomes progressively less important, in some cases ceding value to class.

If we explore the nature of efficiencies that led to the revolutionary yet unremarked-on losses of Brahmin superiority and patriarchy in the procession, the pressing demands of neoliberal time suggest the need for these adjustments. By shifting the process around and allowing the procession to go first to the Brahmin house and then to the Golla Colony, the caste hierarchy, the aesthetics of the procession, and its rasa have all been significantly modified. The Brahmin family separated from the patronage links to the Golla community by having the priests bring the deities to them first; they were no longer entrained to the rhythms, the exuberance, and the delays of the earlier processions.

Unfortunately, there is not enough space here to engage in a complete understanding of the nuances of caste dynamics, the symbolic "giving up" of Brahmin patronage status, and the rise of the dominant caste Golla community. But it is important to note that I do not suggest that this performance shift had any real world consequences in terms of social justice or equality. I find it strange that the changes occurred largely without any political or social commentary.

But these adjustments of time and direction created new and anxious subjectivities along the way. Subjectivity in the contemporary world "denotes a new attention to . . . subtle modes of internalized anxieties that link subjection and subjectivity, and an urgent sense of the importance of linking national and global economic and political processes to the most intimate forms of everyday experience" (Good et al. 2008, 2). We come to a tenuous stability in which change is embedded. It is also supported and made meaningful by a philosophy of adjustment.

"Adjustment" is frequently articulated in Bangalore more widely as an exhortation, as in "*Solpa adjust maadi!* [Kannada: Please adjust!]," and it includes practices of experimentation, improvisation, ingenuity, and creativity as processes of life. Ideally, it implies an openness, acceptance, tolerance, and democratization of that which is not familiar or comfortable. But in terms of mobility, physical and social, adjustment involves recalculating the processes engaged in when faced with an obstacle as illustrated by the processions in Malleshwaram, which were frequently forced to improvise new routes.

Originally a phrase used by local Kannadiga speakers to indicate a tolerance to inefficient conditions, "Solpa adjust maadi" has become a much-beloved Bangalorean meme most often used as an injunction to find an ingenious "hack" around a problem. "Adjustment" in Bangalore signals a righteous and ethical injunction to tolerance in the face of obstacles and problematic enactments. In its strategic form it is negotiation, adaptation, revitalization, and disruption, a change in convention.[34] So "adjust *maadi*" is the directive for a journey, moving from a fixed concept of the way things "should be" or "used to be" to what they can be, an ethical enactment of enduring virtue. To adjust is an alternative to the agency of anger or the virtue of patience. It allows for a third response, which creatively rewrites the terms of the engagement with neoliberalism. The ideals of adjustment—extension, switching, making do, sharing, improvising, and influencing—are seen as constitutive rather than as components of a stereotype of Bangalorean culture, and are acceptable to Bangaloreans in their allowance for both an acceptance of, a capture, and a rejection of, a rupture, of neoliberal mores.

The principle of "adjust" is evidence of a shifting field of morality within which uncertainty reigns, allowing for moral ambiguity as a plastic ontology. Furthermore, all groups maintain the principle of "adjust" to allow for the changes that neoliberalism brings to the fore. It is a contingent and instrumental yet deeply moral ethics. I can argue that the moral acquires new thresholds, where defining ethical behavior is increasingly agentive. The improvisation that adjustment allows for includes structures of argumentation to take on a harder edge of equivocation but simultaneously allows for sudden change that is deemed necessary—a creative shift. Here, adjustment is not a passive making do alone but a remaking that creatively changes the terms of the discourse.

Adjustment has been appropriated by the middle class to indicate the enormity of particular adjustment-requiring problems such as the series of rolling blackouts in Bangalore in May 1999, when there were no updates or announcements by the city government. Middle-class youth at the temple laughed ironically and said, *"Total-darkness-gei adjust maadi"* [Adjust to total darkness]." As one blog describes it, it is "a phrase that is uniquely and unmistakably Bangalorean" and therefore establishes a local, embedded, and "cool" identity.[35]

Ethical Wonders

In 2004 Krishna Bhattar claimed that it was the need for wonder through strategic use of *rasa* that was the distinguishing feature of enduring rituals versus those that languish. When I naïvely mentioned belief, he shook his head in the negative. He explained,

> No, Tulasi. It's not about belief anymore. Everyone believes . . . that's why they come to the temple. Otherwise they would not bother. But some rituals are just not "fashion" anymore. They are out of fashion. For example, before, some twenty years before, my father used to do many; many people used to bring their babies to the temple for *namkarana* [Sanskrit: naming ceremony]. Nowadays, very few bring their children for this. But people have started celebrating other rituals more, like *grahapravesham* [house warming], Lakshmi puja, and *Sashtabyapthapoorthi* [sixtieth birthday celebrations for married men]. They do them with *maha* [Kannada: big] style. That's when I understood. The rituals that stay are those where one can do show. Where other people will look and gasp and say, "Allllaaa! Look at that! How nicely they have done."

Not only does the wrestling with new alternatives and established orders create uncertainty as to what is true, beautiful, and good, but it also stimulates doubts about the interior makeup of persons, laying them open to suspicions of ethical emptiness and moral vacuity—an "adharma" of modernity, as Krishna Bhattar termed it. Or as M. N. Srinivas states in *Social Change in Modern India*, in the last few pages of an appendix titled "Changing Values in India Today": "A major change that has occurred with independence and adult franchise is the emergence of political power as more or less the supreme value for a very large number of people. Translating this into traditional terms, it is as though *artha*, the politico-economic realm, has become sovereign, cutting itself loose from *dharma*, the moral realm" (1966, 186). Krishna Bhattar agreed. He would often say, "*Yellame* politics!" (Tamil: It's all politics!) indicating the supremacy of a political understanding of the world.

This public debate about dharma has become coded as a political joust for the heart and soul of the Indian nation, against the seemingly adharmic external forces of globalization and westernization through which the nation has lost touch with itself, the artha of modern life. Indians who are Westernized in dress and deportment are frequently described as embodying a variety of vacuities—a lack of moral bearing and "culture," or *samskruti*, of quality, of value, of spiritual rootedness and fulfillment or as lacking feeling altogether. Dharma and its counter adharma are used as ethical analytical categories to distinguish behavior and belief. What if we take these seriously not as descriptive terms—as they have been understood by scholars—but as existential ethical analytics to be utilized? Is feeling then a lodestone for imagining dharma as a discourse of inhabiting the sense of wonder?

The mobility of Thayaar and their flow through Malleshwaram is seen as the metaphorical flow of dharma and the inexorable flow of time. Aligning with the shifting moral flow of power evokes an idea of dharma as the compassion needed to change challenging circumstances; it is a threshold to transformation. It aligns itself with the metaphors of "flow" in the modernist sense of the fluctuations and permutations of the global economy and the flows of self-realization doctrines, even as it smacks of a "modernizing project" (Ram 2013) emphasizing relentless conscious will, intent, and agency in the creation of change. But here dharma shifts from its usage in the classic Sanskritic sense, as "container" to that which also flows in or in this case *out* of the container, and with which humans must align in the achieving of self-realization.

As we have seen, the Kanu Pandige procession has become a hermeneutic site of resistance and acceptance, of rupture-capture, of ritual experimentation. This transformation champions a moral definition of the common good, accompanied by obligations and rights that members of a changing society must respect in order for the common good to flourish (Hauerwas 2007). As prominent religious studies scholars note, there is an increasing likelihood of confrontation in the public realm, and, in order to minimize the danger of conflict, the retention and protection of multiple ontologies must be encouraged (Asad 1993; Casanova and Zolberg 2002). In the processions, the multiple social practices of imagination enjoin the ritual participants to act emotively as a "way to clear space for dreams to come" (Schielke 2012, 31). This notion inexorably leads to the conceptual expansion that the fluid experimentation of achara demands and that dharma in its most holistic sense of ethics evokes. Dharma includes, usually in hindsight, the flexibility of achara as it wrestles with new situations that modernity throws up for localites. Achara as practice is a form of worlding that best captures the enactment of dharma. It makes a world that is capacious, elevating custom and practice to the space of existential being, allowing the politics of practice to be the only ethical construct.

Simply put, we can argue that these processions are mobile sites of worlding, a generative space of wonder. Worlding here is not merely generative—though it is that in the main—but also describes an inhabited world that is improvised and filled with wonder, both awe-inspiring and uncanny, yet yielding a world that is practical, but one which may not be good. The anthropologist Michael Jackson, when speaking of an existential anthropology, sees an interplay between given life situations and the human capacity to transform them. This puts the focus squarely on performance and creative practice: "The world is thus something we do not simply live and reproduce in passively, but actually produce and transform through praxis" (Jackson 2005, xxii). Here, perforce, the will-to-be is a will to create.

Field notes, *UB* City Mall, Bangalore, January 12, 2009

I had agreed to go to the fashionable United Breweries (UB) City Mall in the center of Bangalore with some friends. I suggested we go at 9:00 p.m. and they laughed at me. In keeping with "party time," as they put it, we arrived at the UB City Mall at around 11:30 p.m. My friends decided that they would go to the Skyye bar on the top floor.

We rode the richly illuminated elevator to the bar. As the elevator doors pinged shut behind us on the fourteenth floor of the tower, the all-black suited group of doormen-bouncers chorused, "Welcome to the Skyye!"

As I entered, I found a group of young adult children of the elderly devotees of the Krishna Temple—Anand, Arjun, Vasudeva, Sarathy, and others—many of whom worked for Fortune 500 companies in the IT industry of Bangalore. I recognized them though I did not know them well. They looked startled to see me, and I realized in that instance that their parents did not know of the outing.

The floor of the Skyye bar was lit a pale blue, and dance music radiated into the evening sky. Behind the bar was a neon tower—a squatter version of the Empire State building in New York City—lit in purple and gold with the iconic gold-plated Pegasus logo of the United Breweries on top. Waiters circulated in silence, carrying large trays with crystal glasses filled with 100 Pipers, a locally made Scottish whiskey, and United Breweries' iconic Kingfisher beer, the drink that had made the city famous.

I soon lost sight of the group I had arrived with as they mingled with the crowd to find and greet people they knew. I wandered around, watching the glitterati of the city arrive: men in power suits and fancy Indian tunics,

FIGURE INTERLUDE 2.1. UB city mall at night. The Skyye bar is at the top of the tallest tower, center right. Photo by Sharath Srinivasan.

women with shining hair and glittering jewelry. One of the waiters told me his name was Kashyap; he was twenty-two and had arrived in the city "some years back" from Mandya, a provincial market town some sixty miles away. About Bangalore, he said, "I don't like it. *Thumba expensivu* [Kannada: It's very expensive]." I asked him how much the cover charge for the bar was as I had not been allowed to pay it by my friends, a sign of their hospitality. He said, "It's ₹ 7,500 per person, Madame" (approximately $140, a month's salary for many Indians).

The dance floor was crowded and more people seemed to be pouring in. I leaned over the glass parapet, over low-slung Bangalore, and looked down onto the sweeping greenery of rain trees. The verdant canopy stretched below me, obscuring the noise and dust, the insane traffic, the choking piles of garbage, and the infrastructural detritus of a rapidly growing city. I followed the glass parapet around the bar and squinted to look farther into the distance. Sarathy joined me. He pointed to various landmarks: the "heritage" style post office annex; the midcentury modern-style life insurance building; and the granite government building, the beautifully lit Vidhana Soudha.

From the eyrie, one could still map the beautiful undulating topography of the Bangalore region that I had known in childhood and that held such meaning for me—the gray granite outcrops, the open small lakes, the large thickets of trees. The landscape of the Deccan, cast forever into the imagination of its inhabitants, made a distinctive geography and affective locale.[1]

Archana, a local entrepreneur and wealthy boutique owner, the daughter of another patron of the Krishna Temple, joined us at the parapet, holding a glass of Diet Coke. I gestured to the landscape and her face softened unexpectedly. "So pretty it is, no? So nice and green. I couldn't live anywhere else. You know, some survey they did said Bangalore is now the best city in India to live." She pointed to Malleshwaram. I could just make out the slight rise of a spine of hillocks to the north, beyond the immediate city center, and, at the top of one of its hills, a few tiny spires, of the temple towers. Archana continued, "See, can you see that hill? Behind that is my grandmother's house." She then saw someone she knew, waved, and glided away.

As the moon rose, the city beneath us lit up. Its center was a blue-white light filled with traceries of highways and blocklike offices, while the distant suburbs were pale, golden-yellow clusters of homes. The very edge of the city was filled with velvety black holes where tanks, temples, and open spaces lay. Through the patchwork of lights one could map the growth of the city, and the dimly lit villages on the horizon seemed to be waiting to be engulfed by the bright lights. When I pointed out how pretty the lights looked, Sarathy said, "Better enjoy them now. How many power cuts there were in summer. Full-load shedding there was . . . *everyday!*"[2] He added, "My mother was fed up! I was in London on work and she WhatsApped me every day.[3] No lights, no fan, no AC! It's crazy. Only the multinational corporations had current!" Everyone around us nodded in agreement.

The bar was crowded with young Bangaloreans, all dressed in the latest fashion: Prada, Gucci, Jimmy Choo, and equally famous Indian designers, Manish Malhotra, Sabyasachi, and Gautam Ghilot. Knowing fashion was a metric of distinction among this gilded class of global Indians, emblematic of the "new" India. A young, well-dressed woman came up to me and broke my reverie: "Someone told me you were studying Malleshwaram. I grew up there. Now I'm in New York. Just home for the holidays." I noticed she was holding a thin, black cigarillo. "I'm studying corporate law." One of the localites' children waved to the young woman. "Hey Sandhya! Here for the hols? I'm here with some of the guys." "The guys" I knew to mean the IT industry youth, young careerists whose ideas and innovations had made Bangalore a boomtown over the past two decades. Sandhya asked me to take a photograph of the group, and "the guys" came over, smiling against the neon-lit, pseudo Empire State building, holding their drinks in practiced ways. Narayan, who had also grown up in Malleshwaram, told me he had finished at Harvard, and returned "home" to start a biotech company. "Why stay in the States? Today in Bangalore, the sky's the limit!" Suddenly, he and Sarathy looked at their beeping cell phones. "Okay, got the call from the client in the UK. He's woken up now. See you later, *maccha* [dude]!" They turned to me. "See you at the temple? I think we will go tomorrow early for the puja *Bhogi pandigai* (spring festival), no? Beginning of Pongal. Temple will be full!" As they left they warned me not to tell their parents of our meeting at the bar, and they generously added that they would not tell their parents of meeting me there either.

CHAPTER THREE

IN GOD WE TRUST: ECONOMIES OF WONDER AND PHILOSOPHIES OF DEBT

Not everything that can be counted counts, and not everything
that counts can be counted.
—William Bruce Cameron, *Informal Sociology*

Runanubhanda Rupena
Pashu Patni Suta Aalaya
Runakshaye Kshyayaanthi
Tatra Parivedana.
[Cows, spouses and the home are the result of previous birth bondage and debt.]
—*Padma Purana*

A Treasure Trove

When I started fieldwork, I was so anxious that I frequently could not draw
breath. To calm myself, I would retreat to the quietest place in the Ganesha
Temple, out of the way of foot traffic. This was a space between the *hundi*—a
large, green, metal lockbox in which the daily offertory collections would
be placed—and the temple accountant's desk piled high with ledgers, token
books, and account books. There I could quietly regain my equanimity while
also observing and taking notes without being drawn into the breathless

whirls and eddies of the temple's social relations. I placed a small piece of carpet on the floor, sat down, and leaned against the cool granite of the outer temple wall.

I became so attached to my spot that localites referred to it jokingly as my "office." When they saw me outside on the street, they would stop in mock dismay. "What? No office today?" Every day I sat there between the "clink" of coins dropping into the hundi and the rustle of paper money (Kannada: *hanna*) as the accountant counted the takings, but I unthinkingly ignored the play of money all around me. In December 1998, however, the prodigious power of money slid into the forefront of my ethnographic vision in a way that was impossible to ignore.

On the morning of December 31, 1998, I found Dandu Shastri, the chief priest of the Ganesha Temple, doing *alankaram* (decoration) of the Ganesha deity. For several months prior, he had been urging devotees who traveled abroad frequently on business trips to donate any currency from the countries they visited. He cheerfully accosted every businessman, software engineer, government official, and any other whom he knew to have traveled out of India, and asked them to empty their pockets.

I found him in the sanctum, which was brimful with Italian lira, German deutsche marks, U.S. dollars, Japanese yen, Singaporean dollars, Thai bhat, Indonesian rupiah, and Saudi dinars. He was dividing the currencies into piles, folding them carefully into fan shapes and tying them into long garlands edged with tinsel. The *kiritam* (crown) of the deity was covered in newly minted gold coins, which he had requested a devotee to buy at the gold bourse in Dubai to ensure that they were of twenty-four-carat purity. The deity also wore a new, shining gold *kavacha* (breastplate), which Dandu was unveiling for this ritual occasion.

As with most Hindus, I knew of the fabulously wealthy Vaishnavite Tirupati shrine in Andhra Pradesh, a state in South India, where the deity was dressed in a traditional *kasu mala* (coin necklace).[1] And I was used to cinema stars and politicians who wore garlands of Indian currency at film premiers or at successful elections.

As Dandu Shastri decorated the sanctum with the paper chains of currency, he told me that he intended to keep the temple open until 2:00 a.m. to enable devotees to get darshan on New Year's Eve: "Rupee, gold, Italian money, U.S. dollar . . . all hanna, all the same. Only men have made it different. Everyone wants prosperity on New Year, and what is better than seeing God on that day? People go for party, disco, pub-shub. This will make them come to the temple also. It is all Lakshmi [goddess of wealth, Vishnu's consort]." Dandu knew, as did I, that practices of sectarian affiliations have

loosened in Bangalore and, as I noted elsewhere, that today Hindus of different sects visit temples based more on their private need for solace, and hope
for a possible divine intervention, than on sectarian affiliation (T. Srinivas
2006). Dandu Shastri clearly saw an opportunity in the cash necklace for expanding the devotee base for the Ganesha Temple, but I was concerned about
the seeming crass materialism of the necklace and I asked, "Wouldn't decorating the deity with currency make people equate happiness with wealth?"

Dandu Shastri looked at me askance. He cast the necklace as an aspirational desire: "People know that God has the wealth of all possible worlds.
We can only show a small fraction of that in our alankara. But today, people
want to be as wealthy as God! Everyone all desire Lakshmi, but they know
that she will come to only few. So we give them hope that she will visit them
this year by making this *kasu alankara* [money decoration]." Musing about
money, Dandu added, "There is something mysterious and oddly wondrous
about money. People feel its power. It's like the power of God."

How? I asked.

Dandu answered: "Well, we don't understand the power of money. If
someone knows you have money, they treat you differently. You are like a
king, like a god. You can buy what you like, do what you like. We know we
should not do that. In God's eyes, all are alike, rich man or poor man, but
we humans . . . we are blinded by money. So by dressing Ganeshappa in the
money, it's 'two-for-one' [in English]!"

On New Year's Day 1999, I visited the Ganesha Temple in the morning.
The queues to see the deity stretched for a mile or more, as they wound down
Eighth Cross and onto Sampige Road. I found several khaki-clad policemen
patrolling the queue.

I asked the inspector of police, identifiable by the stars on his uniform,
what time they had arrived. He hit his head in frustration as he shouted at a
young boy to get out of the way of oncoming traffic and said, "We came in the
middle of the night. Dandu Shastri called us because he could not control the
crowd. They all wanted to see 'Kasu Ganesha' [Money Ganesha] today only." I
had never heard this form of the Ganesha deity mentioned before, but apparently the inspector had identified this alankaram as a new avatar of the deity
itself. Seemingly, money and its enchantments adhered to the deity forming
new avatars in a time of capitalism.

Many of my friends and informants found me in the queue, and crowded
around me excitedly as they all wished me a happy new year. They all
chorused, "*Yeshtu chanagi alankara madidarai* [Kannada: How well they have
done alankaram]," "You must see it!!" and "*Aashcharya* [Amazing]."

FIGURE 3.1. Banashankari Devi deity decorated with currency and gold necklaces. Photo by the author.

I met Dandu Shastri early the following morning, as he was cleaning the sanctum and bagging the many coins. He told me that over twelve thousand devotees had visited the temple the night before. He added that the New Year's darshan was so successful that he would repeat it the following year but make it even better since it was the "millennium" celebration. Gesturing to the *murti* (image) of Ganesha behind him, he said, "Trust in God! He will tell us what to do. It will be bigger and better." Vishwanatha joined the discussion: "Maybe we can do alankaram out of cashpoint cards.[2] . . . Andhra Bank are full gold! Very nice! They are giving the cashpoint cards out if you have good job. That fellow Rao [*he gestured to the temple accountant's desk*], his son got one!" Dandu turned to me triumphantly, "*Pathengla?* [Tamil: See?]"

A NEW FIDUCIARY culture has leaked into Bangalore. Money, as we know, is an incredibly powerful agent of profound social and cultural transformation (Parry and Bloch 1989, 3), but understandings of its transformative power are still deeply rooted in the Euro-American historical and cultural economic tradition.[3] Money, in its various incarnations as credit and debt, has bled into the local culture from the global, as liberalization has opened India's previously closed gateways to broader capital access. The modern marketplace is always in the making and innovating, which is a "major driver of economic prosperity and social well being" in India as elsewhere (Hallam and Ingold 2007, 1). Appropriately, in Bangalore and in India as a whole, innovation and improvisation, known to management specialists in India as Jugaad, an indigenous form of bootstrapping, is a central theme and dynamic of becoming part of a modern economy.

Following Dandu's aesthetic *sadhana* (practice), I explore money as part of the everyday calculus of ritual life through its usage as adornment for the deity to create *an economy of wonder* that interweaves with and illuminates the monetary economy. The aesthetic of adornment is more than mere decoration, for it includes a register of social aesthetics, fusing intellectual, sense-making activity with local aesthetic criteria for coherence and beauty. The aesthetic of money as adornment interrogates both aspirational capitalism and ritual aesthetics in powerful ways, rethinking the inscrutability of capital and the occlusions of ritual sacrifice. While economists consider currency to form a singular "frictionless surface to history" (Graeber 1996, 6), in Malleshwaram conflicting understandings of fiduciary knowledge, of durability and materiality, of monetized trust and abstractions, all intersect and act coevally. Dandu's actions foreground the pleasure of seeing and the delight in aesthetic judgment as a location for wonder (Vasalou 2015, 140–47), since wonder, as Philip Fisher (1998) tells us, is the outcome of visuality. Aesthetic experimentation with currency that appeals to our visual senses changes the way we see. These experiments consciously oppose the practical use of money, to focus us on seeing the brilliance and lustrous shine of coinage and gold, and to look at the visual splendor of plastic credit cards and paper money. Economies that build wonder allow us to move between the worlds of "as-if" possibility and "just-so" workability, as they do between the working processes and practices of dharma (what we should do) and achara (what we do) (Saler 2012, 13). They, and we, veer between shared imaginative potential—such as the above-described ritual adornment—and the need for the normative and restrictive constructions necessary to survive in the world, such as money as our primary means of exchange. Situated between the ordinary and the extraordinary, we can assess the potentials and perils of a modern enchantment that capitalist economies provoke. Localites engaged the potency of money in two innovative ways that enable and legitimize capitalist aspiration: they made money part of the "perfect world" of ritual interaction, thereby creating new spaces for it to reside in[4] and simultaneously, they slipped money from the realm of transaction to the realm of wonder.

For Dandu and others, this landscape of money as cash, or a means of exchange, and its physicality as gold, an aesthetic object, as well as its virtual correlate of credit cards, offer the potential to wonder by providing a capacious sense of access to resources. Dandu took the obligation of alankaram seriously as he knew the success of the improvisation and its ability to remain generative were tied to its moral acceptance by devotees. When he first debuted the alankaram, he referred to the "need" or "want" (Tamil: *vendiyade*) for money in everyone's lives and said that "asking" for (Tamil: *kezavai*) money to do good things for one's family was not wrong, so long as "wasting" money did not become a "habit" (Tamil: *pallakam*). Here, habit has a double aspect: that of the sedimentation of experience, on the one hand, and a generative capacity for responsiveness to a particular milieu, on the other (Hage 2014).

But the entry of global capital and the growth of internal markets has led to tremendous economic inequality in a country already marked by social and religious inequalities, rendering many in the nation wealthy beyond dreams of avarice (akin to modern Maharajahs) but leaving millions with aspirations of wealth impoverished. Given the lack of government-based social and economic security policies, many are more vulnerable than ever before. Localites improvise, acting both pragmatically and poetically in regard to money and resources, dramatizing the moral dangers coiled within a productive capacity to reunderstand the economic reality of the marketplace.

Prabha, a tall woman with a gentle expression and iron-gray hair, was a temple devotee who became my friend. On more than one occasion, she proudly announced that her son who was a technology officer in an IT company earned "in crores" (tens of millions), but the next day, when shopping for groceries she would be annoyed at the inflated prices, glower at the vendor, and ask rhetorically, "How can people eat? Everyone has become so greedy." The wider global dynamics of money—the market—provides the space where inequality, inscrutability, and unethical behavior all meet (Harvey 2009; Appadurai 2015). Among the middle classes of Bangalore, both ends of the risk spectrum have emerged. While some who work with and for the global IT industry have seen enormous profit, others are mired in debt, cycles of joblessness, and the feelings of inadequacy and fear that boom-and-bust cycles perpetuate. Localites improvised around the precarity that the global market created and exacerbated, acting both pragmatically and poetically in regard to money and dramatizing the moral dangers coiled within a productive capacity to reunderstand the economic realities of the marketplace.

During such times of large-scale precarity, money becomes particularly potent in a moral sense, overflowing with both saturnine *and* redemptive qualities. Seen as "bitter" (Shipton 1989, 37), "hot" (Walsh 2003, 299), and "polluted" (High 2013, 676), money is difficult to domesticate, and its presence and acquisition are the grounds for moral unease (Appadurai 1986b; Robbins 2004). Dandu's consideration of the visible shininess of gold and excessiveness of currency shrouded such moral unease creatively in a habit of wonder.

There is something different—something modern and capitalist, non-Hindu, or perhaps deeply Hindu—about Dandu's fascination with money. Money in the temple suggests a continual reimagination, reinvention, and reconfiguration of the world and life. These worlds are solipsistic, somewhat antisocial as they suggest the blessing of wealth for a lucky few, but images of success are iconic and profoundly seductive. They bring an imaginary world to life and populate it, making it into a shared aspirational public encounter, a common "good."

In an interview in February 1999, while talking about money and wealth, Dandu Shastri seemed more conflicted than usual. Suddenly, he said that he believed that *yellai* (Tamil: poor people) were very good people and that *vittiyacam* (Tamil: lit. difference, treating people differently) based on what they had was wrong. He added that economic inequality made it incumbent on those who were blessed to "take care" of those who were not. This was a classic patronage argument—or so I thought. But then he added, "I believe this running after money is wrong! It makes us all *pannam pisachi* [money vampires]! But what to do? It is a way of life! How can we change it?" His critique of capitalism was heartfelt. He believed that the acceptance of greed should be questioned and resisted. He clearly disliked the inequality that capitalism brought, and thought that encouraging aspiration was a way to resist capitalist imperatives. Money alankaram was his activism.

Dandu understood the problem of making wealth moral, and so he monetized the ritual economy and ritualized the monetary economy, thus making the boundary between the two permeable, allowing devotees the freedom to question the assumption that money is a transcendental object beyond cultural context (Parry and Bloch 1989). The very ways in which Dandu understood money in aesthetic terms as excessive and spectacular and also as moral and as dharmic demonstrated how and to what extent he was reconfiguring dharma's conceptual parameters. The morality of money and its potential use for aesthetic value include a resistance to accepted regimes of value, thrift, sacrifice, and saving.

In our discussion, Dandu suggested that the ritualized usage of money was bewitched and bewitching, bathed in the imaginative power of wonder, both historically and in the present. On one occasion, Dandu spoke of the temple of Tirupathi, a Vaishnavite shrine in South India that held a treasure second in value only to that of the Vatican. Dandu spoke of the Tirupathi myth where the temple treasure was payment in exchange for a divine debt that the deity of the temple had incurred. Dandu described visiting his friend, a priest at the Tirupathi temple, and viewing the gold crown and other jewels of the deity in the treasury, which he said was filled with "uncountable" treasures. He spoke with appreciation of the enormous cache of gold jewelry and money the temple owned; "long chains of kasu mala from head to toe of the deity, kilograms of gold coins, so pure, 24 carat, that your fingernail leaves a dent on the coins." But then he waved widely to encompass the world around us, the trees, the sky, and the land, and added that god's treasure was to be marveled at in its volume and consequence. It was clear that he was torn between advocating the philosophical and moral repudiation of wealth, yet he was enthralled by the gold and money he had seen and its sheer power to fascinate. Dandu added that in contemporary India "everyone wanted to be like god" to have "uncountable wealth." He seemed to suggest that the Tirupathi deity's wealth and prosperity is perceived as emulatable in a mortal frame.

The visual surfeit of money as treasure in ritualscapes performs a dual function: it not only invites devotees to marvel at the unimaginable radiant wealth of God but also offers them hope to be similarly prosperous themselves. The economy of wonder, of money in ritualscapes, allows for a divine aspiration, at once both immanent and grounded. It reimagines reality, creating a new public sphere of the imagination around money and wealth. These subjunctive possibilities bring forth the very hopes and aspirations that enmesh devotees in the sense of wonder.

An alankaram with money only works as aspirational if people trust in the power of the deity to deliver on the promise and accept the priest as a trustworthy messenger who does his job with sincerity. Money is about such a promise and represents a material form of the promise to pay, of credit and debt. The economy of wonder that emerges in Malleshwaram is in a sense a subjunctive promise of prosperity.

The money alankaram conjoins reason with wondrous feeling, the sensation of beauty, and the sublime, to create an "as-if" condition of potentiality.

It functions to push back the rational economic logic of habit, shifting to a pleasure in money as aesthetic conquest. This allows for the interweaving of resistance and acceptance—rupture and capture—to create an economy built on wonder in which new regimes of value become transparent. Virtual money—the dematerialized forms of fiduciary innovation such as credit and debit cards, stocks and shares—are used within ritual practice in unexpected ways, subverting the expectations of rational banking (Holmes and Marcus 2006) and shifting the discourse both to the beauty of the card as object, as Vishwanatha does in the opening vignette, and to its almost magical capacity to act as a gateway to unanticipated fiscal resources.

The unworking of its practical use and workings of money as aesthetic render it a multiplex object, and the ontologies of the market are brought into focus yet made blurred (Maurer 2002; MacKenzie and Millo 2003). A paradox emerges with regard to trust and trustworthiness. As will become apparent in the forthcoming pages, distrust is corrosive of the aspirational. Distrust of the rituals, and of the specialists who perform them, creates a limit to the condition of wonder.

In *The Accursed Share*, Georges Bataille has argued that the shift in economics from restriction to excess, a shift that has occurred in urban India over the past two decades, is transformative of ethical worlds. It follows that, in Bangalore, the drama shifts from aesthetics to ethics, from sufficiency to anticipation (Bataille [1949] 1991). This new aesthetics that enlists the enchantments of money often leads, as my conversation with Dandu Shastri demonstrated, to an ambivalent ethical regime. It requires a contingent creative ethics to deal with this ambivalence embedded in the everyday interactions with money where the ordinary and the extraordinary are braided together (Das 2015b, 4–5). Focusing on the aesthetics of money allows us to interrogate the meaning of the everyday as an ethical realm in which such creative ethics emerges. The question for Prabha and Dandu Shastri is simple: Can ritual practitioners cocreate an improvisational ethics that aspires simultaneously and equally to this-worldly prosperity and other-worldly transcendence?

Twinkling "Excess"

I caught the deity's eye. He looked back at me, enigmatic beneath a crown of gold studded with large rubies and diamonds. The small body of Ganesha, the resident deity of the temple, was obscured by gold armor three times the size of his body, making him appear magically larger. His elephantine ears were coated in a thick, gold plate with more diamonds. The *Garbha Gudi* (sanctum sanctorum) was surrounded in flashing chains of blue-and-white lights, echoing the brilliance of the diamonds.

I asked if it was not excessive (Kannada: *hecchu*) to have the deity covered in diamonds and gold. Dandu was amused. "Excessive?" he said. "You have been in the U.S. too long! There nobody wears any jewelry and everyone is in black color! Have you seen how much jewelry women wear in Bangalore nowadays? So much!" Many of the devotees agreed. Prabha said with annoyance, "Have you seen these girls? They will wear so much gold, *rombamai jaasthi* [Tamil: excessive]!! Ayyo! *Kocchum kollayama irrukum* [It will have fringes and tassels]." As Pierre Bourdieu (1998) famously put it, excess is norm-breaking (or rather it is the perpetual transcendence of norm). But with norms being constantly tested as they are in Bangalore, does excess become the grammar of life?

Joyce Burkhalter Flueckiger, in her magnificent study of the Gangamma tradition in Tirupathi, suggests that excess is an essential part of the gods' own nature. Gangamma, a goddess best known for her excess (*ugram*) of hunger and desire, leads worshippers to feed, adorn, and impersonate her in ways that only some humans—women more than men—can bear. During Gangamma's festival, female celebrants intensify and multiply what they already do on a daily or weekly basis for the goddess (Flueckiger 2013, ix). The intensification and multiplication, a commitment to an "aesthetic of excess," are a way for the devotee to *become* the goddess Gangamma. God is excess, and so, assuming that the familiarity of a state of excess will attract the goddess's attention, devotees wear excessive decorations and gold to attract her gaze. As Flueckiger notes, "The excess is created and visible on several levels: through multiplicity, distribution, and increased intensity" (2013, 52), offering a different understanding of material agency. It reminds us that, in this case, ritual action to create excess is much more important than narrative/ linguistic "knowledge" or analysis of a condition of excess. The practice of excess creates an ambiance that is symbolically more than the sum of the material objects.

Nothing is understood as excessive once excess is the norm. Being clothed in gold and diamonds is necessary to signify the deity's super-humanness in a human world of excess. But perhaps *excess* is the wrong word, since it usually carries a pejorative undertone indicating crossing a boundary of good taste, of transgression, and of going beyond "enough." Dandu suggests that wealth on a human scale and its display ritually enact the natural state of divinity as excessive and overflowing. So perhaps divine *excess* captures symbolically

FIGURE 3.2. The Ganesha Temple decorated in an "excess" of golden American corn. Photo by Sharath Srinivasan.

that which the human life cannot. Human life is the absence and want of divinity. Dandu suggests that excess introduces the spectacular into the ordinary, allowing potentially for a transformation of the tedium of the mundane into divine wonder. If so, then what Flueckiger terms an "aesthetics of excess" is in fact mere necessity for creating a condition where wonderment can take hold.

Dandu underscored this fungability of divine wealth and human want. He said: "You see human want is everywhere. Divine wealth is only in some places when God wants it. But human need is everywhere." Dandu skillfully transposed the want of the sacred into economic want, making the case that want is ethical construction replete in the contemporary world: "Today anything less than excess is deemed to be a lack or a want. People in Bangalore, they want everything: *kasu, chinna, mane, bhoomi* [wealth, gold, house, and land]! Why should we not offer the god some part of this as thanks?" Manjunath, a young coworker of Prabha's who had accompanied her to the temple, agreed. "Madame," he said as he addressed me with care, being younger and seeing the interaction as official since I was taking notes. "Nowadays people do not talk in thousands anymore, or even lakhs; they talk only in crores![5] Even small independent house is three to four crores! Where can ordinary people go?" This consensus that excess has become a basic threshold of need leads devotees to aspire to worldly success in the form of uncountable wealth.

WHILE I WAS at the Ganesha Temple in 2011, a vast treasure of gold, gemstones, and ancient coinage was found in underground vaults of the Sri Padmanabhaswamy Temple in the neighboring South Indian state of Kerala. Dandu's son, Vishwanatha, and the other priests were agog at the news; they speculated endlessly on how much it was worth. In a story worthy of Hollywood and Indiana Jones, the deity of the temple, a slumbering form of the Hindu deity Vishnu, was believed to be seated on six great vaults holding unimaginable treasure.

Deities can own property in India, though the law treats them as minors (as presumably we cannot know a deity's will), and they must be represented by an official guardian, in this case, the erstwhile Maharajah of the former Kerala kingdom of Thiruvanathapuram.[6] The news focused on the opening of the vaults and the endless counting and evaluation required. Images showed temple accountants physically weighing gold coins on a scale and approximating value with calculators. The news readers, filled with awe, repeatedly stated that "counting is going on for days," and "no one can accurately estimate the wealth of the temple."

The gods of Indian temples have historically been wealthy beyond measure.[7] What Dandu Shastri and Krishna Bhattar understand as divine excess comes from deep within the classical recesses of Hinduism. Gods validate and promote the classical *purushartha* (wealth, money, financial security) as divine blessing and beneficence, and so we can make the claim that Indian religious worldviews see no contradiction between the religious (or so-called spiritual) and the monetary (Parthasarathi 2011). They are interlinked and, in fact, one could argue that money constitutes divine metonymy in the imaginative arena of ritual worlding in Malleshwaram temple publics. In ancient India, temples acted as local banks, their money being loaned to the community for various transactions (Fuller 1988, 55–56).

Jake Halpern (2012), writing in the *New Yorker* of the treasure found in the Kerala Temple, mentions his puzzlement that no one had clamored to have the treasure vaults of the temple opened. But he was unaware that the deity was a person with a will, a sovereign lord, a king-god authority "at the moral, economic and iconographic center of the Hindu temple" (Appadurai and Breckenridge 1976, 190; Appadurai 1981). Offerings were made to the king-god as benevolent despot by devotees whose vows reflected wishes for a peaceful, successful, and healthy life. Halpern quotes William Harman, a scholar of Hinduism at the University of Tennessee: "People make deals with deities, and if they receive what they want they pay up." So any treasure inside the Sri Padmanabhaswamy Temple, Harman said, embodied "centuries of vows." The excess, the visual surfeit of the deity, is thus evidence of decades if not centuries of the pleas of devotees and a scorecard of the deity's benevolence toward them, expressed in treasure.

On receipt, the "material" of these vows—the devotees' offerings—are redistributed in the form of shares (Tamil: *panku*) to the royal courtiers, the ritual actors (*yajamána*), and worshippers at large.[8] The temple recirculates the offerings through the community, which, however paradigmatically and however provisionally, commanded resources such as those that are necessary and appropriate for the support and materialization of the ritual processes. The authority to command and redistribute resources places the deity at the center of a transactional nexus in which the deity is expected to be generous. So excess of treasure is interpreted not as a divine hoard but as the expression of the deity's magnanimity and generosity in the world.

The Golden Calf

Field notes, Krishna Temple, Malleshwaram, August 15, 2003

Krishna Bhattar was doing an alankaram celebrating the cowherd aspect of the sovereign deity Krishna. He decorated the deity in a pastoral aesthetic, with mango leaves, natural-looking bouquets of leaves and grasses, and garlands of wild flowers. Suddenly he stood back and shouted out, "Where is the golden calf? Where is the golden kavacha [armor] for the god?" One of the young priests-in-training brought a three-foot-long box from a locked steel door in the back of the temple. Krishna opened it and took out a golden sculpture of a calf. He stood it behind the deity and garlanded it with a simple necklace of tulasi (holy basil) leaves. He then took out a thick gold armor that had dangling ribbons, and he used the ribbons to attach the armor, covering the deity. The deity and the cow behind him shone in the morning light.

Having finished the alankaram, Krishna bowed to the deity. He then turned to me and said, "Eighteen lakhs! We got this golden calf and armor made last year. Many of the sevakara [patrons] contributed. They like to see it."

THE INDIAN LOVE affair with gold as a stable economic idiom has long been remarked on by popular commentators. In his magisterial article on gold wealth in India, Ajay Gandhi notes that though it is a poor country India holds roughly "ten percent of global gold supplies," and is consistently among the "world's largest consumers" of bullion (2013, 93).[9] Indians possess at least 20,000 tons of gold worth $1.6 trillion, according to a 2012 estimate of the World Gold Council (Gandhi 2013, 93–94).[10] Gold plays a large symbolic role to denote wealth and status in Indian society as a whole, but it is also real investment.[11] Localites value gifts of gold symbolically, more than the metal itself.

In August 1998, when Prabha's daughter, a lawyer, married a software engineer in Texas, she was clothed in gold for the ceremony.[12] She was described lovingly by other women in the temple as "*Chinnada bombe*" (golden doll). In a global economy, gold is inevitably "termed a 'dead investment' or as 'unproductive investment'; economists talk of putting 'gold to work'" (Gandhi 2013, 93), a singularly unpopular idea in India. Gold, silver, and monetary wealth are all considered wondrous, as having a morality all their own.[13]

Precious metals that dazzle are sensorial stimulants used for decoration and adornment of the deity.[14] Krishna spoke of the gold armor as exactly describing the god within, radiant and effulgent (*hiranya*), shining and dazzling (*ujjwala*). To Krishna Bhattar, the gold armor and diamond crown are all merely necessities to convey the radiance and capaciousness of divinity to the mortal mind. He said that God's light was "*suryan polle*" (Tamil: like the sun) in that divinity both lights up the world and gives life. He argued that gold and diamonds used for alankaram are poor, ordinary human substitutes to represent this extraordinary, divine radiance. So alankaram, the decoration of the deity, is the everyday repetition of the possibility of making the lurking extraordinary emerge in the ordinary. And through the experience of the ordinary, the unseen extraordinary is experienced as well, hopefully with dramatic intensity.

The power of the light captured in such shimmery objects has a mesmeric quality.[15] Sparkling diamonds and burnished gold are deemed marvelous not only for their market value but also for their aesthetic brilliance and visual resonance (Greenblatt 1991, 11–15). According to Dandu, they imitate the sky, dazzling like the golden sun, "*suryan polle*," and the diamond-like stars, a cosmological metaphor overflowing with wonderment and beauty. As in Vedic alchemy, gold is illuminating and cosmic; it radiates divine energy and power. To Dandu, Vishwanatha, and the devotees it is not merely the monetary value of the gold that is wondrous but also, and perhaps above all, the shine.

Different societies give their own characteristic values and meanings to the shapes, colors, and textures of their shiny objects (Hamell 1983, 47–49;

Saunders 2003, 15–17). Yet, despite these differences, attitudes toward brilliant objects emerged from and reinforce a worldview that regards light, color, and shimmering qualities as indicators of the magical and cosmological world of power and beauty. Such potent objects are the preserve of the local elite and are offered to gods to placate them. Dandu Shastri spoke lyrically about the shiny gold alankaram: "Alankaram is about immersing yourself in the deity. The mood is like the joys of love, music, poetry or just the perfume of a flower. *Sringara* [beauty] is key in creating this mood. Through the alankaram, we gain access to a private world of feeling, a connection between us and the god."

The value of shiny objects was democratized further in the late 1990s and first decade of the twenty-first century as Bollywood cinema gave this shiny aesthetic its own acoustic imprimatur in "*chamak-dhamak*," song sequences that spoke to the aesthetics of bling and glitz. In Bangalore, copying this aesthetic became de rigueur: saris were sequined, bindis were studded, nose rings were aglitter. Even men's designer shirts and pants sported the occasional glitter patch. This also coincided with the entry of strobe lights and computerized lighting displays in urban centers in the early twenty-first century. Temples fascinated, compelled, entrapped, and delighted spectators with their colorful and magically brilliant costumes, jewels, and illuminations.

Prabha, who always wore lots of exquisite gold jewelry, was vociferous in her criticism of my arriving at the temple in an oppositional ambivalent "wiped-down-state" (Tamil: *thodachi vittapilla*). I did not wear my wedding necklace and diamond earrings as befitted my upper-caste and married status. She explained the devotees' fascination with the gold kavacha of the deity in the most concrete and visceral terms to me: "It is the shine, Tulasi! How gold shines! The sparkling [Tamil: *palla-palla*]." The brilliance of the gold and the diamonds in the darkness of the temple vaults was lost on me but not on the residents of Malleshwaram. They saw it as a magical shimmer. It is no accident that in Hindi *chamak* (shine) and *chamatkar* (magic) share a root verb. These shared linguistic origins are subtly interlinked in devotees' minds to create a network of magical possibility and wonder around the shininess of excessive displays of gold.

For ritual specialists and practitioners, creating a visual shining surfeit is a moral act, one that not only enhances the power of the deity and the freedom of ritual creativity. Dandu Shastri was clear that decorating the deity in various currencies was partly in order to regenerate a sense of wonder. When I asked him what made him decorate the deity in currency, he explained:

In getting money, we should not forget it is God who gives money to us. We must remember that. We can run after money but only if God blesses us will we get the money. See how many poor people there are. It's not like they do not want money or they do not work hard. It is all our karma and God's *daya* [mercy] who gets money and who does not. I wanted to show that no matter where you are in the world . . . whatever money you use it is all God's blessing.

That the notion of blessing is used not merely as a descriptive device but as an analytic speaks to the fungability of piety and money. If one is suitably pious one can (with the recognition of God) convert one's hard work into capital.

By 1999, well into the economic liberalization of India, alankaram of the deity exploited a sense of make-believe and illusion, enigmatic shifts of scale, and brilliantly innovative use of different rich and dazzling materials. Collections of treasures of gold and gemstones, fossils and diamonds, bronze, silver, stone, glass, lacquer, and fabrics painted or dyed into phantasmagoric patterns covered the deity in layers of decorative design. The deity was camouflaged in radiantly beautiful and richly eclectic materials, all of which the temple owned and stored. In this new focus on tinsellated excess neoliberalism, the hypercapitalism of consumption was made explicit with the focus on design and display. Devotion to the deity was evidenced by rich gifts that in turn symbolized the status and power of the giver, displaying the connections between high-status individuals and cosmic beings.

The power for devotees of this radiant excess illustrates the power of the subjunctive promise within the context of aspiration, hope, and, by implication, invention. The money alankaram inverts the notion of karma. Rather than having good karma and therefore being wealthy, it posits the idea that if one makes money, one can be blessed. This, then, is a transactional system much larger than sacrifice or the worship cycles of adoration. It has profound implications in our understanding of what constitutes piety, moving from the descriptive to a prescriptive. The transformation of money from merely a mundane object into a marvelous one opens a world of wonder.

The Promise of Plenitude

Field notes, Ganesha Temple, Malleshwaram, December 30 1998

The day before the currency alankaram, I found Dandu Shastri seated inside the sanctum of the temple. He was literally on top of a huge pile of currency, both coins and notes, that had been emptied from two boxes and one basket at his feet. He was sorting the notes; he gave me a handful of notes and urged me to do the same. I sorted them by the nation-state to which they belonged—Thai bhat in one corner, Indonesian rupiah in another, Italian lira, Armenian dram, Saudi dinars, British pounds, American dollars, and more. When I was done, Dandu looked at the piles I had neatly sorted and laughed. "No, no, not by the country!" he said. "You should sort the hanna by color and size. See how I am sorting them? You are organizing them as though it will go to a bank! This is just 'foreign'!" In his organized piles, as opposed to mine, the brass-colored British pound sterling coins were lumped together with real gold coins, the green Indonesian notes of twenty thousand rupiah were piled up in swathes with the green Indian five-rupee notes and green American dollar bills. What mattered was their aesthetics and the fact that they all counted as foreign money.

Currency, as Dandu Shastri rightly understood, is particularly significant as a material object, as a potent symbol of money and of modern capitalism. Although economists consider currency to form a "frictionless surface to history" (Graeber 1996, 6), the truth is that conflicting understandings of nationhood, fiduciary knowledge, durability and materiality, and monetized trust all intersect and act coevally in it. Marcel Mauss argues that only when precious things are "made into currency"—namely, "have been inscribed and impersonalized, detached from any relationship with any legal entity, whether collective or individual, other than the state that mints them"—can one properly think about money ([1923] 1967, 100–102n).

As the piles of currency grew—orange in one corner, purple in another, green in a third—I asked Dandu how he had come upon this money. He replied: "See, these people who come to the temple, many of them go to 'foreign' for jobs and for holiday. So I said when you come back just bring all the change you have to the temple. I asked Vishwanatha, my son, to keep baskets and hundi [lockbox] in the courtyard. Every time someone came who had been to foreign I asked them, 'Do you have money?' See, I even asked you and you gave me some dollars. So everyone was very nice. They all put it into the hundi."

As we were speaking, some young men walked past, carrying computer cases and wearing identifying badges of a high-tech multinational company. Dandu had them turn out their pockets, and several green and purple deutsche marks tumbled out. He added them to the pile and began intricately folding the piles of notes into fan shapes, securing them into garlands with metal ties.

Dandu moved several of the younger priests helping him to an office where they had space to work and patiently demonstrated how to fold and secure the fans without puncturing the banknotes. He watched and berated the priests who had torn or poked holes in the notes: "Be careful, you louts! If you tear these notes, the goddess Lakshmi will never come to you." The priests worked quickly and efficiently, and by the end of the day, all of the thousands of notes that had been collected were tied together in woven fan-shaped, color-coordinated garlands that cascaded like fractal loops. Dandu nodded, pleased with the result.

The devotees commented favorably on the folded fans and the garlands as they walked past the group of priests hard at work. In Dandu's alankaram, folding speaks to the multiplicity of power and the virtue of God. The process of folding allows for what Diane Mines has termed a "density," where the iconographic surfaces of the notes are layered and duplicated. Mines's study of density in Tamil religious publics argues that this density floods the vision and gives a feeling of amplification, expansion, and excess, whereby the "bigness" of the god is enhanced: "density demonstrates the productive capacity of the god, the temple, the event, the place and the community" (2005, 163) and, I would add, of the priest as well. A politics of bigness and the divinely magnanimous nature that such bigness implies rest in an aesthetics of plenitude. The layered density and material excess represented in the folding of the paper money is integral to the production of value, describing a reduplication in which a process of folding (Tamil: mattaku)—"'repetition,' 'folding,' or 'refraction'—contributes to that density by saturating the visual field with repeated or refracted signs" (Mines 2005, 163; Bate 2010, 130–31). The folding allows for excessive play of texture and aesthetics of overdensity.[16] In this gesture and his explanation, Dandu flattens the stratified universe of meaning, folding the finite in and out of itself to indicate an infinite variety and the metaphorical infinity of wealth, thus staging a resistance to discourses of want and thrift. The politics of piety in this instance operate through and between, rather than against, wonder. This is the paradoxical beauty and truth of Dandu's aesthetics: things can only be counted insofar as they remain uncountable.

Dandu was sensitive to the hanna, and its aesthetics—its color, shape, size, and foldablity: "Look at the U.S. notes; all the same size, green. How do they know what they are giving when paying? Five or ten, all is the same!" Or, "See this pretty hanna? These saffron notes? They're from Italy. It says ten thousand, like it's a lot of money, but Raghavendra told me you can only buy one plate of *idli* [steamed rice cakes] with it!" As he reworked the surfaces of the banknotes into elaborate folded shapes, he remark on the notes: "See this blue color? So nice!" He pointed at a sheaf of blue one-hundred-deutsche-mark notes, which he paired with another sheaf of Armenian one-hundred-dram notes of a similar greenish-blue. He then set them aside and said, "Nice! The color goes well together and we can put them together!" In organizing the hanna based on color and form rather than value, Dandu ritualized the authorship and authenticity of the relationship between nation and bank, between debtor and creditor. The affective and aesthetic matters were made more significant than the purchase value. The nonconvertability between currencies was the very point of the many currencies on display, for the money centered on the ritual imagination of the devotees. For Dandu, the money of the different nations is a discontinuity in capital. By using it as ornament, tying it together metaphorically and aesthetically to create relationality, he transgresses and subverts this discontinuity.

But there was one currency that Dandu recognized as special—the U.S. dollar. He separated it from the rest and strung the sheafs into a single garland. The priests pointed to it and wanted to touch and feel it. It was enchanting because of the status and exceptional value of the U.S. economy in Bangalore. As the priests understood it, the software engineers, who made up most of the top earners of the city, all owed their newfound wealth to America. That the U.S. dollar was to be displayed, worshipped, and admired indicated its unfamiliarity and the seduction of its sheer economic power.[17]

Krishna Bhattar echoed and indeed, on some occasions, surpassed Dandu in deploying intricate folding and stacking. The stacking of flower petals, fruit in various variegated colors, garlands, silk, and cloth all contributed to the desired effect. Krishna Bhattar suggested that the folding promoted a sense of movement. "It is as though the god dances," he said. The consideration of movement allows for a possibility of the intrusion of divine life into the everyday, and the aesthetics of movement that this replication provokes, as well as the grandeur of the image bedecked in endless chains of gold, allows for an evocation of the sublime presence—a gesture to the infinitude that divinity is believed to be (Nancy 2007, 36).

Through the *malai* (garland), the politics of capital is tied to something expansive beyond its normative usage, something other than itself. The etymology of religion is *religio*, in Latin meaning obligation or bond and implying that the bond is both given and unanticipated simultaneously. By exploiting this tie, Dandu demonstrates that ritual observance is not at all given and immutable but is continuously being adapted and "bonded" to new meanings and values (Rubenstein 2008, 120). Wonder here is polyvalent in that it allows thought to range to its own farthest limits while yet being present in the world. Wonder is nothing other than that which happens at the limit where structuring of sense is revealed.

For Dandu, the mysterious seductive power of hanna is analogous to the mysterious power of the deity, and by dressing the deity in the hanna, he believes he enhances the power of the deity: "People will remember that only from God comes the blessing of wealth." Public spheres and their dimensions often enable the priests to acknowledge or argue for the legitimacy and the relevancy of the deity in everyday lives, and they legitimize the relation between piety and wealth as inextricably woven with divine greatness and human excess. Living in the world of infinite becoming is thus a blessing of the deity. It is not solipsistic or escapist but rather an act of faith creating a fellowship with divinity and with others of the community. The as-if condition of speculation is a moral one.

In Malleshwaram, ritual improvisations engage a world that is permanently liminal, constantly verging on new states, always already possessed of other natures in potentio. Rituals are transformative practices that engage practitioners' sensitivities to a cosmos that is always pregnant with new forms. Dandu deployed bigness and plenitude to indicate the many facets of the power of the temple, the deity, and the community.

The malai of hanna (garland of cash) is all about transformation: transforming the currency from a system of earthly exchange to one of cosmological transcendence, of sacrifice from mere hanna to an offering to the god. The garland itself is the transformation of the money. By using currencies from different countries to decorate the deity, Dandu and the devotees destabilized the accepted meaning of the money by separating it further from the nation-state for which it stands. Stripped of its provenance, with its national identity less significant than its aesthetics registers, hanna became an object to be used in the register of spectacular excess. The reputation of the temple and the efficacy of the god—the ability of the deity to create largesse—are at stake in the production of visual surfeit. The politics of bigness include the possibility of creating infinite realities of plenitude and expand it along several dimensions, including power, prestige, wealth, fertility, amplitude, and ability, that confirm the power of the deity. Thus, grandness and excess are transactions in power, and status and access to them are either ocular or real, increasing one's status and value—an aesthetics and politics of plenitude that rests in the manner of offering.

"*Mintingu*" and "*Minchingu*"

For younger devotees, Dandu's alankaram was an acceptance and demonstration of the flow of wealth through the city. Ravi had been a college student when I began the study and had since graduated and found a job. He was always particularly well dressed, in expensive shirts and watches that set him apart. I asked devotees about him. "*Avan na? Aayyayo! Mintingu, Mintingu!* [Kannada: Oh him? He is minting money!]." In 2006 "minting" was a phrase I began to hear around the temple, as applied to men and women alike to denote their lofty earning capacities.

By 2010 "minting" was the description of choice of devotees when they admired someone's ability to create wealth. Shubha, a beautiful woman who had worked as director of an art gallery and came occasionally to the Krishna Temple, said of Radha and her husband, a high-wage couple who both worked for Yahoo, "They are simply minting! M-i-n-t-i-n-g." Drawing out the word emphasized how much money was being earned (an excessive amount): "They live like Maharajahs! They have two cooks on standby and their house has two kitchens—one for her to cook and one for the cook—and they have two drivers also. Radha was covered in diamonds last time I saw her! She was full *minching* [Kannada: twinkling]. Not bad for them!"

This act of "minting" is the direct outcome of the money alankaram, a direct supplication to a world of wonder. While normatively it is men who are expected to be "minting," women are expected to display the wealth. They must shine, be radiant and wear sparkling clothes and jewelry, and "minch." Minting and minching are signs of normative gender-appropriate behavior. Women who came to the temple wearing less jewelry than their status demanded were often subject to questioning by others: "Why, what happened?" To this they might make excuses for not dressing up at the ready—"My diamond choker is in the bank locker. I couldn't go"—or they would cite their mood: "Just didn't feel like dressing up!" Occasionally if the status and wealth of the family was well known, the woman's lack of ornamentation and jewelry would be seen as a morally superior position that underlined her status: "She could buy all of Krishnaiah Chetty jewelry shop but see how simply she dressed! So nice!"

Being blessed with money and consumption power is a new imaginative horizon—a frontier of plenitude—for middle-class Indians. Devotees explained to me that this plenitude or the promise of it can be attained by virtue and piety. This piety of prosperity both aligns itself with neoliberal middle-class Indian objectives and aspirations to wealth and productively subverts them by supplanting them into a ritual economy—an economy of transcendence and grace. There is no guilt about accumulation here, nor a desire for thrift, merely an aspirational thirst that needs slaking. People look toward the gods to model that aspiration, toward their greatness and magnanimity.

I asked Dandu how he felt about this movement toward wealth creation and control. I assumed he would parse the difficult ethical choices inherent in making money, considering social and moral corruption. But his notion of the morality of wealth was slightly different from mine. It revolved around the dharma of wealth creation in a prescriptive fashion. "So long as you do good things for many people, God will bless you with money," he said emphatically. So, as my friends and informants suggested, a person who is wealthy is seen as having the god by his or her side. "It is all God's blessings" was a phrase I heard repeatedly from localites to express their good fortune.

Alternatively, one's good fortune in being wealthy is often ascribed to "having good karma" or "having done good things in a previous life" or having "good parents." Here, "blessing" is used as a category to denote both luck and a sense of being rewarded for constant morality and piety. The use of this category indicates that devotees acknowledge this reward as recognition of their piety, but at the same time they also note that this recognition is at the behest of the playful will of God. But it also demonstrates their anxiety about their aspirations not being met (Dickey 2013).

For Dandu and the devotees, capital accumulation can only occur if one submits to Kasu Ganesha (Money Ganesha) and appeals to his mercy and grace. Thus a seeming paradox occurs, wherein devotees who want money give money to the deity who already has so much, in order that they might get more in this life.

Giving creates a greater possibility of the blessing of getting. Money and its aesthetics allow for new imaginings of piety, a new passion located in the self and its needs and wants—new "regimes of value" (Appadurai 1986b, 15, 57). Here, the determination of what is excess and what is necessity is riven with questions. Since the notion of performing piety deals in certain respects with ethical self-realization (Mahmood 2005), it also has larger implications for an understanding of how individuals live together in the contemporary moment and what it takes for them to do so. Even if one sets aside the transactional nature of giving to the deity, collecting money for gold armor for the deity as a necessary philanthropic enterprise in a country of overwhelming poverty raises some troubling questions. Krishna and Dandu see the only way out of this bind of precarious living and aspirational wealth in the power of innovation, resignification, and subversion, where each new iteration is a

FIGURE 3.3. Ganesha deity alankaram using a gold kavacham (armor) above the main deity. Photo by the author.

creative act in itself that reorients understandings of the present and potential for the future, in which wonder becomes a goal and process all in one.

Wonder as imagination provokes the question of the wishful thinking or the longing that allows localites to live both in the everyday and in the space of the imagined future. Michael Puett argues that this "as-if" reality is constant and enduring, that we are constantly creating pockets of "as-if" realities, and that the disjunction between these pockets and the patterns that we fall into in our lived reality is the basis for us to transform ourselves. What we are seeking is not to become more like the person we are in these ritual as-if spaces but rather to learn to respond well to actual situations, an ability we can gain through the work of training ourselves via ritual activity (Puett 2015, 550). But if we decide to emphasize anticipation and aspiration, the disparity between the deity and the devotee becomes a productive line of fiction wherein the realm of possibility exceeds the realm of reality. The future can then

FIGURE 3.4. The Ganesha deity decorated with gold coins. Photo by the author.

be conceived as different from the present and past, an essential element of creative thought. In the plurality of practices in which wonder is a willfully cultivated response, we focus on what is most ordinary and most regular, in order to see it as an extraordinary thing.

Being Poor

Colonel Gopal, a retired military man with a large moustache and prosperous girth, talked about the excess attributed to being a good devotee and the to him troubling focus on the appearance of wealth rather than on productivity: "See all this? Nobody does a simple garland of tulasi leaves or flowers anymore. All American diamond, *chingani chingani* [Kannada: bling], they want! Not even real diamonds they put for God! Just American diamonds (crystals). God will be satisfied with a small garland of flowers given with faith. But they think God is like them. All simply show! Today everyone only thinks they are a king if they have two houses, cars, this and that. Even the auto driver, he has a Samsung phone! What to do? No values anymore! *Thooo!!* [*indicating disgust*] Everyone spends money to show off!."

Many elderly localites such as Colonel Gopal and Chellappa are alarmed by this fiscally motivated understanding of blessing that rests in appearance alone and the shifting nature of spending. For them Dandu's money alankaram and the "as-if" condition it creates reflect an ethical life of deprivation in which spending money rather than thrift is the end result. For Colonel Gopal saving and being saved go hand in hand. "Simply spending to show off" he deemed as inherent lack of fiscal control toward a hollow demonstration of status.

The ambivalence around the acquisition of wealth for localites like Colonel Gopal and the instability of the moral meaning of money, saved or spent, introduce a need for redemption. For Colonel Gopal those without money or without the capacity to save it, lack a productive pathway to redemption. For Dandu, on the other hand, a focus on the ability to spend and consume is central to the scaffolding for aspiration, for acquiring more money and power. Lack for him, and those like him, is the underbelly of excess.

After the Kasu Ganesha alankaram, in a bid to reorient the localites toward what mattered in terms of faith, Chellappa told the many devotees who were listening about the myth of Sudhama, the friend of Lord Krishna, whose penury was legendary.

Sudhama was very poor and lived in a hut with his lovely wife and child. He was hungry, and his family was hungry, but he was a good ethical man. He was very pious and worshipped Lord Vishnu every day. He had known Krishna, the cowherd prince, as a young man, and one day Krishna invited him to his palace. He went to visit his friend, leaving his starving wife and children in rags at home. They were crying with hunger.

He had nothing to give his friend so he took some parched rice as a gift. He walked for three days and came to Krishna's beautiful palace in Dwaraka. Krishna met him. They wandered through the palace together and suddenly Krishna said, "I am so hungry!" Sudhama took out his parcel of parched grain and fed him one handful after another. After three handfuls, Lord Krishna said, "I think that is enough for you." Sudhama wondered what Krishna meant. He spent a happy time with his friend for a few days.

Then he decided to go home. He walked back home thinking of the nice time he had had with his friend.

He was puzzled when he came to his street. His hut was gone! There was a huge palace where his hut had been. A beautiful bejeweled woman, whom he did not recognize, stood in the doorway. She rushed to greet him with a silver *lota* filled with fresh milk. It was his wife. His child was dressed in the finest silks. He looked into the treasury and there was enough money for seven generations.

He realized then that Lord Krishna had blessed him. In repayment for the three handfuls of grain, he had given him a palace, cash, and gold. Sudhama prayed to Krishna, his true friend "in need."

In Chellappa's telling, the myth of friendship between deity and man was also a myth about the ethical value of penury, its dignity. The point of the story was that Sudhama asked for nothing. His worldly success was a "blessing" from the god, an earthly reward for loyalty and devotion. Wealth here is well gotten; it is an acknowledgment of one's piety, moral character, and loyalty.

In Saba Mahmood's study of Egyptian women's pious practices of ṣalāt, the Muslim ritual of daily prayer, she does not assume an a priori outcome of the conventional performances that make up ritual activity. Rather, she suggests that it is necessary to inquire into the variability of relationships as well as the ideal of conventional ritual behavior matched by the process of ethical formation with regard to mobility, affect, and aspiration (Mahmood 2005). Ritual in this formulation is perceived as formalized action. As Mahmood argues in an earlier work, ritual is "the space where individual psychic drives are either channeled into conventional patterns of expression or temporarily suspended so that a conventional social script may be enacted" (2001, 827–28). For the Egyptian women with whom she worked, prayer was and is part of the weavings of daily life, part of "routine living." The practices of prayer do not require "the suspension of spontaneous emotion and individual intention," nor do they require "a space for a cathartic release of unsocialized or inassimilable elements of the psyche" (828). Rather, as Mahmood suggests in an illuminating twist to Michel Foucault's idea of dispositifs or self-cultivation, "mosque participants identified the act of prayer as a key site for purposefully molding their intentions, emotions, and desires in accord with orthodox standards of Islamic piety. As a highly structured performance—one given an extensive elaboration in Islamic doctrine—prayer (ṣalāt) was understood by the women . . . to provide an opportunity for the analysis, assessment, and refinement of the set of ethical capacities" (828). Where the act "induced sentiments and desires in themselves," in accordance with a moral-ethical program, the articulation of "differential relationships between informal activity and rule-prescribed social behavior" (827) leads to a "rehearsed spontaneity" during salat.

Dandu and the localites stand Mahmood's proposition on its head. Rather than examining the proscribed behaviors and potential deviations, he explores the sensory aspects of ritual, the aesthetics of it, and the embedded emotions of desire, and then works backward into its politics. So in the contemporary templescape, habitués interpret wealth as a blessing that is a materialization of piety, which in turn cultivates a capitalist disposition. In Malleshwaram, to be chosen is indexed not by piety but by wealth. One is not pious to be close to God or to have moral worth, but one should aspire to be wealthy in order to be acknowledged as pious. The directionality of proof has changed. This shift concerns Colonel Gopal.

In Chellappa's story of Sudhama, the unworking of the threads between thrift and piety toward excess and piety is not merely what has happened incidentally but rather what *must* happen normatively to reiterate the value of faith. Chellapa told the story to underscore both the gratitude of god to a faithful devotee and god's mysterious ways of repayment for loyalty. But many localites took this story to be an exhortation of a transaction between themselves and the deity. Anand and Sarathy, the young software engineers I met at the Skyye bar told me, "We gave for the gold kavacha because the old man told the story about Sudhama and god giving him lots in exchange for the rice." Anand added, "Let's hope he does that for us also!" Signs of wealth are interpreted as signs of faith in this scenario and giving to the god is a transaction with a hoped-for multiplication.

Being rich is to be close to God, and to be poor is, presumably, to be forgotten by God. For devotees, garnering wealth and displaying it is a form of piety, of expressing their ethical value; as Krishna claimed, they are "rich" in karma. That this is in keeping with the values of the expanding neoliberal world seems to them to be a fortuitous and instrumental logic, in which the interpretation of saving and thrift—toward a new formulation of salvation involving conspicuous consumption and displays of wealth—becomes the measure of piety. This has profound consequences in terms of understanding the democracy of wealth creation and of social justice around notions of inequality. Economic inequality, a central feature of market capitalism, as many reports and books now show (Piketty 2014), is inversely linked with piety.[18]

I asked Dandu about the poor (Tamil: *yellengal*) and how that was construed. If rich people are blessed, what about poor people, I asked; are they cursed? Dandu looked askance at first at the rawness of my question before he responded.

> You see, poverty, it depends. It is all karma. In the previous life, if you behaved badly, you hurt poor people, then yes, you will be reborn to be poor only. Then you will know how it is to be poor. You are right to call

poverty a curse but it is not like being ill, which is a curse of God; this is man's curse. One man's curse upon another. Some people have more and so some have less. No one should be poor. But if you are poor or if you lose money, there are many mantras, many pujas to help you. God's power can change anything!

I asked how karma could be changed. Dandu's answer was simple. Through prayer anything was possible. Dandu saw poverty as a remediable condition. With the right mantras or pujas, with supplication to divine power, one could change one's fate of being poor.

After talking with Dandu at the Ganesha Temple, I went to the Krishna Temple. Standing at the outer door to the Krishna Temple was Lakshmana, a homeless man who slept in the generous entryway to the temple under the *gopuram* (tower). His clothes were torn and his speech was slurred with bhang, a cannabis-derived drug, as he tried to sell me a withered string of tulasi leaves, shouting, "Tulasi for Tulasi!" Lakshmana had told me he was of the potter (Kannada: *kumbara*) caste and through his drug addiction lost his family and home.[19]

Lakshmana's caste-based pollution boundaries were spatial and temporal.[20] He could not get too close to upper castes, nor of course touch them, because his pollution was so contagious (Marriott 1976). Usually, Lakshmana was hyperaware of his "lowly" caste status in comparison to the dominant and upper castes who came to the Krishna Temple. He was careful to stay outside the temple, only venturing up to the gopuram steps at the entry of the temple and no further even when I thoughtlessly invited him to go in to the temple forecourt with me. Lakshmana did not ever enter the temple, as in all probability he would be rejected for his caste-based ritual pollution of the temple. My unintentional cruelty to him in inviting him to join me, born of my middle-class secular upbringing, makes me cringe, even some sixteen years later.

But that day Lakshmana, high on bhang and determined to make a sale of a tulasi garland, followed me into the temple forecourt. Just as he realized his "mistake," Krishna's father also noticed his presence. He came forward and shouted "Ay!" in a hectoring tone, and chased Lakshmana back beyond the gate, shouting raspily at him as he did so, "What were you thinking?" I was deeply disturbed by Krishna Bhattar's father's behavior and attempted to stop him, but he was intent on chasing Lakshmana out of the temple. I looked for Krishna Bhattar but he was nowhere to be seen.

I saw Krishna Bhattar walk into the temple after Lakshmana was ejected. When I told Krishna Bhattar of his father's behavior, he showed no trace of emotion, and I was disappointed in his reaction.

That day was a sevakara offering celebration to honor the gifting of yet another gold ornament to the deity by one of the temple patrons. Members of some of the temple patron's family had arrived dressed in their finest clothes. The prasadam made for the gifting celebration was a delicious sweet rice pongal dish of which Krishna Bhattar, as usual, received the first serving. His portion was large and, served directly after the *naivedyam* (offering to the deity), it was marked as pure and consecrated. Unusually Krishna Bhattar did not swallow it quickly but carefully set it aside and went to the temple gate. "Lakshmana! Lakshmana!" he called out. Lakshmana appeared warily. I saw Krishna Bhattar say a few words to Lakshmana and bring him into the temple forecourt and seat him down. He then placed the leaf before him and served him some more pongal himself. The temple, usually humming with noise, seemed to still. Everyone looked around watching the tableau. Then they all elaborately resumed their conversations as though nothing unusual had happened.

Later, Padma was approving: "Poor fellow! I am glad Krishna Bhattar brought him in and fed him. That is what temple priests should do!" Alamela Ajji echoed her reaction: "Nowadays everyone is welcome at the temple! When I was young, yes we had these rules. This *Holeya* [Dalit subcaste of Karnataka] must not sit there. His shadow must not fall on you. Rules like that. But today we are not like that." Alamela Ajji, who was in her seventies, rejected the toxic marginalizations of caste pollution boundaries and their enforcement (Dumont [1966] 1980, 835). She added emphatically, "Today the temple must embrace all peoples." When I thought about it further, perhaps it was less generous than I imagined. Did the openness to having Lakshmana invited in to eat prasadam occur because he was familiar and there was a sense of upper-caste noblesse oblige and feeding him was an act of charity that kept the feudal hierarchy intact (Raheja 1988; Berreman 1991)?

With these uncomfortable musings, I turned to the younger devotees in anticipation of their openness and inclusivity. They were militant in their anger at Krishna for inviting Lakshmana into the temple. "This Krishna gives too much encouragement to all these fellows!" Arjun, another young software engineer with a greasy pompadour, whom I had met at the Skyye bar, said angrily. "This fellow . . . Lakshmana. He is always drunk or drugs [*sic*]." His friend Vasudeva added blithely, criminalizing Lakshmana's behavior, "These type of fellows, they steal. They are poor. They steal things. Krishna Bhattar should chase him off!" I was stunned by what I saw as an illiberal streak in these young devotees. The experience of wonder as I had imagined it led to greater empathy, a stronger sense of common good, an obvious ethical claim. But it was clear that to the boomtown bourgeoisie, the evidence of Lakshmana's poverty, his dirtiness and torn clothing, was criminal. It was a moral indictment and a physical repudiation. This was no civil society, but the underbelly of neoliberal economics. Although Dandu did not want to say so explicitly, in Malleshwaram, not only was caste pollution still alive and well, it amalgamated with neoliberal stigma where poverty was a curse and being rich a blessing, and everyone understood that implicitly. In this particular case caste seemed subordinated to class, yet both enunciated a violence against the marginal. Troublingly in Malleshwaram the pursuit of wonder led not to the ethical goal of inclusivity but to individual gain and the criminalization of the poor.

"Cashacarda?": Philosophies of Debt

Field notes, Krishna Temple, Malleshwaram, January 13, 2013

I stood in the Krishna Temple and watched the, the government-appointed accountant, Mr. Sampath Kumar, at his desk. He was busy examining his account book and doing some complicated calculations on his little handheld calculator, his fingers flying over it, a series of mechanical clicks indicating the totals being tallied. As I watched, a few young men strode up to his desk. He looked up, lifting his chin and raising his eyebrows to silently ask them what they wanted. They all chorused, "Archane beku, Saar [Kannada: We need individual worship, sir]." Mr. Sampath Kumar took out a small, yellow ticket book and wrote several receipts. Mentally calculating the amount due, he opened the cash drawer with a key, then looked up from his desk and asked, as he did routinely, "Cashacarda? [Cash or card?]." One of the young men brought out a silver Citizens Bank credit card and the other a dark blue Canara Bank credit card. Mr. Sampath Kumar, took a portable electric swipe tablet out from the cash drawer, swiped the two cards, wrote out receipts, and handed the receipt and cards back to the two men.

As Jack Weatherford chillingly notes, currencies are "dying," and the world monetary system has begun to "cough and stumble" to its grave as governments cannot control debt or inflation and international bodies such as the IMF and World Bank are paralyzed (1997, xii). Yet, as the old monetary system staggers to its end, the "electronic whirr of encoded chips on plastic cards passing through electronic readers" (xii) is well begun. The credit card as instrument gives access to property in its most capacious sense; in its ability to buy far more than one has capital for, it holds the promise of endless abundance and of the good life, a promised and promissory future.[21]

Some seven years earlier, in 2006, credit card advertisements started appearing on billboards and stuck on the walls in Malleshwaram: "The City Never Sleeps," "Citibank credit," "Not enough money for shopping? Syndicate Bank Gold card," and one featuring a smiling woman holding a credit card: "You can have the world with MasterCard. Don't leave home without it."[22] These ads moved beyond mere consumption, into the subjunctive futurity of how Bangaloreans wish to see themselves. They promised access to a modern, global future in a finance-scape embedded with luxury goods and high-end products and processes—a subjunctive futurity. The *Economic Times* argued that forms of advertising about credit cards carry the heft of gold-standard persuasiveness in that they radiate with promise of an imagined future.[23]

Krishna Bhattar explained the need as he saw it for a credit card payment system for puja: "*Indaa paisa-waisa yellame poovendithan; ippo yellame 'credit' le vangarango* [Tamil: This currency will all have to go; everyone buys things on credit. Shopping malls, petrol pumps, even CTR takes credit/debit cards.[24] So now we decided we also will take card]." Despite Krishna Bhattar's claim of the credit card's ubiquity in Bangalore, to industry analysts, India has one of the smallest "penetration rates" in terms of credit cards, with only eighteen million users in the country as of 2006.[25] I asked Shubha what she thought of the credit card boom in Bangalore; she responded, "Now even my *maali* [Hindi: gardener] and *dhobi* [Hindi: washerman] have a cell phone and credit card. These poor people don't know. It is just like the local moneylender, huge percentage of interest, only now they are in debt worldwide."

Until 2007, indigenous banking systems had always relied on usury, and debt economies had been part and parcel of both the rural and urban Indian economies.[26] The urban poor, who routinely pawned items of value and retrieved them when possible, constituted a dark shadow-banking system of unregulated financial intermediaries (Acharya and Richardson 2009). The *Wall Street Journal* reported that moneylenders were, in fact, doing brisk business in rural and urban India until the wide-scale adoption of credit cards in 2008 and 2009, enabled by both banks allowing for credit lines and mass-scale advertising of the consumption potential enabled by the cards.[27] Credit and debit cards are now mundane and routinized to such an extent in Bangalore, despite their seeming "low penetration rate," that they have become an accepted part of the financial landscape of India (Bhagwati and Panagariya 2012). I asked Krishna Bhattar about cards and he replied: "See, this credit card looks like a new thing, but it is not. You know the idea of *runa* [debt]? Our life itself is because of runa. When the wheel of karma goes around then you cannot escape the payment of runa."[28]

Since the passage he was referring to explained debt in the karmic sense, I asked him if this applied to simple debt like credit cards. He laughed, explaining:

> Some people might say I am reducing our *samskruthi* [Sanskrit: culture]. That to say all runa is the same is wrong. That is true. The runa of being indebted for life, like you are to your mother and father, that debt is different. But the principle is the same. You must repay this debt. We look after our old parents. That is repayment. Maybe not enough . . . interest will be added and maybe you have to live another life for the karma to be finished. But what I am saying is because we have this philosophy, we can understand debt and repayment very easily.

The idea that debt is in some senses punitive and retributional is embedded in popular Hindu philosophy. Debt was unfungible, not easily interchangeable or forgotten, and interest kept accruing on it.[29] It was unclear to me whether he was drawing the philosophy out to make the market explicable or drawing the market logics into the philosophy, but in blurring the boundaries between the two, he made it possible for a conflation between debt and theology.

Krishna's example is not an isolated incident. Philosophies of debt are in fact central to Hindu religious thought. In the poetry of the Brahmanas and the Vedas—the foundations of Hindu thought—we find reflections on the nature of debt (Graeber 2011, 56). There is a constant concern with debt as moral bondage that needs expiation. In the earlier Vedas, debt is a metaphor for life's gamble, standing either for death or some long-term, almost demonic inner suffering (Rig Veda, chapter 10, hymn 34). But by the time of the later Brahmanas, the distilled philosophical awareness was that man's life is promissory and a form of debt in itself: "Man being born, is a debt; by his own self he is born to Death and only when he sacrifices does he redeem himself."[30] The development of ideas of debt involve life cycles—that we are born in debt to the gods and we repay debt through sacrifice and care.[31] We repay debts to our parents by having children ourselves and debts to our teachers through learning and transmitting knowledge; finally, debts to all men are repaid by offering them hospitality. In sum, then, we create a notion of common good enshrined through and in a common debt. Debt becomes bound to divinity, to ancestors and progeny, and to the ethical-social world. In other words, relationships are the cause of previous life debts. The relationships we have within life end when the debt is discharged, when the account is balanced. In this impermanent world, then, debt is constantly accrued and needs to be discharged.

Krishna Bhattar used the term *runanabandha* (the Karmic debts [runa] lead to bondage or attachment [*bandha*]) in referring to a life bound by debt. He argued that all life is the creation of karmic debts involving all those with whom we interact. These karmic attachments pull us into the wheel of existence again and again. Runanubandha (the bond that results from karmic debts) is at the root of repeated lives. The patterns of runa and karma are myriad, exceedingly intricate, and perplexing. Devotees argue that debt is the reason for karmic rebirth. My friend Padma said, "Till all the karma stored in the spirit is burnt away or exhausted, there is no liberation from rebirth. Human life is nothing but a memory of runanubandha, the story of the countless karmas that we make, and live through."

Soiled Money and the Makings of Distrust

On May 12, 1998, an older male devotee with greased hair and thick bristly moustache, his paunch barely contained in his blue T-shirt, came to the Ganesha Temple. He leaned against the accountants' table, his shirt buttons straining to hold his stomach in, and bought a token for an *archane* (individual blessing). Customarily, during the archane, the priest offered the camphor flame (*deepardhane*) to the deity, after which it was offered to the devotee as a transmuted form of a blessing from the god. It was customary to drop a small amount of money in the offertory plate around the flame. Priests usually scooped up all the paper currency to prevent their incineration but left coins in the plate.

This time, however, when the man in the blue shirt put a note on the offertory plate, the priest stopped and asked him brusquely, "Don't you have change? *Chillare illava?* [Kannada: No coins?]." Priests usually accepted almost any denomination of currency with gratitude and a nod of thanks, so this was unusual. The man in the blue shirt countered, "If you don't accept it, who will?" The priest responded, "*Ayyo! Full haalu aagu bittide!* [Kannada: It's fully spoiled!] I can' t take it." I looked over. Sitting in the plate was a five-rupee note that had clearly seen better times. It was folded and refolded into eight small bits and had split along the seams, each square dog-eared and dirty.[32] The eight parts had been carefully reattached with sticky tape, like puzzle pieces. Red ink squiggles all over the note indicated numerous passages through the banking economy. It had then at some point been placed with care into a cloudy plastic sheet, which in turn had been taped shut. Trapped beneath the grime, Mahatma Gandhi's imprimatur on the banknote peered at us. The devotee had been trying to pass this economic relic onto the offertory plate. The priest and the man in the blue shirt were debating the acceptance of the soiled note.

A week or so later, I found myself in possession of a similar soiled note. People often palmed these soiled notes off in a transaction when the buyer was not alert. Soiled and mutilated notes were seen as symptomatic of the opposite of wealth: a lack of a blessing, a polluted relic that symbolized a void.

When I handed her the dirty note, Padma, my tall friend at the Krishna Temple, who had previously showed no qualms over handling small change, suddenly demonstrated her squeamishness. She said, "You should not touch these notes. They are so dirty. *Cheee!* Who knows who has been touching them. It looks like a rag." Chellapa joined us. "*Ababah!*" he said, expressing disgust.

> These dirty notes. They are like a curse! When I was young my father used to bring his salary in crisp, clean notes and he would directly take it to the *puja* room and place it in front of the goddess Lakshmi. But nowadays who bothers with that? Money means nothing so we throw it here and there. We do not think of them as goddess Lakshmi's blessing. I have seen these fellows spit on their fingers before counting notes [Kannada: *yenjallu*]!

A couple of weeks after this soiled note incident, another male devotee, dressed in a "safari suit," the unofficial uniform of the petit bourgeoisie in Bangalore, approached the Ganesha Temple accountant. He was holding a large vinyl purse under his arm. This was the common method of carrying large sums of currency. I could not make out their words, but the quietness of the conversation and a sort of slyness in his gaze attracted my attention. It was unusual in the temple. After the sibilant conversation with the accountant, he looked glum and went toward the sanctum. After a few minutes, he returned and sat on the temple threshold for an obligatory five minutes, in deference to the belief that one should never rush away from the deity. He was ill-at-ease, the underarms of his shirt stained with sweat rings.

Abruptly, he opened his purse and removed several large bundles of rupee notes stapled together. From my own visits to the local bank, I knew these bundles to be worth ten thousand rupees each. The rusty staples required meticulous abilities to release the notes without tearing. My mother would produce a number of tools when my father got cash from the bank and when he went to work on the rusty staples, convinced that he would hurt himself in attempting to release a few notes. More often than not, the released notes would bear large dents from the rusty staples, looking worse for wear instantly.

With everyone watching, the man took all the notes and hastily stuffed them into the slot of the hundi. Some fell out, and I helped him gather them up and stuff them in again. Vishwanatha looked at my face and then asked the accountant pithily, "*Yeno? Blackaa?* [Kannada: What? Is it black money?]." Vishwanatha elucidated for my benefit since he thought I was hopelessly naïve. "There are many kinds of soiled notes. Some are physically dirty and others represent dirty and secret transactions—the black money of the economy." The accountant nodded and added, "Raid *irrubekku* [Kannada: Must be a raid]." Vishwanatha smiled at me and said, "*Ippo nambe yellarume pano pissachi airrukum* [Tamil: We are all money vampires now]."

The accusation of a vampiric greed and love of money has real-world consequences that increase the precarity of priests' lives. The state, in the form of the Muzrai department, through the legal armature of the Karnataka Act no. 33 in 2001,[33] devolved upon itself the power to seize and oversee temple funds if illegal usage of money or "mismanagement of temple funds" was alleged.[34] The act specifically named pujari, archak [ritual priest] or the "holder of a similar office by whatever name called" as the parties responsible for "rendering religious service in or maintaining the institution." By 1998 the state of Karnataka had forty-three thousand temples, matts, monasteries, dargahs, mosques, and other sacred institutions under its fiduciary care, a symptom of widespread charges of priestly mismanagement that Vishwanatha was commenting on with irony. The usage of the word *mismanagement* is telling, as it draws together neoliberal understandings of the governance of the sacred with the economy.[35]

The Limits of Wonder

One day I attended a luncheon for members of the city's professional class. Some of them were occasional visitors to the Krishna Temple, having married into the patrons' families or as the children of longtime devotees. All the women wore ornate saris and salwars in the latest fashion, and had perfectly coiffed, smooth hair. They looked elegant and well cared for. The men were in suits or fancy jeans, and many of them carried cocktails. One of the invitees who knew me and my work inquired jokingly, "How are your priests?" I responded that I was astonished by how hard they worked. Instantly, several voices arose. "They are all *chooths* [bastards]." One woman, with henna-colored hair, shouted, "Brahmanical hegemony!" I was astonished at the vituperative response. Finally, Sri, a quiet yet confident man whose family came from Mysore, said:

> I think this priestly class should just be abolished! No point. They just inherit the job. Two weeks ago we had some priest come home for a function. He came one hour late! He did not even know the *shlokas* [Sanskrit: recitation of texts] properly. I don't know why we have to pay these loafers. It's not like anyone else gets paid if they do a lousy job. I can't go to my company and say, "Look, I am two hours late and I don't know how to code, but my father held this software job, so I am an expert." *Avaru kobbu jaasthi aagobittidey!* [Kannada: They have gotten too fat!]

The accusations of "fatness" (Kannada: *kobbu*), a metaphor for greed and graft, were repeated to me ad nauseum as my study of temple ritual continued. Women would say, "*Kobbu jaasthi,*" which translated as "Too much fat." Men, less restrained, often used a cruder term, "*kobbu thikka*" (Kannada: fat arse). By 2013 everyone seemed to agree on the fatness of the priests, linking the adipose to moral turpitude.

I returned to the Ganesha Temple after lunch, and found Mr. Iyer talking about getting rid of one of the temporary "consultant" priests who came to the Ganesha Temple occasionally, who was grossly overweight and was also known to be slovenly. "I've seen him . . ." [*Here Mr. Iyer gestured drinking by placing his thumb against his lips and his fist in the air miming a bottle.*] Then he added, "*Kobbu pujari melle nambike yidubardu!* [Kannada: you should not trust a fat priest!]." I frequently heard other devotees also talk of kobbu in reference to their distrust of priestly activity and motives: "He said he would do it, and took the money, but God only knows? *Anvanegai kobbu jaasthi!* [Kannada: He is too fat!]." Or alternatively, "*Avana? Kobbu!* [Kannada: What him? Fat!]."

Vasavi, an old school-friend of mine who by now was a human resources manager in an IT company, and a devotee of the Ganesha Temple, noted:

> Now there is no difference between the pujari [priest] and us. Before they were educated, they knew everything, so we could give them respect. We had a pujari, you remember, Hasaru mama? He used to come to my grandfather's house to do the weekly puja for the *spatikamani.*[36] You know you have to do that puja in a madi [Tamil: pure] way, no? He would walk miles to come there and do the puja and he was an old man. He knew all the pujas and the shlokas and he knew everyone in

the family by name and their nakshatra (star date of birth).[37] He would spend a lot of time doing the puja correctly, you know, "*spashtama sholvango* [Tamil: recite clearly]." Nowadays they all carry a cell phone and they are too busy! They take on two or three assignments at the same time. They come late always. Even with that they are all booked!

Then she added, sotto voce, "Some of them eat meat and drink and all. We only call them as required now!" Other localites spoke of priests' inability to "keep to time," their inveterate unpunctuality, and their disregard of people's schedules. "All day we wait for these guys. Then he comes three hours late, does some *gol-maal* [Hindi: rubbish] and leaves!'

Of course, diagnosing the morally corrupt "fat" priest is not new in Hinduism. Dumontian hierarchies suggest that "the Brahmins in principle being priests, occupy the supreme rank with respect to the whole set of castes" ([1966] 1980, 49), but the corrupt and lazy, "fat" Brahmin is the subject of a nationwide cultural critique of the Brahmin familiar to South Asianists through philosophical and other literatures as well as the movies. The iconic "fat" priest appears to be uncaring of the rigors of Brahmanical purity that are foundational to his efficacy—care for the supplicant ritual practitioner, or any form of goodness and altruism.

C. J. Fuller, in his brilliant study of the priesthood of the Madurai Meenakshi temple priests over two decades, includes the following critique of the priesthood in his work: "It is often stated or assumed that the Brahmin's superiority in the caste hierarchy is in some manner contingent upon, or determined by their priestly role or sacerdotel function" (1984, 60–62). But many of the bourgeoisie saw priests not as sacerdotal specialists but rather as service personnel. An anthropologist colleague from Delhi said matter-of-factly, "In North India we know that Brahmins are part of the service class. If you have a plumbing problem, you call a plumber. If you have a ritual problem, you call a priest." An accountant whom I knew rather well, who had grown up in Malleshwaram, fondly called Vishwanatha a "*mutalla,*" or "*aasami*" (Tamil: idiot or witless) to indicate both his closeness to and his simultaneous lack of regard for the priesthood.

Opposite to the fat priest is the ideal Brahmin, an exemplar modeled on a reading of the classical religio-legal Sanskrit text the *Dharmasastra*, where the role of the Brahmin is seen as the "regally supported creators and bearers of the classical Brahmanical tradition" (Fuller 1984, 62). I found through conversations that there were several considerations that marked the ideal dharmic priest: one who is "learned," "humble," is "educated in Sanskrit," "knows the Agamas," "recited the shlokas properly," and takes the "time to perform rituals correctly." He should also dress "cleanly," be "pure," "not smoke or drink," "*madi vechchukanom* [Tamil: keep purity rituals]," and "*swami polle irrukanam* [be like the god himself]." Unspoken assumptions included that the ideal Brahmin should have very good relations with all of his clientele, be compassionate and truthful, and remain ascetic in his preferences—a dharmic ideal (Heesterman 1964, 31–52, in Fuller 1984, 64).[38]

The Brahmin, Fuller concludes, "ought to teach and study the Vedas, and perform orthodox Vedic rituals," and simultaneously act as a "representative within society and an ascetic renouncer" (1984, 63). He has to be a "representative of transcendence" (Heesterman 1964, 46) and his sacrifices have to be nonviolent rituals (Biardeau 1976; Fuller 1984, 63). So the most general explanation of the relative inferiority of any priest "depends upon an invidious comparison between him and the ideal Brahmin" (Fuller 1984, 65–66), something that my lunch mates seemed to know instinctively. Devotees do not trust fat priests but feel trapped because ritual is a necessary condition of Hindu life. So, the fatness narrative that the Bangalore bourgeois engage in to discredit priestly authority in actuality underlines their own cultural drift and loss. They articulate a seeming loss of values and thus destabilize what they see as a moral exemplar, yet what they merely achieve is a longue durée reemphasis on the inferiority of the temple priesthood. The localites do not trust the priest.

Dandu Shastri, a rather large priest himself, disliked the discourse of fatness. When I asked him about the notion of kobbu, he asked me accusatorily, "Who said that?" I prevaricated. Then he said, "Ganesha himself is a chubby fellow!" Then touching his own belly, he added, "He likes a little bit 'extra'! You know when we were young we had a saying, '*Aavan sheembi irrukan!*' [Tamil: He is worn thin!]." Those are the fellows you must be wary of because they are worn thin by the poison inside.'"

The problem of trust, or rather of distrust, emerges when social contracts break down and when people do not fulfill their roles. The contemporary loss of trust in the priesthood is apocalyptic for both the priests and the communities they serve.[39] My lunchtime companions' remarks were clear. The guile of the priests becomes suspicious, and their improvisational strategies are seen as manipulative, so "fatness" comes to indicate a growing narrative of distrust that circles around the greed of priests and their lack of transparency, not only in their practices but also in their intentions. Liberalism enhances distrust, and distrust sanctions wonder.

The dissolution of trust in the priesthood is part of the current moral entropic condition of Bangalore, and time acts as a symptom of that distrust. Trust is defined as "a recognition of the agency of the other" but also a belief in the benevolence of the other (Seligman 1997, 85). Distrust is a condition of the modern age. Krishna Bhattar and Chellappa both agreed with the formulation that modernity, particularly the neoliberal now, implied a growing distrust among people. Krishna said, "The times have changed. What can I say? People just are not trustworthy anymore. *Vishwasam panna mudiyade* [Tamil: We cannot trust anymore]. *Nampikkai illey!* [Tamil: No trust!]."

Of more expansive concern is the nature of critique and what it forecloses. For example, Marxist critiques of capitalism in India, while intellectually powerful, are rarely put into practice. They mirror critiques of religion, drawing parallels through language and trope (Pandey 2006; Chatterjee 2010; Sundar and Sundar 2014). Most notably, critiques of religion argue that lack of knowledge and blind faith, or "superstition," dominate practice while the larger cultural structures that dominate the religious imagination remain unexamined, as I have noted in my work on guru movements and magic (2015). Such intellectual hypocrisy finds echoes in the stunning lack of reflexivity and self-critique that my luncheon companions displayed; they were all desperately seeking higher-paying jobs while blindly critiquing the priests, who demonstrated the reality of the precarity and distrust of the capitalist marketplace. This "half-blind" critique forecloses critiques of modern urban India's intellectualism and capitalism, which now dominate, while encouraging a critique of the priesthood. It seems a very modern irony that these "fat" priests work so hard to adorn the deities in the ostentatious trappings of wealth in order to please the public—as described earlier in this chapter—only to fall victim themselves to accusations of greed.

In the plurality of practices to which wonder is a willfully cultivated response, the ritual specialist's effort often turns on enthralling one's attention to the wondrousness treading a knife's edge to turn skeptical clients into trusting devotees. And distrust is the limiting condition of this wonderment.

CHAPTER FOUR

TECHNOLOGIES OF WONDER

The possession of knowledge does not kill the sense
of wonder and mystery. There is always more mystery.
—Anaïs Nin, *The Diary of Anaïs Nin*

When she moves, it will be wondrous.
—Vishwanatha Shastri, Ganesha Temple, Malleshwaram, October 1999

Animatronic Devi

In October 1999, a few weeks before Navaratri, the autumn festival dedicated
to the female principle of the goddess, I found Dandu Shastri and his son,
Vishwanatha, discussing plans for a special alankara for the Banashankari
Devi goddess shrine in the Ganesha Temple.[1] Vishwanatha had become fascinated by the latest mechanical engineering technology, which he discovered through demonstration videos that the IT engineers who frequented the
temple showed him. He assumed that everyone was as riveted by these videos
as he was and continually extolled their virtues to us. Of particular fascination was a twentieth-century robot at a German trade fair that could hold
objects of different sizes and shapes. Vishwanatha was determined to use this
technology for the Banashankari Devi alankara.

Uma, the woman who ran the footwear stall at the temple, was subjected to Vishwanatha's hour-long, incomprehensible discourse on electric circuitry. "Vishwanatha should have done engineering," she said. "He likes engineering *too* much—maybe he can build a new *ratha* [chariot] for the god." Playfully, her son, Jeevanna, added, "Why only a new ratha? *Hossa Devaru kattuthare!* [Kannada: He is building a new deity!] Like god Vishwakarma."[2] Vishwanatha listened and smiled smugly. "Wait and see!" he said. "When she moves, it will be *arpitamada* [Tamil: wondrous]!"

The Navaratri festival culminates in Vijaya Dashami—the tenth day of victory—which celebrates the goddess's victory over evil, personified as a demon-buffalo. In the *Devi Mahatmya*, the compendium of devotional literature about the goddess Devi, the battle is related beautifully as a metaphor for the everyday battle between the ego and consciousness. Mahisha, the demon of the ego (Sanskrit: *ahamkara asura*), disguised as a buffalo, tries to capture the beautiful goddess of higher consciousness (Sanskrit: *chitta*). The goddess is instantly weaponized: fangs develop in her howling mouth, arms sprout innumerable weapons—the sword of discrimination, the bow of determination, and the bludgeon of persistent yogic practice—all with the ultimate nuclear payload of powerful mantras. She roars like the lion she sits on. As she battles Mahisha-Ego, millions of goddesses emanate from her, culminating in Parvati, the goddess of creation. When at last she stops toying with the demon and fights him one-on-one, she pierces his buffalo hide with her trident and decapitates him with her sword.

For days before the celebration, Vishwanatha worked secretively on a mechanical apparatus that he kept covered with an oilcloth in the lower courtyard of the temple. His *veshti* (Tamil: sarong) was stained with motor oil. I knew he had enlisted the help of some of the IT engineers.

Finally, the day of the puja arrived. Vishwanatha disappeared behind the *maryade* curtain.[3] Thudding sounds followed, the curtain was pulled back with a flourish, and the goddess was revealed, her right arm lifted high. In her raised hand, she clutched a shining, tinfoil trident, while at her feet lay a papier-mâché image of the buffalo, its severed head smeared with red ink. As we watched, light bulbs within the sanctum flashed, and the right arm of the deity thudded down, causing the trident to strike the buffalo's body. The assembled devotees gasped audibly in sheer delight; children burst into scattered applause and laughter.

The spectacle was repeated at every puja throughout the nine days of the festival. Each time, crowds of devotees gathered to watch, enthralled at the "machine-Devi's" performance. Vishwanatha was ecstatic.

Deus Ex Machina

The wonder created in the robotic Devi allows for the coexistence of multiple ways of knowing, for many realities to share the same conceptual space. It is beyond the practical—it is both an expression of the conditions in which Hindus have found themselves for millennia and a creative augmentation of the mundane world. It incorporates both exegetical and operational explanations, focusing not merely on ritual or technological efficacy alone, though that is part of the argument, but more so on transformation. It elevates devotees into a heightened reality and enables them to not only participate in the everyday order of the cosmos but also interact with a wider realm of divine or supernatural beings, and make use of special powers. In short, ritual practitioners engage technology as theology.

Michael Jackson, in "Familiar and Foreign Bodies: A Phenomenological Exploration of the Human-Technology Interface," suggests that the question of human–machine relations is both critical and existential, wherein "our fate and destiny are implicated" (Jackson 2002, 333–46). Indeed, in the temples of Malleshwaram, these existential questions become ethical and theological as they compel us to think about our relationship to technology and to divinity, to matter and to spirit.

In experimental Hinduism, worship, which is a community-based ritual of homage to the deity, and prayer, an individual petition to divinity, often seen as separate in Abrahamic religions, are frequently collapsed together. Individual prayer, the subjective communion with God, is often part of the intersubjective experience of worship. Through sharing, we gain an understanding of prayer not as a silent return to the interior of the reflective subject but as an agentive state in which the material and the technological become an apparatus in creating intersubjective wonder. As with prayer, wonder is a subjective and transformative experience, but one made more meaningful by sharing with others. What is compelling here for me is the idea of engagement, even union, between the experiential and the technological; actually merged ways of being, rather than the seaming together of subject and object. The history of worship and prayer (and concomitantly the evolution of religion) in these debates is a progressive movement from the mechanical efficacy of the thing itself toward an increasingly intellectual endeavor, a turn from the outward to the inward. In contrast, Dandu Shastri and the localites resist the narrative of prayer as a history of abstraction in favor of materiality—its aesthetics and its purposes of

FIGURE 4.1. Krishna Temple lighting. Photo courtesy of Andrew Hutcheson.

enchantment—as a form of agency. They return us to the etymological roots of prayer as a "bead," a gloss for both materiality and mechanized rhythms or repetitions.

The material presence of the goddess, her arm plunging the trident outward toward the temple walls, pivots the observer's eye to the future and invites us to explore its seductions; one would be wrong to render the future unequivocally as a valorization of progress. Indeed, the question of the new and its value within ritual has plagued scholars of ritual (Clothey 2006, 148–50). How is the new to be understood and accounted for?

Our experience of the new is an open-ended framing of the process of time in which its "cutting-edge" quality is an aspect of its attractiveness. New technologies and their novelty are associated not only with worldly progress but also with that of the otherworld. Ritual makes manifest what exists but usually remains unseen. For our purposes, the central question is how such innovation moves from novelty to the quotidian, how it is appropriated and incorporated into the mundane over time. Discussing possible futures, the question revolves around the acceptance of and adjustments made for the new and the strange, including the igniting of certain sentiments in aid of discerning what qualifies as new.

The New in Bangalore

Work life, particularly IT work in Bangalore, revolves around the invention and production of new technologies: new software, new biotech, new engineering of all kinds. Technological innovation and the problems and promise of the "cutting edge" are familiar discourse in the "Electronic City." In the 1990s several multinational corporations decided to build "Innovation Clusters" or "Innovation Laboratories" around Bangalore, thus creating new IT places, such as General Electric's (GE) John F. Welch Technology Center, where several of the devotees of the Ganesha Temple worked.[4] Everyday conversations in pubs and restaurants in Bangalore revolved enthusiastically around the "latest" in technology, whether it was the newest phone or the smartest app. Home-grown engineer-entrepreneurs like Mr. Narayan Murthy, the creator and CEO of a Fortune 500 tech company, were heroes. The culture of the city oriented itself aspirationally around new technologies and the skill required to create them.

Bangalore is a field in which the notions of "the possible" and "the real" as mirror images of each other are distinguishable in the everyday. The difference between them lies in the category of existence: the real exists, the possible does not—at least not yet.[5] Existence as a whole implies a process of differentiation of that which *is* (Marrati 2005, 1110). By contrast, creative experience is the process that brings the possible, that which can be, into a dynamic condition of wonder. The creation of wonder via technology's inclusion—or infusion—caused the general ethos of appreciation for technology to infiltrate the temple and rejuvenate the ritual.[6] Priests like Vishwanatha engage with technological apparatus and the ethos of newness. They "enjoy, rather than eschew" technology as an "instrument and agent of religious change and transformation" (DeNapoli 2017, 2–5), thus allowing for an imagined world full of potential.

Technology in Bangalore is allied with a creative force of possibility as well as an accompanying, ongoing process of actualization of new concepts, ideas, and affections. In the national imagination, Bangalore is the place of the new, where ideas are made intimate and real. Tracing this orthography of potentiality and the movement to the real is yet another kind of worlding. This potentiality is key to understanding the durability of ritual in a world that is constantly engaging the new, from making it, to encountering it, to renewing it.

The Mythical Garuda-Helicopter

Field notes, Ganesha Temple, Malleshwaram, February 20, 1999

A year into my fieldwork, Dandu Shastri said that he wanted to install a goddess deity in the Ganesha Temple to attract women devotees. He chose Banashankari Devi, a popular form of the goddess.[7] In the south of Bangalore was a one-hundred-year-old shrine to Banashankari Devi that attracted several hundred women devotees daily. If Dandu Shastri built such a shrine, he was sure he could increase the success and popularity of the Ganesha Temple with women who lived in the northern part of the city.

Dandu Shastri had been pestering me for a month or more to "get" him a helicopter. A helicopter would allow him to shower the shikhara *(cupola) of the new shrine with rose petals,* kum-kum *powder, and* thirtham *(holy consecrated water) at the installation festival for the Banashankari Devi. Before I could act, he told me a week later that he had contacted a civil aviation agency for the job. He asked me if I thought their price of 60,000 rupees (approximately US$1,500) sounded reasonable. I pointed out my lack of experience with hiring private helicopters but said it sounded reasonable to me. The next day, Dandu Shastri commanded Bhairavan, a neophyte priest who had just begun his service at the temple, to get ready to fly. Bhairavan left the temple looking worried.*

The morning of the consecration ceremony, I arrived at the Ganesha Temple at 4:00 a.m. I found Bhairavan giggling with excitement, sporting a gigantic crash helmet with radio receiver. One of the young priests slapped him on the back and said, "Yeno 'Top Gun'! Ready, na? [Kannada: Well 'Top Gun'! Are you ready?]," referring to the popular Hollywood movie starring Tom Cruise as a fighter pilot. Bhairavan beamed in delight. Dandu Shastri caught sight of him and shouted, "What are you doing? Are you going to clean the temple wearing this helmet?" Bhairavan hastily removed the helmet, but a short while later I saw him depart on his scooter, his veshti flying and his helmet under his arm.

At precisely 8:00 a.m., the Mahabhishekam *(consecration bath of the deity) and the enlivening of the deity through the painting of the image's eyes ended. The chanting of the 108 priests reached a crescendo. Suddenly we heard a buzzing sound. The 108 priests, who had been alerted to the possible arrival of the helicopter, stopped immediately and stared at the sky.*

A minute later, the dark shadow of a helicopter rose from behind the temple gopuram. In front of it was a lone bird, a Brahmani kite known as a Garuda, riding the wind gust from the rotary blades. The bird had clearly been disturbed by the noise of the helicopter from its nest in the temple tree. Vishwanatha became incoherent in his excitement, yelling into the microphone, "Helicopter has come. Garuda is here . . . Helicopter . . . Garuda . . . Helicopter-Garuda! Garuda-Helicopter!" In response, many people dashed out of the surrounding houses and streets and peered into the sky with their hands folded in prayer. Mr. Sainath, a retired second division engineer, referred to the Garuda with the words "Krishna vahanam [the mythic vehicle of Krishna]." The helicopter hovered in the clear blue sky, and we were suddenly drenched in red and yellow petals and consecrated water as Bhairavan found his mark. Many of the devotees were visibly moved, and tears streamed down their faces. Mr. Gowda, a friend of Sainath, and an aeronautical engineer with the Hindustan Aeronautics Limited, who had worked on India's signature satellite technology, said, "Wonderful! Wonderful! What a divine sight." I too found myself surreptitiously wiping tears from my eyes.

As I was collecting my slippers from the footwear stall outside the temple later that day, I saw the priest Bhairavan, now returned to earth and flushed with delight. He was in the center of a large group of devotees and young priests, to whom he was lecturing on the dangers and excitement of flight. Ranga, the watchman-guard at the temple, waved his lathi (truncheon) and said, grinning, "See that fellow! Just because he has gone in the helicopter he is acting like Lord Rama, who rode in the Pushpakavimana [the mythic flying chariot of the god Rama]."

When I met Dandu Shastri the next day, he described the surprised and "shocked" reactions of some of the devotees. Then he added, lest I think it was a self-aggrandizing project, "It is all due to the power of Ganesha. That is our seva (Sanskrit: worship). Everything, all this helicopter, everything, it is all the power of Ganesha, the power of Brahman, the ultimate god. It is a kind of 'energy,' you might say. Nothing is Dandu Shastri or Vishwanatha Shastri! No, No! It is all growing because of Swami [Tamil: the Lord]."

But not everyone shared in this wonderment. The next day, tired after the festivities, I stopped to "check in" at the Krishna Temple. Someone asked Krishna Bhattar what he had thought of the helicopter ceremony. Krishna Bhattar said that he "knew it would be a hittu," using the Kannada pronunciation of the English idiom, but he added waspishly that the audience had become undiscriminating, that "navu yellaruve ivaga mixture jana aagubittudivi [Kannada: we have all become 'mixture' folk now]."[8] As he spoke, he churned his arm to indicate how mixed up we had become. He added, "You know how we are. If the neighbor has a new car we want one also! So now every priest will want a heli-

copter vimana for their pujas. Soon the sky will be dark, not with rain clouds, not with birds, but with helicopters!"

THE GARUDA-HELICOPTER DID indeed exemplify the hybrid that Krishna Bhattar asserted was an existential condition of being in the modern world. If we think of Dandu Shastri and the localites as co-creators of aesthetic forms, we are brought immediately to Frederick Jameson's conclusion that in postmodern societies like Bangalore, which have a historical amnesia, a loss of the subjective and true understanding of the past, artists recycle past aesthetic forms into a "pastiche" (1991). Here, hybridization or pastichification allows for the adjustment of the technical within the dimension of the mythic through metaphor and metonymy elevating both beyond the mere pastiche into a new representational form. By which I mean this form not only holds to the truth of postmodernism, that is to say, to its fundamental object, the world space of multinational capital, but at the same time achieves a breakthrough to an unimagined new mode of representing this object that elevates it from pastiche to something greater: an authentic object.

The mythic imagination quickly engulfs the helicopter by conflating it with the Garuda rising from the tree, the vehicle of Lord Vishnu. The immediacy of the transfer from the material (in this case the helicopter and bird) to the mythic depends on devotees' intuition and also allows for improvisation in the ad hoc nature of the fusion of traditional ritual with the Garuda-helicopter. In fact, Victor Turner, in his study of Ndembu ritual, defined the ritual symbol as a "storage unit" filled with a vast amount of information (1967, 1–2). Direct comparison of the helicopter to Lord Rama's vimana, as made by many of the devotees, suggests a metaphorical turn by which the mythic but real Garuda and the not-so-new technology of the helicopter are made imaginative cousins. Joined thus, as things that fly and as the mythic vehicle of Vishnu, they become radically new. Metonymy and metaphor working together allow for the hybridization of the helicopter with the eagle and mythic flying vehicle in the spectator's imagination. Therefore, in the imagination of localites, the real and the fictive together make for a wondrous moment and in the marvel of the Garuda-helicopter the excess of God's benevolence is felt. Wonder here marked the fault lines of order in which a creative edge was visible, and incoherence was a contingent yet valued state.

But I am making distinctions between what wonder is and how wonder is practiced and understood. When I asked Dandu Shastri how we were to understand the wonder of the Garuda-helicopter, he referred to the canon—the *Chāndogya Upaniṣad*, a speculation on epistemological, metaphysical, ethical, and semantic topics of the first century BCE[9]—where he said new things can be recognized and understood as avatars of older principles, making them familiar *despite* their newness and thus facilitating a broader understanding of the cosmos, one that is not disrupted by change and difference, but that has a temporal discontinuous continuity.

In practice, our conceptions of reality are seen in terms of fragments that we appropriate and reconfigure in various ways. The strategy of collapsing the bird, the helicopter, and the flying chariot into each other invites the audience to fuse the three image fragments. Such chains of equivalence that transfer and enhance meaning exemplify creative appropriation and reconfiguration.

I was struck by the sense of disorientation that the hybrid produced in the audience. They were, after all, a technologically savvy crowd of Bangaloreans, yet their reactions breathed wonder. They called the spectacle "super," "life-changing," "breathtaking," and "wonderful." It appeared that the improvisation of acts of wonder within the sensorium of worship allowed for a transformative individual communion with God that had the potential to interrupt stasis. The sudden conflation of the natural bird and the mechanical one thus created a sense of mythic disorientation, an emancipatory vision that conjoined reason and thought with feeling.

Pursuing a moment where wonder can exist results in the creation of a sublime aesthetic moment both as a new category of experience and as a subversion of previously understood relationships between pasts and futures; it resides in a state of disorientation, an edge of incoherence in tension. The practice of wonder as understood by Dandu Shastri and Vishwanatha is very simple; it is to harness this incoherence, domesticate this disorientation, in order to create a singular moment whereby enthusiasm and acceptance for the new would be engendered and, hopefully, repeated. These hybrids provide an admixture of the modern sublime to move beyond the dialectic between imaginary and real life worlds whereby we can use the former to reimagine reality as provisional, practical, enchanted, and complex. In these practices of wonder resides a subjunctive world promising reasonable enchantments beyond those of myth or modernity.

Krishna Bhattar had heard of Garuda-helicopter from localites who moved between the Ganesha and Krishna temples. He was curious. When I appeared at the Krishna Temple a week after the event, he quizzed me about the audience reception. Shreyas raised the most significant question, couched as a critical comment: "But only God can make the Garuda fly!" pointing out the arbitrariness of the event. Krishna Bhattar's immediate response was "That is what God does!" For Krishna Bhattar, the emergence of the new hybrid was not a capricious event but rather one where the conditions for wonder had been successfully met, allowing for the act of God of the Garuda's flight to intervene to create a new event. He said to us, "We cannot always ask for a Garuda but if we prepare properly then we will get the Garuda to fly! Then wonder will break through [Tamil: *vadikkun*]. But we cannot plan for God's *leela* [Sanskrit: play, miracles]!" In fact, then, in thinking about Garuda-helicopter, I argue that there is no empirical question here but rather a taxonomic one: the taken-for-granted difference between matter and spirit. Reflection on worship and technology may force us to reframe our mostly implicit taxonomies of matter and spirit in intellectually freeing ways.

Krishna Bhattar frequently remembered our previous conversations. Some years later, watching Shreyas touch his new iPhone, Krishna Bhattar said, "This phone that lights up and allows you to see people in America. This is marvelous. We can see, we can hold it, we can 'press buttons.' It is like God's *leela*! We cannot perceive it fully, only its edges." Krishna Bhattar gestures to the marvelous nature of the bird in conjunction with the helicopter and the marvel of the iPhone, conjoining them to the miraculous nature of God's "play," yet rendering God's will as beyond human imagining. The marvel is rooted in a reality that humans can perceive and even manipulate. The miraculous is unpredictable and unknowable.

On the other hand, as Krishna Bhattar understood, priests like himself gesture to the seduction of the new (or the newish) by incorporating relatively recent technologies regularly into the daily puja through ritualized acts of improvisation. Thus, newness slips into daily acts of adoration of the god, rendering the immediate in flux. In Malleshwaram, life lies in the ad hoc gluing together of immediate solutions that localites deploy.

But in using the helicopter, Dandu Shastri was also attempting something else, which Krishna Bhattar understood almost instinctively. Dandu Shastri wanted to position his temple as cutting edge, fashionable as opposed to "old" and uncool temples. The new was "modern" (pronounced "modren"), "*Bombhat, sakkath, rivaju!* [Kannada: Cool, awesome, fashionable!]" and "*asai* [Tamil: desire]," or "heavy! Hi-fi! cool! hottu! too good!" all terms widely used to index value, desirability, and cutting-edge presence.

The new was a key part of a strategy for attracting younger and well-educated devotees to the temple. As Krishna Bhattar noted to me in many conversations, modernity's costly objects of desire such as helicopters, cars, televisions, and computers, which had entered the markets of Bangalore just a few years prior, belonged to a conceptual force field in which newer meant better. In this space, having technology, preferably newer technology, also signaled global sophistication.[10] Aspiration to be seen as fashionable and sophisticated flowed through the spaces of Bangalore. The helicopter, though not so new in the modern world of warfare and civil aviation, had assumed fashionability, a certain "of-the-moment" modishness when transported into the realm of ritual. Paradoxically, this time twisting of oldness and newness— of familiarity and strangeness—was muddied by the fact that military helicopters had been built in the Hindustan Aeronautical Laboratory's factories right in Bangalore for many decades. When I asked Mr. Iyer, the aviation engineer, about his tearful response to the helicopter-Garuda, he said, "I've never seen a helicopter in that situation. It was new." So it was not the absolute newness of the technology but the contextual "newishness" that was significant. Residents did not need the creative articulations and disarticulations of the world dictating to them established modes of response; they were capable of reforging reality that already encompassed broader modes of response and thereby fueling wonder.

Ritual practitioners, like Dandu Shastri and Krishna Bhattar, play a "double game." They seek out newness, in image or in context, to "shock" and surprise themselves into a state of wonderment. New and newish technologies are made intimate in Malleshwaram, allowing for an imagining of the possible and its actualization into the real, overturning the dialogics built into tradition and modernity. At the same time, the new technologies are made to feel familiar through reference to known correlates. I was curious therefore about the question of temporality and tedium: when did the newish technologies lose their cutting-edge appeal regardless of context and become tedious? Tedium, after all, is an enemy of wonder.

Anthropologists have been largely unsuccessful in analyzing the importance of fluidity, disorder, and chaos in ritual, focusing instead on how ritual domesticates and brings together: how it creates order and meaning from chaos and disorder. Yet the chaotic and its ability to disrupt the everyday has always intrigued anthropologists. Webb Keane has argued that there is an inherent relationship between "that which is most highly valued and orderly and that which is most devalued and disorderly" (1997, 3). Anthropologists like Michael Puett (2008) maximize the understanding of ritual as domesticating the dangerous and gluing together the fragments of the world. In his readings of specific ancient Chinese ritual he argues that the performance of ritual is a necessity to glue a riven world together, converting it into a harmo-

FIGURE 4.2. Devotees reading prayers under new electrical lighting at the Krishna Temple. Photo by the author.

nious, monistic cosmos, and such harmony is not the opening assumption, nor the enduring state, of ritual.

Localites see much more than a dangerous world that needs to be glued together for harmony. They see a possible outcome of ritual as continued fragmentation, fluidity, excitement, and creativity. This rupture of the everyday is set against the agglutinative forces of tradition, allowing for a capture of the new, and localites wish to dwell and be immersed in this moment of creative fracture. And, according to Catherine Bell, this remaking aspect of ritual, this repetition, is "at the heart of ritual" (1997, 25). Here, lived experience and theoretical apparatus become blurred. The practice of wonder resides in this blurring, where the creation of instabilities of meaning provides an opening to endless new strangeness and possibility.

We often think of newness as indexed to its origins in creativity, in disorder. In American universities and businesses, the word *disruption* is repeatedly used in a positive sense, signifying thinking anew and thinking "outside the box." The concept of innovation embedded within this praxis is rather stale, but in the mature economies of the West, this concept has been linked with institutional research and development spending. Indigenous innovators such as Dandu Shastri and Krishna Bhattar are of a smaller, slipperier order, as are their innovations.[11] Indigenous innovation in India has been often referred to in the business school literature as *jugaad*, a hack or "frugal engineering" around a series of impediments and obstacles (Radjou, Prabhu, and Ahuja 2012). The solution circumvents the problem while attempting to retain the essence of what is required for authenticity in the solution, rather than cutting through the problem or rendering it null and void. Jugaad is slippery. It is usually conceived of as the small, powerless entrepreneur's route to success in a heavy-handed bureaucracy. It could also be argued that such an adjustment around rigid obstacles is antisocial and unethical; the triumph in beating the system by finding threadbare tracks *around* the rules is usually an individual achievement rarely shared or having a notion of the common good. In this view, ethics is a creative habituation that is slippery, encompassing all manner of behaviors and ways of being that are morally questionable.

But as I understood it from Dandu Shastri and Vishwanatha, this ad hoc hack brought to the forefront a new reality in which the present became invigorated with new and joyful potentialities for change, expansion, and transformation.

Envisioning the Sublime

A few years later, while we were speaking about something entirely different, Dandu Shastri confessed to me in a sibilant whisper that the animatronic Devi and the helicopter-Garuda were mere *parvai* (Tamil: spectacle), a viewing pleasure created as an "advertisement" to get devotees to darshan (Sanskrit: sacred sighting of the deity). Although he felt slightly ashamed about the discrediting nature of the spectacle, it was a profoundly progressive impulse in Dandu's thought, that the more palpable and material forms of worship had gradually given way to something more subtle and nuanced. For Dandu Shastri, technology can hold and render wonder, which in turn guides the devotees to a watchful contemplation that might ultimately lead the devotee to surrender to the divinity. In other words, technology acts as materiality of wonder.

Some skeptical devotees suggested that Dandu Shastri and Vishwanatha were simply seeking money, but Dandu felt he was doing good in enticing devotees to view the deity. His hope was that the spectacle would lead to worshipful prayer, which would in turn open the way to pure contemplation of divinity, to surrender to the will of God. In this case worship is not identified fully with the gross materiality of technology, but neither is it purely ethereal. Worship is the correlate of enchantment that adheres to technology and divinity, substituting the visible wonder of the former to indicate the unfathomable wonder of the latter. To ritual practitioners, it is not only the mode of composition or framing that matters. The greater value lies in consideration of practices of wonder as aids in revealing the dimensions of sublimity of the divine.

Dandu talked about God as sublime, as having qualities of greatness—physical, moral, intellectual, metaphysical, aesthetic, spiritual, or artistic—that are beyond human comprehension, measurement, or imitation. In the intellectual history of wonder, the sublime imbued in Dandu's idea of parvai, the optics of seeing, is the capacity for wonder to acknowledge the fluidity of the world, its sublimity. While ritual proscription, liturgical structure, community expectations, seasonal variations, and visual expression all create a somewhat rigid form, technology enables a freeing of the imagination. This imaginative freedom, often expressed through metaphor, helps liberate devotees from the rigidity of ritual form and find a way to wonder. Dandu explained:

> The first time I saw my mobile [cell phone] I couldn't understand how to switch it on. Then Vishwanatha showed me. Like that it is with God. The on switch is hidden. In the Mahabharatha when Krishna allows Arjuna to see him, it's like the light comes on! It is *Vishwaroopa* [Sanskrit: all life images in one]. Arjuna sees the whole universe in Krishna: the earth, the sky, the stars, the sun and moon. He even sees himself! This is wonderment. Where you suddenly can *see*. Everything is illuminated. You see your connection to the smallest ant and the biggest king!

Here, Dandu Shastri speaks of a wonder that makes the individual aware of the intersubjective ties of the universe, the central animating principle of the Chandogya Upanishad and of Hindu philosophy in general. Since thought at the limits of human philosophical speculation cannot grasp divinity, we are pushed back, in Dandu's words, onto wonder, onto a mixture of contemplation and practical *imitatio Dei* as the closest thing to an apotheosis that human life in its material contingency can support. Here, the materiality acts, as Dandu points out, as a *panae* (pot or vessel) for the creator to fill with extraordinary wonder.

Malleshwaram temples create conditions for a new kind of sublime: the "technological sublime" where the traditional Kantian categories of aesthetics (beauty, meaning, expression, feeling) are being replaced by a type of exaltation enhanced by technology—a space of being at the limits of experience.[12] The deep attraction of the technological sublime is its transcendence of human finitude where change and fixity no longer matter. The sublime is a distillation toward essence or a realization of the ultimate nonfixity of reality. Through a recognition of the sublime, we are granted the potential to understand that our worlds—how we see them and live within them—are susceptible to change and remaking through our own conceptions of reality (Jackson 2013).

The marvelous bewitching nature of the Animatronic Devi or the Garuda-helicopter hybrid is that they straddle the edges of truth and fiction. If we think about wonder rationally, we understand that the imagination can change our bodies and our perceptions. As Vishwanatha noted, these marvels are closely related to dreams, and in dreams our imaginations allow us to invest these objects, composite or not, with extraordinary significance, elevating them into sublimity.[13] But there is tension between the transcendence of the sublime—its uncontained nature—and the fixity needed to hold it, as there is between a universe of change and that which is changeless.

Drums of Contention

But it isn't that localites think all technology is wonderful. Some technologies are not unanimously accepted or acceptable in the temples. A fight about a drum set smoldered for over four years and split the Ganesha Temple devotee base.

In March 1999 Vishwanatha had a blowout fight with Sundaram, the *nadaswaram* player and the leader of the temple band of musicians.[14] The temple musicians arrived every morning to perform their seva, their work of offering music to the deity. They had the inherited right to play while the deity was fed, and again at dusk when the deity was put to bed.[15] On festival days, the musicians played for processions and for special worship sequences. For localites, these auspicious sounds of adoration were supportive of devotional behaviors. They were meant to drown out any inauspicious sounds, the *beswara* of daily life, such as sounds of sorrow or conversations about profane subjects, that might intrude on the ears of congregants.

Vishwanatha and the other priests felt that Sundaram's band played out of tune and this untunefulness was purposeful. Vishwanatha often complained of their *apaswaram* (Tamil: untuneful) music.[16] In private, he also grumbled that they cost the temple too much money. He said he was tired of negotiating with them regarding the days the band would play in the temple. One day in conversation with Vishwanatha, Dandu Shastri said, "It's not like they play 'concerts' or in any 'cultural events' or anything. They only play here." Cultural performances, often hosted by civic institutions or by temples in the festival season for middle-class audiences in the city, became a metric of success by which to evaluate musicians, dancers, and other performers.

Dandu saw performing and "earning good money," as he put it, as markers of success in the neoliberal circuit of cultural shows. In contrast, Sundaram thought they were denigrating his lifetime of service to the temple. Temple musicians felt they were *sevakaras*, artists who offered their art to the deity. Sundaram would talk to me about the ways in which different opening sound sequences (Sanskrit: *alaapana*) would evoke certain moods among devotees. Sounds—the whispery notes of a flute or the staccato beating of the drum—were analogous to feeling or rasa for Sundaram.

Despite Sundaram's musical abilities, Vishwanatha Shastri and other surrogates started a campaign to discredit the temple musicians, saying privately when Sundaram was not there, "These fellows they charge too much . . . not like their parents." On another occasion, in Sundaram's presence, another surrogate said Sundaram's band had arrived "too late," suggesting a lack of professionalism. Sundaram looked at me, pleading to intervene on his behalf: "He only called one hour ago, Madame!" So despite my anthropological disquiet, I did plead on the band's behalf, but to no avail.

Vishwanatha's ulterior motive was made clear a week later when he had an automatic drum set installed that was truly "new" technology. I had never seen anything like it, and neither had any of the congregants. It consisted of two traditional wooden and leather drums mounted on a cast iron platform, two brass bells and clangers, and an electric wheel that ran the clappers and drum sticks in a set of six synchronized beats. Mounted in a brightly painted yellow cast-iron cage, it was made by an entrepreneurial industrialist in the suburb of Yelahanka. The cage of reinforced bars allowed the drums to be locked up with a giant padlock. Vishwanatha proudly showed it to me and explained: "You see, now we are not dependent upon the lazy [Tamil: *shomberi*] temple musicians. They say they will come, and they don't show up. So I got this drum set installed. I saw it somewhere else and this fellow built them so I got his number and ordered it. Everyone has been commenting about it." Sundaram and Nanjundappa, one of the oldest musicians in the band, were understandably annoyed by the introduction of the drum set. Nanjundappa commented, "As it is they don't call us for the seva. Now only on festival days they will call us. Before, all day we would be attached to a temple, provide the music for the god, for his waking, sleeping, for archane, for *mangalaarthi*, for everything."[17] Then he added sadly, after listening to the drum set beat its staccato regular sounds, "It has no bhava, no rasa, no feeling. It just plays beats, not music."

But Vishwanatha's delight was not to be diminished. He demonstrated that he could "automatically" switch on the temple bells and music for the mangalarathi by simply flicking a switch in the sanctum. He did so and the temple was filled with an unearthly din. The reaction of the devotees present was not exactly what Vishwanatha hoped for. Colonel Gopal, now a trustee of the temple, jumped at the noise. He shouted, imitating the sound of the drum set, "*Ayyo! Yenu shabdha!* [Kannada: *Ayyo!* What a noise!]." He then proceeded to imitate it, "*Donghu donghu! Donghu donghu!*" Mrs. Iyer, wife of Mr. Iyer the engineer who was at the forefront of the Helicopter-Garuda puja, was simply aghast when she came by for the evening puja and the machine was switched on, saying, "*Abbah! Yenu vipreeta galata!* [Kannada: What a racket!]." The loud and lifeless synchronized sound took everyone by surprise.

Shanthi, a middle-aged and supposedly wealthy philanthropist, courted by all the priests, arrived at the temple in the evening, in the middle of yet another sonic "test" of the drum set by Vishwanatha. She said, "What is all this? Why does the temple need all this? It's all that Vishwanatha's fault. He is crazy for the *lateshtu* [Kannada: latest]. I wanted the god to have a nice new silver *kiritam* [crown], but did they use the money I gave for that? No! This fellow Vishwanatha, he decided that the temple need some new drums and now this temple is like a disco! They give me a headache!!" She added that the desire for technology "*jasthi ag betide* [Kannada: becomes too much]" that najuka explored previously was now subordinated to *labha* (Sanskrit: greed). "These drums, these computerized lights, all this . . . *prabhaava yella hogubittide* [Kannada: the inspiration is lost]!"

Prabha, the root word of *prabhaava*, is often translated as light, illumination, and knowledge. Shanthi was mourning a loss of illumination, a loss of the experience of the sublime, despite the introduction of technology. Moral degeneracy is frequently ascribed to the desire for new technology—a churning in the ethical plane of subjectivity (Gold and Gujar 2002, 102). The technologies themselves are seen as causing degeneracy—fragmenting attention, creating a vivid spectacle where previously there was none, allowing access to a world of pornographic content, ratcheting up desire by producing newer and newer versions, and so on. After listening to an ear-shattering bout of the drum set, Kamala Ajji, an elderly woman who could not see or hear very well, said, "I feel very sad. See . . . did you hear the drums? This is not like the music that we used to have in temples. It's just 'fashion.'" Then she added, "I am deaf but still I can hear this racket!"

Kamala Ajji's mourning was greeted with amusement by some of the younger devotees, such as Arjun with the greasy hair, and Anand, who had mysteriously taken to calling himself "Ash" as an affiliation with his Western outsourcing personality, both part of the group at the Skyye bar. The drum set polarized the devotees, pitting the youngsters who enjoyed the cutting edge and the fashionable against the out-of-date "oldfashiondu." I found that the older devotees were often dismissed by the younger ones as "*thumba old fashioned* [Kannada: very old-fashioned]" by saying "*avarige modern ishta illa* [Kannada: they do not like modern things]." Others hesitantly admitted to a sense of involuntary loss of something ineffable in the hectic advancement toward an undefined goal in which technology played a master part.

Shanthi and Kamala Ajji were in the minority, overruled by the younger, more brash devotees who looked on the technological hybrids with delight. It was a generational conflict where the appropriation of technology, usually Western technology, was contested and debated in the public sphere. Following Akio Tanabe's study of Orissa, Ann Gold notes that the birth of a new "moral society," in which to "legitimize or criticize politico-economic practices in a wider sphere" is made possible, requires some conflict, which Tanabe describes through the ancient Hindu metaphor of "churning," a process that ultimately "generates new forms of discourse and practice regarding the vision of community" (Tanabe qtd. in Gold 2009, 381).

Charles Hirschkind, in his brilliant analysis of Egyptian cassette sermon listeners, suggests that cassette sermons, like these drums, allow for an emergent "ethics of listening" that cultivates new affective moral stances, a counterpublics of listening (2006). So too in neoliberal Malleshwaram, the genesis of a new ethics of listening occurred with the introduction of the drum set. The counterpublics of the ephemeral practices of sound technology allowed for a new generation to practice piety. New virtuosos—younger devotees familiar with Western rock music or popular Bollywood music—were drawn to the temple, through a transformative ethics of listening in which the white noise of the drum set helped focus the attention on the deity, whereas the lyrical playing of the temple musicians focused the listener on the music. According to young localites, the pious could use the staccato beat of the drum set to drown out the external inauspicious noise of the city, the original intention of the music, and focus on the deity. Byre Gowda, one of the Ganesha Temple accountants, said, "The music, when they play, we start to listen. We say it is *apaswaram* or it is nice. So then our thoughts are not on God, no? That is not good!" The devotees developed a rationale over the course of the first year following the installation of the drum set, arguing that the musicians' traditional repertoire of Carnatic songs of adoration were a distraction to worship.

Six months after I spotted the drum set at the Ganesha Temple, there was one at the Krishna Temple. When I asked Seshadri, a young priest, about whether they had seen the one in the Ganesha Temple and copied it, he objected: "*Naavella copy madolla! Yaruu gift madidaru* [Kannada: We don't copy!

FIGURE 4.3. A drum set. Photo by the author.

Someone gifted it to us]." But in fact Krishna Bhattar clarified that while the drum set was the gift of a temple patron, trustees had requested it right after they had seen it in the Ganesha Temple.

By the time I returned to Malleshwaram in 2009, the same synchronized beats rang throughout the neighborhood from multiple centers of worship. The subtle rhythms that Sundaram's playing embodied, his capacious knowledge and musical ability, could not compare to the standard rhythms of the mechanized drum set.

So a new ethics of listening, one that Kamala Ajji attested to, more standardized and mechanical, had spread through the community of Malleshwaram. In modernity, mimetically capacious technologies replaced mimetically capacious individuals, another version of the institutionalized distinction in anthropology between tradition and modernity, and imitation and creativity (Taussig 1993).

While mourning the loss of trained musicians Prabha noted that localites had been trained to accept mechanized computerized drumming as it surfaced in the score of popular Hindi, Tamil, and Kannada film songs, and in popular Bhajans that followed the "filmi" genre, which she noted were played from every shop in the area. "All the songs now have this computer music in between. We are used to it." Devotees were trained through repeated listening to other genres of music to accept staccato drum beats as devotional music.

But while there was some pedagogic listening involved, localites also said that the temple drum "noise was acceptable" because though loud it "stopped quickly," so they could stand it. The ephemeral sounds were acceptable due to their impermanence. Devotees wrongly assumed that since the sound died away quickly, the technology would as well. But in reality the technology remained, and its transformative force in the politics of piety is enduring.

As time wore on, devotees accepted the drums. Shanthi told me some years on that the drums were "acceptable" because they were seen as a simple "adjustment," an ad hoc shift. Technology here enables a creativity in the ritual that matters in its capacity to enable piety, an advance on an already defined path toward an ideal Hindu self. Similarly, the larger acceptance of the innovative and the improvisational marks the temple publics as spaces of constant experimentation.[18] This experimental regime combined with the ideas that public imagination is complex and provisional.

Capturing Divine Biometrics

When I began this study in 1998, I had an older Canon film camera and would sometimes use it to document certain processions or festival alankara to have as memory prompts for significant events.[19] Whenever I attempted to take a photograph of anything near the deity, I was admonished by the priests and devotees alike. Padma, my friend at the Krishna Temple, said emphatically that I should *always* point my camera away from the deity for fear of photographing the god. I knew that the larger pilgrimage temples had a "no photographs" policy prominently displayed on notice boards all over the temple and enforced by security guards and priests, but the ethics of photography in smaller neighborhood temples such as the Krishna and Ganesha Temples had never before been made explicit to me.

Krishna Bhattar echoed Padma on the rule. "God should not be captured in a camera lens," he said on more than one occasion. I asked Chellappa, my elderly mentor from the Krishna Temple, why this was so. He responded first with a normative injunction, "Because God is alive like us and capturing him on a camera lens is wrong." Later he clarified, "You cannot capture him in any photograph. That is only the *murti* [image] you are taking . . . not him. He is much bigger." It was clear that the biometrics of the deity were at issue.

Speaking in Tamil interspersed with English, Dandu Shastri's explication built on Chellapa's injunction.

You see, the Swami inside the "idol" is very powerful. The image, the "idol," holds all this power of the Swami. "Like a battery." So when we do *abhishekam* [Sanskrit: bathe] to the idol we drink the water after, because in passing over the "idol," the water gains the strength of the Swami within. The power "leaks" out. Like when you make "coffee decoction," no? The "coffee powder" is in the "filter," and then when you put water in the "filter," the strength of the coffee leaks out into the water and you get your "decoction." So then anyone who takes a photograph, can take this "power" and keep it.

For Dandu Shastri, the form of the image is thus like a porous sheath, a "filter" that holds the power of the deity within. The power "leaks" out occasionally. A photograph captured some of the deity's essence, which was then lost to the deity. Krishna Bhattar explained the ban on photography through a riddle: "Our power comes from the god. That's all. We try to keep God with us through the photo. But we forget him day to day. Keeping and losing. All are the same."

When I got a better camera several years later in 2002, Krishna Bhattar's earlier philosophical musings on the ethical equity between taking and keeping a photograph and the loss of memories did not get me out of trouble when I took photographs, for devotees often policed me to ensure that I was not stealing a photograph of the deity. If they thought I swung perilously close, they complained to Krishna Bhattar, who would raise his finger in admonition to me if he was busy during the puja. Despite the stricture on my activities, I soon had hundreds if not thousands of photographs of the temple, the devotees, festivals, and occasional out-of-focus shots of the deity.

I spoke with Anand, aka Ash, an avid technology buff and part-time IT entrepreneur, whom I assumed would be against the ban on photography as it limited the reach of technology. But he justified the ban in terms of capitalist ideas of profit: "The big temples like Tirupathi . . . for them these photos of the god, Lord Venkateshwara, they make lots of money. They make calendars, watches, photos, pendants, all that. Why will they then allow you to take photo for free?" Anand's theory of the biometrics of the deity acting as the intellectual capital of the temple seemed particularly viable when in 2002 Krishna Bhattar handed me a calendar of photographs of different alankaras of the Krishna Temple deity. "Who took the photos?" I asked, puzzled by the license of some to capture images of the deity given the strictures on me. Krishna Bhattar replied, "We had a professional photographer from Srinivasa Photo Studio on Sampige Road come to take them on different festival days. To record." Then he went to the *almirah*, a metal lockable cupboard, colloquially called a "Godrej bureau" in the corner of the temple, unlocked it, and after rifling through boxes containing jewels for the deity, documents, money, and silver candelabras, he drew out a cardboard box with a few spools of nega-tives.[20] He made a pun on the word *God*, as he drew out the negatives and said, "This 'Godrej' almirah has so many 'negatives' but it is very 'positive.'"

Archiving the Divine

In 2009 I returned to the Krishna Temple. By this time, I had a digital camera. When I arrived, Krishna Bhattar placed me facing the deity. It seemed that I had carte blanche to shoot whatever I wanted but, I realized I could only shoot processional deities. I asked Krishna Bhattar why the policy regarding pho-tography had changed. He seemed to have forgotten his earlier strictures: "No, I never had an objection. Only some of the older devotees felt . . ." His voice trailed off. "Bad?" I asked. "No, not bad. It was just simply . . ." He declined to continue the thought, but in Bangalore I knew that "simply" meant no real explanation would be forthcoming.

He watched me for a while as I took pictures, out of sight of the older devotees then, viewing the photographs, he said in wonderment: "*Ababah!* So clear it is! With 'digital' we can keep them forever, no?" Then he turned to a teenage devotee and said, "Before we used to get them in album. Small printings and we had to paste them in the album. The photos used to get lost or something would happen. You remember I used to keep negatives in the Godrej bureau?" The permanency of the photo archive mattered greatly to Krishna Bhattar. While the digital nature of the photos made them seem ephemeral to me, for Krishna Bhattar, it gave them increased fixity as a valid historical archive, where the divine biometrics of the deity and the beauty of Krishna's Bhattar's alankaram were captured for eternity. He gestured to Shreyas and said, "These young fellows. They say this is all important infor-mation. So now if you have any photos in your 'set,' will you share with us?"

The "set" of photos, the archive, was a constant mobile space, particularly as photographing the processional deity was encouraged. The younger priests sent me shots and I sent them e-copies of what I took, enlarging both our sets constantly. It became a project to manage and share our albums.[21] Krishna Bhattar was concerned less with psychic apparatus and more with inscription technology's relationship to memory (as it is conceived and as it may func-tion) and to the photographs themselves.

He was amazed by the clarity of the photos of the deity and the amount of information each photograph conveyed. He asked me to show him all the photos I had, so one day I scrolled through my entire collection. He exclaimed, "*Ayyo!* You've taken so many! Look in this alankaram I used the banana leaves rolled up. That must be so long ago . . . I haven't done that for some time. And see the *shaate mala* [Tamil: big garland] in this one. It was made of *roja poo* [Tamil: rose flowers]! It was perfumed." Krishna Bhattar was lost in excavating the imprints in his mind and imagination spurred by the visual information my fragmented archive provided. The transfer of film archives from almirahs to digital cards and the shifting reproduction technology clearly affected Krishna's capacity to recall his memories. Krishna Bhattar was amazed by his own forgetfulness: "I 'totally' forgot this alankaram! 'Total.'" But he also remembered moments of creative improvisation with pleasure: "That year I couldn't get any oranges for the *phala vastra* [Sanskrit: fruit chandelier offering] during Krishna Jayanthi. It was full 'drought' in north. So I made do with guavas wrapped in orange tinsel, orange marigolds, and gold foil. No one noticed the change. In fact, they said it looked better."

By 2004 cell phone technology had permeated the public spaces of India, Bangalore, and the temples of Malleshwaram. Cell phones had caught on very fast in India, and by 2012, 59 percent of Indian residences had a mobile phone.[22] With the democratization of mobile phones, there was easy access to image capture and manipulation, as most cell phones had built-in camera devices. When I arrived in 2008 with an out-of-date Nokia flip-phone, Vishwanatha quizzed me as to why I did not have the iPhone with a built-in camera, the latest seductive gadget on the market.[23]

Most devotees saw the digital albums as ways to share visual images of the deity. Ritual participants with cell phones were constantly at the temple photographing one another, taking "selfies" with the deity and "SMS-ing" (texting) these images to each other, or taking photos and videos of the deity and uploading them to various social media sites. In 2009 Padma was given a new iPhone by her son. She had become addicted to photography, and acted as a semiofficial photographer for the Krishna Temple. She shyly told me she had "over one hundred thousand" photos and videos of the deity documenting the various alankaram, which she said she "shared" with other devotees.

Devotees like Padma became mobile archives and held a great deal of status within the temple community. Whenever Krishna Bhattar wanted to demonstrate his skill at alankara or to recall a certain floral arrangement with the flower vendors, he would call Padma over and ask to digitally review her many virtual albums of the deity. While showing me her many digital albums, Padma said, "Look at all my photos of Perumal and Thayaar *sannidhi* [shrines of the mother]! I have from past five years. If I lose this phone, I will lose all these photos. But my son says, '*Amma,* you have filled up all the memory!' You know I never realized I had taken so many!" Padma captures the intimacy of

FIGURE 4.4. Localites capturing images of Perumal in procession, on their cell phones. Photo by the author.

her relationship with the deity through her digital archive and, in doing so, enhances emotional connections and builds memories and social attachments. But this is no mere repository of technological artefacts. Padma argues that this photo-taking renews her bhakti (devotion) to the deity.

Jacques Derrida, in discussing the nature of the archive and the problems of being inscribed in it, argues that the act of inscribing, or in this case the curating that Padma performs, leads to a compulsive and repetitive desire to return to the archive: "It is to have a compulsive, repetitive, and nostalgic desire for the archive, an irrepressible desire to return to the origin, a homesickness, a nostalgia for return to the most archaic place of absolute commencement" ([1995] 1996, 91). Entwined in the devotees' imaginations, this desire is a repetitive force, the retention of a specific origin through repetition. Derrida asserts that "the technical structure of the archiving archive also determines the structure of the archivable content even in its very coming into existence and in its relationship to the future. The archivization produces as much as it records the event" ([1995] 1996, 17). This idea posits a fluid relationship between the archive and what it archives. The archive, its structure, formulation, and operation, is informed by its contents, along with any number of external bodies of knowledge. The archive is locked into what it memorializes and the construction of that memory.

Padma uses these photo archives to reconnect memory and social obligation and create attachment to local place and a culture. She sees her archive as enabling a normative "love" for India and for Hindu culture in her American grandchildren. She said, "I keep every photo and sometimes I send them as greetings to my children abroad. I'll send them on festival days, like when our *kainkarya* [Sanskrit: vow/worship] is done I'll send a photo of Perumal in the new sari that we gift. I don't know what my son does, but I feel if I send it he will remember and teach his children about our samskruti." As Derrida states, the One (in this case the archive) cannot distinguish itself from the Other without a constant reiteration of itself. In the ceaseless work to maintain one memory at the expense of another, the archive not only maintains and curates memory but buries it as well. Padma's archive is about memory and durability. She believes that through it, she keeps the death of some traditions in abeyance by drawing the next generation into samskruti. For Padma's children and American grandchildren, as well as others who view Padma's digital archive, the archive acts as memory bank and unlocks the faint traces of memory of a visual alankara, which then becomes the site of a true archive, an original authentic record. So the new and the layered not-so-new come into contact through memory.

For Derrida the interrogation of the archive is about the capacity for immortality through inscription. In Derridan archives there are no originary texts, only traces leaving yet more traces and fragments, thus eroding the distinctions we make between original and copy, inside and out, tradition and modernity, history and the now. Padma's picture taking becomes a form of this tracing—an "archi-tracing," as Derrida terms inscription—that permits the emergence of the evident or existent as history in the instant of now ([1995] 1996).

Technologies of Capture

During the Kanu Pandige festival in 2013, I watched as the young priest Shreyas leaned into the Thayaar deities and took a "closeup" on his iPhone. He then turned to me and explained that it was for the temple Facebook page. He added, "You must go and 'like' it." In this case, the visual capture of the deity allowed for a much broader reach, to devotees and others in different geographic spaces and time zones. Photographing the deity, capturing the divine, once a forbidden practice, is now mundane in its ubiquity, an accepted everyday practice of making the ineffable part of the quotidian. Shreyas added, "Soon my brother will see if we can do virtual seva [worship] so we can put up real-time video and people like yourself sitting in U.S. can see Perumal at any time!" The problem of the depletion of the god's energy through photography, discussed earlier, had apparently dissolved. So not only is the divine biometrics of the deity available at all times, to all people, but also the daily liturgy is perpetually accessible through video snippets and still images. The mysterious, sacred foreignness of the temple—the heart of its very transcendence—becomes familiar, portable, and mundane. The wonder of the deity is brought into intimate contact with the quotidian life of the devotee, permanently available and yet still transcendent, domesticated yet powerful.

In contemporary Malleshwaram, as most people have smartphone technology, the question revolves less around the biometrics of the deity and more around the technologies of capture. In late 2016 Vishwanatha Shastri asked me to get him an iPhone 7 so he could get "better shots" of the god. Then everyone all over the world could see his wonder and delight in it.[24]

The technology of capture and the ubiquity of social media also serve to render the biometrics of the deity as public property. The deity's divine biometrics are no longer assailable by my photographs. There is no unique theft of the image possible anymore, since everyone participates. No longer contained within the spaces of the temple, these images are free floating in virtual space and devotees lay claim to them in surprising ways. Most frequently, they are used as evidence of an "I was here" moment. The democratization of capturing the deity visually harbors a repetitive impulse. So the archive is no longer limited to the act of inscription but is extended to other mediated forms. The archi-album here is a regulative ideal, a public space, a strategic concept, and a mediatized principle. As more photos accrued on their phones or on their social media pages, devotees were considered more important patrons of the temple. The concept of patronage was extended beyond the traditional monetary understanding of patronage into new spheres, and the location of the temple was incidental to the status of claiming a devotional index based on the frequency of capturing the divine biometrics.

As the biometrics of the deity became more accessible, they also became subject to interrogation in ways they were not previously. This emerging protocol of rethinking the body of the deity and its biometrics not only gestures to an intimacy with the capturing of the deity in visual images but also allows for an intimacy and comfort with the new or the partially new. Here, the intimacy with technology created a mediated transformative moment with the divine. It was the tumultuous meeting point of truth and reality, albeit an ephemeral, digital kind. But when I asked if this portability, this eternal presence, reduced or eroded the divine force of the deity, I was met with strategic silence. "We are thinking about that," Krishna Bhattar acknowledged.

FaceTiming God

In June 2016 I received a notification from the Ganesha Temple requesting that I "like" their Facebook page. Hesitantly I pressed "yes," and immediately I found myself in an update stream of the temple; thousands of photos of a variety of alankara, devotees' videos, selfies with the deity, written prayers in English and Kannada, and much, much more were shared on the stream. The sheer surfeit of data invoked a kind of ethnographic indigestion and anxiety, a dread of deciding how to intellectually contend with this abundance. I did not return to the page for many weeks.

Later in the same month, my mother, who had been unwell, was told she needed surgery. Worried, my sister and I thought we might perform a simple archane, an individual worship, at the Ganesha Temple to remove any obstacles to her getting well. My sister, Lakshmi, rang the number posted on the Ganesha Temple Facebook page. Vishwanatha's distinctively cheerful voice answered, "*Jai Ganesha!* [Hindi: Victory to Ganesha!]." It was a simple new greeting he had coined to replace the more common "Hello" or Dandu Shastri's "*Namaskara! Hegu iddira?* [Kannada: Namaste! How are you?]." Vishwanatha's "*Jai Ganesha!*" carried shades of a nationalist Hindu greeting, *Jai Hind* (victory to India), the charged call of the postindependence era that to me resembled the patriotic yells of Hindu nationalist parades, but to others recalled the popular song, "Jai Ho!" (Be victorious!) from the globally accepted manual of aspiration and feel-good Hollywood movie, *Slumdog Millionaire.* He had created a hybrid muscular-yet-aspirational branded salutation that increased the force and range of the deity by sheer vocal repetition.

With the aid of an astrologer, Vishwanatha suggested a variety of healing rituals for my mother: a Vedic ritual of *Mrithyunjaya homa* (Sanskrit: sacrificial fire rite to defeat death), a set of 1,008 Navagraha *Japa* and *homa* (Sanskrit: a set of Vedic runic incantations to the nine planets), and a *Dhanvantri homa* (Sanskrit: sacrificial ritual to Dhanvantri, the god of medicine). He said that he would perform the entire set of rituals the following morning and would do a charitable *Anna danam* (Sanskrit: gift of food) to feed the hungry in my mother's honor. Taken together as a combination, they would cast a beneficial healing net around my mother at the time of the surgery and beyond.

It seemed like a massive undertaking to organize in the space of the few hours between our call to him and the start of the ritual on the following day, which was the auspicious *Ekadashi* day.[25] But Vishwanatha was confident of accomplishing it. He asked us questions to, as he put it, "get the data" he required to perform the entire puja: my mother's lineage descent (Sanskrit: *gotram*), her family's deity (Sanskrit: *kula devata*), and her star date of birth (Sanskrit: *nakshatra*). He followed with yet another question: "*Macbook Skype irruka? Phone panna 'live' panalam. Appo Amma sankalpam pannamudiyum* [Tamil: Do you have Macbook Skype? Then we can do a 'live relay' and your mother can participate in the ritual invocation]." It had not occurred to us that we could witness this. In fact, just a few minutes prior, we had been considering who we could request to be at the temple at dawn to start the invocation. Vishwanatha relayed an instruction from his son, Ganesh: "*Ganesh sholran FaceTime pannalam! Adde seri!* [Tamil: Ganesh says we can do FaceTime! That will be the right way!]" We agreed hesitantly to this strange ritual connectivity. He added, "At the start time I will give you a 'missed call'.[26] You can call me on that number." So the next evening, feeling slightly guilty, we responded to his "missed call" prompt, at the auspicious start time of the ritual.

In real time he showed us the entire scene: the sun just risen behind the ficus tree and the koel birds whooping and whistling in the branches above. There he was, beaming, in front of a phalanx of twenty-three orange-robed priests, waiting for our call. The Vedic fire altar was ready behind him, bundles of the auspicious *samhitha* (Sanskrit: the Vedic offering of ficus twigs), ghee, and other offerings all gathered and placed in front of the fire altar. The nine decorated *kalasha* (Sanskrit: urns) for each of the nine planets, representing the entirety of the Hindu cosmos, were just visible in the front of the altar. He greeted us, "*Arumbikalaama?* [Tamil: Shall we begin?]," then began to recite the *sankalpa*, the slow unfurling of the ritual intent, with an instruction to my mother, "Repeat after me!" My mother, seated on a sofa in Boston, repeated his words faithfully, "*Mamma karishyaami . . . ,*" announcing her intent to perform these healing rituals. As the night progressed in Boston, we watched the entire ritual take place ten thousand miles away. The sun rose in Malleshwaram. We witnessed the priests reciting the sacred mantras, and saw fires lit, sacrifices made, coconuts broken, and ghee poured. We watched the rites of gods and planets, the invocation of the planetary gods, their ritual adoration, and the sacrifices. We watched as Vishwanatha and his cohort of

FIGURE 4.5. FaceTiming the Ganesha Temple from the author's cell phone in Boston. Photo by the author.

priests lit the Vedic fire with twigs of the sacred ficus tree, and offered it ghee, rice, and black sesame seeds. The sonorous chanting of twenty-three priests enveloped us. The fire swallowed all the offerings, emitting a funnel of black smoke to effectively link the earth and sky. It transmitted the offerings to the gods, in return for their benefaction and protection of my mother.

Once or twice during the event, Vishwanatha stopped to instruct us about the technology and connectivity: "Now hang up. I will call you again . . . *Jai Ganesha!*" But occasionally during the night, the Internet would die and Face-Time failed as it passed through fiber-optic cables deep beneath the ocean floor. Vishwanatha would disappear while the link rebuffered, the small gray wheel spinning idly on the screen for some time. Then he would reappear, stronger than before, and say, " 'Network'? OK, ah?" During one buffering period, I placed my iPhone in front of a colorful Ganesha statue on the table in front of us. As the call reconnected, we saw Vishwanatha's puzzled face as he looked directly at the god. He was delighted, chuckling, "Oh look! My 'boss' is in America now! Su-per! Su-per!"

Once, when he reappeared after the link rebuffered, he pointed to the low-flickering Vedic sacrificial fire behind him and said jokingly, "Our network is going down. The network of Agni [Vedic fire god] needs more ghee!" He shouted to the priests nearby, "Add more ghee, more samhitha." Then he added, only half-jokingly, "We need Agni, the network of Brahman, and we need this iPhone network to make sure that Amma is taken care of."

BURGEONING NEW TECHNOLOGIES, some of them invented in Bangalore, serve as expanding platforms for worship. The material apparatus of these new methods of "e-prayer" include laptops, tablets, smartphones, and other Internet-enabled devices. These new tools and techniques, as digital artifacts, emphasize to localites the benefits of online social networking as a conduit to the cosmic.

Vishwanatha referred to the "network" multiple times in our conversation, using the word to indicate the virtual computer network, the fire network of the Vedic god Agni that transmitted our sacrificial gifts to the gods, and the cosmic network that linked all living beings. The overlapping networks were a new entangled web that enabled supplicants to mimic the Bangalorean engineers, to cross time zones to work at the "site" of their clients' needs and transcend the limits of geography.

But Dandu Shastri told me in a prognosticatory moment in 2004 that since the dharmic universe was "full of change," one could see new technologies that were emerging (like the cell phone at that time) as mere material manifestations of the entangled "net" of the Hindu godhead of Brahman— of Brahman's cosmic magical energy, a combination of, as he put it, "*yantra* [Sanskrit: techne], *mantra* [Sanskrit: runes], and *tantra* [Sanskrit: magical thought]."

In Hindu theology, Brahman is the universal one, the central godhead, from which all creation emerges and in which all dissolution ends. The idea that Brahman is an entangling net has a long theological history in Hinduism (DeNapoli 2017). In myth, the most significant usage of entanglement is illustrated by a debate that occurs in King Janaka's court between two renowned sages, Gargi Vacaknavi and Yajnavalkya, featured in the *Brihadāraṇyaka Upaniṣad* (3.7–3.8.12). In it, Brahman is explicitly described as the ever-expanding divine cosmic net in which all creation, "moving and unmoving," in the universe is entangled (Olivelle 2008, 44–46). The popular *Upaniṣadic* image of Brahman as the divine "warp and woof of the cosmos" (DeNapoli 2017, 20) allows Dandu Shastri and Vishwanatha to theologize technology.

DeNapoli rightly notes, "Brahman shapes and directs the course of creation through means of changes in technology and he charges human beings with the creation of its manifestation" (2017, 21–23). Dandu and Krishna, through the usage of a helicopter, the iPhone, and other technologies, develop this idea of technology as an agent and instrument of the ever-expanding cosmic energy of Brahman. This commonly voiced definition supports the semantic undertones of the word *Brahman*, which is derived from a Sanskrit root meaning "to grow" and "to expand" (Klostermaier 1996, 76). The concept of Brahman has wrongly been imagined, as DeNapoli notes, in the popular religious discourse as the changeless and permanent cosmic principle that underlies the phenomenal world impermanence (C. Moore 1967).[27]

For Dandu Shastri, Krishna Bhattar, and Vishwanatha, the nature of Brahman is endless, universal, and constantly in flux. Changes in technology are incorporated into the shifting cosmological and moral world of Brahman. Here there is an overlay of divinity on technology, making the two difficult to distinguish, though everyone understands them to be of different substances and values. This slipping of the boundaries of what constitutes real and unreal enables a parallel slippage whereby technology ties into a metaphysical realm in which reality can be created. The range of possibilities here is neither completely unconstrained nor limited; the transformations presume a creative impulse.

In 2009, when I needed cash for a puja at the temple, Vishwanatha directed me to the new automatic teller machine, locally called "cashpoint." We watched as the machine counted and spitted out my cash. Vishwanatha said, "I am still amazed by this cashpoint. *Idde Vishwakarma ode mayaam!* [Tamil: This is the illusion of Vishwakarma!]."[28] Then he told me about Vishwakarma, the mythical master craftsman of the gods who was the official builder of all the gods' palaces, the master designer of all the flying chariots and all divine and magical tools and weapons of the cosmos. He spoke of the origin myth of the *Mahabharata*, the great fratricidal war between the Pandavas and their cousins the Kauravas, where the brilliant illusions of the Pandavas' palace aroused their cousins' jealousy.

Vishwanatha pointed out that in the divine world of the gods, tools frequently doubled as weapons.[29] He said that Vishwakarma the god had harnessed the power of Mayasura, a demon king of illusion, and built wondrous palaces.

Confused by all the myths and by the different gods invoked in discussing these technological networks, I asked Vishwanatha, "Your father said it is Brahman, but you say Vishwakarma. They are different." Vishwanatha thought about this and responded, "It is all the *shakti* [Sanskrit: power], the *lila* [Sanskrit: illusion] of Brahman, yes, but Vishwakarma is the builder who makes the energy into these magical machines and places. You can say either and both will be correct. Like the knife is the tool but the sword is the weapon." Vishwanatha was less interested in the naming and framing exercises than in the efficacy of the technological solution. But in theologizing technology and infusing it with divine wonder, Vishwanatha conflates the wonder of technology with theological wonder. Here the priests' theologizing of technology "performs" the act of creating wonder by a simple use of technology to transport devotees to an alternate state of being, to show them possibilities. This theologizing of technology is in some senses the wondering of the universe.

Wonder of Wonders

Vishwanatha, Krishna Bhattar, Dandu Shastri, and the localites of Malleshwaram blend, fuse, and entangle types and archetypes, a marker of true experimentation and creativity. As Vishwanatha noted in our discussion about the Garuda, the entry of the eagle for him was not random, nor was it fully explained by the noise of the helicopter. It was the moment of divine intercession. Malleshwaram ritual practitioners attribute divine intentionality at work in creation to technology. I have recruited the idea of the new to interrogate improvisation within ritual and the ethical stances that are coterminous with such experimentation. Here, the contextual agency of improvisation—of adjustment—allows for serious recasting of the liturgy and of divinity itself.

Hindu ritual is understood to inherently accept and promote experimentation—a "capacity for old and new structures" to exist side by side without conflict and with adaptation, "the very legitimation within the existing structure that permits their acceptance and implementation of innovating . . . behavior" (Gusfield 1967, 354), even juxtaposition of seemingly conflicting elements. Joseph Gusfield argues that the syncretism of inconsistent elements had long been noted in the acceptance of religious usages and beliefs in India and that the fusion and mutual penetration of different spheres created an almost postmodern sensibility wherein the "admixture" was created rather than being a set of inherited conflicts. The foreignness of the new is domesticated, allowing other foreign practices and objects to become part of the familiar and therefore be integrated into the body of habit. What is surprising is how the new endures as a trope fulfilled by both technology and new moral forms of discourse within the community, and yet how so evident an ethical practice of incorporating the new could have gone unacknowledged for so long.[30]

Some might want to argue, as proponents of Hindutva do, that technology is ancient. One could argue that ancient technologies were, as the name implies, *technologies*, and so the old is always implied in the new. But to comprehend and properly adapt to such situations, one cannot rely fully on the settled past, for—if it truly is settled and static—then it renders the ritual increasingly irrelevant in the face of the future's valuable novelty. Newness as exemplified in modern technology is seductive as the material form of the possible and a key to generativity.[31] I want to make clear that this retrieval of modern technology and claim to its origins in Hinduism is not the argument I am making. Rather, it is the opposite.

If we argue that creativity, perhaps more than we often realize, emerges on the basis of the familiar and the habitual, at the limits of what we know, then it follows that the habitual becomes a function of the new (Ram 2013). The issue here is not whether creativity might be needed in particular cases or situations, for, of course, it usually is; rather, the point becomes that creativity is a general requirement for "traditions" to survive and remain relevant over time. Tradition and creativity are not opposed to each other; tradition is more creative and experimental than the scholarly literature often presumes.

I finally arrive at the problem of authority and authorship—of how selves are maintained and advanced within the traditions to which they bear a sense of obligation; how these technologies are birthed, or, alternatively, how a tradition is inherited by its adherents. In Malleshwaram, as I have tried to show, by achara (custom) new technologies have prestige in that they are disengaged from circulation and exchange (Bohannan 1955; Kopytoff 1986). Deeply familiar notions of creativity and imitation that underwrite prevailing conceptions of tradition are the same ones that overdetermine our contemporary approaches to the improvisation and the incorporation of the new. These notions make the new into the familiar and obscure its ethical dimensions, attenuating our understandings of its authority. This, in turn, has led to an emphasis on rituals as liturgical imperatives, disembodied from the specific modes of engagement that structure their living authority as forms of piety and interaction with divinity.

Unveiling the backdrop of neoliberalism and the seduction of new technology, I have sought to think about the new in ritual improvisation and the mechanisms of appropriation; how mimesis, as in the case of the installation of the drum set at numerous temples, allows for endless repetition and appropriation throughout the templescapes of Malleshwaram. Novelty and iterability are seen as analogous, not oppositional, in the appropriation of new technologies. The cultural and religious traditions of Hinduism appear to bend and stretch elastically, to continuously transform, so that any reading of the ritual tradition of Hinduism purporting a static and dogmatic seamless ritual "tradition"—whether invoked pragmatically or politically—is inevitably flawed. In this dialogic capturing of new, or newish, technologies, a productive liberation occurs, and the embedded meaning of the symbol, language, and material artifact is reconstructed to fit the context. This is a liberating maneuver that allows priests like Krishna Bhattar and Dandu Shastri to adopt neoliberal technologies without also assuming the burden of the freight these technologies carry within the Western context. This liberation is further strengthened through an iterative maneuver by which change is made constant and expected. Ritual improvisation and new technology allow for the expression of ethical self-agency and represent a demonstration of the individual's and the temple community's continued ethical potential while allowing for different figural ways of thinking.

CHAPTER FIVE

TIMELESS IMPERATIVES, OBSOLESCENCE, AND SALVAGE

The separation between past, present, and future is only an illusion, although a convincing one.
—Albert Einstein, *The Meaning of Relativity*

Who really knows? Who will here proclaim it? Whence was it produced? Whence is this creation? Perhaps it formed itself, or perhaps it did not—the one who looks down on it, in the highest heaven, only He knows—or perhaps He does not know.
—"The Poetry of Creation"

"Times Have Changed"

Field notes, Ganesha Temple, Malleshwaram, August 10, 2004

My footwear was regularly stolen when I was doing fieldwork at the temples. Despite being friends with Uma, the woman who took care of the chappals (Tamil: sandals) at the Ganesha Temple, I would return to the footwear counter after a long day to find my shoes missing, leaving me to either limp home or give in and buy a new pair. I became deeply troubled by the conjoined amoralities of the continuous stealing of my footwear with my paranoid suspicions of everyone around me as possible culprits.

Dandu Shastri blamed me, the victim, for my naïveté in wearing "good" footwear to the temple. He diagnosed the times as amoral. "Kala badalagide! [Kannada: Times have changed!]," he said. "You should wear dirty chappals like everyone else. Then no one will want to steal them." "Kala badalagide" had become the explanation of choice for random examples of otherwise inexplicable moral degeneracy. "Money was stolen from the temple offertory? Kala badalagide!" "The priest does not know the correct mantra? Kala badalagide!"

I came to understand that "Kala badalagide" was simultaneously an explanation of singular moral loss and a larger diagnosis of living in a time of moral degeneracy.

WE KNOW OF the anthropology of time—the segmented, the useful, the calendrical, the ritual, the everyday—of the regulation and consumption of time, and of the devices and desires that temporality engages in the understanding of the present and the push to the future (Munn 1992). But until recently, as Anand Pandian has noted, the singularity of time was understood to be not a flow but a fixity, an unchanging quality or structure (2012, 558). What that view has ignored is the nature of living through the chasm of temporality between perennial tradition and endless modernity as most Bangaloreans do—looking backward to a golden past that is just out of reach, and forward to a silver-lined future that is also tantalizingly beyond reach. Exploring the movement of time, its flow, and its many textured, multilayered meanings and uses allows us to preview the taxonomies of multiscalar temporalities in Malleshwaram—the global, the intensely local, the ritual, the cosmological, the diurnal, the life-cyclical, the progressive, and the mechanical—not only to contemplate the aporic segmentation of time in Malleshwaram but to reflect on the nature of this *timeness* itself.[1]

According to the *yoga sutras* of Patanjali, time is an object (Patanjali 4.12) that has an essential quality: a *timeness*—a *tattvam* (Sanskrit: beingness)— that makes it horologically independent of our perception of it. In the *Pūrvamīmāṃsā, vidhi* is used as the term for "the overall order of a ritual" (Clooney 1990, 175) that can be repeated for injunctions, prescriptions or a disciplined set of actions.[2] But Krishna Bhattar, Dandu Shastri, and the localites struggle not only with the tattvam and vidhi of time, but also with the challenge of apprehending the moment across two countercategorizations of time: "modern" and "ritual" time.[3] I propose to explore the intersection of ritual and modern time that coalesces around creative rhythms

(Lefebvre [1992] 2004; Maycroft 2005, 170) and their repetitions (Deleuze 1994).

The theft of my shoes provides one example of why modern time is seen as morally entropic. I explore the twisted reflection of this erosion of morality in the perception of "not keeping to time," a conflict between ritual and modern time enabling us to untie time as a moral and ethical rubric. Here, time is an act not only of becoming but of undoing as well. Hindu ritual time, the tempo of sacred actions and practices, and the praxis of engaging Hindu rituals are seen as mitigating the ills of modern time. Although the many interruptions of modern global time often conflict with ritual time, ritual participants try, in practical ways, to negotiate a way of life that can allow them to intersect with both time spaces. The uncertainty of our knowledge of time—its flow, duration, workings, and meanings—gestures to the mixing of ordering and disordering: the sedimentation, the regimentation and ad hocism, and the bending of time that occurs in ritual process.

Negotiating such ritual time-bending is often fraught with difficulty, for ritual time is also multilayered and constrained. According to the Hindu lunar calendar of festivals, there are auspicious and inauspicious days and times on which to perform various pujas, ritually "dark" times to avoid, and "pure" times that are auspicious. I argue that the play of ritual time as it is juxtaposed with modern work time in Bangalore is a disarticulation of the present and part of a practical piety that allows for a melding of Hindu life with modern capitalist life. It requires a seemingly endless negotiation around timings and projects, and enfolds both the discomfort of embryonic beginnings that create the conditions for the possibility of wonderment and the delight of the interruption of a transformational wonderment, evidence of an "infinite complexity" of time (Munn 1992, 92–93).

To mark the creativity and wonder of ritual time, I begin to locate the philosophical understanding of *ritu* (Sanskrit: season or time as a moral order) set against *ippo* (Tamil: immediacy, instant), which I found used constantly in Malleshwaram to indicate the urgent immediacy of things, in a chronologically granular fashion. Through an interrogation of the temporal in ritual creativity, we can speak to incipient forms of the present, timely forms of attention to modes of emergence, and the originality and freshness of regimes of living in Malleshwaram.

I also examine an architecture of obsolescence in which the creative forces are dulled and creative failure occurs. I seek an understanding of time that has recently passed, its passé-ness, and the notion of the fashionable to distill what failures of history impart to Malleshwaramites. How are the various registers of moral time differentiated? What resources do we have to think about emergence, creativity, and newness when our own concepts and language betray the temptations of the familiar, the customary, and the agglutinative?

Finally, I trace the time of regeneration, through salvage. I argue that the concept of salvage is key as a mechanism of temporal inhabitation that allows for both the rupture and erosion of moral time and its enhancement. According to the *Oxford English Dictionary*, salvage is a marine metaphor synonymous with reclamation, saving, rescue, and reuse. But here it is understood on dry land as recycling from ideas and emotions of the past to build a grammar for the articulation of a vision of a future.

I find useful to disinter Anand Pandian's idea of traditional "fragments" to suggest that salvage allows the reuse of such fragments that allows both new and old to cohere together in ritual, creating a resilient form (2008). Salvage allows the new to comprise fragments of what has gone before, creatively knit together in new ways. I trace the concept of salvage through the history of two temples: a Mariamman Temple and a temple to an underground, spring-fed lake. Time here is a creative force that comes "again," moving the discourse from obsolescence to salvage, the return in a fragmented state of that which is remembered as whole. Salvage provides an ecologically sustainable, morally robust mechanism of regeneration in which the new and the old cohere and resilience and durability are built.

Most importantly, endurance and resilience are the key to the durability of ritual forms across time. Questioning resilience, which I see as elastic, and durability, which I see as firm, requires us to understand the surges of material, aesthetic, and emotive energies that flow through ritual. Here, the fact of generation, of creativity, of contingency, and of improvisation is submerged and rendered opaque, guised in pragmatism or in material or social conditions. Yet generativity that accounts for both the enfolding of the new and the enfolding of the old is a process of production that speaks to the emergence of feeling, form, and life itself; it is an onward propulsion of life.

The Untimeliness of Modernity

On my way to the temples, I would pass a bus stop on the main Sampige Road in Malleshwaram that sported a billboard advertising a call center in a Fortune 500 company. The ad was unintelligible to me as there was no image of a call center or of work. It sported an image of the pastoralist god Krishna in a meadow at dusk surrounded by cows, playing his flute to magically enchant and herd the animals. Underneath was the emphatic slogan "Work is worship!" and below the assurance "We are always 'on call'!" with the name of the company in English.[4]

One day, Krishna Bhattar saw the billboard and quipped: "For me as pujari (Sanskrit: priest) my work is worship! Only it is not *my* worship but other people's worship. So I am like these call center people, *illiya* [Tamil: is that not so]? I am always 'on call.'"

While I appreciated his subversion of the message of the advertisement, of elevating call center work to worship, the irony of linking mythic time to the modern capitalist work ethic seemed lost on him and on other localites.

Modern time for localites is located in the immediate contemporary, as "an actual object domain in the present whose recent past, near future, and emergent forms can be observed" (Rabinow 2008, 5). Although in the West modernity and neoliberalism are seen as a time of increased precarity, for the Malleshwaram middle classes, modern time is one of prolific aspiration and gain set against the tedium of precarity that previous generations had to endure. As one of my female collaborators said, "It's no doubt that now we have no worries. We have enough! My parents waited their whole life and had one small Fiat car; now we have Mercedes, BMW, two, three cars . . . you name it, it's there!"[5] Middle-class Malleshwaramites have yet to feel the vicissitudes of neoliberalism. To them, modern time indicates the rhythms by which professionals work night and day as based on the Gregorian calendar, a client's geographic location, the deadline requirements of projects, school times, and other nondomestic times—a series of punctuated times.[6] Because of the presence of the IT and call center industries in the city, productive business and work take center stage. Bangalorean modern time is based on the mores of global businesses profiting across time zones, of a familiarity with Western business practices, of working for a multinational corporation, and aspiration to a high salary.

"Call center *kelsa* [Kannada: work]" was an industry at the heart of the growth in "service" jobs in Bangalore. The call center industry as a whole epitomized the outside-of-time nature of work in the neoliberal moment. These jobs entered the IT landscape of Bangalore in the 1990s, when technical support jobs and back-end business processing outsourcing (BPO) were sent to India.[7] In the decade following, these call center jobs became sought after because of their high wages, late nights, and the youth of their workforce. White jeeps dashed all over the city day and night, ferrying young adults to offices from which they worked on projects in time zones from Australia to the western United States.

In a *Forbes Magazine* article in 2012, authors Chris Walker and Morgan Hartley describe the virtual time migration of the BPO industry from the perspective of one Indian call center employee, Deep. The article states, "Deep worked graveyard shifts for months on end, basically living on US time in India." Deep described his life and the demands of call center work, saying, "I didn't see sunlight for 6 months at a stretch," emphasizing the deep-seated angst of living on the edge of his own time zone.[8]

For these young workers in Bangalore, time is, to quote Hamlet, "out of joint," composed of interruptions that lie outside normal possibility, in which time might be flipped, squeezed, stretched, chopped up, and diced into smaller and smaller pieces in order to be put to greater use. Indeed, IT workers struggle with being in two or more space-times at once, "being both here and there at the same time, of overcoming the gravity of space" (Beck 2000, 75, qtd. in Upadhya and Vasavi 2008, 20). Their daily "virtual migration" to other space-times creates social and familial disruption and psychological stress (Aneesh 2006, 93–94). Modern time in Bangalore is associated with such physical and moral labor, with the ills of westernization and capitalization, of exploited labor, of endless work, of a singular focus on profit to the exclusion of all else, of the mental and physical exhaustion of the rat race, and, finally, a schedule that is out of sync with Hindu seasons, rituals, festivals, customs, and traditions.

Situated between the local and the elsewhere, IT workers are locked into an out-of-sync rhythm of everyday life in Bangalore, sleeping during waking hours and living in the darkness in order to make a living. Several localites described the call center workers as *vetalas* (Sanskrit: vampires). One middle-aged devotee said of his son who worked in a call center, "My son is like a *pretha* [Kannada: ghost] since he started working in IT. Before he could come any day to the temple. Now he can only come on Friday because it is his 'day off.' " Indeed, the call center workers were ghostlike beings, living on the periphery of daily existence, coming to dawn or dusk services as the timings of their clients allowed. The residual feeling of devotees toward these IT "ghosts" was sadness at their dislocation in time and fragmented social lives. There is a systemic alienation at work here as modern temporality turns people into ghosts and vampires.

In response to the devotee describing his grandson as a vetala, Krishna Bhattar launched into a philosophical lecture about modern time, "It is *Kali yuga* [Sanskrit: the contemporary age of evil]. Here there will be vetalas and *asuras* [Sanskrit: ghosts and demons]. In these times no *satya* [Sanskrit: truth] is possible." Then he added, "The saturnine nature of time, of *kala* [Sanskrit: time], was turned inward, poisoning the moral goodness of man."

But what about the perception of time passing, I asked hesitantly. "*Kalachakra*," Krishna Bhattar declared, "the wheel of time." He added, "In order to create divisions and movements of life and sustain the worlds in periodic time frames, the past is no longer, the future is not yet, and the present cannot be said to be until it is created. It is only through the mind that they come into being, in our minds."

He tapped his skull before continuing his lecture about time and history.

"We think through *smriti* [Sanskrit: memory] and we come to the *itihasa* [Sanskrit: past]; we bring *savadhana* [Sanskrit: attention] for the *ippodike* [Tamil: now] and *apeksha* [Sanskrit: expectation] for the *bhavishya* [Sanskrit: future]." Here two histories and futures are interwoven: first a metahistory, in which the future is uncertain and perilous as the present is precarious and corrupt; and the second a smaller, individual, almost granular history, linked more immediately to the fragmented now in which the future is predetermined. Here, time, though itself fragmented for instrumentality, is a series of interruptions—moments of wonder in which multiplex realities are made manifest.

Avvelle and Ritu

Krishna Bhattar told me of the localites, "Even if they have call center kelsa they will always come to the temple. It gives them peace and hope." Indeed, localites who worked in the IT and call center industry would arrive sleepy-eyed and yawning after their workday had ended. I could see that they were tired, and when I asked why they had come to the temple when they were so tired, they said that performing ritual gave them "relief" and "hope," and removed "tension."

Shekhar, a young man with a fondness for brightly colored shirts, aviator sunglasses, and pocket protectors who frequently visited the Ganesha Temple late in the evening or early in the morning after his night shift, told me he worked at Microsoft. He said pointedly that coming to the temple regularly, doing puja, participating in the festivals, and watching the pujas all gave him "peace."

Shekhar spoke with melancholy about the rarity of meeting his friends, and the focus it required to get to the temple in the daytime.

> Everyone is busy, no? Before we used to go out . . . movie-geevee, club-shub.[9] We used to come to the temple every day before college and just we used to time-pass! But now no one has time. *Thumba busy! Avvelle nalli gudi ge baruthivi!* [Kannada: We are very busy! We come to the temple at odd times!] Only Tuesdays because it is Ganesha, or we come

on festival days like Sankasth Chathurthi . . . like that. We cannot come every day like previous. Impossible!

Anand, his friend and coworker, added: "Bangalore is the city that never sleeps. When I first came here ten years back everything was closed by 10:00 p.m. Now bars are open during the morning for workers who come off the nightshift. *Hucchu!* [Kannada: Crazy!] It's all crazy!"

The neoliberal economy requires a dematerialization of skills and resources that leads everyone in Bangalore to make use of *avvelle* (Kannada: incorrect, inconvenient, time out of time) time, an "unright time," out of sync for ritual interaction. Shekhar said triumphantly, as though he had found the ideal solution, "Everyone keeps to different shifts based on time zones of the clients. . . . But only the temple keeps to timings. They should have 'shifts' of pujaris so we can come and go. Twenty-four-hour darshan there should be! If the city is twenty-four hours then the temples should be also." Avvelle is an out of time unscheduled time-space, according to Shekhar. As time unaccounted for it was "rare," and busy schedules left it uncertain. The discussion of his temple-going schedule revealed his melancholic sense of loss that his work schedule had made the temple inaccessible to him.

Within the milieu of neoliberal capitalism, ritual cosmological time comes to be seen as the disjuncture to work time, which is normalized as "routine." Localites used the phrase, " he's back to routine" to suggest settling into the everyday. Seema Bijlani, who arrived at the Ganesha Temple dressed like a movie star in a bright green tinsel sari with long strands of jasmine flowers in her flowing black hair, said she worked for a large, multinational company (MNC) as a manager in its finance sector and travelled a great deal. She would always say when she returned to the temple, "I'm back to routine!"

Seema wanted Dandu Shastri to perform a *Sathya Narayana katha* and puja (Sanskrit: a storytelling and worship event) in her house, but they had been wrangling over dates: "Nowadays, it's a big rush to get a good priest on a good day. They are all booked in advance. And these MNC companies, they don't give leave for you to perform these pujas so it becomes difficult. Everyone wants to do the puja on Saturday or Sunday and the pujaris are all booked solid!" Seema had arrived at the Ganesha Temple to "book" a "good day" to do the puja. Dandu Shastri pulled out his calendar of rituals and determined the auspicious days in the next month to do the puja. Seema simultaneously looked at her phone, and as she scrolled through her calendar, they found each day of the month to be unacceptable, either because it was inauspicious or for work-related reasons. Dandu Shastri said, "No, we can't do that day. It is *amavasya* (new moon)." Then he would propose a day and Seama would say, "No. No. I have to be in Dubai for work." When they finally found an opening some three weeks later, Seema said worriedly, "Can we do it that day? Is it a good day?" Dandu nodded as he spoke to the uncertainty, the rarity of finding "good days" that also worked with a work schedule: "Not the 'best' day but it is all right! We will do some *parihara* [Sanskrit: sacrifice] and make it work. It's not easy to find another day. You'd better book it *now* itself." Seema pulled out a wad of cash and paid a deposit, saying to me as an aside, "I didn't get my first choice but at least I got one day." She added: "The problem is these MNC jobs. They have few holidays. They follow the U.S. . . . . They don't keep our Hindu calendar, no? My friend in Indian Bank, he gets all holidays plus leave to go to his native place and all. But I only get some Indian holidays and only two weeks leave in the year." Then after casting a glance at Dandu and noticing he was preoccupied, she added, "These Brahmin-types are also not adjusting, eh?"

When I told Krishna Bhattar this fieldwork anecdote of the scarcity of a "good" time, strategically excising Seema's embedded critique of the priesthood, he nodded and expanded on this notion of time-out-of-time: "Now time is all avvelle. No one can do ritual at the good time all the time. Too much demand for us and not enough coordination. So we do at odd time and do parihara to make up." Then he added,

See, the seasons [Sanskrit: ritu] themselves are odd. It's hot in winter. Before we only used to get good cucumbers in summer, melons also. Now they are all the time. Or the flowers for the god. Before we used to get jasmine, different kinds that were seasonal. The festival alankara were seasonal. We used to use the *parijatha* flower in January because it blooms in the winter and the needle-shaped jasmine flower in summer. But now the needle jasmine is in the market all the time, but the sweet smell is gone! Only the parijatha is 'on schedule.'

Chellappa was a descendant of a family of sevakar and lived in a large house across the street from the temple with his children and grandchildren. Wrapped in a red woolen shawl and wearing a blue "monkey" cap, he wandered over to join in: "My mother, she is now dead, used to say that ritual and ritu were the same. That one could only do some rituals in some seasons. We would go my grandfather's place in the village and only what he grew we gave to the temple. So the prasadam would have beans and squash that we grew." Ritu is invariably linked in the imagination to agrarian rhythms of what is natural and of a "right" cosmological ordering, a moral order of value that had been interrupted.

The group got larger as Padma spotted us chatting and came over to join us. She corroborated Krishna Bhattar:

> Krishna Bhattar is right. We don't eat properly according to the ritu. The seasons are all one and so also with people. We all work all the time. We used to eat seasonally, fruits and vegetables also. The seasons meant that often we could not get some fruits or vegetables, so my mother and aunts would make do with whatever they had. Even temple prasadam was more varied than now. We used to begin the year fasting and then eat *bevu-bella* [Kannada: bitter neem leaves and cane sugar] to start the year. Elders said it was to leave behind the bitterness of the past and to find the sweetness in the new year. But also it cleaned the stomach. But now everyone eats chips all the time. No one fasts. Everyone has "sugar" [colloquialism for diabetes] and is tired!

Seasonal time is made obsolete by the neoliberal notion of constant standardized plenty. Padma points to the illnesses that the constant abundance creates. This lost seasonality is spoken of as a lost time of innocence when humanity lived in accordance with "natural" rhythms.

Abstract time, standardized into regimes of time according to the demands of global economics dominated by Western-style capitalism and the mores of the Gregorian calendar, was replaced by a quantified, rationalized, and reified time system enfolding several different local times into one large unit. Often lost were local, seasonal, and ritual understandings predicated on temporal units based on cosmological occurrences. As the rituals require specific auspicious times and seasonal fruits and vegetables, they are rendered irrelevant in Seema's working world; it is a slow yet insidious violence of erasure.

Slipping Away

At the same time, the violence of such change led to a sense of urgency about time in general and a heightened awareness that time was precious and was slipping away. Chellapa's grandson Arun worked in one of the largest call center offices in Ulsoor. He said of his work, "I have to be there by 8:00 p.m. because I do the first shift for U.S. East Coast. I finish at five in the morning and catch the Sumo [an SUV car service] and come home and just sleep. Office has cafeteria, gym, everything! I don't go out. Time is precious, no?"

There is a constant feeling of running out of time. Dandu Shastri spoke to this when he said repeatedly, "Everyone is watching their phone or watch always. . . . They want things, 'Fast, fast!' Everyone is running all the time nowadays! They must 'catch up.'" But he added that this focus on work time in ever smaller fragments made for stressful living. "All this pressure about time is no use. Too much pressure! Not good for anyone to be like this." Dandu Shastri felt that the act of fragmenting time into a series of moments that are then countable, usable, auditable, and categorized to indicate their usefulness or uselessness runs counter to time as fluid, cyclical and regenerative. He saw this vision of time as a Western preoccupation. "In America I have seen. They all are like this only! They set alarm for everything, waking up, eating, bath, everything! Time for them is more important than food or money. But for us in India time is not like that. Always we are late. They say Indian Standard Time, no?"[10]

Dandu Shastri knew that for Shekher, Anand, Arun, and their friends at call centers, time is fixed and inflexible, a precious resource to be managed and eked out to the greatest potential. The "best" use of time is one in which social advancement is the focus. It involves a rigid self-discipline, in which "time pass"—leisure activity to pass the time such as movie watching or even "loafing" at street corners—is seen as a waste of a precious resource meant for self-betterment. Time pass for leisure activity has become time spent earning one more degree or holding an additional part-time job while one waits for certainty and stability (Jeffrey 2010).

So ritual life is pragmatically fitted into the larger rubric of self-betterment, a "practical piety" (Herzfeld 2015). Arun said, "I come to the temple to pray every week because it makes me calm." Dandu Shastri states that "everyone" comes to the temple to pray that "God takes care of them," which includes material, physical, and emotional care. Anand said, "I come to the temple to pray for my family and myself also! I pray that God will take care of me and my family." Shekhar laughed and added, "Eh *hudiga! Sullu hellu beda!* [Kannada: Eh boy! Don't tell lies!] Sometimes he prays for things like a new car or house because he wants to get married, but like that for fun!!" Anand added in frustration, "First, I have to find time to come here, no?"

In order to keep alive the space-time of ritual, intense negotiation by ritual practitioners is often required. If ritual is what keeps the moral world in order, then the moral danger of "getting spoiled," as one Krishna Temple devotee put it, of losing their moral bearings, is very real in Bangalore.

When Wonder Fails

Obsolescence, part of the emotional and social world of neoliberal anxiety, worried everyone who worked in IT. Software engineers were always talking about the obsolescence of their latest product, crying, "It will be wiped out by the next generation in two years if we are lucky!" But while the ethos of obsolescence and throwaway culture had entered Bangalore, in contrast many ritual participants spoke repeatedly of the loss of thrift and the moral value of saving.

The Ganesha Temple sat on a big, granite boulder. In the origin story of the temple, children from the neighborhood were playing on the rock and found the Ganesha idol there. As such, not only was the deity magical but also the boulder on which the deity had been found. The boulder "gave birth" to the deity and thus acted as a "mother" to it—the *terra cognita* of divine space. As with all temples in South India, the boulder was painted with white lime embellished with red ochre stripes.

In 1998, when I returned to start fieldwork, Dandu Shastri was excited to show me what he had done to the sacred boulder. It had been chipped away to form a cave-like structure about twenty feet long and fifty feet deep. It was covered with a painted concrete tableau. "Look, it is Mount Kailasa [the sacred mountain on which the god Shiva supposedly lives] . . . Can you see?" Dandu said. In the background of the tableau were tight triangles simulating snow-capped peaks of blue and white, which according to devotees were "the Himalayas." In the foreground, seated on a mountaintop of the divine mountain Kailasa, was the divine family of the titular deity, Ganesha. Shiva, Ganesha's divine father, was painted a grayish blue with staring eyes, matted black locks, concrete snakes writhing in his painted hair, and a fountain coming out of his head to symbolize his mythic capturing of the river Ganges in his locks. Nearby was Shiva's consort Parvati, painted gleaming white to denote her fair skin and wearing a red sari dotted with gold and a gold crown. To Shiva's right was the sculpture of the main deity of the temple, Ganesha, painted a creamy flesh color, sculpted with a heavy hand, standing and paying obeisance to his parents. Next to him, lost in the concrete sculpted hillocks, was Ganesha's vehicle, his pet rat. His brother Skanda, a forest deity, stood on the other side of the divine parents, next to Shiva's vehicle Nandi the bull. Skanda stood, his weapon of a gold trident in front of him, next to his spirit animal, an iridescent silver and green peacock. Tiny concrete hills poked up in front of the observer, painted blue and white to denote the Himalayan snows, and a river snaked its way through the miniaturized mountainous landscape.

FIGURE 5.1. The tableau on the boulder at the Ganesha Temple. Photo by the author.

All the images were crafted in the tradition of the popular Amar Chitra Katha comic book images and painted in the same virulent color scheme. Vishwanatha flipped a switch and water began to pour out of Shiva's sculpted head, simulating the river Ganges believed to flow from his locks. The water flowed along a channel and into a blue-lit pond complete with concrete lotus pads and flowers at the front of the tableau, separated from observers by a low wall. People at the temple were delighted by the show. Some threw coins into the pool. Dandu Shastri was proud to show me the tableau and kept switching the fountain on and off. "Recycle," he said, watching the fountain; he believed it would appeal to middle-class sensibilities of thrift and water saving in drought-ridden Bangalore.

Dandu Shastri seemed anxious for praise, so I mumbled a few half-hearted words, at which he looked very disappointed. I was unhappy at my own lack of appreciation, but I was puzzled by the aesthetics of the tableau and did not understand its purpose. Apparently, Dandu Shastri conceived of the tableau as a technologically creative moment—a predecessor of the animatronic Devi—to be grasped for its newness and fashionability. Much time, money, and planning had obviously gone into its creation.

Dandu Shastri took devotees to the tableau throughout the month. He hoped to convince me that the tableau was fashionable. He said that *every-*

one commented on the beauty of the tableau and the realism of the image. I was clearly in a minority, and each time someone commented on the beauty of the tableau in my presence, Dandu would look at me intently to be sure I had absorbed what was said.

When I returned in 2006, I found that the tableau was forgotten. The garlands on the deities were dried up, and the fountain was in disuse. The pipes were rusted and the water basin that formed the lake at the base of Mount Kailasa bore traces of slime. Devotees no longer threw coins into it. The younger priests told me it was *washetu* (Kannada-English: waste) and the space could have been better used as a hall to rent out. I thought of asking Dandu Shastri what he intended to do, but I judged it to be too sensitive a topic for discussion. Every time someone mentioned the tableau, Dandu would tense up and say, "*Addu Na? Biddu!* [Kannada: Oh that? Leave it!]." The materiality of the event deemed it dated, and because of its permanence, the tableau was no longer acceptable. Whatever is new in the now happens in relation to what is perceived as old in the imagined past.

Roy Rappaport argues that "rituals composed entirely of new elements are, thus, likely to fail to become established.... Rituals composed entirely of new elements are, however, seldom if ever attempted. 'New' rituals are likely to be largely composed of elements taken from older rituals" (1999, 32; cf. Moore and Myerhoff 1977, 8–9). And Axel Michaels (2016) argues that ritual change only happens because of technological or social change and people refrain from changing rituals even if they believe them to be ridiculous. I argue quite the reverse: rituals fail when there is not enough of the new to render them relevant.

By 2010 Dandu Shastri had built two extra halls against the side of the boulder face, rendering the hillside unrecognizable. He tried to hide the tableau and never referred to it when talking about the amenities of the temple. He seemed embarrassed by it. One younger devotee who worked in a computer graphics company stared at the scummy pond, commenting, "Nowadays with special effects, theme parks and all, who needs this? We are all used to top quality entertainment now. India is doing great things in the virtual arena, you know? We are going to work on many stories from Ramayana, Mahabharata, all that. Audiences are used to watching that level of tech. This is simply out-of-date!" The permanence of the tableau was compared with the dynamism and sophistication of the evolving field of computer graphics and found wanting.

I want to think about failure as it speaks to an aspiration for a time of change and for hope. What is our analytical approach to failure? Experimentation in temple publics can render failure to be inherently, even constitutively, a part of performance. When convention is reiterated in a space where experimentation has become the norm and the novel is validated, it opens the door to misfires. Irony, resistance, creativity, and ingenuity—all bloom in radical failure. Culturally normative repetitions act as installed models in the form of preexisting scripts. In the case of Dandu's tableau, the script was so strong that the fountain required both a mythic and a conventional form. Convention is reiterated, and reiteration is an accepted route to success. But the very fixity of the fountain is in opposition to what novelty prizes: dynamism. Here perpetuity is associated with obsolescence and being out of touch.

Dandu Shastri's fountain failure was embarrassing to him, but it was one bump in a long road of experimentation toward success. The animatronic Devi, built several years later, was a descendant of the fountain. Its resounding success enabled Dandu to overcome the feelings of lagging behind that the fountain represented to him.

These kinds of events can be seen as a retroactive performative chain. They are reversals in an ongoing strategy of forward experimentation in which repeated failures constitute success at some point. These failures create a new plateau whereby a chain of polythetic performances is created. Each performance moves closer to the cutting edge; seen in totality, they produce deliberative chains that lead to a successful innovation. Failure is temporary and delimited as it lays the grounds for the next reversal, ultimately leading to the genuinely cutting edge. This progression is always seen in hindsight and so its promise is retro-performative. The tableau suggested that the mythic past of Lord Shiva's family in Mount Kailasa is directly connected to aspirations for the future in Malleshwaram.

Dandu's ambitious expectations for the tableau indicate capacious aspirations to inspire and touch the imaginations of viewers. Such an experiment sets its horizons partly through practices meant to build aspiration into a muscular system in which the greater the failure, the greater the innovation. It seeks to multiply the occasions in which to exercise aspiration. As such, the tableau "fails forward," to quote Krishna Bhattar, toward the next success. It changes the context of both the experiment and the expectations for it. We can thus reimagine failure not as the opposite of success but as a characteristic of success in miniscule increments. It is experimental and evolutionary, and it mirrors our experiences as anthropologists in the field of learning through failure.

Time Lords

Priests and devotees agree that *Kali yuga* will end in *pralaya* (Sanskrit: the complete dissolution of the known universe).[11] Nevertheless, measures are taken to counter the fatalism that one might expect in light of the certainty of the inevitable dissolution. The inauspicious hours that each day holds are to be avoided or mitigated in order to curtail their dangerous potential to derail the positive effects of ritual performances, prayer, and worship. Called Rahu Kala, these are segments of time in which nothing fortuitous can be begun. Named after the head of the astrological dragon who is believed to regularly swallow the sun, Rahu is dangerous. The dragon's time occurs every day in segmented measures of approximately two hours, the saturnine underbelly of wondrous time.

Devotees knew various mnemonic devices to chart the approximate times of Rahu Kala during the week, and they would regularly warn each other about not performing activities that required the gods' benign influence during Rahu Kala.[12] "Don't begin your ritual on Friday in the morning; it's Rahu Kala." "Don't have your son's *Nischitartham* [Sanskrit: engagement] on Thursday at two o' clock. Wait until four o'clock; then Rahu Kala will be over." Knowing Rahu Kala timings is a sign of being a pious and observant Hindu: "My grandmother told me to go to office late today. Today I was expecting to hear about my promotion due to exam results, but because it was Rahu Kala when I was supposed to leave, she made me wait so I got to office late." Rahu Kala is the hallmark of saturnine time that foreclosed on any positive potential.

How can one avoid such saturnine time every day? This became the central question that many devotees brought to Dandu Shastri. In the words of one devotee: "I cannot be stopped all the time by Rahu and Shani [Sanskrit: Rahu and Saturn]! We must do something." Devotees had to continue with "life" as dictated by capitalist interests—including school and work life—and configured by Western and secular calendars that had no place for evil time.

The twin mechanisms to deal with Rahu were avoidance and placation. Most ritually observant localites tended to avoid Rahu Kala altogether by not beginning anything auspicious during those times. Others would get mitigatory pujas done in advance of a day when they could not avoid activities during Rahu Kala. Others would circle the shrine to the nine planets, the celestial gods of astrology. Dandu Shastri called all these rituals "insurance." He explained, "In Satya Yuga, there were *Rishis* [Sanskrit: sages] who could through their penance stop time and make it go in different ways. They were like time lords! If they wanted Rahu Kala not to be there for anytime, he [Rahu] would be useless. Like that they were powerful. They would tell the heavens how to be! But nowadays no one can stop time! And with all these things happening, we all need insurance."

During my visit to the temples in 2013, Prabha and I were trying to calculate the Rahu Kala for an auspicious event later that year. Vishwanatha pointed to his cell phone and said, "Eh, why do you bother? I have app for that." Called Shubh Kaal Pro, the iPhone application locates the phone's coordinates and, based on the day and time, calculates the Rahu Kala segment for the day required. The advertisement for the application is "Lucky times on the go!" Vishwanatha had helped the engineer to devise the app, and he was pleased with it because it democratized the calculation of auspicious ritual timings so that "now the priests were not the only ones who could calculate every day." He added, "It is a good thing. Now each person is independent. Not just for Rahu Kala calculation. It calculates *dina* [Kannada: day], nakshatram [Sanskrit: star dates], *thithi* times [Sanskrit: auspicious times for offering ancestor sacrifices], yoga and *karana* [Sanskrit: use] times. If some priest wants to cheat you in U.S., you can just use it, set to Boston; you will know if it is a good time or not."

Dripping Time

In borrowed chappals I stood in an ordinary-looking coconut orchard on Temple Street in Malleshwaram, at the base of the Kadu Malleshwara spine of hills, facing the low-slung granite walls of a temple barely eight feet high. "*Ayyooo! Accariyama irrukke* [Tamil: It's simply astonishing]," I heard. Vasudeva, a friend and colleague of Anand who had met us that evening at the Skyye bar, waved his arms to indicate just how astonished he was. "I did not know this temple was here. But why me alone? Nobody knew!" The temple seemed to be crouching in the orchard, its unusual square shape and low spire matching its small tight wooden door. Unusual for Bangalore, we could hear the gush of overflowing water nearby mimicking the expected sounds of endless city traffic.

Just before I began fieldwork in Malleshwaram in 1997, this dusty coconut orchard on Temple Street where boys played cricket in the evenings was "Notified for Acquisition," a maneuver—usually termed an NOA—that allowed the government and property developers to annex land that was public property for private profit. At the time, this politico-developer nexus was at its height, and although amoral, the takeover of public lands for private profiteering was legal. Public lands with their inclusive uses were appropriated for private development into luxury homes and shopping malls.

The developer of the coconut orchard had begun to excavate for the construction of an enormous luxury apartment complex. After a week of excavation, a workman fell through what seemed to be a sinkhole in the earth. Padma told me the dramatic story: "Everyone clustered around to help, to pull him out, but when they looked into the hole, they found him paddling on the surface of a large pool. He found himself looking at a jet-black Nandi statue from whose mouth water gushed into a beautiful granite-edged dark pool in an underground stone grotto." More digging and more astonishment ensued. Colonnaded hallways surrounded the stepped floor of the pond and were beautifully carved with the aquatic ecology of tortoises and fish and double-headed snakes, emblems of the Mysore royal family. Thick granite columns supported a vaulted ceiling, and a magnificent open-air vault covered the pool. To Padma, the pool was miraculous as its water, supplied by an underground aquifer, never diminished.[13]

Word spread about the miracle pool and rumors began: the water dripping onto the *lingam* (Shaivaite deity) from the mouth of the Nandi statue had healing powers; the pool belonged to the Kadu Malleshwara temple but had been covered up; in the encryption someone had died, and his ghost haunted the pool and kept it safe these many years, and so on.

Avinash, a friend of Vasudeva, joined us, summoned by a text. A thin young man with fifties-style glasses, he lived next door on Temple Street. We all stared at the water dripping into the pool, fracturing our reflections into liquid concentric swirls.

> There was this *Ajji* [Kannada: old lady]. She used to live there in that house when I was a boy. She was very old . . . maybe nineties or something. She always said that there was a miracle temple here. We all thought she was mad. But when we had water troubles and there was no water, she always said that when she was a girl the Kadu Malleshwara Temple had a tank that was never dry. She said one day it disappeared. I think this must be this tank that has gone into the *bhoomi* [Kannada: earth].

The developer was unwilling to let go of his investment but was prevailed on to stop excavation after several resident groups protested. The Archaeological Survey of India assumed responsibility for the dig, unearthing more and more of this "Tank Temple," in which the pool itself was the temple. In a parched city where officials had abdicated their duty to supply clean water to residents, the overflowing water of the Tank Temple was simply unbelievable for localites who had linked the desertification of the city to the loss of the riparian habitat. For them, the excavation of the ancient Tank Temple illuminated the connections between present-day life and the past as a "place" to be opened, imagined, thought about, and inhabited (Pandian 2012, 547).

The timelessness of the Tank Temple was enhanced because it locked into the topological imagination of Bangaloreans.[14] Prakash, a local resident, said to me, "The central *kere* [Kannada: tank] is a deep, deep whirlpool. No one knows how the water gets circulated from there to the Nandi's mouth, but it does." Anu, his wife, said, "Some people say it is linked by a stream to Sankey Tank, the lake near Palace Orchards where everyone goes for their Ganesha immersion, but who knows? But definitely it is very, very old. It is five thousand years old."

In 2001 informants told me that the age of the Tank Temple was verified by experts from the Archaeological Survey of India, who were called in by the local residents. The temple was anywhere between two thousand and seven thousand years old. Ravi, a material science doctoral student at the Indian Institute of Science, claimed excitedly that the "latest technology" of "carbon dating" was used to verify its age. He said, "It had to be dated for the Archaeological Survey, but my grandmother was just so thrilled to see something that old that stood the test of time to show us how Hinduism, how our culture, is so strong. It's amazing to think it is so old. It's a heritage building." Vasudeva added, "Are you talking about heritage architecture? Only a couple of bungalows are still here and there. People have made them into public buildings or you can rent them for functions, like that! They cost a bomb! But they have all the heritage architectural details like teak columns and marble floors, all that."

Heritage connoted a sense of history, a "collective immortality in the face of individual mortality" (Herzfeld 2015). I asked Krishna Bhattar about this idea of history, memory, and its packaging as heritage for neoliberal consumption, and he replied in his philosophical style, "Memory can lead to deepening a search for something that is in a dimension beyond time itself. This is the use of memory for liberation. Liberation acts to free us not only from the past but from future expectations also."

But Krishna Bhattar's placing of the notion of heritage in temporal cycles of past and future enabled me to understand that disinterring the rhythms, tempos, beats, cycles, durations, sequences, and repetitions of mutually im-

FIGURE 5.2. The Tank Temple. Photo courtesy of Andrew Hutcheson.

plicating structures of time allows us to pursue a few ways of acknowledging the productivity of interrogations of time through an immersion in the liquidity of space-time (Adam 2003). It locates the now and indicates a differential repetitiveness like a circular movement of the watery whirlpool of the Tank Temple.

The rationalization of time in neoliberal modernity diminishes the wondrousness of untimely and contingent events. Time becomes closed and marked, yet ritual time needs to remain open ended, porous, and mysterious. Here I am drawing on Pandian's (2015) useful recent work on time but am pushing further to the consideration of salvaging time in a loop as ethically creative. As Lefebvre notes explicitly, there is "no rhythm without repetition in time and space, without reprises, without returns, in short without measure," but "there is no identical absolute repetition definitely . . . there is always something new and unforeseen that introduces itself into the repetitive" ([1992] 2004, 6). This tiny fragmented newness in the endlessly repetitive gestures to a time out of time—a wondrous time—that lurks in unexpected places. It is a created time field in which the cosmological, the intended but unexpected, and the serendipitous and frighteningly wondrous emerge. The ethics of created wonderment unfold through the texture of time itself.

The Urgency of the Now

The preciousness of ritual time focuses localites and priests on the fierce urgency of the immediate, the ippo, and how it plays out. In terms of the subjective experience of time, the immediate now is a limit that separates what went before from what comes after. For example, Krishna Bhattar would say when instructing the neophyte priests about something needing to be done for the daily ritual, "Ippovai! Now! Not later!" or "Before we did this, but ippo we do this." It is a moment of the now that acts as a boundary along the continuum of time.

But Krishna Bhattar thinks of this boundary not as rigid but as a porous boundary allowing leakage from the past into the present and future. However, when he uses it as an exhortation to other priests, commanding "*Ippovai pananaum!* [Tamil: It must be done *now!*]," it is framed as an indivisible and duration-less instant in which time coalesces. For Krishna Bhattar, ippo is a juncture holding past and future together, enabling a differentiation within the continuum of time to collect all the moments as past and those as future. The ippo is a distinguishing metric related to change and magnitude.

Krishna Bhattar seemed to suggest that ippo was more than time—it was a manner of moral subjectivity, a presence in the present: "All the distractions of the mind and senses away from the god are in the present now. Ippovai." So it is the now, but the now is not a function of *kala* [time] alone but rather an injunction to be present.[15] Krishna Bhattar said, "This is a sign of being present . . . no absence!"

Krishna Bhattar shared the subjective quality of time engagement through what he termed four "stages" of awareness of time, of being constantly "present" in the now through the entire day:

> The first stage is *jagruti* [Sanskrit: awakening], like one gets up with the sunshine, one awakens into awareness. The second stage is like the *swapna* [Sanskrit: daydream], in which by dreaming you become more aware of yourself. The third stage is full awakening and the *Mandukya Upanishad* refers to this person as *tejasa* [Sanskrit: one who is shining, brilliant]. Next is a stage of sleep like we do at night called *nidra* [Sanskrit: sleep], but this is no ordinary sleep . . . this is the state of real insight. Last we come to the full state of consciousness that goes beyond the daily routine of day and night. We call it *turiya* [Sanskrit: comatose] because in this state the self is awestruck. It is in wonder, transcending time itself. Language cannot describe this state, this

FIGURE 5.3. A localite at the Tank Temple checking the time on his cell phone. Photo by the author.

time. The *Mandukya Upanishad* says it is supreme good, infinite peace. It is neither consciousness nor unconsciousness . . . it is the *atman*, the true self.

For Krishna Bhattar this sense of wondrous selfhood is beyond the tedium of the everyday, even beyond knowing itself. He said with emphasis that for this self-knowledge, "the most important time is ippo. Now!"

For Krishna Bhattar, the concept of ippo and its ad hoc immediacy, *ippo-dike* (for now), allow for endless creativity, negotiation, improvisation, and adjustment. Like Aristotle's immediacy, Krishna Bhattar's ippo constitutes both instant and present, rendering the moment subjective and natural at once. Fernand Braudel (1992) deals with this freezing of time into one instance when he talks about the subjectivity of time, recognizing that for each now there is a past that has already happened and is thus closed to intervention except in the imagination. Past events cannot be changed, and anticipated events may be affected only insofar as the action arrives "in time." In fact, both assert that the unity of objective time synthesizes the multiplicity of subjective temporal experiences.

Time's Arrow

The sociological trick that pretends to "freeze time" by examining structural relationships at one point in time ("synchronically") cannot help us understand the subtleties of ritual creativity. Such freezing of time in a section—what Louis Althusser calls an "essential section" (coupe d'essence) in his reading of Hegel—wherein a vertical break is made at any moment in historical time, where such a break in the present reveals all the elements of the whole (1970, 17).

But though Althusser claimed that this section of time reveals a specific structure of the social totality, in which all the elements of the whole are given in a co-presence and are legible in it, in Malleshwaram the ippo cannot reveal the character of the social formation, of economy and society structured as a totality, because there is no single now in which all elements of a social formation come into play; there is no single de jure preliminary presence of time. Rather the ippo is two meanings in one: the moment as a moment of a development (which invokes the continuity of time); and the moment as a moment of time, as the immediate fractured present.

According to Krishna Bhattar we have to think of the moral context of time, its qualitative character. The influential notion of qualitative time actually derives from the characterization of inner durée as a qualitatively differentiated but unsegmented, temporal movement, a moral innerness (Bergson [1889] 2012, 5, 118–19, 170, 171; Munn 1992, 95). Thus, time is both about the measurement of the instant of the now and about the now's present, living nature in contrast to the timelessness of the soul and of the eternal godhead. Krishna Bhattar said as I quizzed him:

> You keep asking about kala. Our *jeevana* [Kannada: lives] are like a *kshana* [Kannada: moment]! You know the comparison of our time with the time of Brahma? You know the sage Narada?[16] They say he lived for a thousand years. But when he is born, Brahma goes into the toilet with his kalasha [Kannada: water pot] to wash himself, and when he comes out he sees Narada's dead body being taken away! The moral is God's time is eternal. It is not measurable by humans. Most of it is spent in contemplation. All that we see around us is but a kshana, a moment.

With the introduction of the cosmological domain, temporality shifts from a measurable abstraction of usefulness to an internal, moral, godlike dimension. But Krishna Bhattar continued:

The problem is we do not see God's time. We cannot live so long and we are not so wise. We only see small things, our lives and our small successes. Our vision of time is small. The way we see time is like the flight of a *bana* [arrow]. That when an arrow comes from Sri Rama's bow, like in the story of the Ramayana, the arrow we see it moving forward, never back. We always experience life as this going forward, and so our experience of time is always as though it is lost falling behind us.

Krishna Bhattar's understanding of time is as an illusion of forward motion with a multiplicity of smaller steps or pieces—a fragmentation.[17] For him, the problem of time is not only its fragmentation into usable units that he equates with capitalistic desires, to reveal that our perception of time is flawed. Krishna Bhattar had more to say about the so-called arrow of time: "But we must remember that it is not an arrow. That is only our eyes, our *sanna* [Tamil: perception]. Time goes forward and back. We see time as forward moving, as the flight of an arrow, and this influences our understanding of the past and the present." Modern progress implies movement in time from the unchanging past to the dynamic future, but such movement can also be called an erosion, in space from the isolated hinterland to the bustling city, and in culture from static and isolated tradition to fashionable and entangled modernity (Shove, Trentmann, and Wilk 2009).

Krishna Bhattar uses the well-known image of the flight of time's arrow to indicate not only a sense of linear progression but also our faulty perception of time *as* linear and progressive. For him, the knitting together of fragmented time is retroactive. While each fragment—each moment—is individualized and countable, the very fact that they are linked together is what makes each moment meaningful. In Krishna's understanding, the psychology of time telling cannot be understood except in the succession of a series of moments in which the teller of time is aware of his own presence.

But as Krishna Bhattar commented when he regarded a billboard with the slogan "Work is worship," his notion of time is inflected by the religious and moral. After all, he spends every day, from a little before dawn to well after midnight, organizing temple activities, praying, worshipping, performing rituals, reading, and teaching. For him, god is the maker and consumer of all time. It is God, Krishna Bhattar told me, who decides how the yugas should be, how long they should last. It is God who determines the ritu, the seasons, in Boston. It is God who knows and understands time. He continued, "You think anyone can tell when you will die? No! Only Yama, the god of death, can do that. Not even astrologers will tell you the moment of birth or death. It is left in God's hands. Why? Because God is master and fount of all time. The seasons pass because of God's will."

For Krishna Bhattar, time is theological, the product of Brahman's will: "No. Time is not a product. It is the essence of the Brahman." He added, "Creation begins when God makes his energies active and ends when he withdraws all his energies into a state of sleep. God is timeless, for time is relative and ceases to exist in the absolute. The past, the present, and the future coexist in him simultaneously. There is no ippo there, no difference, no timekeeping!" Time is eternal and controlled by God, who is also time's very being. By returning to the Brahman and citing existing theological understandings of God, Krishna seeks to reintroduce wonder into alienated, modern time. For Krishna Bhattar, time in this sacred sense is formless and open, mysterious and wonderful.

Salvaged Gods

I stood in front of the Mariamman Temple with a number of long-distance drivers on the dusty edge of the road, drinking hot tea from a cart. Mariamman, the patron goddess of the temple, is a form of Devi known to ward off infectious diseases. The temple stood on the outskirts of Malleshwaram in a sort of borderland between the locality and the Indian Institute of Science. Forty years ago, it was the edge of the city. Mariamman temples frequently occupied the liminal spaces between forest (Tamil: *kadu*) and town (Tamil: *uru*) because it was thought that infectious diseases could be kept out of the town by strengthening its porous boundaries (Mines 2005). Often needing placation, Mariamman was widely worshipped until the mid-twentieth century as smallpox, cholera, and other epidemics swept through rural and urban India. With antibiotics, penicillin, and other medicines readily available in Bangalore, Mariamman lost her following.

When I began fieldwork in 1998, the Mariamman Temple was in disuse. The ceiling had caved in and the doors were locked. Dandu Shastri convinced the board of his temple to install his nephew as the priest and to repair the roof. I largely ignored the Mariamman Temple until 2000 when Dandu pointedly told me that some devotees were going to take their new car there for *vandi puja* (Tamil: car blessings). I went along and found the temple buzzing with hundreds of devotees and their new cars. I found the priest herding the devotees into a line, hitting his head in exasperation at the chaos. The salvage of the Mariamman Temple and its growth indicated the casting of a new futurity—the past, grasped and brought forward into the present to create aspirations for the future.

When I drove past the temple in mid-1999, I noticed some roads under construction and a traffic circle being built opposite the temple. Then, in November, on the day of the festival of Saraswathi Puja, dedicated to the goddess of learning, tools, and trades, I noticed a small line of new vehicles parked at the circle. The temple was newly white-washed and a youngish priest was performing worship by the vehicles. I stopped and asked what was happening.

The young priest, who happened to be the son of Dandu Shastri's nephew, said, "Yes, you see Mariamman is a goddess of illness but what is the big illness today that kills people? It is traffic. Accidents happen every day so I started this small puja for lorries [trucks] because we are on the highway route north. Soon lots of lorries started coming here. Now everyone comes for a puja for their new vehicles to get them protected."

When I returned in 2006, I found that the Mariamman Temple had grown. It had replaced an adjoining copse with a giant parking lot. The temple now hired four priests to cater to a throng of bright-washed vehicles waiting for the "drive puja," as one priest called it. The goddess had been renamed "Circle Mariamman" in reference to the traffic circle, and Malleshwaram residents now referred to the temple by the goddess's new name.

This conversion of the Mariamman Temple into a sort of talisman against the deadliness of traffic accidents in Bangalore has given it a contemporary relevance in a city in which congestive traffic jams, deadly accidents, parking altercations, drunk driving, road rage, and other vehicular incidents continue to increase. In September 2011 the IBM Global Commuter Pain Survey deemed Bangalore to be the sixth worst city in the world for driving with commuters who spend an average of over thirty minutes stuck in traffic.[18]

One vehicle owner at the Mariamman Temple called Mariamma "Circle Mariamma, traffic goddess," and by way of explanation added, "*Thumba traffic Bangalore nalli* [Kannada: Lots of traffic in Bangalore]." Then he added, "This traffic, it is the disease of this time. Traffic jams! Every day in the papers . . . don't you read? This one died, that one died in traffic accident, bus killed them, lorry dashed them! Only *Amma* ["Mother," indicating the deity] can protect us!" as he gestured to the temple door.

The taxi driver, Murugan, and I waited for over three hours to get to the front of the line for the blessing. Murugan had brought all the materials for the car blessing puja, including four limes that were a sacrificial offering, a coconut, some flowers, fruit, incense sticks, and money. The priest came out of the temple and in contemptuous silence jerked his chin to indicate Murugan's "turn." The front of the priests' silk dhoti was covered in ghee stains and

FIGURE 5.4. The Circle Mariamman Temple in 2016. Photo by the author.

his hands were dirty. He carried a silver plate with a gold coin embedded in it, indicative of the wealth of the temple. Without any words of greeting he gestured to Murugan to place the limes under the tires of the vehicle. The belief, as Murugan explained it to me, was that the limes assuaged the blood lust of the car, and sacrificing the limes by driving over them prevented the car from demanding any life. The priest, who never introduced himself, went through the motions of a cursory blessing and Murugan drove over the limes as sacrifice. The incense was lit, the coconut broken, and we were hustled along as the priest went off to the next customer, a large man in a brightly painted lorry. We left quickly after Murugan gave the priest a 500-rupee note as the queue of cars behind us grew.

The revivification of Mariamman as a traffic goddess speaks not only to the dangers of hypercapitalism in a city of endless traffic jams but also to the endless reinvention and salvage of the portfolios of the deities. Salvage escapes our immediate vision, as our view is temporally partial at best. Salvage and repetition are in themselves creative acts, weaving improvisation within and into the fabric of time. The recycling of divinity to create solutions to contemporary problems is not only about the durability of the divinity or even about the innovation of Bangaloreans in reassigning this deity and accepting her new avatar as a traffic goddess.

This act of salvage speaks to the ability of priests and devotees to co-create and deploy alternate structures of living as a way of addressing problems of ontological insecurity and uncertainty. What is celebrated in this case of deity-and-temple recycling is the epistemology of reinvention that creates an opportunity to address a problem of living. Salvage gestures to the changing value of obsolescence in which the ethics of the forgotten are seen as providing the chance to rethink and restructure, as a gateway to the new. To forget is not to lose permanently but rather to creatively reuse that which is found.

But the mechanics of this transformation are not gentle. They can be violent, as in the cases of the suppression of certain gods, festivals, or temples; the shunting of time for festivals or pujas; the erasure of other gods, demigods, and sages; or the sundering and reworking of links between "successful" festivals and processions like the Kanu Pandige and the Golla community, or even, potentially, the silencing of whole lower caste groups, and the appropriation of their festivals, gods and temples. The salvage and reworking of gods, festivals, and temples toward contemporary value and potentially greater durability requires intuitive understanding of their appeal, and a refabrication of their aesthetics and meanings. Durability requires persistent experimental reworking. Continuity thus implies a multiplicity of moments and elements and their interpenetration, visible only in hindsight.

This "retro" movement of time in salvage is a cultural device that allows for a new way of telling history by which possibility and agency are enhanced. In colonial times, Bangalore was described with metaphors that "blend[ed] the connotative meanings of time, distance and cultural development together" and objectified the concept of tradition as located in a distant time and place (Wilk 2003, 421). Progressive time, seen as oppositional to tradition, accrues to the administrators themselves. This "repurposing" of development toward progress highlights the agency of participants in building capital and enhancing capabilities essential to progress in their own vision of the future. The practice of salvage unearths older meanings and forms and recasts them, no doubt a violence done to history, but in some cases localites deemed it a necessary violence. Salvage builds a capacity for the inclusion of previously paradoxical and oppositional tropes as coping mechanisms in a capitalist world. Localites see it is as an agentive and hopeful set of devices and practices.

The trope of recycling that Malleshwaramites unconsciously evoke and employ is an abrogation of the culture of plenty and waste, which they see proliferating around them. Chellappa, a trustee of the Krishna Temple, privy to the accounts, constantly complained about the "washetu" of valuable and expensive resources like oil, water, sugar, and so on. Localites who were more sensitive to environmental pollution like Prabha spoke of how much waste was produced in Bangalore and how garbage littered the streets in Malleshwaram. Mr. Iyer blamed the culture of "throwaway," which he claimed Bangaloreans had learned from the rich West. They all routinely exalted thrift as a bygone value.

Salvage here was seen an apparent turn to a culture of value and thrift—something that Dandu Shastri argued was much needed in today's world. Priests and devotees regain and restructure a new frame that creates opportunity for more productive "regimes of living" (Collier and Lakoff 2004). Here salvage is not an end point but a point along the way, providing impetus and propulsion to greater change, whereby the portals of the future remain wide open to creative evolution, even though many of these changes may seem contradictory or contestatory (Bergson [1907] 1911).

Where salvage is a way of being, newness is seen a locus of accretions of microscopic changes, not only in a relentless forward movement as described by the "arrow of time" metaphor but also in a kaleidoscopic scattering and flowing. The relationship to the past is one of efficiencies, of both longing and rejection—a rejection of the limitedness of the past as well as a nostalgic reaching for its safe enclosures. In Bangalore, the past is aggregated into a social contract and understanding of culture in which the tacit consent of the middle classes to the "retention" and "defense" of an Indian "culture" creates a narrative of disjuncture between those on the track of gentrification and those harking back to gentler days.

In an ironic twist to the logics of creativity, as the past is politicized and reworked through a neoliberal radicalized Hindu narrative, it becomes the origin of the present in a direct trajectory. This allows the fictitious saturnine retracing of the wonder of modern creativity back into an imagined Hindu womb crystallizing in the Hindu nationalist project. For example, it allows Prime Minister Narendra Modi to argue that ancient India invented plastic surgery and helicopters, as images drawn from myth are given a modern spin. Rama's Pushpakavimana (flying chariot) becomes the modern helicopter as time becomes suffused with middle-class aspirational goals, and the future becomes a project of reclamation—a reclamation of a golden past that is distinctly Hindu.

The political effort to remake the past is, by extension, an effort to remake the present and the future into a radicalized hegemonic nationalist form—a repellent form of chronometry.

Granular Time Telling

For the Bangalore bourgeoisie, the priests themselves—who are or aspire to be part of this same rising middle class—represent the moral entropy of the world that modernity ushers in. A common damning critique of the priesthood was their incurable unpunctuality, their lack of an ability to "keep to time," by which is meant modern time. Devotees would comment frequently on the priests "being late." "Keeping to time" was a way of showing one's familiarity with modern professionalism and moral ability.

In 1998 Krishna Bhattar and Vishwanatha both wore big gold watches to show that their notions of time were modern, and that they were trustworthy. Vishwanatha said proudly to me, "You will be able to go at seven o'clock on the dot! When I say seven, I mean seven . . . not like these other fellows who say seven but mean eight o'clock! We keep time here!" Keeping to modern time was thus proof of trustworthiness, and they were proud of falling in line with the neoliberal gestalt.

The priests also understood that ritual time ran counter to modern time. Dandu Shastri posited the problem of the priests' lack of punctuality as service to a higher master: "I understand they are busy. They have work and all. But I am also busy. I am serving God. For him all the time is valuable. I am not wasting time. I have to do things in the order in which he wants." Dandu's criticism of modern measured time is that it constrains the will of God.

While, on the one hand, emphasizing their punctuality and the value of modern time allows for a capture of the neoliberal gestalt, on the other hand, priests rationalized their unpunctuality as a resistance, a rupture of modern time. This rupture-capture process involved a granular rethinking of time frames.

My last conversation about time with Krishna Bhattar was in 2013. He was sitting in his living room with a number of young priests, all vying for his attention. He said, "Tulasi, you have been asking me about time for a long time now, and I have given you so many answers. Still you are not satisfied. All right, so you want me to describe time? The time has come! I will tell you what time is. It is *pamsudhana*!" I wasn't familiar with this Sanskrit word, so he translated into everyday Tamil, "*manl kuviyal*" (a heap of sand).

According to Krishna Bhattar, this heap of sand allowed for a "mounding up" of instances one upon the other, gesturing to a layering of memories and imagination. It was not unidirectional like the arrow of time metaphor. Instead, it indicated an accumulation of moments in the chaotic fashion of real-time experience—a subjective understanding of time: "Pamsudhana is the way we experience life." Strangely enough, Nancy Munn echoes Krishna Bhattar's usage of sand to get at the crystalline quality of time. In her article on time, she likens it to Borges's "book of sand," for "as one opens this book, pages keep growing—it has no beginning or end" (Munn 1992, 92). For Krishna and Dandu, time is infinite, a true metaphysical phenomenon, stretching in a series of fractal-like moments that are experienced linearly.

Experience is the key word here: reality is a subjective experience; it is perception. The information perceived—*experienced*—represents the connection between the observer and the observed; it encapsulates the link between the subject and the object, the relationship between what we conceptualize as the external world and what it feels like to experience this external world from within.

The duration of time in the Malleshwaram perception becomes a continuous progression of possibilities that grows into the future with microscopic changes and swells as it advances (Bergson [1907] 1911, 6–7). What is past is what is known. Memory and history, such as that of the Tank Temple, are part of the pamsudhana, the heap of sand. The past is thus always present within entropic states—a cycling of the past into futurity as a sort of condensate of history.

At this point, Professor Seshadri, an astrophysicist at the Indian Institute of Science, joined our conversation. He initially tried to give me his own explanation for time and its progression and regression, but after listening to Krishna Bhattar, he said, "Yes, this idea of time as sand is a very old idea. See, even the Romans used sand in their hourglasses." I suggested that in fact the actuality of using sand for timekeeping and the metaphor of time as granular were somewhat different. But then he added something fascinating. He said, "The point of the sand heap is that it flows away. It can never retain its shape. It always moves toward disorder. This is the second law of thermodynamics, the law of entropy. It's called the Fundamental Principles of Equilibrium and Movement. Everything in the world is subject to entropy—that is, everything dissolves and dissipates. This entropy is the rule of order and of disorder."

The Hindu notion of a dharmic erosion toward *pralaya* (annihilation) can be seen as a theology of moral entropy, a descent to the chaos of end times.

In the eschatology of this millennial vision, the four great yugas (Sanskrit: epochs/time cycles) of Hindu cosmological time are Sathya (Sanskrit: age of truth), Dwapara (Sanskrit: the second age), Thretha (Sanskrit: the third age), and Kali (Sanskrit: the age of evil). We are thought to be currently living in the last epoch.

I asked Krishna Bhattar what the point of doing ritual was, given that the world would soon end. "What is the use of doing these puja?" he repeated incredulously, uncertain if I was serious. "We must do it. Only if we do it can we overcome the bad forces of this age of evil." According to Krishna Bhattar, here ritual was prophylactic, protecting the ritual practitioner in an age of evil but also critical in keeping moral decay in check as far as possible. Ritual domesticates the danger and disorder of entropy by allowing humans to harness the power of the universe, gods, and forces to do their bidding in reknitting the world (Puett 2005, 75–80). The domestication and repair work that ritual performs is in fact the mooring of human morality, providing a vision in the imagination of the hoped-for future against the perceived reality of entropy.

But, after a few minutes of silence, Krishna Bhattar provided a different response, reflecting on questions of originality and creativity.

> The other day you asked me how I can do things for adbhutha. I said that Perumal tells me what to do. Yes, it is him alone. It is. Because for us humans, custom makes us think only one way is possible. This is why it is so difficult for us priests to think differently. Because we do things in one way. It put a "limit" on what we can think.
>
> So when I do something different in the alankara or in the ritual, I am changing something. Not the mantras, because they are important, but something small. That small something makes people like the ritual. Like I might make the sari more modern. Or maybe use more modern decorations like use modern flowers or different modern fruit. This changes the way we think about the sari or about the fruit. It makes us more accepting of it. We don't then think this is different or wrong. We think it's different, maybe it is nice. Then we turn our mind, our heart, to see this new thing as nice.

Here, Krishna Bhattar ruptures the idea of pamsudhana, the heaps of sand, condensates of memory and history, to argue instead for originality. While he ascribes the creativity and original thinking of creating wonder to the deity, he is well aware of his hand in it. The rupture of old custom is the origin of a new paradigm.

The Future, the Past, and the Immortal Present

On January 15, 2013, we were sitting in Krishna Bhattar's living room in the evening. The previous day had been long, with the performance of the Kanu Pandige procession. The evening was quiet and Krishna Bhattar came and sat on the floor in front of me, ready for a chat. Valù, his wife, brought him a silver lota of hot milk. When she left, I thought it an opportune moment to ask Krishna Bhattar about the concepts of time that bothered me. I took out my notebook. He smiled, as by this time he was used to the signs of my "interview," as he called it. I started asking about the fluidity of time and the concept of uncertainty. "I always know what time is until you ask me about time and then I do not know what it is anymore," he said jokingly. Then, his smile fading away, he said seriously, "Time is always moving. It is endless. Like a river, no, like *sagara* [ocean].[19] . . . Always unfolding, always." He pointed to his eldest son, Krishna, who was busy sorting through several gigantic garlands while being served milk by his young wife. "Look at that young man! When you first came here he was starting school. Now he is like I was when you came here. Time moves so fast. We sit in boats on these waves of time and what can we do? We count the waves!" The metaphor of shifting ephemeral time, its endless rhythmic pulsing and flux—a wave—is appealing both visually and philosophically.

Krishna Bhattar added, "Time, kala, is ungraspable even though we are always trying to account for every moment." Time is ungraspable for Krishna Bhattar because it enshrouds everything. Because everything changes "with," "in," "through," "because of," or "over" time, then time must literally permeate everything, making it unknowable. He added that unknowing was valorous: "You always ask me questions about time seeking to know it, but it is not about *jnana* [Sanskrit: knowledge], it is about unknowing. That is what leads to *vairagya* [Sanskrit: true liberation], unknowing. It is not about ignorance but it is about acceptance [Sanskrit: *parabhkati*] of being in a space of not knowing. Being a teacher you find that difficult I think."

After he said this, Krishna Bhattar fell silent for a long while. The sun was setting and the room lit up with the rays of the setting sun. Then it became gray and then finally dark, and I could barely make out the lines of Krishna Bhattar's face. Prabha came in to switch on the lights, and Krishna Bhattar looked at me, smiled, and said in astonishment, "See what a long conversation we have had about time. The sun has set! So I can say one thing . . . Time only measures itself. And only God can measure real time. Only he is its true meaning. All time ends in God's presence." Staying in the space of unknowing as opposed to knowing allows for liberation from the terror of having to know. We cannot comprehend wonder through knowledge; only unknowingness can help us surrender to the divine unknown, to comprehend and feel wonder.

A PLACE FOR RADICAL HOPE

The only philosophy which can be responsibly practiced in face of despair is the attempt to contemplate all things as they would present themselves from the standpoint of redemption.
—Theodor Adorno, *Minima Moralia*

Astonishment is necessary.
—Krishna Bhattar

Creativity in Turmeric

A year before I began this study, my parents and I visited my patrilineal ancestral temple, dedicated to the deity Narasimha, a hybrid man-lion incarnation of Vishnu, in a town some fifty miles west of Bangalore. We left home at dawn. But despite our early start, we arrived just a little too late for the morning rituals. The sanctum was curtained off as the alankaram was being finished. In most temples, people were often distracted by other things during this time—chatting or leaving the temple—but in this temple, attendees' attention was focused intensely on the closed curtain. I soon discovered the reason for this rapt attention.

Abruptly, without any musical warning, as was de rigueur in most temples, the curtain was drawn back. A child, waiting with her mother, screamed in fear at the spectacle unveiled before us.

In the darkness sat a yellow-maned lion. Lit by a guttering lamp, the deity's ferocious eyes seemed to stare, and his talons seemed to drip with blood. A disemboweled dying body lay across its lap.

I remember being shocked by the violence of the gruesome sight. Yet I understood, almost at a cellular level, the wonder of the spectacle's deep enactment of transformation for the audience. I looked more carefully. The lion deity was painted in turmeric; the "blood" was red kum kum powder, artfully placed on the talons and teeth of the deity. I learned that day that this temple had perfected this frightening yet wondrous alankara over generations.

I BEGAN THIS study attempting to get beyond both a simple updating of our understanding of ritual life in South Indian temples and the unique pedagogical value of temple life—worthy quests in themselves. But in the periphery of my vision was a sense of existential precarity and ethical erosion that accompanied everyday life in Bangalore. Under the tutelage of the localites, I began to understand that ritual is a site of creativity and resistance; that ritual creativity is greater than practical adjustment and more meaningful than mere pragmatism; that ritual creativity could perhaps provide a safe space from which to contemplate this precariousness, and to generate new ways of thinking.

But as I continued doing fieldwork, I realized that the larger aspiration for this work was to render an update on social and religious changes in modern India. In a prescient article written in 1962 for the *Economic Weekly*, my father observed that India was changing—its institutions, culture, society, and, most particularly, religion. He argued that it was difficult to see how the religion could endure, as "Hinduism has been much too dependent on institutions such as caste, joint family and the village community for its survival. All these three critical institutions are undergoing change due to the operation of a variety of forces, social and economic" (M. N. Srinivas 1962b, 110). He continued:

> This ought to be a matter for concern because it is necessary to provide the younger generation with a sense of purpose and of values. Nationalism may provide the former for the people, but it will not provide the latter. Even internationalism will not be enough. . . . If the bulk of the people derive their Weltanschauung [their philosophy of life] from their religion, and if this religion is very largely dependent upon a triad of

social institutions viz caste, joint family and village community, which are changing in important respects, what will be the consequences for the people concerned and their country?

One can (and should) argue about whether *Hindu* values are good for Indian society in the twenty-first century, but what M. N. Srinivas noted is that in India religion is the bedrock from which most people get their values, and without values a society is morally adrift. Indeed, this urgent tracing of societal-institutional change and the concordant need for an existential ethical paradigm that he articulated over half a century ago is no less urgent today.

Through watching and participating with Dandu Shastri, Krishna Bhattar, and the localites, I came to understand that every creative ritual act has the capacity to do this moral work of resistance, acceptance, rupture, and capture in a fraught time. The attentiveness to detail, an improvisation to make it work, that, when sedimented, can be seen as *radical ritual creativity*—ritual acts are an improvised worlding that enable ritual practitioners to imagine new horizons to their futures. This worlding, the center of meaning, requires an expansive imagination to engage creativity in the ebbs and flows of everyday life. In turn, ritual practitioners understand wonder as an imaginative construct—as both sublime delight and existential wound—and apply a strategic imagination that allows both an expansive resistance to and acceptance of the terms of modern life. Such an application forces consideration of religion not as text or in relation to text but as it is lived, experienced, and practiced toward singular ends.

Seeing ritual as both a template *for* and *of* change enables us to better apprehend how ritual is constitutive and denotative of mobility across ideological, temporal, and social domains. Here, the experimental and evolutionary *is* the ethical because it posits another ontological horizon that can undercut existing power structures. Experimental Hinduism in Malleshwaram is a way of receiving yet refusing the power of neoliberal modernity as it exists, and transforming it into something other, something liberal, something that enables survival and even flourishing. Viewed retrospectively in terms of the juxtaposition of power, a small change is enormous in its consequence. Remote from nostalgia, the past is grasped and brought forward into the present to create aspirations for the future.

As the Narasimha turmeric alankaram suggests, wonder has long been a part of the ritual experience. It is not unique to Malleshwaram, nor of course to the modern period—merely the tools of its evocation are. I doubt that modernity challenges existing wisdom about creativity, tradition, and meaning. Detailing the micro shifts of specific ritual improvisation over a decade and a half—some large, some small, some miniature—allows us to understand the resistances, appropriations, and challenges of such religious experimentation. Representing neither diffusion of Western ideas outward, nor distinctly Indian forms, the understanding of creative ritual practices attuned to wonder involves a transnational history of modernity, one shaped by global conversations about creativity, change, and society.

Ritual practitioners and specialists suggest that a recovery of wonder is a new heuristic for generating insights into Indian ritual in a way that is distinct from Western philosophical understandings of the wonderful, even while it might apply to them. Wonder is salient in the aesthetics of many Indian religious communities, more prominent in Hindu discourse of aesthetic appreciation, more relevant to key Hindu cosmological notions, such as power and ethics, and more suited to describe creativity within religious publics.

In Malleshwaram I observed an emergent Hindu philosophy of liberation from the colonized imagination. Dandu Shastri and Krishna Bhattar enable an epistemological decolonization—a decolonizing of the imagination. It teaches us that we as scholars and anthropologists are grounded in a deeply Eurocentric interpretation of religion and knowledge but that the polytropic ambiguity of Hinduism and its essential experimentation allow us to question our understandings of what counts as ritual and how it is to be performed, as well as what counts as religion and how it is understood. The pursuit of wonder propels a decolonization of thought and is an urgent and timely response to the many things that are broken in our world—the economic, emotional, and ecological degradation that surrounds us. Now, more than ever, calls for an existential generosity, an anthropological sensibility, and a faith in humanity yet to come are needed. We need ways of hanging on, and of courting openness and care as livable realities.

Listening to Dandu Shastri and Krishna Bhattar, Vishwanatha, Suresh, Padma, Prabha, Chellappa, Raju, Mrs. and Mr. Iyer, Mr. Ramanuja, "Top Gun" Shiva, and my other friends and interlocutors requires taking wonder seriously as a grounded analytic. It requires thinking about the world as ecologically and temporally emergent in an endless process of worlding, a durable creativity.

But let me be clear, as we have seen, such creativity and wonder need not necessarily lead to "good" or liberal outcomes, and could in fact do the opposite. But everyday Hinduism, this experimental Hinduism—the way most Hindus learn what it is to be Hindu—is worked from the ground up. It is the antithesis of the rigid, crystalline, nationalist, and fundamentalist Hinduism that is a top-down appeal to the bitter populist forces and fears, and it offers new ways to understand the category of "religion" not in relation to

FIGURE C.1. Localites at the Krishna Temple. Photo by the author.

the text, or to its definitional history in the West, but as a living and breathing discipline.

The challenge ahead therefore is as it always has been—to take power responsibly, working with and through it to produce and activate knowledge not against power but against the prevailing assumptions that have regulated the production and use of knowledge and creativity that aid the weakest and most vulnerable. I suggest that the tracing of an emergent creative ethics attempted here might even allow us to break away from forms of absolute categories of knowledge and economy—the totalitarian impulses of our time.

Thresholds of Possibility

Three years later, it was dusk in Malleshwaram and I was waiting for Krishna Bhattar in the Krishna Temple. It had been a warm April day and the evening air was filled with the sounds of birds calling as they settled to roost in the temple tower. I sat on the pavilion threshold, waiting.

Krishna Bhattar came and sat down with a tired sigh. He neatly folded his veshti under him and his shawl around him as he said, "Have you heard the Narasimha myth?" Of course, I knew the myth, but before I could speak, he continued:

There was this ferocious evil demon king called Hiranyakasipu. He was terrible. . . . He did evil things, killing, cheating, doing bad things to women. He was a horrible demon. But he had a beautiful pure son, a devotee of Lord Vishnu. His name was Prahalada.

There was one thing Hiranyakasipu wanted above all else. He wanted immortality. But that was reserved only for the gods. He did some difficult penance whereby he won a boon from the gods. He demanded of Indra, the king of the gods, "I want to live forever." Indra denied his demands. But Hiranyakasipu was determined and clever. So he said, "I want to die neither in heaven nor in hell, neither in day nor in night, neither inside nor out, and by no weapon." He thought that way he could never be killed and never die.

Hiranyakasipu grew undefeatable and soon ruled all the worlds. The gods realized they could do nothing to stop him because of the boon Indra had granted. So, Indra went to Lord Vishnu and told him of Hiranyakasipu's "terrorism" ways [sic].

One day, Hiranyakasipu was fiercely harassing his son, Prahalada. He wanted Prahalada to bow only to him. Prahalada started chanting the lord's name as a refuge, "Narayana Narayana." Hiranyakasipu was angry, and he kicked one of the pillars in his palace as he shouted, "Where is this Narayana of yours who you keep calling? Is he here?"

The pillar broke open, just like that! [Krishna Bhattar hit the step with his fist for emphasis.] A fearsome creature, neither man nor beast, emerged. It had the head and tail of a lion and the body of a man. It was Narayana in the Narasimha [Sanskrit: man-lion] avatar.

Lord Narasimha lifted Hiranyakasipu with great strength and took him to the threshold of his palace. He waited until dusk, like it is right now. As the sun was sinking, he tore open Hiranyakasipu's stomach with his talons and he killed him.

I expected Krishna Bhattar to conclude the story with a moral takeaway about evil in the world, but unexpectedly he said,

This story teaches us that we are all like the demon Hiranyakasipu. We can only think in limited ways. We focus upon what we want. We

cannot see many possibilities. Nor can we see that things keep changing. Hiranyakasipu could not see that his son Prahalada was not just
his son but also had become a close devotee of Narayana. He was blind.
And we are all blind like that. My children are growing but to me they
are still my little sons. So there is just one thing definite—the only constant is change [Sanskrit: *parivarthanameva siddhiranthu*]!

AS WE HAVE SEEN, Malleshwaram's wonder discourses and practices—the
stories, speculations, rumors, and claims; the practices, crafting, making, and
doing of things people have described as, and reacted to as, amazing, perplexing, miraculous, and wonderful—undermine the disenchantment and uncertainties of a precarious modernity. In this work I have attempted to rethink the
ritual process. I have focused more on what ritual *is* rather than what it *does*,
more on the process of ritual than its outcomes of social solidarity or its efficacy. A focus on its granularity as process highlights evidence that creativity
is a part of ritual and a cause of its durability. Through a microscopic process
of rupture-capture, Malleshwaramites perform everyday ritual not only to
engage modernity but to disrupt it in productive ways and create new ways
of worlding.

The twinned process of rupture-capture is a resistant acceptance, a function of haphazard operations and creative thinking. Its modes of expediency
and its necessarily excessive self-production (in particular, its fascinating
capacity to generate more than it needs, to produce in excess of any functionality or systematicity) result in the very excesses (the sites of over- or
underinvestment in power's uneven spread over culture) that enable and
at times insist on the conversion of power into its ever-newer forms, into its
unpredictable and stimulating future. This, at its very core, is resilience.

As Arjun Appadurai says, anthropology "must redefine itself as that practice of representation that illuminates the power of large-scale, imagined life
possibilities over specific life trajectories" (1996, 55). Such a redefinition gives
a sense of the enormous possibilities at play. Wonder undoes older ontological assumptions of dystopic visions and creates new joy-filled ways of being
that enable localites, to see further, to enjoy more, to experiment repeatedly,
to improvise and create.

Dandu Shastri and Krishna Bhattar's capacity to feel wonder, to play, and
to make others feel wonder is a vital, joyous source of their creativity. The
delighted disorientation that ritual practitioners experience is essential to the
magic of wonderment. Creativity and play help us in flight from the normal

toward the wondrous. And what wonder does in the world is important. This is no mere escapism; escapism suggests a removal from reality, a lack of responsibility. Rather, wonder suggests the hope and possibility of an alternate reality, a better future more conducive to joy and care. It celebrates a dexterous opportunism.

Wondering as a practice allows localites to mine the unknown and invite the mysterious in order to arrive at a different kind of knowing. This route to knowing is a mysterious one, replete with random encounters and serendipitous searches, demanding creative patterning that relies on getting lost in a new way of seeing radiantly and joyfully. The sense that what lies distant is close and that the unexceptional is the inexhaustible is the herald of wonder. Wonder in this world is about the poetics of a practice that allows for a true and meaningful *ars vivendi*, an art of living.

Localites recognize the role of wonder in reimagining an ethical horizon—a creative ethics—wherein humans and the beings they worship reposition their lives and themselves within the everyday. Through creative ethics, ritual practitioners fuse and change the Hindu category of dharma into a fluid ethical analytic wherein an infiniteness of interpretive possibilities resistant to standardization in the bounded terms of Western philosophy are at play. Ethical life here cannot and should not be imagined as composed of grand gestures of excess or of a simplicity of inhabitation but rather as a joining and coming together of what have traditionally been considered ethical *and* unethical—the lacing together of opposites through the fantasy of wonderment. This genesis of a new understanding of the ethical aligns ritual with the modern in new and unpredictable ways. The incongruences between the two should not lead anthropologists to adopt a reductively instrumental or economic reading of creative Hinduism in which other human values are ontologically privileged.

Toward an Anthropology of Wonder

For a long time, I was uncomfortable with this book; I was uncomfortable with what it said as well as with its lacunae. It has taken me a decade and a half to be comfortable with the fact that this work dwells on the threshold—the baffled edge of wonder.

Yet part of what feels funny about my journey into wonder, sometimes darkly so, is the realization that a serendipitous stumble into the mysterious—in this case, ritual creativity and change—can lead to practical inquiry regarding invention in ethnographic method. How can one learn to find what one does not know one is seeking? Part of the burden of my work in Malleshwaram has been to show that to let something happen to you in a singular moment and to recognize it as such is as much work as the so-called active mode of engagement. What we glimpse in the peripheral vision of our intellectual life as we focus on something else may in fact be the thing we are seeking.

And so I claim wonder for anthropology: for its understanding of the ineffable quality of change, for the study of the existential nature of being human and enduring the vicissitudes of that, for its focusing us on the experimental and the everyday, and for its commitment to hope. In my view philosophy where wonder has resided has delimited it, by attempting to comprehend the source of the wondrous, a rather mundane, black-or-white articulation; but an ethnography of wonder renders it in glorious technicolor. For me, then, wonder is also about the ethnographic practice, a rethinking of anthropology as both a yearning for ethical life and an embodiment of a morally responsible form of being in the world.

I began this work suggesting that this book be read as a folio composed of fragments of creative experiments. But at the end, I realize that what I offer here is more a manual of wonder combined with a ledger of possibility. I suggest that the anthropology of wonder encourages creativity but bends it toward a recognition of justice. Reopening anthropology to the big question of wonder requires that it be rebuilt on a new foundation: a critical realism that is focused on human survivability, creativity under extreme conditions, and endurance shaped by joy and hope.

I may not have sufficiently emphasized the joy with which localites went about the daily improvisational adjustments of the ritual practices. In *The Passions of the Soul*, René Descartes suggests that "the first [passion] is the surprise of Wonder . . . when joined to joy." Both joy and wonder may involve a desire to be surprised by the everyday, or a capacity to appreciate the surrealism of the real ([1649] 1989). Wonder in Malleshwaram is a resistance to the tedium of the modern and encourages us to like surprises—and to be surprised by what we like. Thus we are allowed to be seduced by that which we need not know, absorbing the fertile spirit of a place where words, hands, and imaginations are given license to roam. It seems we may need wonder to stay alive to the pleasure of not quite knowing things—not an infinite delay of resolution but rather an open-ended resolution that privileges the experimental and the creative.

Dandu Shastri joked, Krishna Bhattar laughed, and devotees sang and had fun. They found meaning and value in the smallest of tasks, and pleasure in the smallest of things. If stopped in traffic for a procession, localites would stop and enjoy the spectacle. If frustrated by waiting in a queue, they would play joyful Bollywood music about love on their cell phones. If caught in a monsoon rainstorm, they would shelter under a handy tree and eat a road-side snack, commiserating with the nearest person. If ground down by urban practices of catching water, of no electricity, of lack of money, they would pray for grace. If faced by difficulty, they would turn to hope.

As Babu observed, "Lord Narasimha, when he came to the threshold, he was not just killing. That here this destruction is creation. So we must understand that when we are at the edge of something in life, so we are also at the center of something far more important. This center is pathless. It is with necessary hope [Tamil: *avashyama*] we make the path. With hope [Sanskrit: *Niriksha*]!" Wonder offers to carve out a space for *radical hope* to burgeon. Barack Obama argued for such "audacious" hope in the face of the enormity of neoliberal economic downturns, abiding corruption, terrible wars, and the exhaustion of cynicism. "Hope is not blind optimism," he said. Rather, it is "that thing in-side us that insists, despite all evidence to the contrary, that something better awaits us if we have the courage to reach for it, and to work for it, and to fight for it. Hope is the belief that destiny will not be written for us, but by us, by the men and women who are not content to settle for the world as it is, who have the courage to remake the world as it should be" (Obama 2008). This radical hope that Obama beautifully described is what rituals of wonder allow for. It, in turn, allows localites to face a world that can seem hopeless and find value in life, to move forward with joy.

I write this in America in the shadow of an election that shocked the world with its outcome and where for many, hopelessness now feels close at hand. More than ever, a book on wonder seems a necessary and timely way forward. We need a sense of possibility, a liberal and joyful vision of the world. We need a radical sense of hope more than ever before. "What makes this hope radical," Jonathan Lear writes, "is that it is directed toward a future goodness that tran-scends the current ability to understand what it is" (2008, 163). Radical hope is not so much something you have but something you practice; it demands flexibility, openness, and what Lear describes as "imaginative excellence." Lo-calites seek and find radical hope through wonder; with wonder, they weapon-ize hope against moral erosion, loss, fear, and despair. They fashion wonder, in both discourse and practice, in order to cultivate radical hope.

Their hopefulness allows for durability and a way to survive in Mallesh-waram. It makes endurable—and sometimes even joyful—the unendurable. It allows Dandu Shastri and Krishna Bhattar and the localites to live and to laugh. Radical hope allows them, and us, to survive, to endure, and to overcome.

AFTERWORD: THE TENACITY OF HOPE

We are always changing. Everything around us is changing. Everything is new every day.
—Dandu Shastri

On August 6, 2012, I was looking at the Bangalore newspapers over tea in Boston when I saw a small notice in the *Deccan Herald*: "Malleshwaram Priest Dies in Traffic Accident." I wanted to read further but could not. I had an ominous pit of fear in my stomach. I called home to Bangalore and told my mother of my unnamed fears; could it be Krishna Bhattar? She calmed me. I called Krishna Bhattar and was instantly relieved to hear him pick up and say "Tulasi, ah?" in his familiar calm tone. After some pleasantries and a "catch up" on all that was going in in Malleshwaram, he gave me Vishwanatha's number. I tried calling him, but there was no answer. My fears doubled.

A day later, I was at some academic conference or another, unable to sleep, when I finally managed to get through to someone at the temple. He said simply, "*Dandu Sahstrigal poyatar* [Tamil: Dandu Shastri is gone]."

I vaguely remember the carpeting of the hotel room of the conference center, rising to meet me as I slumped onto the floor, stunned. Dandu Shastri was only in his late sixties. He was full of vigorous plans and dynamic schemes when I had last seen him. His death seemed so unnecessary. How could this happen?

I called my mother, unwilling to believe the news. She called Vishwanatha and got through. He relayed the bare bones of the story to her. Dandu Shastri had left early to go to a private home on the outskirts of the city, "the Outer Ring Road," to do a grahapravesham. On the way home his small car had been broadsided by "an Alto," a bigger vehicle in the traffic maelstrom that the streets of Bangalore had become. He never recovered, dying in the hospital. "What to do? God took him," he said wearily.

Six months later in January 2013 I returned to Malleshwaram, still saddened by the loss. I thought it might be the last time I would return to the temples as an ethnographer, and I wondered about my ability to transmit what I had learned about wonderful living in a precarious world. Unable to face the Ganesha Temple without Dandu Shastri, I went first to the Krishna Temple to pay my respects to Krishna Bhattar.

For the first time since I had arrived in 1998, Lakshmana, the opium-smoking flower seller, did not greet me at the temple entrance. He usually badgered me loudly to buy some flowers and then would take his meager earnings to buy some bhang cheroots. This time I found him missing. I was surprised but thought he might have stopped off at the street corner to smoke, as he sometimes did.

As always, I did not have to say much for Krishna Bhattar to understand how I was feeling. He greeted me gently with "I heard the news about Dandu Shastri. I did not know him well. But I knew you knew him and through you I felt I knew him." I waited, and then I asked about Lakshmana the flower seller. He said, "Ah yes, Lakshmana became sick sometime back. He wanted to go to his village. He asked us for money and we gave him some. He never came back!"

I confessed to Krishna Bhattar my sadness, anger, and loss. I told him I felt the unthinking development of my hometown had taken Dandu Shastri away and then poor Lakshmana as well. He listened and then with his voice dropping in empathy, he quietly said,

> Our whole life we spend searching for the wonder of God but when he calls someone we love we are surprised, for we are not ready to let go. But that does not mean our misrecognition and loss is the only thing that is real. When we reach him ourselves, when our *prana* [Sanskrit: breath] leaves us, and we surrender unto him, then we can understand that wonder of life, feel it as real, and then, only then, can our *atman*

[soul] rest eternally. That is the true delight, the summation of nonexistence. Like a water droplet returns to the ocean, we return to our Lord. Then we can finally rest in eternal delight, having merged with him!

At that time, I was focused on my irretrievable losses, irritated by what I then heard as platitudes, empty philosophizing in the face of an irreparable wound. "Droplets returning to the ocean?" I thought irritably.

I snapped at Krishna Bhattar in my self-indulgent irritation: "What does one do until then? Until one reaches our Lord? Until this droplet reaches the ocean?"

He tilted his head and patted the threshold on which he sat as an invitation to join him, smiling as I accepted. "What to do until then? You have to ask, Tulasi? You know this ending is just another beginning, yes? So until then, what can we do? We 'ad-just'!"

INTRODUCTION: WONDER, CREATIVITY, AND ETHICAL LIFE IN BANGALORE

1. Bhadrapaada usually falls in the month of September in the Gregorian calendar.

2. This *bhajan* (hymn) is very popular across India for its rousing tune. It can be roughly translated as "I seek refuge with Lord Ganesha."

3. Man-made lakes are referred to as tanks in Bangalore.

4. I focus on everyday Hindu ritual life as a site of wonder, purely for its enduring and perverse pleasure, for as anthropologists know, ritual is a frayed site of inquiry for us.

5. Frits Staal (1930–2012), in his lifelong work on Hindu Vedic rituals, developed a well-known theory on the meaninglessness of rituals (1989); anthropologists Bruce Kapferer (1983), Stanley Tambiah (1979), and Richard Schechner (1974, 1993, 2002) concentrated on ritual performativity in South Asia; and Caroline Humphrey and James Laidlaw (1994), writing on Jaina forms of worship, unpacked liturgical rituals. But besides one notable exception (Clooney 1990), the value of the indigenous theories of ritual, for instance the Purvamimaṃsa school, or the theory on (rasa) aesthetics of theater and dance performances (Pollock 2016) have not yet been sufficiently recognized in ritual theory. Most recently, Axel Michaels (2016) has written a comprehensive study of South Asian ritual life that does justice to indigenous theories of ritual life.

6. Ritual is said to be derived from *ṛta*, "order, truth," or from the Indo-European root *srew*, "to flow" (cf. Turner and Turner 1978, 243–44). In the first case, the cosmological order is in the foreground; in the second, the dynamic aspect is in the foreground (Michaels 2016).

7. The sage Bhartṛhari thought that it was this fracture, the *sphoṭa*, or splitting of the absolute itself, that echoed in time and space, through which the world came into being—an existential creativity. This breakage, the crack, is an empty space for creation to manifest. Creativity endures in this space of brokenness.

8. Hindu rituals and their links to the *Dharmashastras* have been descriptively compiled by Indological scholars such as P. V. Kane (1958) and Jan Gonda (1977, 1980).

9. The larger inspiration for this work grows out of a simple premise: that one can tell the all-encompassing story of radical religious change in a complex society like modern India through recording fragmentary creative shifts in practice in urban spaces where wonder discourse and practices inspire greater creativity.

10. We tend to think of expressive creativity as the purview of the arts, such as narrative and poetry (Lavie, Narayan, and Rosaldo 1993), or in the context of media studies, craft, and making (Hallam and Ingold 2007; Ingold 2013), or in the making of movies (Pandian 2015), often to suggest it is the finished work of a lone heroic auteur or a group of artists.

11. The one exception is Sherry Ortner (1978), who early on demonstrated that among the Sherpas of Nepal, rituals are a forum to negotiate status, question existing power relations, and develop new social structures.

12. The study of ritual focusing on its doing has inevitably circled around ritual efficacy (Seligman et al. 2008; Puett 2013), and in accordance with this rubric, changes in ritual practice were seen inevitably as a "mistake" or at best as "practical piety," a "façade of structural consistency that hides the internal tensions and accommodations generated between doctrine and practice by the human foibles and social ambiguities of everyday life" (Herzfeld 2015, 22).

13. In Greek, *thaumatazein*, the sudden descent of wonder, is thought to be evanescent, a descent from the cosmological to the human.

14. Tracing the intellectual history of Western thinking about wonder establishes a comparative framework for an ethnographic approach to wonder, rendering an account of what generates wonder when the ontological premises at stake are those of neither the Cartesian dualism that are the understood characteristic of modernity nor the relational nondualism commonly imputed to anthropological "others" (Scott 2016).

15. As Jerome Miller suggests, wonder creates a new understanding of certain experiences, charging them with ontological significance, because they "transform our knowledge of what is by awakening us to realities of which we would otherwise be oblivious" (1992, xii).

16. Natural philosophers such as Thomas Hobbes, Luigi Galvani, and Robert Boyle sought to explore otherness and conducted experiments in the physical and natural sciences in order to grasp the properties of life and the world. Explorers and collectors went to find and to bring back curiosities to fill the *Wunderkammers*, the cabinets of wonders of the European elite (Daston and Park 2001).

17. There are four Vedas, the ancient Hindu religious treatises that encapsulate the moral philosophy of Hindus—the Rig, Atharva, Sama, and Yajur Vedas. Each one is a compilation of thousands of stanzas set in poetic meters to be recited orally. The Sama Veda is unique in terms of its recitation. Believed to be the origin of Indian music, it is recited in a special cadence, with voices of different registers coming together to create a harmony.

18. There are uncanny similarities between what ritual practitioners do in crafting rituals and our work as ethnographers in telling people's stories—their thoughts, expressions, performances, and actions. I intertwine my voice with that of the localites,

with their critical insights, to cast theory in a new narrative register, one that connects the creativity of storytelling with the crafting of ritual in urban temple publics.

19. Two thousand hectares of lakes were infilled, and, in between 2005 and 2010, approximately fifty thousand trees in the city were felled.

20. The mapping of the city became a problematic and hazardous enterprise in this era, for land transformations were hidden, with land "going missing" from books, harassments and threats directed at evaluators and cartographers, and eruptions of turf wars between crime bosses and development syndicates. The local and national newspapers (both in English and Kannada) had stories of crime waves sweeping through the city, tales of murder and mayhem and of the toppling of politicians and corrupt business leaders over land grabbing (Nair 2007, 188–89). It allowed for cynicism, a breaking of the notion of the "common good" and civility, which had wide-ranging consequences for Bangalorean culture. Because of the vast amounts of unaccounted-for capital flowing through the land market in Bangalore, two outcomes were inevitable: first, a building boom in Bangalore that began in the late 1980s and took the form of three different waves lasting until 2011; and second, the influx of several crime and political syndicates, both national and global, aspiring to convert their dubious wealth into saleable assets.

21. The philosopher of religion Mary-Jane Rubenstein suggests that wonder responds to "a destabilizing and unassimilable interruption in the ordinary course of things, an uncanny opening, rift, or wound in the everyday" (2008, 10).

22. Land prices rose from Rs. 500 per square foot (US$10) in 1998 to Rs. 50,000 per square foot (US$1,000) in 2012. More recently, land prices have increased still further with built prices going up to Rs 80,000 per square foot. T. J. S. George, a Bangalorean journalist, writes of the cultural shifts that the IT revolution brought to Bangalore, underlining the insider-outsider dynamics that have played through the city as it has grown: "The old agreeable Bangalore was now replaced by an aggressive Bangalore where no one had time for his neighbours. Everyone was chasing success as measured by a new consumerist value system. A gladiator culture took over with the spirit of combat as its perennial feature. If the pre-IT immigrants made an effort to merge into Bangalore, the new combatants were too disparate to try" (2016, 29–30).

23. To become "Bangalored" in the United States was to be told that one's job had been shipped overseas, but in India, Bangalore has become iconic as an example of successful development.

24. In 2006 India accounted for 65 percent of the global offshore IT services and slightly less than 50 percent of business process outsourcing (BPO) services (Nasscom 2005–6), though the numbers have fallen since then as capital has found newer and cheaper labor. The BPO service industry also saw a boom, generating US$7.2 billion (Nasscom 2005–6) in the same time period.

25. Leela Fernandes suggests that the new middle class "shifted from older ideologies of a state managed economy to a middle class culture of consumption" (2006, xv) where the Indian citizen-consumer is the aspirational ideal. The boundaries of the Indian middle class and its mosaicked composition becomes a key indicator to its vitality.

26. Bangalore's official population of 8.2 million in the 2010 census puts it distinctly behind the major urban centers of Mumbai (approximately 13 million) and Delhi (approximately 10 million). After a decade and a half of economic "liberalization," as the entry into the free market was known in India, the growth rate for India stood at a formidable 9 percent, of which Bangalore contributed a GDP of US$83 billion. According to a picture-based story in Yahoo's finance pages: "A large skilled labour force, growth in manufacturing sectors and considerable foreign investments rank India as one of the fastest-growing economies in the world. The economic growth rate of the country is at 6.5% for 2011–12 and the CIA World Factbook estimated the GDP of India to be $4463 billion derived from purchasing power parity as of 2011." "India's Top 15 Cities with the Highest GDP," accessed November 3, 2012, https://in.finance.yahoo.com/photos/the-top-15-indian-cities-by-gdp-1348807591 -slideshow/.

27. Arjun Appadurai (1981) and C. J. Fuller (1984, 1988), in their magisterial studies of ritual life in South Indian Hindu temple publics, organized the everyday of ritual practitioners within the temple as servants of the king-god. The temple was a seat of redistributive economics where hierarchies were reanimated. In their reading, the lines between what is ritual space and nonritual space are held fast. One got the sense that the ritual world ended at the temple walls.

28. Meera Nanda suggests in her polemic *The God Market: How Globalization Is Making India More Hindu* (2011) that the number of adherents to all forms of religiosity has increased since the era of economic reform of the early 1990s.

29. I am referring to the ongoing critical discussion in religious studies of the provenance of a "non-western" religion (King 1999; McCutcheon 2001; Pennington 2005), arguing that the particularities of context and the problems of universalization create a new set of challenges for religious studies (Ramanujam 1989).

30. I knew as an adult, largely from hearsay, that one of my grandmothers who had passed away when I was very young "kept" madi (Tamil: ritual purity), by which it was understood that she kept to a religious and caste-based vegetarian diet that she cooked herself in a kitchen that was ritually cleansed. She would not eat food cooked by anyone else, and she would clean her own clothes and objects of use, ritually sanctifying them after every usage.

31. I was as puzzled as my American classmates by Louis Dumont's assertion that India's anti-individualism spoke to caste as a communitarian interdependence, where economic relations, unlike those in the individualist West, were incapable of exploitation, structured to hold the community together, or, as he put it, "an economic phenomenon [like exploitation] presupposes an individual subject," whereas in caste society, "everything is directed to the whole . . . as part and parcel of the necessary order" ([1966] 1980, 107).

32. The diversity and skill of opposition to Dumontian theory struck me as all of a piece (Marriott 1969; Kolenda 1973; Appadurai 1986a; Berreman 1991). I came away thinking that those writing about caste were doing interesting and valuable scholarship, but they were still merely adding to a body of knowledge already defined (Harriss-White 2003; Pandey 2013). For more on the flexible system, see M. N. Panini,

"M. N. Srinivas—Theory and Method" (talk given at National Institute of Advanced Sciences, Bengaluru, January 2017).

33. A mangalyam is a gold necklace with caste symbols identifying the female wearer as married.

34. Picking up on Sartre, the scholar of religion Robert Orsi asserts that "research is a relationship" between people (2005, 174). Moreover, he suggests that as scholars of religion become preoccupied with themselves as interpreters of meanings, they forget that they also participate in the network of relationships between heaven and earth.

35. Were these localites my "own" society? I wondered. The problem, of course, is with ownership and who or what one considers one's own.

36. John Ruskin, a leading Victorian essayist, Oxford artist, thinker, and social critic, brings together these questions of self-creation and the sublime. For him, the sublime, the wonderful, is a sister to the art of self creation (1849). But wonder, as opposed to wondering or dreaming, is the sudden bewilderment of (mis)recognition, of fascination, is an eruption into perception of another order, one that is creative and generative. And that is what we, as anthropologists, feel. Fieldwork itself is an object of wonder because it is not simple and transparent but vivid, occluded, and complex. Indeed, to wonder is to engage in a cognitive as well as an emotional process.

37. Hopefully, I do not have to point out that patriarchy forces women to do much of the "interpretive labor" to imagine life from a male point of view, an essential violence of omission (Graeber 2005, 407–8).

38. New biographies of Dr. Ambedkar, the Dalit legal scholar and writer of the Indian Constitution (Omvedt 1994; D. Gupta 2000, 218), tracing the historical and contemporary violence of the state on peoples who were "pariahs" (Viswanath 2014), or even the telling contemporary illusion of "merit" in the premier educational systems of new India (Subramanian 2015, 292–95), still dealt with male realms of power and achievement. They all supported the view that systemically caste might be dying, but it was constantly "revitalized" as individual castes gained and regained power (M. N. Srinivas 2003).

39. I turned to Lynn Bennett's (1983) study of Brahmin women in Nepal and Isabelle Clark-Decès's (2005) work on marriage and funerals to find spaces where women lived and breathed. As Bennett notes in her study of upper-caste Brahmin-Chetri Nepali women, women present an oddity within a patrifocal society like Hindu India (1983, 317).

40. Axel Michaels, in his magnum opus on South Asia ritual life, creates a Linnean taxonomy of Hindu ritual (2016). In it are six different families of rituals—*karma kriya* (ritual actions that define karma), *mangala* (auspicious ceremony), *samskara* (life cycle ritual), *kalpa* (set of rules for ritual action), puja (worship, adoration rites), *yajnya* (sacrificial rites), and utsava (festival rituals, usually processionals) (Michaels 2016, 7–9).

41. The etymology of *Muzrai* indicates it is an ancient Indo-Persian word meaning weight and/or measure. The "Muzrai department" is what people call the Department of Religious and Charitable Endowments or the Karnataka Government because I suspect the department measures in the income of all "public" Hindu temples and Islamic mosques under its purview.

42. Prior to the passing of the Hindu Religious Charitable Endowments Act, Hindu religious temples and shrines of the state of Karnataka were governed by five independent acts by territory: (1) the Karnataka Religious and Charitable Institutions Act, 1927; (2) the Madras Hindu Religious and Charitable Endowment Act, 1951; (3) the Bombay Public Trust Act, 1950; (4) the Hyderabad Endowment Act, Regulations, 2349F; and (5) the Coorg Temple Funds Management Act, 1956. All the disparate acts were conflated into the Hindu Religious Charitable Endowments Act, of the Government of Karnataka, 1997, accessed August 13, 2017, http://dpal.kar.nic.in/33%20of%20 2001%20%28E%29.pdf.

43. Here *oikonoma* (management) is usefully linked epigrammatically to economy and thrift (Agamben 1998, 4–5). The Hindu Charitable Act of Karnataka states that the state can "initiate action and hold inquiry for misconduct either suo-moto or on complaint received against an Archaka (priest), including an Agamika (liturgical scholar), Thanthri (ritual specialist), or Pradhan Archakar (chief priest), or on temple servants and to impose an appropriate penalty for proven misconduct." Hindu Religious Charitable Endowments Act, chapter III, section 16, accessed August 13, 2017, http://dpal.kar .nic.in/33%20of%202001%20%28E%29.pdf.

44. Studies of ritual process (Gennep [1909] 1960; Evans-Pritchard 1956; Turner 1974; Gluckman 1977) have focused rigidly on the performance of ritual society as a validation of the norms within society, a domestication of all that is dangerous and revolutionary. The Turnerian idea of antistructure was that ritual afforded a space for such limited revolutionary states to exist without affecting larger society. When the ritual ended, or soon thereafter, practitioners fell back into the hierarchy of structure, where "disturbances of the normal and regular" only give us greater insight into the normal (1974, 34–35). In keeping with such theories of religion, ritual worlds have been understood as atypical sites of creativity. Many changes in ritual have been regularly misdiagnosed as a "disruption," a "mistake," a "flaw," a "distortion," an "error," and a "failure" (for example, see Huesken 2007; Grimes 1988). Improvisation in ritual brings to mind Johan Huizinga's work *Homo Ludens* (1955), in which he defines play as marked out in space and time and creating a reality that is manipulatable.

45. Ritual acts are thought to "do" two things: repair the broken, entropic moral world and domesticate dangers within it (Seligman et al. 2008). Enactment of ritual is understood as therapeutic for the world, rendering it anew, transformative, constitutive of the terms of positive community, of recognition by the state, and individual devotion (Bell 1997).

46. The deity came from an old temple in Kudaloor, a town some hundred miles from Bangalore, where the temple had fallen into disuse due to lack of funds.

47. Dharma is a Vedic cosmological set of principles that give order and consonance to the world, morality to a social community, and a code of conduct to an individual. The *Dharmashastras*, a written compendium of ethics, are a comprehensive and cogent understanding of how dharma operates in the everyday lives of Hindus as both a cosmic and social moral order (Olivelle 2008, 503). Yet, as the anthropologist Joyce Flueckiger notes, what may be considered dharmic behavior is unclear: "It is not clear what the minimal practices or theologies might be that identify a person as Hindu. In daily life,

there is no assumption that there is a single *dharma* appropriate for all to follow" (2015, 6). Instead, there is custom, or achara, which leavens the rigidity of dharma. The moral code is built into and out of the symbolic, social, and material practices of everyday Hindu ritual life; the images, mythologies, institutions, performances, textual and vernacular traditions, art and material culture, festivals, and foodways that encoded the shifting moral, economic, political, cultural, and gendered expectations of people's worlds are the means by which novel dharma interpretations are imagined, constructed, and embodied (Flueckiger 2015). From the Sanskrit root *dhr,* meaning "to hold, support, maintain," dharma is the socio-moral grounding of Hindu identity and operates at both universal and individual levels. At the universal level, dharma is that which "holds the world together," a metaphysical concept often translated as "religion" or "way of life."

48. Although rarely mentioned in the Vedas themselves, they are world building and normative all at once (Olivelle 2008, 492). Barbara Holderege suggests that dharma establishes each part in its proper place and ensures that every aspect of the cosmic system is properly balanced and coordinated with every other aspect and thus contributes the maximum to its own evolution and to the evolution of the whole system (2004, 213–14). Written and complied between the fifth and second century BCE, the *Dharmashastra* corpus of the literature includes the *Dharmasutras,* academic treatises written in aphoristic form concerned with rules and conduct; the *Dharmashastras,* treatises on dharmic legal and social codes of conduct written in prose; and various commentaries (*bhyasa*) and digests (*nibandha*), which analyze the meanings of specific sutras and organize sutras according to content.

49. Jennifer Ortegren's dissertation (2016) makes a similar distinction between dharma and achara.

50. The Dharmic code does give elaborate instructions on ethics by caste and stage of life, called *varnashramadharma,* or gender, where *stridharma* dictates the code that women should follow, codified in the main for the three "superior" *varnas* or castes— Brahmin, Kshatriya, and Vaishya. In her analysis of the narrative construction of Hindu dharma among Sringeri Brahmins, Leela Prasad suggests that ethical practice is an "imagined text": "Underlying ethical practices is a dynamically constituted 'text' that draws on and weaves together various sources of the normative—a sacred book, an exemplar, a tradition, a principle, and so on. Such a text is essentially an imagined text. It is a fluid 'text' that engages precept and practice and, in a sense, always intermediary. In this imagined text the normative manifests as emergent, situated in the local and the larger-than-local, the historical, and the interpersonal" (2007, 119).

51. Creative ethics may be rooted in violence, a disruption, in failure of that which is familiar and stable, resulting in inevitable moral dilemmas that are unresolvable. It comes closest to what Veena Das imagines ethics to be, as "the expression of life as a whole," where often the ethical and unethical are less opposed than "knotted together" (2015a, 3–4).

52. It is tempting to associate creative ethics with a subaltern underprivileged position of complete resistance, but Dandu Shastri and Krishna Bhattar are not subalterns and neither is the ritual practitioner at the temples. This is a post-subaltern-global-moral-epistemology-in-the-making.

53. I see this as affording a much-needed provocation to a different model of theorizing and writing. It does not offer a concrete argument but rather gives possibilities.

54. Of course, what counts as thickness in ethnographic research has changed. Where it was once exhaustiveness in detail and description, it has shifted to a revelatory narrative unveiling highly integrated and systemic aspects of a culture (Ortner 2006).

CHAPTER 1: ADVENTURES IN MODERN DWELLING

1. As Michael Puett theorizes, subjunctive spaces encourage both the appreciation of perspective and the imagination of horizons (2014).

2. Sacred enspacements are, as Gerard van der Leeuw ([1933] 1986) argued, political. He identified four kinds of politics in the construction of sacred space: a politics of position, where every establishment of a sacred place is a positioning; a politics of property, where a sacred place is appropriated, possessed, and owned; a politics of exclusion, where the sanctity of sacred place is preserved by boundaries; and a politics of exile, a form of a modern loss of, or nostalgia for, the sacred. I suggest that not only must these politics be rethought with reference to emergent sacred spaces in Malleshwaram, but we need to think of ritual as process not as politics, to focus on the dynamism that ritual allows for.

3. One elderly resident, Chellappa, a devotee of the Krishna Temple, suggested that this divine vision, this eye of the lingam, allowed the whole of Malleshwaram to act as a magical lens and "see" the unseeable.

4. The kanne of the Kadu Malleshwara was in homage to a myth concerning the devotion of a forest dweller, Kannappa, who gave his eyes to cure the seeming blindness of god Shiva.

5. The presence of tanks as the appropriate landscape of romantic encounter wove a continuous thread in Kannada movies, bringing the folk love of water into the contemporary. Kings were valued for building public works such as steps into or leisure areas near the river.

6. The neighborhood of Malleshwaram, known in local parlance as a "locality," ran the length of a jagged set of granite hillocks that dipped on both sides into shallow hollows originally occupied by small lake beds but were now covered in small individual housing estates known as "colonies." To the immediate south of Malleshwaram was Swimming Pool colony, and to its north was the Rajajinagar Colony.

7. This grounding was due to an aesthetic understanding of the city that resonated through, and was kept alive by, everyday ritual performance—processions to caves, riparian festivals, woodland rites, and pilgrimages to deities that guard hillocks. Many of the city's foremost shrines were dedicated to gods and goddesses of landscape rocks (Rajajinagar Hanuman Temple), caves (Gavipuram Temple), and hills (Basavangudi Nandi Temple), creating a seamless link between topos, mythos, and divinity. Topological elements and their power in the landscape of the imagination of residents created and sustained an aesthetic understanding of the city that still reverberates

through ritualized performance. For localites, ritual enabled them to find continuity in discontinuity, to tell the story of the rents and tears caused by uneven land development, the entry of capital, the changing geographies of mobility, and the sutures of infrastructure and imagination.

8. The Malleshwaram I remembered from the late 1980s was a charming Victorian-style suburb of beautiful houses surrounded by big gardens. The neighborhood was socially and culturally diverse by this time, and the residential streets looked aesthetically pleasing with wide tree canopies and big gardens. Secular Hindu Bangaloreans who lived elsewhere in the city would venture into Malleshwaram to buy Brahmin foodstuffs, condiments, and pickles, to get materials for a puja, or to go to a temple or attend a "function" in one of the many civic institutions like the Women's Institute or the Vedantha Samaja.

9. But there was other less visible loss as well. As John Harriss observed, the transformation of cities like Bangalore, and neighborhoods like Malleshwaram, became progressively less welcoming to working class and urban poor: "The process of exclusion is of course the shift in the design of middle-class housing towards intensely privatized gated communities and condominiums, in place of the old more open housing colonies" (2007, 4–5). Malleshwaram became a vertical terrain of "flats," emphasizing a groundlessness to its urbanity and a privatization to its commons.

10. According to an independent website that belongs to a civic collaborative of "concerned citizens of Bangalore," the number of registered vehicles in Bangalore has skyrocketed. In 2009 alone over 3.6 million vehicles were registered in Bangalore; of those, 606,427 were cars and 2,607,536 were two-wheelers, an unimaginable increase. "Number of Vehicles Registered in Bangalore," September 22, 2010, accessed December 7, 2016, http://praja.in/en/gyan/number-vehicles-registered-bangalore. For more in-depth data on traffic pollution, water problems, etc., in Bangalore, see related pages at this website.

11. Here the decay of the landscape, its developed erosion as it were, signals the outbreak of *le mal d'archive* (archive fever) (Derrida [1995] 1996, 12)—it animates the capacity of the archive to deconstruct the teleology of these models that dominate our thinking about spaces of dwelling.

12. For Michel de Certeau, walking through the city, a mundane everyday reality, is an exercise of attunement to the jouissance of the city, which in turn makes the spaces alive (1984). For Sigmund Freud (1919), the uncanny of spaces remembered is not about reality of space but is an affective feeling based on interaction with a fantasy, a resemblance of a home/unhome-like space.

13. Radicalized Hindu memory required the physical rebuilding of lost precious landscapes, such as the birthplace of Rama, the bridge he supposedly built with the help of an army of monkeys to Ceylon, and certain Himalayan shrines that had fallen into ruin, were disputed, or were claimed with a vital virulence and recast as a national project of regeneration of a Hindu past.

14. The Ram Janam Bhoomi project of building a Hindu temple at the supposed site of the birthplace of the Hindu god Ram was controversial, to say the least. The site was host to both a mosque, the Babri Masjid built in 1528 under the orders of the

Mughal emperor Babur, and a temple believed by Hindus to be the birthplace of Lord Rama, the hero of the epic Ramayana. In a few short decades postindependence, it became the center of religious battles. With the rise of fundamentalist Hinduism also known as Hindutva, a militia of emboldened guerilla youth swarmed the mosque and brought it down one night in 1992. The Hindutva objective was to build an enormous temple on the site to discredit and disallow any Muslim presence.

15. This was a newish way to raise money for temple building. Traditionally, steps leading to the shrine would be auctioned to patrons, who would have their names carved on the steps. The belief was that the patrons would receive merits when pilgrims to the holy sites stepped on their names. This auctioning of building materials had been reconstituted as selling bricks for the Rama Temple. In some cases, the bricks were said to have the name of the donor etched on them.

16. According to a story by the Indian Express news service "BANGALORE, July 3, 1997: Tuesday's gangster shoot-out in Bangalore may have signalled the entry of international and Mumbai underworld figures into the garden city. Worried police officers say that Bangalore is now likely to be the bone of contention between Dubai-based don Dawood Ibrahim and Mumbai don Chota Rajan. Muthappa Rai, who police believe is a member of the Dubai don's gang, is suspected to have planned Tuesday's shoot-out at Banashankari, which claimed the life of gangster Seena alias Srinivasa. Rai had fled the city two years back after killing a rival, Amar Alva. Mumbai's underworld don, Chota Rajan, now based in Singapore, appears to have realised that Dawood who is losing clout in Mumbai, has shifted his attention to Bangalore. Rajan is reported to have selected Bangalore as he and his gang members are sure that Dawood will one day return to Bangalore where his henchmen have bought sizable property."

17. These apartments boasted more luxury amenities than ever before: indoor gyms, swimming pools, security and concierge services, parking for one or more cars, tropical landscaping and indoor courtyards, modernist elevators sheathed in milky white marble, mirrored doors, and carved gilded gates.

18. As de Certeau notes in his essay on walking in the city, one's experience of the urban is actually a poetics and rhetorics of individuation, a construction and evocation of selfhood that separates the individual from the "legible" order of the city instituted by planners (1984, 157–58). For localites, as for de Certeau, the everyday experience of the city is different from the official, as it takes place in the gaps of power structures, and it gestures to affect and poetics more than to logics and analytics.

19. A brief history of Malleshwaram commences with an epidemic of the plague in the *pette* (city) (circa 1890) when colonial governors worked with local administrators to carve a sanitary and salubrious neighborhood out of clean virgin forest to the north of the city and named for the twelfth-century Kadu Malleshwara temple in the forest. Malleshwaram was planned as early as 1892 and was executed in 1898 "with some urgency" due to the intensity of the plague epidemics that swept through the then city. The neighborhood was to be a "distinctive social and material milieu" that could withstand "a deluge of six inches" of continuous rainfall during the monsoon and yet emerge unscathed (Nair 2007, 66–69). With its wide streets, logical

grid, conservancy lanes, and big homes, it was thought to keep pestilence at bay. Most of the early residents were upper-caste families, but other caste and religious groups such as Vaishyas (Sanskrit: traders), Agassa (washermen), and Gollas (milk vendors) also built homes in the neighborhood. The early residents were bourgeois professionals—teachers, doctors, lawyers, newspaper magnates, and other prominent urban citizens.

20. The wide, tree-lined avenues were remnants of British colonial planning. For the British, the indigenous area of the city—known as the pette—with its narrow lanes, multiple family residences, and lack of open space, was considered the very worst in city planning that "nourished disease and death" (Nair 2007, 46). The Indian city had "the elusive contradictory, negotiated, tentative and fluid meanings" (Hosagrahar 2005, 45), where British attitudes and anxieties rendered the native city full of fearful problems. When the British planned portions of the city including Malleshwaram in the late nineteenth century, they insisted on wide roads and big housing plots.

21. As Smriti Srinivas notes, the shift from a layout of gardens to that of a grid was achieved through multiple regulations and laws passed from federal to local authorities and not through one urban planning body (2001, 48), thus leading to confusions between form and meaning.

22. Disorientation, part of Guy Debord's critical and political reading of city space, became in itself a familiar feeling in wandering around Malleshwaram. This repeated disorientation suggests a "critique of dominant images of urban form and their appropriation and mutation into new diagrams" representing the city as "supremely open to change, as a sensitive register of the desires of its inhabitants" (McDonough 2005, 8), which allowed for a "weaving of alternate tapestries" (Smith qtd. in Eade and Mele 2002, 12) flowing through the city's "isolatable and interconnected properties" (de Certeau 1984, 94). The concept of dérive, as a "passionate shift [dépaysment passionel] through the hurried change of environments" (McDonough 2005, 7–8) where the known city recedes, and an emergent one of unknowns and unseen, unmapped affect, and sensual meaning—a sensorial and subjective mapping exercise—was at play, bringing la vie quotidienne (the de Certeauian "everyday") to life in strange and uncanny context.

23. Jürgen Habermas's notion of the public rested in a concept of the civic where citizens came together to discuss problems with state-based authority. But it also implies a spatial concept, an arena where meanings are articulated, distributed, and negotiated, as well as the collective body constituted by, and in this process, "the public." Habermas's ([1962] 1989) notion of the public is set within the larger embourgeoisement of European society and the decline of its publics, similar in some ways to the rapid neoliberalization of Bangalore and the decline of public space.

24. For an excellent though condensed social history of the neighborhood and its essential inclusivity, see S. K. Aruni, "Made for all Communities," The Hindu, March 6, 2013, http://www.thehindu.com/news/cities/bangalore/made-for-all-communities /article4481321.ece. Aruni is the deputy director of the Indian Council for Historical Research, Bangalore.

25. As Lauren Berlant notes, "The past was present in the way locality was constructed in a zone of precarity" (2011, 684; see also Biehl 2005).

26. The palimpsest of Malleshwaram is a layered text in which previous traces can be detected, where buildings and roads undergird and overlay experiences, values, and meanings. As Jeffrey Kroessler (2015) notes, "No city without a tangible, tactile history, without the capacity for denizens and visitors to reach into the past while experiencing the present, can be truly vital."

27. The Kannada Cheluvaliga movement raised calls of a "return" to linguistic purity, "*hesaraayithu Karnataka, usiruaagali Kannada* [Kannada: the name is Karnataka, now let the breath be Kannada]," seen as ethnic purity and a movement away from the excessive Westernization and cosmopolitanization of the space of the city.

28. The Karnataka state government had supported the rise of such Kannada culture purity movements through subsidizing language classes, Kannada language movies, and other Kannada cultural activities.

29. Mestri is a Dalit caste group of Karnataka, recorded in the Scheduled Caste and Scheduled Tribe Act (1978). The Mestri were traditionally stone masons. But confusion reigns as to their caste category, as there is a marked overlap in people's minds between the Mestri caste in Karnataka and the Mistry caste of Gujarat, who claim to be Vishwakarma Brahmins, descended from Lord Vishwakarma, the builder of the universe.

30. Lakshmi is the goddess of wealth and domesticity and is worshipped for prosperity and peace, in particular by married women.

31. It was Jean Baudrillard (1975) who noted that human-environmental interactions are subordinate to the dominant modern perspective not only because they are popularly imagined as preceding it in social evolutionary time but also because they are represented as "mere" beliefs.

32. The Cosmic Purusha is a wellspring of all creativity. In early Vedic theology, the Cosmic Purusha is described as a being whose sacrifice forms the universe, but in later Hindu theology, it evolved into an abstract form opposite to matter (*Prakriti*). This antimatter is represented as a magical person, in a diagram or *mandala*, as the soul of beingness and harmony.

33. Our argument should be informed by Mircea Eliade, who argues that ritual "enables people to experience the ontologically real and meaningful, to regenerate cyclical notions of time, and to renew the prosperity and fecundity of the community" (Eliade 1993 qtd. in Bell 1997, 11), and so "ritual makes creation over again" (Eliade 1993, 346).

34. Citing a revealing number of judicial cases over the acquisition of land by the city government, Janaki Nair (2015) notes that the BDA did acquire 10,458 acres out of the 19,054 slated for acquisition by 1991, but only 5,750 acres were used for housing. For more information, see T. V. Sivanand, "CAG Finds Fault with Denotification of Land Acquired by Housing Board," *The Hindu*, December 26, 2014, http://www.thehindu.com/todays-paper/tp-national/tp-karnataka/cag-finds-fault-with-denotification-of-land-acquired-by-housing-board/article6726757.ece.

35. In 2016, after I finished fieldwork, without any warning Prime Minister Modi engaged a "demonetization" policy to cut out the black money in the marketplace by only allowing people to deal in bank-authorized cash. This demonetization caused untold hardship for the middle classes, who largely dealt in cash, and people had to stand in long queues at banks to get a rationed amount of "white money" from their bank accounts to spend every day. The entire economic system froze for several months, demonstrating the amount of black money that lubricated the system on an everyday basis. The newspapers castigated Modi for a self-inflicted economic crisis.

36. In Hindu philosophical and moral understandings of time, there are four *yugas*, or epochs, in which morality is slowly eroded. The analogy is made to a cow with four legs in the first *satya yuga* or the epoch of truth, with three legs in *treta yuga* or the second epoch, two legs in *dwapara yuga* or the third epoch, and finally balancing on one leg in the last epoch of *kali yuga*, our contemporary time period, in which sin is rampant.

37. Gilles Deleuze and Félix Guattari argue that the essential relation in life is not between matter and form nor between substance and attributes, but rather between materials and forces (2004, 377). For them, materials with variable and different properties, enlivened by the forces of the cosmos, mix together through and into the generation of things, enfolding one into the other.

38. The Cosmic Purusha is a Vedic concept. It is believed that the sacrifice of the Purusha is the origin of creation. In Later Vedic and Upanishadic texts, Purusha changes into a universal principle and is set in opposition to Prakriti or matter. The Vedicpurusha is drawn materially as a seated man whose body forms the cosmos.

39. He told me that he called himself a "doctor" because like all doctors, he "diagnosed" a problem and healed it.

40. Leaving aside the undeniable effects of modern repression, and without seeking to account here for what Freud called "the return of the repressed," the symptoms are specters that haunted localites.

41. The Gomukha site is believed to be the most sheltering in Vaastu standardization. It is therefore also the most valuable site, as Hindus who believe in Vaastu will pay a premium for it in the open market.

42. One crore is approximately US$650,000, or 100 million rupees.

CHAPTER 2: PASSIONATE JOURNEYS

1. Pongal, the larger festival of which the Kanu Pandige is a part, is centered around the "pongu" or boiling over of a dish of fresh milk and newly harvested rice in a new clay pot—the *pongal pannai*—a potent aspirational symbol of the hoped-for material abundance of the harvest and a flourishing of self, family, and community. This ritual marks not only the everyday, the ordinary, the routine, the days of the year, the months, and the seasons but also the time of life itself. The festival cries of "*Pongallo, pongal* [Tamil: May the milk boil]" and greetings of "*Paal pongitha?* [Tamil: Did the milk boil over?]" expressed a hope and anticipation of flourishing and a greeting of

the subjunctive condition of prosperity. It is the simple aspiration to live a better life than before, deeply tied to the anxiety of economic and social mobility but framed in ritual terms.

2. I do not suggest that the Kanu Pandige is unique in this aspect but rather the opposite—that many Hindu festivals link seasonality and the Hindu lunar calendar, and though modern and Western notions of time govern many aspects of urban life in India, festivals, whether Hindu or Muslim, are often movable feasts based on the lunar calendar rather than the Western Gregorian calendar.

3. To view a video of the Kanu Pandige procession please visit https://www.youtube .com/watch?v=7U3Ha1HQgI8&feature=youtu.be.

4. I am grateful to Marilyn Goodrich for this idea.

5. The patron's family had become a patron to the temple through inheritance of the yajamana, or sacrificer status, from his father. Most of the larger patrons of the temple had inherited their status, being the sons or grandsons of the original builders of the temple. They were all uniformly upper-caste Brahmin families to whose homes the gods occasionally paid a visit on festival days. But there were newer occasions to become patrons that were more egalitarian. Many dominant caste families had become patrons of the temple by contributing to a new pavilion, or a new golden cradle for the deity, or clothes, silver lamps, or even a new vehicle for the processions. For these "new" patrons, the status of having the god visit was not available but they received the status of having their names carved on the building they donated and being recognized by the priests and the community or worshippers for their good works. Their families often received "special" treatment from the priests, including reserved seating close to the sanctum, extra prasadam, and other ritual perks.

6. Obviously she was a privileged middle-class woman and the complaints of waiting would be very different from a poor woman's.

7. The liberalization of the economy has broken up the social welfare state and reorganized corporations to reduce jobs, while simultaneously media images and globalization have given people an appetite for prosperity and success, and the two combined have pushed people into spaces of limbo. Emergent fields of fluid power, through the global reorganization of capital and the industrial state nexus, allow for endless waiting as refugees and migrants, marginal groups and workers all wait in limbo for beginnings.

8. But according to Jarrett Zigon, morality and ethics are different. Morality is not "thought out beforehand," nor is it "noticed when performed." It is "simply done" (Zigon 2008, 9). Ethics, on the other hand, is a "kind of reflective and reflexive stepping away from the moral discourse or habitus. It is brought about by a moral breakdown or problematization" (Foucault 1984, 388, qtd. in Zigon 2008, 18). Ethics is a conscious movement away from the taken-for-granted quality of morality, a critical stance, and necessitates, as Zigon notes, "a working on the self" as it presumes "conscious question or dilemma" with regard to the moral habitus and necessitates working through this dilemma (2008, 18).

9. Rasa is thought to be the cumulative result of "*vibhava* [Sanskrit: stimulus], *anubhava* [Sanskrit: involuntary reaction], and *vyabhicari bhava* [Sanskrit: voluntary

reaction]" (Schechner 2002, 29). This raises questions regarding how the whole sensorium is or can be used in performance and interrogates the intellectual distinction we hold between theater and spectacle and the tensions subsumed therein (Beeman 1993, 369).

10. An aesthetic founded on emotive gesture and the logics of sensuality is markedly and experientially different from one founded on the Greek *theoria* or analysis. Theoria is a way of seeing, a contemplation, related to *theorema*, "spectacle" and/or "speculation" (Schechner 2002, 30), and this binding of "knowing" to "seeing" is the root metaphor/master narrative of Western thought. Whereas in the Hindu tradition, feeling is also bound to knowing, it is postulated as a different kind of knowing located in the interaction of emotion between the performer and the spectator.

11. Bhakti is an individualized, overwhelming sense of belief that connotes (from its history as a Hindu reform movement of the fifteenth to seventeenth centuries) a normative communitarian ideal of prayerful submission. And as Christian Lee Novetzke brilliantly notes in his tracing of the receptions of bhakti, manifestations of this subjective belief are in essence "performances that are part of, or help form, publics of reception" filled with affect (2007, 255).

12. Richard Schechner notes that rasa aligns with aesthetics and performance. It is "sensuous, proximate, experiential. Rasa is aromatic. Rasa fills space, joining the outside to the inside" (2002, 29).

13. As Schechner notes in his creation of the neologism *rasaesthetics*, the *Natya Shastra* is not a complete text but "fragmented, sub-merged, misplaced, and unread," and this fragmentation and subsequent interpretation and reinterpretation evoke the nature of mobility over time and space, as well as the "aliveness" of the tradition as "active, oral and corporeal" (2002, 28).

14. While Krishna Bhattar and others recognized emotion and feeling as important, the anthropologist Stanley Tambiah suggests that ritualized behavior was not meant to express intention, emotions, or states of minds of individuals who performed the ritual but to "distance" individuals from spontaneous expressions because such expressions could be "contingent, labile, circumstantial, even incoherent or disordered" (1985, 132), and ritual was a means of deploying, channeling, and divesting these incoherent emotions and chaotic states, and antisocial ways of being toward a Durkheimian social effervescence that brought the community together. But Bruce Kapferer has argued otherwise: that ritualized behavior employs "conventional," as in conventions of, rather than "genuine" or authentic individual emotion (1979), and this is particularly significant in our understanding of how ritual operates through theatrics because affect is considered to be primordial and therefore foundational—an intensity owned and recognized.

15. In "performing passions," as the sociologist Donald Brenneis notes, "participants are engaged with the symbols in the interactional creation of a performance reality, rather than merely informed by them as knowers" (1987, 236). So considering knowledge alone is not enough; rather, it is the imagination, passion, emotion, and the senses that understand ritual.

16. *Abhinayadarpanam* is usually dated between the tenth and thirteenth centuries AD.

17. I am made sensitive to the fact that my bewilderment is only made sensible through disruption at this point and the question of the familiar being creative is not attended to here. What of the ordinary made extraordinary? These and other such questions will anchor chapter 5.

18. *Jati* literally translates as species. It is used in that sense to describe the good pedigree of agricultural animals.

19. Gollas in Karnataka are a subcaste group of Yadavas with fictive kinmanship to the god Krishna as a cowherd. In North India, Gollas would be on par with the North Indian Yadava caste group the Ahirs, who are traditionally herdsmen. See Singh 1998, 44–45; Yadava 2006.

20. *Art silk* was a local term used for artificial silk.

21. When I was growing up in Delhi, my mother always received a letter on Kanu Pandige day. The letter would contain three auspicious, turmeric-stained yellow threads with withered jasmine flowers, to be worn on the wrist. They were sent by my grandmother, along with some money, for my mother and her two daughters to celebrate the festival.

22. Viraha as an established emotion of the *navarasa* (Sanskrit: nine tastes) is termed *virahabhakti*.

23. Originally the Sanskrit text the Natya Shastra carried an affective categorization matrix of the navarasa in which the eight emotions, other than wonder, were associated with different gods and colors—*shringaram* (love, attractiveness), *hasyam* (laughter), *raudram* (fury), *karuṇyam* (tragedy, mercy), *bhibhatsam* (disgust), *bhayanakam* (horror, terror), *viryam* (heroism or bravery), and *adbhutam* (wonder, amazement). A ninth rasa was added by the dramatist Abhinavagupta in the eleventh century—*shantham* (peacefulness, contentment)—and the entirety, referred to popularly as the navarasa, fueled the twelfth-century understandings of the bhakti devotionalist reform movement within Hinduism. It is usually in reference to either performance or this reform movement that the navarasa is used in contemporary popular religious discourse in Bangalore today.

24. It is important to note that in Hindu devotional literature of the bhakti movement, even the pain of loss that the devotee feels when separated from God is understood to be joy and an evocation of *Parama prema* (supreme love) for the deity.

25. An experience of wonderment is one of the imaginative experiences that could be included in David Shulman's (2012) explanation that thought or desire (Sanskrit: *bhavana*), the intention (Sanskrit: *sankalpa*), and the imagination (Sanskrit: *kalpana*) link together to form a reality (Sanskrit: *klp*).

26. In 2013, with the aggravated rape and assault of a young woman in Delhi city, the anxiety of the urban condition became painfully obvious. Other everyday events such as governmental corruption, the problem of urban housing, and poverty despite the promises made at the liberalization of the Indian economy brought home the precariousness of the urban poor and the middle classes.

27. Indeed, even today in India, men are rarely kept waiting. Adult men are served food first usually by women or younger men in the family. They are offered all the ritual elements such as the camphor flame before women in the temples. So waiting

would suggest a reversal, an unnatural state of being that would induce anger and frustration.

28. Ann Gold tells a typical story of *nindasthuthi* devotion. In her telling, *Jungli Rani* (Queen of the Forest or the Uncivilized Queen), a vernacular tale told in Rajasthan, is a case of devotional power, where the girl threatens to hurt God and shatter his *murthi* (image) into pieces (Raheja and Gold 1994).

29. According to the Reserve Bank of India and the Finance Ministry, the numbers are staggering:

150 million: People who earn between Rs 3.4 lakh and Rs 17 lakh a year [a lakh is 100,000 Indian rupees]. Their number is growing at 13 per cent.

800 million: People who earn between Rs 45,000 and Rs 3.4 lakh a year. Their number [is] growing at 3.2 per cent.

89 per cent: Percentage of tax payers earn between Rs 0–5 lakh per annum. The maximum burden is on those earning Rs 2 lakh to Rs 5 lakh—the lower middle class.

22.8 per cent: The household saving rate in 2010–11, a sharp fall from 25.4 per cent in the previous year, showing an erosion of savings.

12.1 per cent: Growth in personal loans in 2011–12, down from 17 per cent in the previous year as consumers cut down on spending.

Source: Nayar 2012.

30. The Aam Aadmi [Hindi: ordinary man] Party (AAP), born out of the India Against Corruption (IAC) activist movement, was launched in 2011. Millions of Indians peacefully protested against widespread corruption in government. Arvind Kejriwal, founder of the AAP, along with other prominent leaders like social activist Anna Hazare and former police officer Kiran Bedi, demanded an anticorruption bill to cleanse the government of corruption. The Delhi State Assembly elections of 2013 provided the first political platform to the AAP to officially contest elections.

31. Nita Kumar describes an alternate reality in the experience of time for the artisans of Benaras. They were constantly and notoriously unpunctual. Time for them is akin to a feeling, where doing what moves one is of prime importance, rather than keeping to appointments. It is not, as Ramanuja suggested, that time has no importance but rather that time is too important. It cannot be sacrificed for any purpose "arbitrarily"; it has to be lived "to the full, every bit of it." So there is no real sense of hurry, no sense of time "slipping" or flying by. Time is not an external that is to be spent gainfully but is a way of feeling. The way you feel, "what you are moved to do, is what time it is" (N. Kumar 1988, 96–97), an aesthetic and sensual register of time. This sense of feeling alters one's sense of time and of reality in toto.

32. Raja Rajeshwari is a female deity, a form of Shakti or Parvati, the consort of Shiva. Thayaar, however, was supposedly Vaishnavite in that they were consorts to Krishna, a form of Vishnu. The procession was thus a syncretistic link between Vaishnavite high-caste ritual and folk Shaivite ritual.

33. Traditionally foreigners, that is, non-Hindus, were termed *mleccha* (foreign or having no caste), and they had no caste. As such, then, they were prevented from

assuming positions of any consequence, or indeed partaking at any level, in ritual sequences. In the past decade, as more Bangalorean Hindus have had mixed racial and cultural marriages, the foreign-born member of the family is merely treated as the rest of the family in terms of caste and status, though usually no official conversion ceremony or purificatory rite is held.

34. When using a convention, one can rightly think of text-structured behaviors. Ironically, however, Clifford Geertz himself provided the most lucid account of shifting ritual and emotion in his essay "Blurred Genres," in which he suggests that drama is beyond text and also beyond convention. That is, "prima facie, the suggestion that the activities of spies, lovers, witch doctors, kings, or mental patients *are moves or performances* is surely a good deal more plausible than the notion that they are sentences" (1980a, 30, emphasis mine). In fact, Geertz's understanding of ritual as a "blurred genre"—as something plastic—and a manipulatable game is in reality closer to what we find in Malleshwaram.

35. There is even a blog titled *Solpa Adjust Maadi* that describes the phrase as "unmistakably Bangalorean." See *Solpa Adjust Maadi*, accessed December 7, 2016, http://solpaadjustmaadi.blogspot.com/.

INTERLUDE: UP IN THE SKYYE

1. People from this topography were known as Dakhani in the north to distinguish them from those of the Indo-Gangetic plains.

2. *Load shedding* is a term used all over India to describe scheduled rolling black-outs when energy is at a premium.

3. WhatsApp is a free technology allowing information sharing that is very popular in India.

CHAPTER 3: IN GOD WE TRUST

1. The kasu mala is a traditional South Indian piece of jewelry made by knitting gold coins together to form a long necklace. It is usually worn by Hindu women and traditionally by the upper caste and wealthy. Women who had kasu mala traditionally had high status, often from very wealthy and powerful families.

2. Cashpoint cards are credit/debit plastic cards issued by banks.

3. Even today, as Bill Maurer (2006, 17) notes, anthropologists have remained loyal to the promises offered by the evocative symbols of devils and demons, narratives of great pollution, and teleologies of decline and despair as the common threads in the discussions around money.

4. A *New York Times* article quotes a Mumbai businessman about the prosperity rituals for Ganesha and the anxiety over money and rising prices in India: " 'People are coming because they are insecure—about rising prices, about the way ladies are treated,' Mr. Dahibawkar said. 'The government is not just to them. Only God.' " Ellen Barry, "Uncertain Times in India, but Not for a Deity," *New York Times*, September 18, 2013.

5. One lakh is 100,000 rupees; one crore is 1 million rupees.

6. Historical trade in Kerala pepper, luxury spices, and perfumes led to uncountable wealth. Pliny the Elder in 77 BC noted that India had become a "sinkhole" for Rome's gold. The Dutch, French, Portuguese, and British who conquered India often complained similarly.

7. Historians have estimated that in the eighteenth century, one-third of all gold bullion in the world was in India, in the vaults of temples like Thiruvanthapuram (Parthasarathi 2011).

8. The temporary accumulation of treasure at temples reminds one of the essence of antiproduction—a temporary accumulation of specific goods that the society deems of intrinsic value (Bataille [1949] 1991). In antiproduction, all lines of allegiance flow to the person of highest consequence. It is the economic system of the sovereign deity where the patchwork system of debt and reciprocity all flow to the deity in a form of unidirectional debt formation—debt for life, debt for success, debt for education, debt for health, and so on. The tribute to the deity is in lieu of payment of such debt, the payment of centuries of debts in the form of vows.

9. Gold is among India's largest imports; from "6.9 per cent of total imports in 2008–2009, costing US$29.9 billion, it increased to 11.5 per cent in 2011–2012, amounting to US$56.5 billion—an increase of 200 per cent" (Gandhi 2013, 93).

10. http://profit.ndtv.com/news/corporates/article-indians-to-buy-less-gold-in-2012 -own-20-000-tonnes-worth-1-trillion-survey-305540, last accessed August 16 2017.

11. In 2001 gold was US$271 per troy ounce; by February 2013 it had reached US$1,575 (Gandhi 2013, 93).

12. Almost all of the gold in India is imported; Indian mines satisfy less than 1 percent of domestic demand. Thus, gold—more than any other single commodity or service—"results in a net outflow of money from the country" (Gandhi 2013, 93).

13. This is particularly true of the precious metals that make gold jewelry, such as the gold that makes up a woman's *thali* (her marriage necklace), which denotes caste status.

14. Ellen Barry notes that in the Ganesha festival in Mumbai, wealthy devotees offered gold cradles, gold umbrellas, and other items made of gold and gems to the deity to thank the god for their gift of wealth. Barry, "Uncertain Times in India, but Not for a Deity."

15. The aesthetics of technology and newness that I have explored in chapters 1 and 2 fit in with this aesthetic of shiny newness and excess. Technology also shimmers or creates shimmer in people's lives, allowing for excessive illumination.

16. This is also true in the haute cuisine of French patisserie making, or the haute couture of mille-feuille silk folding.

17. This aesthetics of speculation is not unique to Bangalore but is also true of Vietnamese money offerings to spirits, in which fake money is burned to domesticate the demonic spirits of ghosts and hungry ancestors. Heonik Kwon notes a marked resistance to "foreign" currencies being used to appease the spirits, particularly to the fake American dollar (do-la) when it was introduced as spirit money (Kwon 2007, 75).

18. The International Monetary Fund (IMF) issued a report that stated, "Nations should admit that 'trickle-down' theories of wealth and prosperity do not work,"

along with a policy that spoke to the problem of growing structural inequality within nations. This followed an Oxfam report on income inequality. See Jon Queally, "IMF Report Admits IMF's Obsession with Capitalism Is Killing Prosperity," *Common Dreams*, June 16, 2015, accessed June 18, 2015, http://www.commondreams.org/news /2015/06/16/imf-report-admits-imfs-obsession-capitalism-killing-prosperity.

19. This section of the India-wide potter caste known as a Kumbhara was believed to call themselves Prajapati after the Vedic god of creation (Saraswati 1979, 46–47).

20. As M. N. Srinivas notes in his 1951 exegesis on the interdependence of the various castes in the village of Kodagahalli in Mysore, each caste had a separate caste-court with juridical control over caste fellows and the right to punish fellow caste members for offenses such as entering spaces where they were forbidden by virtue of their caste. The caste-courts were termed *gadi*, which means frontier or boundary, articulating the spatial circumscribing of the caste (1951, 1053–54). Interestingly, in his article Srinivas notes the caste-court case of a potter caste of Mysore that attempted to claim superiority over similar potter caste members in the surrounding villages such as Kodagahalli, Pura, and Arakere. They lost in every village but one.

21. Credit card advertisements create not only an attachment to an object but "attachments to an attachment," a pursuit of an elusive desire that can be gratified immediately but is not satiated or instantiated; rather, it is promised through a circuit of deferrals that lubricates a series of mobilizations (Žižek 2009). Credit card pujas with deferred payment systems were promissory vows that proved very popular.

22. "The concept of using a card for purchases was ostensibly described in 1887 by Edward Bellamy in his utopian novel, ironically titled *Looking Backward*. Bellamy, according to various chronicles, used the term credit card 11 times in this novel, although this referred to a card for spending a citizen's dividend rather than borrowing," Chidanand Rajghatta, "Till Debt Do Us Part," *Times of India*, February 20, 2013, accessed September 20, 2013, http://blogs.timesofindia.indiatimes.com/ruminations /entry/credit-card-nation-till-debt-do-us-apart.

23. Malini Goyal, "Rise in Credit and Debit Cards Spending Signals India's Transformation into a Cashless Economy," *Economic Times*, October 6, 2013, accessed April 7, 2017, http://economictimes.indiatimes.com/news/economy/indicators/rise-in -credit-debit-cards-spending-signals-indias-transformation-into-a-cashless-economy /articleshow/23596180.cms.

24. CTR is an acronym for Central Tiffin Rooms, a beloved local restaurant.

25. Interestingly, debit cards are much more popular in India. In 2005–6, the number of debit cards in the market was just 49.8 million. In 2007–8, the numbers grew to 102.4 million and, in 2009–10, to 181.4 million; accessed August 22, 2017. http:// indiafacts.in/money/credit-card-and-debit-card-users-in-india/.

26. Sandeep Singh, "Village India Relies More on Money Lenders Than Banks," *Indian Express*, July 24, 2007, accessed October 30, 2013, http://www.indianexpress.com /news/village-india-relies-more-on-money-lenders-than-banks/206480/.

27. Ketaki Gokhale, "As Microfinance Grows in India so Do Its Rivals," *Wall Street Journal*, December 15, 2009. This article argues that small credit lines were thought

to give agency to borrowers, but in point of fact, moneylenders and loan sharks still dominate the money-borrowing landscape of rural India.

28. The idea of runa or debt in Indian philosophy largely is a rationale for renunciation. The *Mahāsubhāṣitasaṃgraha* has the whole verse, whose purpose is to justify renunciation: ṛṇānubandharūpeṇa paśupatnīsutālayāḥ / ṛṇakṣaye kṣayaṃ yānti kā tatra paridevanā / [Cattle, wife, sons, home—these are examples of debt relationships. When the debt is finished, the relationships are too; what is sorrowful about this?]

29. The debt is the fructification of *sanchita karma* (the accumulated karma of past lives), which leads to *samskaras* (aptitudes and inclinations) and *vasanas* (desires). The karma ripens to become the debt (*prarabdha*), but the individual is presumed to have the free will to act in the current life (*kriyaman*), an agentive form of karma. The karma that envisages the future, a subjunctive karma (*agami karma*), is also agentive but in the imagination, where the future is thought to reside. Thus agami (intent and planning) leads to kriyaman (freshly executed actions of the present), which becomes sanchita (accumulated), to later surface as prarabdha (destiny).

30. *Satapatha Brahmana* 3.6.2.16 qtd. in Graeber 2011, 399.

31. Sacrifice acts as a tributary payment "interest," as it were, to postpone the inevitable. In the ancient texts of the *Shavaite agama*, the *Panchartara agama*, and the *Sri Sukta*, sacrifice was embedded in the daily worship cycle of the temple, described colloquially as *pahal path* (day ritual) and *ra path* (night ritual). The daily and annual cycle of time was for the work of sacrificial offering, a constant and enduring repayment cycle.

32. These dirty notes were a significant problem in turn-of-the-twenty-first-century India. The Indian state, despite promises of liberalization that the eager public had lapped up for a decade, had in fact hit a credit crunch, of which the soiled notes were a symptom. The largely cash-based economy of the country at the time meant that every bank note circulated through several hands, often many times a day. The notes fell to pieces in trading, so much so that one-, two-, and five-rupee notes were trading far above their value. Dandu was particularly adept at redistributing new and used currency to garner favor with various patrons. In a bizarre experiment, the state had decided, paradoxically, that they would not print any new "small denomination" notes while they reclaimed and destroyed defaced ones. But there was a deep chasm between governmental intention and action. The national newspaper *The Indian Express* gave the stringent conditions under which notes could be exchanged. The reporter Manju quoted Mr. B. S. Iyer, assistant manager of the State Bank of India, who said that "Banks like to shirk the responsibility of exchanging old notes. Most banks refused to accept soiled notes at their cash counters." Manju A. B., "Exchange Torn Currency Notes for New," *Indian Express*, May 18, 1997, accessed August 20, 2017, http://expressindia.indianexpress.com/fe/daily/19970518/13855263.html.

33. The Karnataka Act no. 33, or the Hindu Religious Charitable Endowments Act, answered "a long-standing public demand to bring about a uniform law for the regulation of all Charitable Endowments and Hindu Religious Institutions in the state." Prior to the passing of this uniform act, the Hindu religious temples and shrines of the state of Karnataka were governed by five independent acts by territory: (1) The Karnataka

Religious and Charitable Institutions Act, 1927; (2) The Madras Hindu Religious and Charitable Endowment Act, 1951; (3) The Bombay Public Trust Act, 1950; (4) The Hyderabad Endowment Act, Regulations, 2349F; and (5) The Coorg Temple Funds Management Act, 1956.

34. "All rights, title and interest vesting in the inamdar including those in all communal lands, cultivated lands, uncultivated lands, whether assessed or not, waste lands, pasture lands, forests, mines and minerals, quarries, rivers and streams, tanks and irrigation works, fisheries, and ferries shall cease and be vested absolutely in the State Government, free from all encumbrances." Hindu Religious Charitable Endowments Act, chapter II, section 4(g), p. 8, accessed July 13, 2012, http://dpal.kar.nic.in /pdf_files/16%20of%201960%20(E).pdf.

35. As Giorgio Agamben notes, the Greek term *oikonoma* (management) is usefully linked epigrammatically to economy and thrift (Agamben 1998, 4–5).

36. Spatikamani is a kind of fossil found in the rivers of the Himalayas and worshipped by Hindus as a symbol of Vishnu's divinity and purity.

37. Nakshatra is the star date of birth by the Hindu lunar calendar.

38. The religion scholar Deepak Sarma, in questioning his own "insider-outsider" Brahmin status, writes that when the Brahmin is a *Brahmabandhu*, an "unworthy" or "wicked" Brahmin who lacks proper piety as evidenced by laziness, gluttony, greed, intemperance, and unpunctuality—a loss of the ideal temperament—or one who is only nominally a Brahmin, or one who forfeits their eligibility through unwanted and trangressive acts, then one reconstitutes oneself as unworthy to bear the title (2001, 82–90). I am aware that this brief engagement with caste will seem overly simplistic to many fellow anthropologists; however, my interest is not to get into a complex discussion of Brahmanical hegemony but rather to look at corruption in terms of this understanding of the loss of an ideal type.

39. Distrust is a condition of the modern age, according to Russell Hardin (2006, 138).

CHAPTER 4: TECHNOLOGIES OF WONDER

1. Navaratri, literally "nine nights," is a pan-Indian Hindu nine-day festival dedicated to the female principle, Devi or Shakti. During the nine nights, the mother goddess is worshipped in different forms, and the festival culminates on the tenth day, called Vijaya Dashami (the tenth day of victory). In Bangalore, the capital of the state of Karnataka, Navaratri is part of the festival of Dussehra, a public celebration with statewide school and official holidays, big temple celebrations, and much gift giving and feasting.

2. Vishwakarma is a principle god of the Vedic Hindu pantheon, the divine architect of the universe, a creator and maker.

3. Curtain of "respect" that was drawn in front of the sanctum to visually block the deity from the devotees when he or she was being bathed, dressed, eating, or performing any other intimate activity.

4. Engineers in the GE laboratory alone filed ninety-five patents for new inventions in the United States between 2000 and 2003. Statistics like GE's phenomenal output

of new technologies were commonly discussed in the new pubs, new homes, new restaurants, and new golf courses in Bangalore.

5. By contrast, the conceptual pair of the virtual and the actual displays a very different logic. The virtual and the actual are both real; that is, they are different registers of reality, and the passage from the virtual to the actual is about differentiation.

6. Technology in Bangalore follows Jean-Luc Nancy's argument, of a "logos itself as ethos." Nancy's understanding of living with technology, the "abiding in the escape of the absence" (Nancy 2007, 90), is as the seat of wonderment and the unerring presence of wonder that allows intimacy and the possibility for any new creation.

7. The original Banashankari Temple was in the town of Bagalkot in north Karnataka. The temple was built by the seventh-century Kalyani Chalukya kings who worshipped the goddess Banashankari as their tutelary deity. Banashankari or Vanashankari was the consort to Shiva and the goddess of the forest.

8. Mixture, a popular teatime snack food, is a mix of different fried savory chips, nuts, and lentils. Krishna Bhattar used it to indicate both popularity and mixing.

9. In the Chandogya Upanishad, a compendious text, part of the Sama Veda, the first principle is said to be "the rule of substitution." This is equivalent to Quentin Meillassoux's "correlate." Patrick Olivelle in his magisterial work on the Upanishads describes an exchange between a seer and student in which this rule is explicated to describe the universal interconnectedness of all beings and of all time.

"You must have surely asked about the rule of substitution, by which one hears what has not been heard before, thinks of what has not been thought of before, and perceives what has not been perceived before?"

"How indeed does that rule of substitution work, sir?"

"It is like this, son. By means of just one lump of clay one would perceive everything made of clay—the transformation is a verbal handle, a name [*vācārambhaṇaṃ vikāro nāmadheyaṃ*]—while the reality is just this: 'it's clay.'

"That, son, is how this rule of substitution works."

Chāndogya Upaniṣad 6.1.3–6

10. The appropriation of the helicopter from the world of military and industrial flight into a world of cosmological flights of the imagination leads us to consider the process of appropriation. Appropriation may not merely be of practice, knowledge, or context but of some combination of the three.

11. I had previously called this discourse and the practice that arose from it "religious entrepreneurship" and termed Krishna and Dandu as religious entrepreneurs (T. Srinivas 2006). But *entrepreneurship* is a weak word for this ability to innovate under constraints that demonstrate a strength of flexibility and maneuverability, a resistance to the dominant forces of modernity, as well as a deep appreciation for a plurality of possible meanings.

12. Perplexity, bewilderment, and a loss of bearings are all heightened by the sudden realization of the sublime within the ordinary. The notion of the sublime in the Kantian romantic sense, as an aesthetic, is combined with Rudolf Otto's sense of the sublime as enfolded into the numinous of wonder (Kant [1790] 2007; Otto [1923] 1958). Technology is in itself not sublime, as Brian Larkin suggests in his study of electricity (2013, 328–30), but technology facilitates action that turns the devotee to wonder.

13. For a different perspective, see Brosius 2012.

14. The nadaswaram is a kind of recorder or flute.

15. Temple music, like other services rendered to the temple, often belonged to families, guilds, or caste groups that had inherited rights to play at a particular temple.

16. C. J. Fuller and Haripriya Narasimhan have suggested that this evaluation of temple musicians as playing "inferior music" is not uncommon (2014, 203).

17. *Archane* is personal worship for an individual or family. *Mangalaarthi* is worship with the camphor flame, the critical moment for *darshan* or sacred witnessing of the deity by the devotee.

18. As Michael M. J. Fischer notes in his analysis of the place of cinema in contemporary Iran, the cinema is a kind of "messianic space" in which modernity and religious discourse are set in agonistically generated multiple hybridizations of form and content, leading to a *heightened experimental regime* in which the taken-for-granted assumptions of everyday life become questionable (2004, 225).

19. I was brought to a consideration of the place of the camera as a new technology in eras past when I read M. N. Srinivas's classic ethnography *The Remembered Village*, in which he notes he was called the "chamara" man, for the camera that he carried. The irony that *chamara* in Kannada meant the yak tail whisk used to fan gods and kings was not lost on Srinivas (1980, 20). He described the surprise of the villagers and their cautiousness in having their photographs taken for fear of its magical power to steal parts of their souls.

20. An almirah is a big steel bureau and safe manufactured by the Godrej company in which many Indians stored their valuables.

21. Derrida, in his lectures titled *Archive Fever*, speaks to the passion of the archive. He deconstructs inscription as an act central to the archive, as a printing on the psyche, distinct from memory ([1995] 1996).

22. "New data from the country's 2011 census shows 59% of Indian households have a mobile phone. Only 47% have a toilet on the premises (and that includes pit latrines that don't use running water)," Annalynn Kurtz, "In India, More Cell Phones Than Toilets," CNN *Money*, March 14, 2012, accessed July 21, 2014, http://economy.money .cnn.com/2012/03/14/in-india-more-cell-phones-than-toilets/.

23. The iPhone was released in June 2007 and was not yet available widely in India. Vishwanatha saw it as a desirable good. Later, in 2016, he requested that my sister get the newest version of the iPhone for the temple. He was particular about the amount of memory and the look of the iPhone. He wanted "all black."

24. For many years Vishwanatha Shastri had requested several technological artifacts, cameras, recording devices, and so forth. I had always refused, unsure of the ethics of engaging in such a relationship with the priesthood.

25. *Ekadashi* is the eleventh day of the new moon cycle in the lunar-based Hindu calendar. It occurs twice in the Hindu calendar month, during the *Shukla Paksha* (period of the brightening moon also known as waxing phase) and the *Krishna Paksha* (period of the fading moon also known as waning phase). An auspicious day dedicated to the ancestors, it is marked by fasting and atonement.

26. The "missed call" is an ingenious hack found in the subcontinent replacing voice mail messaging as a cost-free alternative. A caller dials a phone and the receiver allows the phone to ring and calls the recorded number back. It allows for a number to be recorded without costing the initial caller any money. "Missed Call," Wikipedia, accessed October 22, 2016, https://en.wikipedia.org/wiki/Missed_call.

27. Antoinette DeNapoli argues that Brahman has been imagined in the classical texts in different ways, including the changing and expansive aspect that is probably found more in the Puranic literature and early Upanishadic and Vedic literature, but that in popular discourse a particular meaning has become fixed for Brahman, due to colonial neo-Hindu rhetoric that sought to construct a Hindu divinity that could compete with, if not outdo, the colonial Protestant idea of God (2017).

28. In the Mahabharata, the Pandavas' palace city was called Indraprastha and was built by Vishwakarma. He was such a master architect that floors shone like pools of water and ponds and lakes seemed dry. He possessed the ability to turn solids into air and vice versa, the sign of master craftsmanship.

29. See Kirin Narayan and Kenneth George on Vishwakarma (2017).

30. But I am sensitized to the politics of appropriation in the incorporation of the new. I suggest that appropriation is an opposition to the idea of creativity as the product of lone genius (Lavie, Narayan, and Rosaldo 1993). Appropriation as part of improvisation allows us not only to incorporate the new but also to locate creativity in discursive and dialogic frameworks of community enterprise.

31. This argument is separate from the politicization of technologies that the Hindu Right has recently engaged in, arguing that postmodern technologies were always known in ancient Hinduism.

CHAPTER 5: TIMELESS IMPERATIVES, OBSOLESCENCE, AND SALVAGE

1. Paul Ricoeur echoes this separation between endless timeness and subjective perception of time as moving, reading the phenomenon of time and its nature through what he calls the "aporia of temporality," by which he means the struggle between the instant of time itself and the subjectivist perception of the instant (1984, 19–28).

2. For Roy Rappaport, the term *ritual* denotes "the performance of more or less invariant sequences of formal acts and utterances not entirely encoded by the performers" (1999, 24). For him, "formality, i.e. adherence to form, is an obvious aspect of all rituals" (qtd. in Michaels 2016).

3. Here the ideas of possibility, creativity, and wonder at the intersection between modern and ritual time bring us to thinking about Henri Bergson's durée, of a duration that seeks to make visible the creative and inventive quality of time, where the creative impulse develops from the unexpected, the serendipitous, and the surprisingly regenerative. Bergson has argued that every moment in our lives is "a kind of creation," and so time is not incidental to processes of creativity but endemic to it ([1907] 1911, 7–8). The concept of duration "in which the past, always moving on, is swelling unceasingly with a present that is absolutely new" ([1907] 1911, 164) allows us

to foreclose on the untimeliness of newness as it spills into an emptiness of durative time. It allows us to move from the apparent novelties of the present "toward the temporal textures of experience" (Pandian 2012, 548) through which newness is encountered in the first place, a place in the time that foretells of the emergent.

4. The second phrase played with the Indian English idea of being on a call, which was shortened colloquially to "I'm on call," a slogan of being permanently available for advice.

5. I found that in conversations about change, time shifted. In fragments from conversation notes, field diaries, and recorded interviews, through a focus on ritual time and large shifts in modern time, time scales intertwined with each other, and as they did so they gathered modes of thought, action, care, and attention around each fragment of time. Following each ritual episode where temporality was interrogated, I tried to have discussions of time, where a certain way of both imagining and inhabiting time was confronted, in the hope that its generative force would be drawn into and through the text, illuminating the unfolding nature of time.

6. For Paul Rabinow, a definition of modern time as modern "in style" or "existing or occurring at, or dating from, the same period of time as something or somebody else" (2008, 1–2) gestures to the effects of the capitalist imperative of modern time in Bangalore. As Henri Lefebvre notes explicitly in *Rhythmanalysis*, there is "no rhythm without repetition in time and space, without reprises, without returns, in short without measure," but he insists, correctly, that while "there is no identical absolute repetition definitely . . . there is always something new and unforeseen that introduces itself into the repetitive" ([1992] 2004, 6). Far from being thought of, as Walter Benjamin notes, as "progression through homogenous empty time" (1968, 261), or Fredric Jameson's idea of time as a sense of temporality that depends upon the macroeconomic history of the world system (2003), there is, as Jane Guyer notes, a "convergence of temporal emphasis on public forms of representation and argumentation" (2007, 410), where a significant part of the analysis of the postmodern condition and globalization has revolved around the problem of time. Temporality considered here is neither episodic nor specific alone, but rather it is "punctuated" (Guyer 2007, 309).

7. In 2006 India accounted for 65 percent of the global offshore IT services and slightly less than 50 percent of BPO services, though the numbers have fallen since then as capital has found newer and cheaper labor. In 2005–6 the IT industry generated earnings of US$17.8 billion, an enormous amount of foreign exchange for a poor country like India. The BPO service industry also saw a boom, generating US$7.2 billion in the same time period.

8. Chris Walker and Morgan Hartley, "The Culture Shock of India's Call Centers," *Forbes*, December 16, 2012. In this article, Walker and Hartley report on the cultural training that call center employees receive in India to prepare them for having a conversation with U.S. customers and understanding their values. The trainer in this article, a young man by the name of Deep, once was a call center employee himself. The article focuses on Deep's biography as a young man with a large disposable income, off working hours, his recovery from a debilitating drug habit, and his successful training techniques to impart a facility with U.S. cultural mores and customs.

9. In Bangalore it is common to rhyme words in order to give them emphasis within the sentence.

10. The popular joke is that Indian Standard Time (IST) is also an acronym for Indian Stretchable Time.

11. A yuga is a unit of Hindu mythic categorization of time similar to an aeon. The yugic system is morally entropic and ends in pralaya, a spectacular flood that is the beginning of the apocalypse. The apocalypse commences when the Hindu god Shiva dances his dance of destructive-creation, the tandava. The universe lies fallow until the entire system starts again. In Hinduism, the four yugas are likened to the four legs of the cow of morality. As each age passes, one more leg is amputated. The current age is Kali Yuga, the age of evil, the precursor to the end-times.

12. Devotees recited to me in English the acrostic "Mother Saw Father Wearing The Turban Slowly," and through the coded days of the week, they would work out the standard times for Rahu Kala on those days.

13. It is unclear when the temple got submerged under layers of soil, but in 1998, according to the story told by many of Malleshwaram's citizens, the Nandeeshwara Temple (also called the Nandi Theertha Temple) was part of a complex of four temples that made up the Kadu Malleshwara complex—the Kadu Malleshwara Temple, the Lakshmi Narasimha Temple next door (where Krishna Bhattar's brother is the chief priest), the Nandeeshwara Temple, and the Gangamma Temple (dedicated to the river goddess of the Ganges), of which only the Kadu Malleshwara temple was recognized by the government as having historic value and thus protected by the Archaeological Survey of India.

14. Various informants gave me different dates for the temple, ranging from the time of Shivaji (1638–68) to over eight thousand years ago. The *Times of India*, a national newspaper, set the approximate age at seven thousand years, though it is unclear where this figure came from. Meghana Mathur, "7000-Year-Old Temple in Malleshwaram," *Times of India*, October 14, 2001, accessed December 14, 2016, http://timesofindia .indiatimes.com/city/bangalore-times/7000-year-old-temple-in- Malleswaram/article show/129602326.cms. The article describes the discovery of the Tank Temple in Mallesh-waram and its dating by the Archaeological Survey of India.

15. One could argue that this is similar to Aristotle's understanding of the now, except for Krishna Bhattar this is not naturalistic, nor is it separate from the perceiver.

16. Narada is a Vedic sage who plays a prominent role in a number of Hindu mythic texts, notably the Ramayana and the Bhagavata Purana. Narada is ancient India's most traveled sage with the ability to visit distant worlds and realms (Sanskrit: *lokas*). He is a musician and a scholar believed to have compiled the Naradasmriti.

17. This is reminiscent of E. E. Evans-Pritchard's notion of lineage time. Evans-Pritchard argues that lineage/descent constructs, as forms of long-term time, or time-reckoning in the now, the well-known form of an abstract space of structural distance (1951). Lineage time, for Evans-Pritchard, is "not a continuum, but a . . . relationship between two points," with a "constant number of steps" (1951, 105–8) between ancestors and living persons. Because it is noncumulative, "engaging a limited set of non-progressive positions rather than an incremental movement," the genealogical grid

creates only an immobilized "illusion" of time (Munn 1992, 98). Tellingly, the space of both Evans-Pritchard's structural time and Krishna Bhattar's understanding of time is coequal in that it is not concrete and qualitative but geometrical (cf. Munn 1992, 58, 67) and quantitative. In this it follows or rather intersects with Bergson's understanding of time as spatial, defined in terms of units of distance rather than minutes (Munn 1992, 98–99).

18. The IBM Global Commuter Pain Survey states that "On average, drivers in Nairobi, Mexico City, Johannesburg, Beijing, Bangalore, and Moscow spend the longest amount of time (36 minutes or more) on the road to get to their workplace or school." From the IBM Global Commuter Pain Survey, September 8, 2011, accessed August 29, 2017, http://www-03.ibm.com/press/us/en/pressrelease/35359.wss.

19. Babu Bhattar echoes Bergson, who describes this very oceanic sense of liquidity. For Bergson, intuition is what allows us to contend with the present as an "interval of duration," a movement of ceaseless and indivisible transformation. But this endless transformative state has its own rhythms, revealing other durations as Deleuze so strongly brings to our attention—the waves of an inner ethical ecology—that intuit a rhythmic attunement and synchronicity with the everyday present. In ritual time, the liquidity of untimeliness and the rhythms of contingency make for a time of creativity, offering a generative and regenerative way of both imagining and inhabiting time. These regenerative rhythms allow for both the rupture of time in its many incarnations as well as its productive capture, a promissory locating and imaging of the future.

REFERENCES

Acharya, Viral V., and Matthew Richardson. 2009. *Restoring Financial Stability: How to Repair a Failed System.* Hoboken, NJ: John Wiley.

Adam, Barbara. 2003. "Reflexive Modernization Temporalized." *Theory, Culture and Society* 20, no. 2: 59–78.

Adorno, Theodor. 2006. *Minima Moralia: Reflections from Damaged Life.* Translated by E. F. N. Jephcott. London: Verso.

Agamben, Giorgio. 1998. *Homo Sacer: Sovereign Power and Bare Life.* Stanford, CA: Stanford University Press.

———. 2005. *State of Exception.* Chicago: University of Chicago Press.

Althusser, Louis. 1970. "From Capital to Marx's Philosophy." In *Reading Capital*, Part 1, by Louis Althusser and Étienne Balibar, translated by Ben Brewster, 11–69. London: New Left Books.

Amin, Ash. 1994. *Regional Incentives and the Quality of Mobile Investments in the Less Favoured Regions of the EC.* Oxford: Pergamon.

Aneesh, A. 2006. *Virtual Migration: The Programming of Globalization.* Durham, NC: Duke University Press.

Anonymous. 1981. "The Poetry of Creation." Book 10, Hymn 129. In *The Rig Veda: An Anthology.* Translation by Wendy Doniger O'Flaherty. New York: Penguin.

Appadurai, Arjun. 1981. *Worship and Conflict under Colonial Rule: A South Indian Case.* Cambridge: Cambridge University Press.

———. 1986a. "Is Homo Hierarchicus?" *American Ethnologist* 13, no. 4: 745–61.

———, ed. 1986b. *The Social Life of Things: Commodities in Cultural Perspective.* Cambridge: Cambridge University Press.

———. 1990. "Disjuncture and Difference in the Global Cultural Economy." *Public Culture* 2, no. 2: 1–24.

———. 1996. *Modernity at Large: Cultural Dimensions of Globalization.* Minneapolis: University of Minnesota Press.

———. 1998. "Putting Hierarchy in Its Place." *Cultural Anthropology* 3, no. 1: 36–49.

―――. 2004. "The Capacity to Aspire: Culture and the Terms of Recognition." In *Culture and Public Action*, edited by Vijayendra Rao and Michael Walton, 59–84. Stanford, CA: Stanford University Press.

―――. 2015. *Banking on Words: The Failure of Language in the Age of Derivative Finance*. Chicago: University of Chicago Press.

Appadurai, Arjun, and Carol A. Breckenridge. 1976. "The South Indian Temple: Authority, Honour and Redistribution." *Contributions to Indian Sociology* 10, no. 2: 187–211.

―――. 1995. "Public Modernity in India." In *Consuming Modernity: Public Culture in a South Asian World*, edited by Carol A. Breckenridge, 1–20. Minneapolis: University of Minnesota Press.

Asad, Talal. 1993. *Genealogies of Religion: Discipline and Reasons of Power in Christianity and Islam*. Baltimore: Johns Hopkins University Press.

Augé, Marc. 2008. *Non-Places: An Introduction to Supermodernity*. London: Verso.

Barth, Fredrik. 1967. "On the Study of Social Change." *American Anthropologist* 69, no. 6: 661–69.

Bataille, Georges. [1949] 1991. *The Accursed Share: An Essay on General Economy*. New York: Zone Books.

Bate, Bernard. 2002. "Political Praise in Tamil Newspapers: The Poetry and Iconography of Democratic Power." In *Everyday Life in South Asia*, edited by Diane Mines and Sarah Lamb, 354–70. Bloomington: Indiana University Press.

―――. 2010. *Tamil Oratory and the Dravidian Aesthetic: Democratic Practice in South India*. New York: Columbia University Press.

Bateson, Gregory. 1936. *Naven: A Survey of the Problems Suggested by a Composite Picture of the Culture of a New Guinea Tribe Drawn from Three Points of View*. Stanford, CA: Stanford University Press.

Baudrillard, Jean. 1975. *The Mirror of Production*. St. Louis: Telos Press.

Bayart, Jean-François. 2007. *Global Subjects: A Political Critique of Globalization*. Cambridge: Polity.

Bayly, Susan. 2001. *Caste, Society and Politics in India from the Eighteenth Century to the Modern Age*. New York: Cambridge University Press.

Beck, Ulrich. 1992. *Risk Society: Towards a New Modernity*. London: SAGE.

―――. 2000. *What Is Globalization?* Cambridge: Polity.

Beeman, William O. 1993. "The Anthropology of Theater and Spectacle." *Annual Review of Anthropology* 22:369–93.

Bell, Catherine M. 1997. *Ritual: Perspectives and Dimensions*. New York: Oxford University Press.

Belliappa, Jyothsna Latha. 2013. *Gender, Class and Reflexive Modernity in India*. Basingstoke, UK: Palgrave Macmillan.

Benjamin, Walter. 1968. *Illuminations*. Edited by Hannah Arendt. Translated by Harry Zohn. New York: Harcourt, Brace and World.

Bennett, Lynn. 1983. *Dangerous Wives and Sacred Sisters: Social and Symbolic Roles of High-Caste Women in Nepal*. New York: Columbia University Press.

Berger, Peter L., and Thomas Luckmann. 1966. *The Social Construction of Reality: A Treatise in the Sociology of Knowledge*. Garden City, NY: Doubleday.

Bergson, Henri. [1907] 1911. *Creative Evolution*. Translated by Arthur Mitchell. New York: Random House.

———. [1889] 2012. *Time and Free Will: An Essay on the Immediate Data of Consciousness*. Mineola, NY: Dover.

Berlant, Lauren. 2011. "A Properly Political Concept of Love: Three Approaches in Ten Pages." *Cultural Anthropology* 26, no. 4: 683–91.

Berreman, Gerald D. 1968. *Stratification, Pluralism and Interaction: A Comparative Analysis of Caste*. Berkeley: Center for South Asia Studies, University of California.

———. 1991. "The Brahmanical View of Caste." In *Social Stratification*, edited by Dipankar Gupta. Delhi: Oxford University Press.

Béteille, André. 1991. *Society and Politics in India: Essays in a Comparative Perspective*. London: Athlone.

Bhagwati, Jagdish N., and Arvind Panagariya. 2012. *India's Reforms: How They Produced Inclusive Growth*. New York: Oxford University Press.

Biardeau, Madeleine. 1976. "Le sacrifice dans l'hindouisme." In *Le sacrifice dans l'Inde ancienne*, edited by Madeleine Biardeau and Charles Malamoud, 139–54. Paris: Presses Universitaires de France.

Biehl, João Guilherme. 2005. *Vita: Life in a Zone of Social Abandonment*. Berkeley: University of California Press.

Biehl, João, Byron Good, and Arthur Kleinman. 2007. *Subjectivity: Ethnographic Investigations*. Berkeley: University of California Press.

Biehl, João, and Peter Locke. 2010. "Deleuze and the Anthropology of Becoming." *Current Anthropology* 51, no. 3: 317–51.

Bissell, David. 2007. "Animating Suspension: Waiting for Mobilities." *Mobilities* 2, no. 2: 277–98.

Bohannan, Paul. 1955. "Some Principles of Exchange and Investment among the Tiv." *American Anthropologist* 57, no. 1: 60–70. doi:10.1525/aa.1955.57.1.02a00080.

Bourdieu, Pierre. 1998. *Acts of Resistance: Against the New Myths of Our Time*. Cambridge: Polity.

Braidotti, Rosi. 2011. *Nomadic Theory: The Portable Rosi Braidotti*. New York: Columbia University Press.

Braudel, Fernand. 1992. *Civilization and Capitalism, 15th–18th Century: The Structure of Everyday Life*. Berkeley: University of California Press.

Brenneis, Donald. 1987. "Performing Passions: Aesthetics and Politics in an Occasionally Egalitarian Community." *American Ethnologist* 14, no. 2: 236–50.

Brosius, Christiane. 2010. *India's Middle Class: New Forms of Urban Leisure, Consumption and Prosperity*. London: Routledge.

———. 2012. *Empowering Visions: The Politics of Representation in Hindu Nationalism*. Cambridge: Cambridge University Press.

Butler, Chris Adrian. 2012. *Henri Lefebvre: Spatial Politics, Everyday Life and the Right to the City*. Abingdon, UK: Routledge.

Bynum, Caroline Walker. 1997. "Wonder." *American Historical Review* 102, no. 1: 1–26.

Caldeira, Teresa Pires do Rio. 2000. *City of Walls: Crime, Segregation, and Citizenship in São Paulo*. Berkeley: University of California Press.

Cameron, William Bruce. 1963. *Informal Sociology: A Casual Introduction to Sociological Thinking*. New York: Random House.

Carrette, Jeremy R., and Richard King. 2005. *Selling Spirituality: The Silent Takeover of Religion*. London: Routledge.

Casanova, Jose, and Aristide R. Zolberg. 2002. "Religion and Immigrant Incorporation in New York." Paper presented at New School University, 2002.

Castells, Manuel. 2000. *The Rise of the Network Society*. Oxford: Blackwell.

Chatterjee, Partha. 2010. *Empire and Nation: Selected Essays*. New York: Columbia University Press.

Chawla, Devika. 2006. "Subjectivity and the 'Native' Ethnographer: Researcher Eligibility in an Ethnographic Study of Urban Indian Women in Hindu Arranged Marriages." *International Journal of Qualitative Methods* 5, no. 4: 13–29.

Clark-Decès, Isabelle. 2005. *No One Cries for the Dead: Tamil Dirges, Rowdy Songs, and Graveyard Petitions*. Berkeley: University of California Press.

Clifford, James. 1988. *The Predicament of Culture: Twentieth-Century Ethnography, Literature, and Art*. Cambridge, MA: Harvard University Press.

Clooney, Francis Xavier. 1990. *Thinking Ritually: Rediscovering the Pūrva Mīmāṃsā of Jaimini*. Vienna: De Nobili Research Library.

Clothey, Fred W. 2006. *Ritualizing on the Boundaries: Continuity and Innovation in the Tamil Diaspora*. Columbia: University of South Carolina Press.

Collier, Stephen J., and Andrew Lakoff. 2004. "On Regimes of Living." In *Global Assemblages: Technology, Politics, and Ethics as Anthropological Problems*, edited by Aihwa Ong and Stephen J. Collier, 439–63. Malden, MA: Blackwell.

Coomaraswamy, Ananda K. 1977. *Coomaraswamy: I, Selected Papers: Traditional Art and Symbolism*, edited by Roger Lipsey. Princeton, NJ: Princeton University Press.

Cox, Brian, and Andrew Cohen. 2011. *Wonders of the Universe*. New York: Harper Design.

Das, Veena. 2015a. "Ethics as the Expression of Life as a Whole." Research paper. Academia.edu. https://www.academia.edu/14431568/Ethics_as_the_Expression_of_Life_as_a_Whole.

———. 2015b. "What Does Ordinary Ethics Look Like?" In *Four Lectures on Ethics*, 53–125. Chicago: University of Chicago Press.

Daston, Lorraine, and Katharine Park. 2001. *Wonders and the Order of Nature, 1150–1750*. Rev. ed. New York: Zone Books.

Davis, Donald R. 2004. *The Boundaries of Hindu Law: Tradition, Custom and Politics in Medieval Kerala*. Turin: Comitato "Corpus Iuris Sanscriticum et fontes iuris Asiae Meridianae et Centralis."

Debord, Guy. [1956] 1958. "Theory of the Dérive." Translated by Ken Knabb. *Situationist International Online*. http://www.cddc.vt.edu/sionline/si/theory.html.

de Certeau, Michel. 1984. *The Practice of Everyday Life*. Translated by Steven Rendall. Berkeley: University of California Press.

Deleuze, Gilles. 1994. *Difference and Repetition*. New York: Columbia University Press.

Deleuze, Gilles, and Félix Guattari. 2004. *Anti-Oedipus: Capitalism and Schizophrenia.* New York: Continuum.

DeNapoli, Antoinette Elizabeth. 2017. "Dharm Is Technology: The Theologizing of Technology in the Experimental Hinduism of Renouncers in North India." *International Journal of Dharma Studies* 5, no. 18: 2–36. https://internationaljournaldharmastud ies.springeropen.com/track/pdf/10.1186/s40613-017-0053-0?site=internationaljourn aldharmastudies.springeropen.com.

DeNapoli, Antoinette Elizabeth, and Tulasi Srinivas. 2016. "Introduction—Moralizing Dharma in Everyday Hinduisms." *Nidan: International Journal for the Study of Indian Religions* 28, no. 2.

Derné, Stephan D. 2008. *Globalization on the Ground: Media and the Transformation of Culture, Class, and Gender in India.* London: SAGE.

Derrida, Jacques. [1995] 1996. *Archive Fever: A Freudian Impression.* Translated by Eric Prenowitz. Chicago: University of Chicago Press.

Descartes, René. [1649] 1989. *The Passions of the Soul.* Indianapolis: Hackett.

Dharia, Namita. 2015. "Artifacts and Artifices of the Global: Practices of US Architects in India's National Capital Region." *Global South* 8, no. 2: 49–64.

Dickey, Sara. 2012. "The Pleasures and Anxieties of Being in the Middle: Emerging Middle-Class Identities in Urban South India." *Modern Asian Studies* 46, no. 3: 559–99.

———. 2013. "Apprehensions: On Gaining Recognition as Middle Class in Madurai." *Contributions to Indian Sociology* 47, no. 2: 217–43.

Dirks, Nicolas. 2001. *Castes of Mind: Colonialism and the Making of Modern India.* Princeton, NJ: Princeton University Press.

Dissanayake, Wimal. 2005. *Melodrama and Asian Cinema.* Cambridge: Cambridge University Press.

Doniger O'Flaherty, Wendy. 1976. *The Origins of Evil in Hindu Mythology.* Berkeley: University of California Press.

Dumont, Louis. [1966] 1980. *Homo Hierarchicus: The Caste System and Its Implications.* Rev. ed. Translated by Mark Sainsbury, Louis Dumont, and Basia Gulati. New Delhi: Oxford University Press.

Duncan, James S., and David Ley. 1993. *Place/Culture/Representation.* London: Routledge.

Durkheim, Émile. [1898] 1973. "Individualism and the Intellectuals." In *On Morality and Society: Selected Writings*, edited by Robert N. Bellah, 43–57. Chicago: University of Chicago Press.

———. [1915] 1995. *The Elementary Forms of Religious Life.* Translated by Karen E. Fields. New York: Free Press.

Durrell, Lawrence. 1957. *Justine.* In *The Alexandra Quartet.* London: Faber.

Eade, John, and Christopher Mele. 2002. *Understanding the City: Contemporary and Future Perspectives.* Hoboken, NJ: Wiley-Blackwell.

Einstein, Albert. 2010. *The Meaning of Relativity: Four Lectures Delivered at Princeton University, May, 1921.* Charleston, SC: Nabu Press.

Eliade, Mircea. [1957] 1961. *The Sacred and the Profane: The Nature of Religion: The Significance of Religious Myth, Ritual and Symbolism within Life and Culture.* Translated by Willard R. Trask. New York: Houghton Mifflin Harcourt.

———. 1993. *The Encyclopedia of Religion*. New York: Macmillan.

Embree, Ainslie Thomas. 1990. *Utopias in Conflict: Religion and Nationalism in Modern India*. Berkeley: University of California Press.

Evans-Pritchard, E. E. 1951. *Kinship and Marriage among the Nuer*. Oxford: Clarendon.

———. 1956. *Nuer Religion*. New York: Oxford University Press.

Ferguson, James. 1999. *Expectations of Modernity: Myths and Meanings of Urban Life on the Zambian Copperbelt*. Berkeley: University of California Press.

Fernandes, Leela. 2006. *India's New Middle Class: Democratic Politics in an Era of Economic Reform*. Minneapolis: University of Minnesota Press.

Fischer, Michael M. J. 2004. *Mute Dreams, Blind Owls, and Dispersed Knowledges: Persian Poesis in the Transnational Circuitry*. Durham, NC: Duke University Press.

Fisher, Philip. 1998. *Wonder, the Rainbow, and the Aesthetics of Rare Experiences*. Cambridge, MA: Harvard University Press.

Flueckiger, Joyce Burkhalter. 2013. *When the World Becomes Female: Guises of a South Indian Goddess*. Bloomington: Indiana University Press.

———. 2015. *Everyday Hinduism*. Hoboken, NJ: Wiley-Blackwell.

Freud, Signumd. 1919. *Essay on The Uncanny*. Accessed March 12, 2018. http://web.mit.edu/allanmc/www/freud1.pdf.

Friedman, Thomas L. 2005. *The World Is Flat: A Brief History of the Twenty-First Century*. New York: Farrar, Straus and Giroux.

Fuller, C. J. 1984. *Servants of the Goddess: The Priests of a South Indian Temple*. Cambridge: Cambridge University Press.

———. 1988. "The Hindu Temple and Indian Society." In *Temple in Society*, edited by Michael V. Fox, 49–66. Winona Lake, IN: Eisenbrauns.

———. 1997. *Caste Today*. Delhi: Oxford University Press.

Fuller, C. J., and Haripriya Narasimhan. 2014. *Tamil Brahmans: The Making of a Middle-Class Caste*. Chicago: University of Chicago Press.

Gadgil, Madhav, and Ramachandra Guha. 1995. *Ecology and Equity: The Use and Abuse of Nature in Contemporary India*. London: Routledge.

Gandhi, Ajay. 2013. "A Superlative Form: How Gold Mediates Personhood and Property in Mumbai." *Etnofoor* 25, no. 1: 91–110.

Geertz, Clifford. 1957. "Ritual and Social Change: A Javanese Example." *American Anthropologist,* 59, no. 1: 32–54.

———. 1973. *The Interpretation of Cultures: Selected Essays*. New York: Basic Books.

———. 1976. *The Religion of Java*. Chicago: University of Chicago Press.

———. 1980a. "Blurred Genres: The Refiguration of Social Thought." *American Scholar* 49, no. 2: 165–79.

———. 1980b. *Negara: The Theatre State in Nineteenth-Century Bali*. Princeton, NJ: Princeton University Press.

Gennep, Arnold van. [1909] 1960. *The Rites of Passage*. Translated by Monika B. Vizedom and Gabrielle L. Caffee. Chicago: University of Chicago Press.

George, T. J. S. 2016. *Askew: A Short Biography of Bangalore*. New Delhi: Aleph Book Company.

Ghannam, Farha. 2011. "Mobility, Liminality, and Embodiment in Urban Egypt." *American Ethnologist* 38, no. 4: 790–800.

Ghurye, G. S. 1969. *Caste and Race in India*. Bombay: Popular Prakashan.

Glaeser, Edward L. 2011. *Triumph of the City: How Our Greatest Invention Makes Us Richer, Smarter, Greener, Healthier, and Happier*. New York: Penguin Books.

Gluckman, Max. 1977. *Politics, Law and Ritual in Tribal Society*. Oxford: Basil Blackwell.

Gold, Ann G. 2009. "Tasteless Profits and Vexed Moralities: Assessments of the Present in Rural Rajasthan." *Journal of the Royal Anthropological Institute* 15, no. 2: 365–85.

Gold, Ann Grodzins. 2016. "Portrait: Ann Grodzins Gold." *Religion and Society* 7, no. 1: 1–36. doi:10.3167/arrs.2016.070102.

Gold, Ann Grodzins, and Bhoju Ram Gujar. 2002. *In the Time of Trees and Sorrows: Nature, Power, and Memory in Rajasthan*. Durham, NC: Duke University Press.

Gonda, Jan. 1977. *The Ritual Sutras*. Wiesbaden: Otto Harrassowitz.

———. 1980. *Vedic Ritual: The Non-Solemn Rites*. Leiden: E. J. Brill.

Good, Mary-Jo DelVecchio, Sandra Tessa Hyde, Sarah Pinto, and Byron J. Good, eds. 2008. *Postcolonial Disorders*. Berkeley: University of California Press.

Gould, Harold A. 1987. *The Hindu Caste System*. Vol. 1. Delhi: Chanakya.

Graeber, David. 1996. "Beads and Money: Notes toward a Theory of Wealth and Power." *American Ethnologist* 23, no. 1: 4–24.

———. 2005. "Fetishism as Social Creativity: Or, Fetishes Are Gods in the Process of Construction." *Anthropological Theory* 5, no. 4: 407–38.

———. 2011. *Debt: The First 5,000 Years*. Brooklyn: Melville House, 2011.

Green, André. 1999. *The Work of the Negative*. London: Free Association Books.

Greenblatt, Stephen. 1991. *Marvelous Possessions: The Wonder of the New World*. Chicago: University of Chicago Press.

Grimes, Ronald L. 1988. "Ritual Criticism and Reflexivity in Fieldwork." *Journal of Ritual Studies* 2, no. 2: 217–39.

Gupta, Akhil, and James Ferguson. 1992. "Beyond 'Culture': Space, Identity, and the Politics of Difference." *Cultural Anthropology* 7, no. 1: 6–23.

———, eds. 1997. *Anthropological Locations: Boundaries and Grounds of a Field Science*. Berkeley: University of California Press.

Gupta, Dipankar. 2000. *Interrogating Caste: Understanding Hierarchy and Difference in Indian Society*. New Delhi: Penguin Books.

Gusfield, Joseph R. 1967. "Tradition and Modernity: Misplaced Polarities in the Study of Social Change." *American Journal of Sociology* 72, no. 4: 351–62.

Guyer, Jane I. 2007. "Prophecy and the Near Future: Thoughts on Macroeconomic, Evangelical, and Punctuated Time." *American Ethnologist* 34, no. 3: 409–21.

Habermas, Jürgen. 1989. *The Structural Transformation of the Public Sphere: An Inquiry into a Category of Bourgeois Society*. Hoboken, NJ: John Wiley.

Hage, Ghassan. 2014. "Critical Anthropology as a Permanent State of First Contact." Theorizing the Contemporary, *Cultural Anthropology*, January 13. https://culanth.org/fieldsights/473-critical-anthropology-as-a-permanent-state-of-first-contact.

Hallam, Elizabeth, and Tim Ingold. 2007. *Creativity and Cultural Improvisation*. Oxford: Berg.

Halpern, Jake. 2012. "The Secret of the Temple." *New Yorker*, April 30.

Hamell, George R. 1983. "Trading in Metaphors: The Magic of Beads." In *Proceedings of the 1982 Glass Trade Bead Conference*, edited by Charles F. Hayes III, 5–28. Research Records No. 16. Rochester: Rochester Museum and Science Center.

Han, Clara. 2011. *Life in Debt: Times of Care and Violence in Neoliberal Chile.* Berkeley: University of California Press.

Harari, Josué V. 1979. *Textual Strategies: Perspectives in Post-Structuralist Criticism.* Ithaca, NY: Cornell University Press.

Hardin, Russell. 2006. *Trust.* Cambridge: Polity.

Hardt, Michael, and Antonio Negri. 2000. *Empire.* Cambridge, MA: Harvard University Press.

Hardy, Friedhelm. 1983. *Viraha-Bhakti: The Early History of Kṛṣṇa Devotion in South India.* Delhi: Oxford.

Harriss, John. 2007. "Antinomies of Empowerment: Observations on Civil Society, Politics and Urban Governance in India." *Economic and Political Weekly* 42, no. 26: 2716–24.

Harriss-White, Barbara. 2003. *India Working: Essays on Society and Economy.* Cambridge: Cambridge University Press.

Harvey, David. 1989. *The Condition of Postmodernity: An Enquiry into the Origins of Cultural Change.* Oxford: Blackwell.

———. 2009. *Social Justice and the City.* Athens: University of Georgia Press.

Hauerwas, Stanley. 2007. *The State of the University: Academic Knowledges and the Knowledge of God.* Malden, MA: Blackwell.

Heesterman, Johannes Cornelis. 1964. *Brahmin, Ritual and Renouncer.* Vienna: Indologisch Institut, Universität Wien.

Heidegger, Martin. 1975. "Building Dwelling Thinking." In *Poetry, Language, Thought*, translated by Albert Hofstadter, 141–61. New York: Perennial Library.

Hertz, Robert. 2006. *Death and the Right Hand.* London: Routledge.

Herzfeld, Michael. 2015. "Practical Piety: Intimate Devotions in Urban Space." *Journal of Religious and Political Practice* 1, no. 1: 22–38.

High, Mette M. 2013. "Polluted Money, Polluted Wealth: Emerging Regimes of Value in the Mongolian Gold Rush." *American Ethnologist* 40, no. 4: 676–88. doi:10.1111/amet.12047.

Hiltebeitel, Alf. 2011. *Dharma: Its Early History in Law, Religion, and Narrative.* Oxford: Oxford University Press.

Hirschkind, Charles. 2006. *The Ethical Soundscape: Cassette Sermons and Islamic Counterpublics.* New York: Columbia University Press.

Holderege, Barbara. 2004. "Dharma." In *The Hindu World*, edited by Sushil Mittal and Gene R. Thursby, 213–48. New York: Routledge.

Holmes, Douglas, and George Marcus. 2006. "Fast Capitalism: Para-Ethnography and the Rise of the Symbolic Analyst." In *Frontiers of Capital: Ethnographic Reflections on the New Economy*, edited by Melissa S. Fisher and Greg Downey, 33–56. Durham, NC: Duke University Press.

Horkheimer, Max, and Theodor W. Adorno. 2002. *Dialectic of Enlightenment: Philosophical Fragments.* Translated by Gunzelin Schmid Noerr. Stanford, CA: Stanford University Press.

Hosagrahar, Jyoti. 2005. *Indigenous Modernities: Negotiating Architecture and Urbanism*. London: Routledge.

Huesken, Ute. 2007. *When Rituals Go Wrong: Mistakes, Failure, and the Dynamics of Ritual*. Numen Book Series 115. Leiden: Brill.

Huizinga, Johan. 1955. *Homo Ludens: A Study of the Play-Element in Culture*. Boston: Beacon.

Humphrey, Caroline, and James Laidlaw. 1994. *The Archetypal Actions of Ritual: A Theory of Ritual Illustrated by the Jain Rite of Worship*. Oxford: Clarendon.

Hutton, J. H. 1963. *Caste in India: Its Nature, Function and Origins*. Bombay: Oxford University Press.

Ingold, Tim. 2011. *Being Alive: Essays on Movement, Knowledge and Description*. London: Routledge.

———. 2013. *Making: Anthropology, Archaeology, Art and Architecture*. London: Routledge.

Irigaray, Luce. 2004. *Luce Irigaray: Key Writings*. London: Continuum.

Isin, Engin F. 2004. "The Neurotic Citizen." *Citizenship Studies* 8, no. 3: 217–35. doi:10.1080/1362102042000256970.

Jackson, Michael. 2002. "Familiar and Foreign Bodies: A Phenomenological Explanation of the Human-Technology Interface." *Journal of the Royal Anthropological Institute* 8, no. 2 (June): 333–46.

———. 2005. *Existential Anthropology: Events, Exigencies, and Effects*. New York: Berghahn Books.

———. 2013. *Lifeworlds: Essays in Existential Anthropology*. Chicago: University of Chicago Press.

Jain, Pankaj. 2011. *Dharma and Ecology of Hindu Communities: Sustenance and Sustainability*. Farnham, UK: Ashgate.

Jameson, Fredric. 1991. *Postmodernism, or, The Cultural Logic of Late Capitalism*. Durham, NC: Duke University Press.

———. 2003. "The End of Temporality." *Critical Inquiry* 29, no. 4: 695–718.

Jeffrey, Craig. 2010. *Timepass: Youth, Class, and the Politics of Waiting in India*. Stanford, CA: Stanford University Press.

Kane, P. V. 1958. *History of Dharmasastra: Ancient and Mediaeval Religious and Civil Law*. Pune, India: Bhandarkar Oriental Research Institute.

Kant, Immanuel. [1790] 2007. *Critique of Judgement*. Translated by Nicholas Walker and James Creed Meredith. Oxford: Oxford University Press.

Kapferer, Bruce, ed. 1979. *The Power of Ritual: Transition, Transformation and Transcendence in Ritual Practice*. Adelaide, Australia: Department of Anthropology, University of Adelaide.

———. 1983. *A Celebration of Demons: Exorcism and the Aesthetics of Healing in Sri Lanka*. Bloomington: Indiana University Press.

Keane, Webb. 1997. *Signs of Recognition: Powers and Hazards of Representation in an Indonesian Society*. Berkeley: University of California Press.

Keen, Sam. 1969. *Apology for Wonder*. New York: Harper and Row.

Kidambi, Prashant. 2007. *The Making of an Indian Metropolis: Colonial Governance and Public Culture in Bombay, 1890–1920*. Aldershot, UK: Ashgate.

King, Richard. 1999. *Orientalism and Religion: Postcolonial Theory, India and "the Mystic East."* London: Routledge.

Kleinman, Arthur. 1995. *Writing at the Margin: Discourse between Anthropology and Medicine.* Berkeley: University of California Press.

Klostermaier, Klaus K. 1998. *Hinduism: A Short Introduction.* London: Oneworld Publications.

Kolenda, Pauline. 1973. "Caste, Religion and Power: An Indian Case Study." *Journal of Asian Studies* 33, no. 1: 144–45.

Kopytoff, Igor. 1986. "The Cultural Biography of Things: Commoditization as Process." In *The Social Life of Things: Commodities in Cultural Perspective*, edited by Arjun Appadurai, 64–91. Cambridge: Cambridge University Press.

Kripalani, Manjreet, and Pete Engardio. 2003. "The Rise of India." *Business Week*, December 7. https://www.bloomberg.com/news/articles/2003-12-07/the-rise-of-india.

Krishna, Sankaran. 2011. "Forgetting Caste While Living It: The Privileges of Amnesia." In *Caste in Life: Experiencing Inequalities*, edited by D. Shyam Babu and R. S. Khare. Delhi: Pearson.

Kroessler, Jeffrey A. 2015. "The City as Palimpsest." Working paper, CUNY Academic Works. http://academicworks.cuny.edu/jj_pubs/42.

Kuehn, Julia, and Paul Smethurst. 2009. *Travel Writing, Form, and Empire: The Poetics and Politics of Mobility.* New York: Routledge.

Kumar, Ashwini. 2005. *Vaastu: The Art and Science of Living.* New Delhi: Sterling.

Kumar, Nita. 1988. *The Artisans of Banaras: Popular Culture and Identity, 1880–1986.* Princeton, NJ: Princeton University Press.

Kwon, Heonik. 2007. "The Dollarization of Vietnamese Ghost Money." *Journal of the Royal Anthropological Institute* 13, no. 1: 73–90.

Lambek, Michael. 2010. *Ordinary Ethics: Anthropology, Language, and Action.* New York: Fordham University Press.

Larkin, Brian. 1997. "Indian Films and Nigerian Lovers: Media and the Creation of Parallel Modernities." *Africa: Journal of the International African Institute Africa/ International African Institute* 67, no. 3: 406–40.

———. 2013. "The Politics and Poetics of Infrastructure." *Annual Review of Anthropology* 42 (October): 327–43.

Lavie, Smadar, Kirin Narayan, and Renato Rosaldo, eds. 1993. *Creativity/Anthropology.* Ithaca, NY: Cornell University Press.

Leach, Edmund Ronald. 1971. *Rethinking Anthropology.* London: Athlone.

Leach, Edmund Ronald, and S. N. Mukherjee, eds. 1970. *Elites in South Asia.* Cambridge: Cambridge University Press.

Lear, Jonathan. 2008. *Radical Hope: Ethics in the Face of Cultural Devastation.* Cambridge, MA: Harvard University Press.

Leeuw, Gerardus van der. [1933] 1986. *Religion in Essence and Manifestation.* Translated by Hans H. Penner, James Edward Turner, and Ninian Smart. Princeton, NJ: Princeton University Press.

Lefebvre, Henri. [1992] 2004. *Rhythmanalysis: Space, Time, and Everyday Life.* London: Continuum.

Levi-Strauss, Claude. 1963. "Social Structure." In *Structural Anthropology*, translated by Claire Jacobson and Brooke G. Schoepf. New York: Basic Books.

———. 1966. *The Savage Mind*. Translated by J. Weightman. Chicago: University of Chicago Press.

Liechty, Mark. 2003. *Suitably Modern: Making Middle-Class Culture in a New Consumer Society*. Princeton, NJ: Princeton University Press.

Lutz, Catherine A., and Geoffrey Miles White. 1986. "The Anthropology of Emotions." *Annual Review of Anthropology* 15:405–36.

MacKenzie, Donald, and Yuval Millo. 2003. "Constructing a Market, Performing Theory: The Historical Sociology of a Financial Derivatives Exchange." *American Journal of Sociology* 109, no. 1: 107–45.

Mahmood, Saba. 2001. "Rehearsed Spontaneity and the Conventionality of Ritual: Disciplines of Ṣalāt." *American Ethnologist* 28, no. 4: 827–53.

———. 2005. *Politics of Piety: The Islamic Revival and the Feminist Subject*. Princeton, NJ: Princeton University Press.

Manderscheid, Katharina. 2009. "Unequal Mobilities." In *Mobilities and Inequality*, edited by Timo Ohnmacht, Hanja Maksim, and Manfred Max Bergman, 27–50. Farnham, UK: Ashgate.

Marrati, Paola. 2005. "Time, Life, Concepts: The Newness of Bergson." *MLN* 120, no. 5: 1099–111.

Marriott, McKim. 1969. "Homo-Hierarchicus." *American Anthropologist* 71, no. 6: 1166–75.

———. 1976. "Hindu Transactions: Diversity without Dualism." In *Transaction and Meaning: Directions in the Anthropology of Exchange and Symbolic Behavior*, edited by Bruce Kapferer, 109–42. Philadelphia: Institute for the Study of Human Issues.

Martineau, Jonathan. 2015. *Time, Capitalism and Alienation: A Socio-Historical Inquiry into the Making of Modern Time*. Leiden: Brill.

Massey, Doreen. 1993. "Power-Geometry and a Progressive Sense of Place." In *Mapping the Futures: Local Cultures, Global Change*, edited by Jon Bird, Barry Curtis, Tim Putnam, and Lisa Tickner, 59–69. London: Routledge.

Masuzawa, Tomoko. 2005. *The Invention of World Religions, or, How European Universalism Was Preserved in the Language of Pluralism*. Chicago: University of Chicago Press.

Mathur, Anuradha, and Dilip da Cunha. 2006. *Deccan Traverses: The Making of Bangalore's Terrain*. New Delhi: Rupa.

Maurer, Bill. 2002. "Anthropological and Accounting Knowledge in Islamic Banking and Finance: Rethinking Critical Accounts." *Journal of the Royal Anthropological Institute* 8, no. 4: 645–67.

———. 2006. "The Anthropology of Money." *Annual Review of Anthropology* 35:15–36.

Mauss, Marcel. [1923] 1967. *The Gift: Forms and Functions of Exchange in Archaic Societies*. Translated by W. D. Halls. New York: W. W. Norton.

Maycroft, Neil. 2005. "Review of *Rhythmanalysis: Space, Time and Everyday Life*, by Henri Lefebvre." *Capital and Class* 29, no. 86: 170–75.

Mazzarella, William. 2003. *Shoveling Smoke: Advertising and Globalization in Contemporary India.* Durham, NC: Duke University Press.

McCutcheon, Russell T. 2001. *Critics Not Caretakers: Redescribing the Public Study of Religion.* Albany: State University of New York Press.

———. 2007. *Studying Religion: An Introduction.* London: Routledge.

McDonough, Tom. 2005. "Delirious Paris: Mapping as a Paranoiac-Critical Activity." *Grey Room* 19 (spring): 6–21.

McGranahan, Carole. 2014. "Ethnographic Writing with Kirin Narayan: An Interview." *Savage Minds*, February 3. http://savageminds.org/2014/02/03/ethnographic -writing-with-kirin-narayan-an-interview/.

Mead, Margaret. [1935] 2001. *Sex and Temperament in Three Primitive Societies.* New York: HarperCollins.

Mehta, Suketu. 2005. *Maximum City: Bombay Lost and Found.* New York: Vintage.

Michaels, Axel. 2016. *Homo Ritualis: Hindu Ritual and Its Significance for Ritual Theory.* New York: Oxford University Press.

Miller, Jerome A. 1992. *In the Throe of Wonder: Intimations of the Sacred in a Post-Modern World.* Albany: State University of New York Press.

Mines, Diane P. 2005. *Fierce Gods: Inequality, Ritual, and the Politics of Dignity in a South Indian Village.* Bloomington: Indiana University Press.

Molé, Noelle J. 2010. "Precarious Subjects: Anticipating Neoliberalism in Northern Italy's Workplace." *American Anthropologist* 112, no. 1: 38–53.

Moore, Charles Alexander, ed. 1967. *The Indian Mind: Essentials of Indian Philosophy and Culture.* Honolulu: East-West Center Press.

Moore, Sally Falk, and Barbara G. Myerhoff, eds. 1977. *Secular Ritual.* Assen, Netherlands: Uitgeverij Van Gorcum.

Munn, Nancy. 1992. "The Cultural Anthropology of Time: A Critical Essay." *Annual Review of Anthropology* 21:93–123.

Nair, Janaki. 2007. *The Promise of the Metropolis: Bangalore's Twentieth Century.* New Delhi: Oxford University Press.

———. 2015. " 'The City Is History': New Indian Urbanism and the Terrain of the Law." *Südasien-Chronik—South Asia Chronicle* 4:165–99.

Nancy, Jean-Luc. 2007. *The Creation of the World, or, Globalization.* Albany: State University of New York Press.

Nanda, Meera. 2011. *The God Market: How Globalization Is Making India More Hindu.* New York: Monthly Review Press.

Narayan, Kirin. 2014. In "Ethnographic Writing with Kirin Narayan: An Interview," by Carole McGranahan. *Savage Minds*, February 3. http://savageminds.org/2014/02/03 /ethnographic-writing-with-kirin-narayan-an-interview/.

Narayan, Kirin, and Kenneth George. 2017. "Tools and World-Making in the Worship of Vishwakarma." *South Asian History and Culture* 8, no. 4: 478–92.

Nasscom-McKinsey Report. 2005. *Extending India's Leadership of the IT and BPO Industries: Background and Research.* New Delhi: Nasscom.

Nasscom Report. 2007. *Strategy Review: The IT Industry in India.* New Delhi: Nasscom.

Nayar, Lola. 2012. "Was It Just a Mirage Then?" *Outlook*, June 11.

Niebuhr, H. Richard. 1951. *Christ and Culture*. New York: Harper.

Nin, Anaïs. 1969. *The Diary of Anaïs Nin*. Vol. 1, *1931–1934*. New York: Mariner Books.

Novetzke, Christian Lee. 2007. "Bhakti and Its Public." *International Journal of Hindu Studies* 11, no. 3: 255–72.

Obama, Barack. 2008. "Address after the Iowa Caucuses." Des Moines, January 3.

Olivelle, Patrick. 1998. *The Early Upanisads: Annotated Text and Translation*. New York: Oxford University Press.

———. 2008. *Upaniṣads*. Oxford: Oxford University Press.

———. 2009. *Dharma: Studies in Its Semantic, Cultural, and Religious History*. Delhi: Motilal Banarsidass.

Omvedt, Gail. 1994. *Dalits and the Democratic Revolution: Dr. Ambedkar and the Dalit Movement in Colonial India*. New Delhi: SAGE.

Ong, Aihwa. 1999. *Flexible Citizenship: The Cultural Logics of Transnationality*. Durham, NC: Duke University Press.

Orsi, Robert A. 2005. *Between Heaven and Earth: The Religious Worlds People Make and the Scholars Who Study Them*. Princeton, NJ: Princeton University Press.

Ortegren, Jennifer. 2016. "Dharma, Class and Aspiration: The Shifting Religious Worlds of Urban Rajasthani Women." PhD diss., Emory University.

Ortner, Sherry B. 1978. *Sherpas through Their Rituals*. Cambridge: Cambridge University Press.

———. 2006. *Anthropology and Social Theory: Culture, Power, and the Acting Subject*. Durham, NC: Duke University Press.

Otto, Rudolf. [1923] 1958. *The Idea of the Holy: An Inquiry into the Non-Rational Factor in the Idea of the Divine and Its Relation to the Rational*. Translated by John W. Harvey. New York: Oxford University Press.

Pandey, Gyanendra. 2006. *Routine Violence: Nations, Fragments, Histories*. Stanford, CA: Stanford University Press.

———. 2013. *A History of Prejudice: Race, Caste, and Difference in India and the United States*. Cambridge: Cambridge University Press.

Pandian, Anand. 2008. "Tradition in Fragments: Inherited Forms and Fractures in the Ethics of South India." *American Ethnologist* 35, no. 3: 466–80.

———. 2009. *Crooked Stalks: Cultivating Virtue in South India*. Durham, NC: Duke University Press, 2009.

———. 2012. "The Time of Anthropology: Notes from a Field of Contemporary Experience." *Cultural Anthropology* 27, no. 4: 547–71.

———. 2015. *Reel World: An Anthropology of Creation*. Durham, NC: Duke University Press Books.

Pandian, Anand, and Daud Ali, eds. 2010. *Ethical Life in South Asia*. Bloomington: Indiana University Press.

Parry, Jonathan. 2000. "'The Crisis of Corruption' and the 'Idea of India': A Worm's Eye View." In *The Morals of Legitimacy: Between Agency and System*, edited by Italo Pardo, 27–56. Oxford: Berghahn Books.

Parry, Jonathan P., and Maurice Bloch. 1989. *Money and the Morality of Exchange*. Cambridge: Cambridge University Press.

Parthasarathi, Prasannan. 2011. *Why Europe Grew Rich and Asia Did Not: Global Economic Divergence, 1600–1850.* Cambridge: Cambridge University Press.

Patel, Geeta. 2012. "Advertisements, Proprietary Heterosexuality, and Hundis: Postcolonial Finance, Nation-State Formations, and the New Idealized Family." *Rethinking Marxism* 24, no. 4: 516–35.

Penkower, Linda, and Tracy Pintchman, eds. 2014. *Hindu Ritual at the Margins: Innovations, Transformations, Reconsiderations.* Columbia: University of South Carolina Press.

Pennington, Brian K. 2005. *Was Hinduism Invented? Britons, Indians, and Colonial Construction of Religion.* Oxford: Oxford University Press.

Piketty, Thomas. 2014. *Capital in the Twenty-First Century.* Translated by Arthur Goldhammer. Cambridge, MA: Harvard University Press.

Pinto, Sarah. 2019. *The Doctor and Mrs. A: Psychiatry, Religion, and Counter-Ethics.* Delhi: Women Unlimited Press.

Piot, Charles. 1999. *Remotely Global: Village Modernity in West Africa.* Chicago: University of Chicago Press.

Pollock, Sheldon I. 2016. *A Rasa Reader: Classical Indian Aesthetics.* New York: Columbia University Press.

Prasad, Leela. 2007. *Poetics of Conduct: Oral Narrative and Moral Being in a South Indian Town.* New York: Columbia University Press.

Puett, Michael J. 2005. "The Offering of Food and the Creation of Order: The Practice of Sacrifice in Early China." In *Of Tripod and Palate: Food, Politics, and Religion in Traditional China,* edited by R. Sterckx, 75–95. New York: Palgrave Macmillan.

———. 2006. "Innovation as Ritualization: The Fractured Cosmology of Early China." *Cardozo Law Review* 28, no. 1: 23–36.

———. 2008. "Human and Divine Kingship in Early China: Comparative Reflections." In *Religion and Power: Divine Kingship in the Ancient World and Beyond,* edited by Nicole Maria Brisch, 199–212. Chicago: Oriental Institute of the University of Chicago.

———. 2013. "Critical Approaches to Religion in China." *Critical Research on Religion* 1, no. 1: 95–101.

———. 2014. "Ritual Disjunctions: Ghosts, Philosophy, and Anthropology." In *The Ground Between: Anthropologists Engage Philosophy,* edited by Veena Das, Michael Jackson, Arthur Kleinman, and Bhrigupati Singh, 218–33. Durham, NC: Duke University Press.

———. 2015. *Path: What Chinese Philosophers Can Teach Us about the Good Life.* New York: Simon and Schuster.

Rabinow, Paul. 2008. *Marking Time: On the Anthropology of the Contemporary.* Princeton, NJ: Princeton University Press.

Radjou, Navi, Jaideep Prabhu, and Simone Ahuja. 2012. *Jugaad Innovation: Think Frugal, Be Flexible, Generate Breakthrough Growth.* San Francisco: Jossey-Bass.

Raheja, Gloria Goodwin. 1988. *The Poison in the Gift: Ritual, Prestation, and the Dominant Caste in a North Indian Village.* Chicago: University of Chicago Press.

———. 1993. "Caste Ideologies, Protest and the Power of the Dominant Caste: A Reply to Gregory and Heesterman." *Social Analysis,* no. 34 (December): 17–32.

Raheja, Gloria Goodwin, and Ann Grodzins Gold. 1994. *Listen to the Heron's Words.* Berkeley: University of California Press.

Ram, Kalpana. 2013. *Fertile Disorder: Spirit Possession and Its Provocation of the Modern.* Honolulu: University of Hawai'i Press.

Ramanujan, A. K. 1989. "Is There an Indian Way of Thinking? An Informal Essay." *Contributions to Indian Sociology* 23, no. 1: 41–58.

Ramberg, Lucinda. 2014. *Given to the Goddess: South Indian Devadasis and the Sexuality of Religion.* Durham, NC: Duke University Press.

Rappaport, Roy A. 1999. *Ritual and Religion in the Making of Humanity.* Cambridge: Cambridge University Press.

Rawat, Ramnarayan S. 2011. *Reconsidering Untouchability: Chamars and Dalit History in North India.* Bloomington: Indiana University Press.

Reader, Ian, and George J. Tanabe. 1998. *Practically Religious: Worldly Benefits and the Common Religion of Japan.* Honolulu: University of Hawai'i Press.

Ricoeur, Paul. 1984. *Time and Narrative.* Chicago: University of Chicago Press.

Robbins, Joel. 2004. *Becoming Sinners: Christianity and Moral Torment in a Papua New Guinea Society.* Berkeley: University of California Press.

Rubenstein, Mary-Jane. 2008. *Strange Wonder: The Closure of Metaphysics and the Opening of Awe.* New York: Columbia University Press.

Ruskin, John. 1849. *The Seven Lamps of Architecture.* London: Smith, Elder and Co.

Saler, Michael T. 2012. *As If: Modern Enchantment and the Literary Prehistory of Virtual Reality.* New York: Oxford University Press.

Saraswati, Baidyanath. 1979. *Pottery-Making Cultures and Indian Civilization.* New Delhi: Abhinav.

Sarma, Deepak. 2001. "When Is a Brahmin a 'Brahmabandhu,' an Unworthy or Wicked Brahmin? Or When Is the 'Adhikārin,' Eligible One, 'Anadhikārin,' Ineligible?" *Method and Theory in the Study of Religion* 13, no. 1: 82–90.

Sartre, Jean-Paul. [1960] 1963. *Search for a Method.* New York: Vintage Books.

Sassen, Saskia. 2000. "Spatialities and Temporalities of the Global: Elements for a Theorization." *Public Culture* 12, no. 1: 215–32.

Saunders, Dumbarton. 2003. " 'Catching the Light': Technologies of Power and Enchantment in Pre-Colombian Goldworking." In *Gold and Power in Ancient Costa Rica, Panama, and Colombia: A Symposium at Dumbarton Oaks, 9 and 10 October 1999,* edited by Jeffrey Quilter and John W. Hoopes, 15–48. Washington, DC: Dumbarton Oaks Research Library and Collections.

Schechner, Richard. 1974. "From Ritual to Theatre and Back: The Structure/Process of the Efficacy-Entertainment Dyad." *Educational Theatre Journal* 26, no. 4: 455–81.

———. 1993. *The Future of Ritual: Writings on Culture and Performance.* London: Routledge.

———. 2002. *Performance Studies: An Introduction.* London: Routledge.

Schielke, Samuli. 2012. "Surfaces of Longing: Cosmopolitan Aspiration and Frustration in Egypt." *City and Society* 24, no. 1: 29–37. doi:10.1111/j.15481744X.2012.01066.x.

Schwartz, Susan L. 2004. *Rasa: Performing the Divine in India*. New York: Columbia University Press.

Scott, Michael W. 2016. "To Be Makiran Is to See like Mr Parrot: The Anthropology of Wonder in Solomon Islands." *Journal of the Royal Anthropological Institute* 22, no. 3: 474–95.

Seligman, Adam B. 1997. *The Problem of Trust*. Princeton, NJ: Princeton University Press.

Seligman, Adam B., Robert P. Weller, Michael J. Puett, and Bennett Simon. 2008. *Ritual and Its Consequences: An Essay on the Limits of Sincerity*. Oxford: Oxford University Press.

Sheller, Mimi, and John Urry. 2006. *Mobile Technologies of the City*. London: Routledge.

Shipton, Parker MacDonald. 1989. *Bitter Money: Cultural Economy and Some African Meanings of Forbidden Commodities*. Washington, DC: American Anthropological Association.

———. 2009. *Mortgaging the Ancestors: Ideologies of Attachment in Africa*. New Haven, CT: Yale University Press.

Shove, Elizabeth, Frank Trentmann, and Richard Wilk, eds. 2009. *Time, Consumption and Everyday Life: Practice, Materiality and Culture*. Oxford: Bloomsbury Academic.

Shukla, D. N. 1993. *Vastu Sastra: Hindu Science of Architecture*. 2 vols. New Delhi: Munshiram Manoharlal.

Shulman, David Dean. 2012. *More Than Real: A History of the Imagination in South India*. Cambridge, MA: Harvard University Press.

Shyam Babu, D., and R. S. Khare. 2011. *Caste in Life: Experiencing Inequalities*. Delhi: Pearson.

Siegel, James T. 2011. *Objects and Objections of Ethnography*. New York: Fordham University Press.

Singh, K. S., ed. 1998. *People of India: Rajasthan*. Mumbai: Popular Prakashan.

Sinha, Surajit. 1967. "Caste in India: Its Essential Pattern of Socio-Cultural Integration." In *Caste and Race: Comparative Approaches*, edited by Anthony V. S. De Reuck and Julie Knight, 92–106. Boston: Little, Brown.

Sloterdijk, Peter. 2014. *Globes: Macrospherology*. Translated by Wieland Hoban. Cambridge, MA: MIT Press.

Smith, Jonathan Z. 1987. *To Take Place: Toward Theory in Ritual*. Chicago: University of Chicago Press.

Solnit, Rebecca. 2005. *A Field Guide to Getting Lost*. New York: Viking.

———. 2016. *Hope in the Dark: Untold Histories, Wild Possibilities*. Edinburgh: Canongate Books.

Srinivas, Lakshmi. 2016. *House Full: Indian Cinema and the Active Audience*. Chicago: University of Chicago Press.

Srinivas, M. N. 1951. "The Social Structure of a Mysore Village." *Economic Weekly* 3, nos. 42–43: 1051–56.

———. 1956. "A Note on Sanskritization and Westernization." *Far Eastern Quarterly* 15, no. 4: 481–96.

———. 1959. "The Dominant Caste in Rampura." *American Anthropologist* 61, no. 1: 1–16.

———. 1962a. *Caste in Modern India: And Other Essays.* Bombay: Asia Publishing House.

———. 1962b. "Changing Institutions and Values in Modern India." *Economic Weekly* 14, nos. 4–6: 131–37.

———. 1966. *Social Change in Modern India.* Berkeley: University of California Press.

———. 1973. "Itineraries of an Indian Social Anthropologist." *International Social Science Journal* 25, nos. 1–2: 129–48.

———. 1980. *The Remembered Village.* New Delhi: Oxford University Press.

———. 1992. *On Living in a Revolution and Other Essays.* Delhi: Oxford University Press.

———. 2003. "An Obituary on Caste as a System." *Economic and Political Weekly* 38, no. 5: 455–59.

Srinivas, Smriti. 2001. *Landscapes of Urban Memory: The Sacred and the Civic in India's High-Tech City.* Minneapolis: University of Minnesota Press.

Srinivas, Tulasi. 2006. "Divine Enterprise: Hindu Priests and Ritual Change in Neighbourhood Hindu Temples in Bangalore." *South Asia: Journal of South Asian Studies* 29, no. 3: 321–43.

———. 2015. "Doubtful Illusions: Magic, Wonder and the Politics of Virtue in the Sathya Sai Movement." *Journal of Asian and African Studies* 52, no. 4: 1–31.

Srivastava, Sanjay. 2007. *Passionate Modernity: Sexuality, Class, and Consumption in India.* New Delhi: Routledge.

———. 2012. "National Identity, Kitchens and Bedrooms: Gated Communities and New Narratives of Space in India." In *The Global Middle Classes: Theorizing through Ethnography*, edited by Rachel Heiman, Carla Freeman, and Mark Liechty, 57–85. Santa Fe, NM: SAR Press.

Staal, Frits. 1989. *Rules without Meaning : Ritual, Mantras, and the Human Sciences.* New York: P. Lang.

Stiglitz, Joseph E. 2002. *Globalization and Its Discontents.* New York: W. W. Norton.

Subramanian, Ajantha. 2015. "Making Merit: The Indian Institutes of Technology and the Social Life of Caste." *Comparative Studies in Society and History* 57, no. 2: 291–322.

Sundar, Aparna, and Nandini Sundar. 2014. *Civil Wars in South Asia: State, Sovereignty, Development.* Los Angeles: SAGE.

Sweetman, Will. 2003. *Mapping Hinduism: "Hinduism" and the Study of Indian Religions, 1600–1776.* Halle, Germany: Franckesche Stiftungen.

Sweetman, Will, and Aditya Malik. 2016. *Hinduism in India: Modern and Contemporary Movements.* New Delhi: SAGE.

Tambiah, Stanley Jeyaraja. 1979. *A Performative Approach to Ritual: Radcliffe-Brown Lecture.* London: Oxford University Press.

———. 1985. *Culture, Thought, and Social Action: An Anthropological Perspective.* Cambridge, MA: Harvard University Press.

Taussig, Michael T. 1993. *Mimesis and Alterity: A Particular History of the Senses.* New York: Routledge.

Tsing, Anna. 2005. *Friction: An Ethnography of Global Connection*. Princeton, NJ: Princeton University Press.

Turner, Frederick. 1986. "Reflexivity as Evolution in Thoreau's *Walden*." In *The Anthropology of Experience*, edited by Victor Turner and Edward M. Bruner, 33–45. Urbana–Champaign: University of Illinois Press.

Turner, Victor. 1967. *The Forest of Symbols: Aspects of Ndembu Ritual*. Ithaca, NY: Cornell University Press.

———. 1968. *The Drums of Affliction: A Study of Religious Processes among the Ndembu of Zambia*. Oxford: Clarendon.

———. 1969a. "Forms of Symbolic Action: Introduction." In *Forms of Symbolic Action: Proceedings of the 1969 Annual Spring Meeting of the American Ethnological Society*, edited by Robert F. Spencer, 3–25. Seattle: University of Washington Press.

———. 1969b. *The Ritual Process: Structure and Anti-Structure*. Chicago: Aldine.

———. 1974. *Dramas, Fields, and Metaphors: Symbolic Action in Human Society*. Ithaca, NY: Cornell University Press.

Turner, Victor, and Edward M. Bruner, eds. 1986. *The Anthropology of Experience*. Urbana–Champaign: University of Illinois Press.

Turner, Victor, and Edith Turner. 1978. *Image and Pilgrimage in Christian Culture*. New York: Columbia University Press.

Upadhya, Carol, and A. R. Vasavi, eds. 2008. *In an Outpost of the Global Economy: Work and Workers in India's Information Technology Industry*. New Delhi: Routledge.

Urry, John. 2007. *Mobilities*. Cambridge: Polity.

Vasalou, Sophia. 2012. *Practices of Wonder: Cross-Disciplinary Perspectives*. Cambridge: James Clarke.

———. 2015. *Wonder: A Grammar*. Albany: State University of New York Press.

Viswanath, Rupa. 2014. *The Pariah Problem: Caste, Religion, and the Social in Modern India*. New York: Columbia University Press.

Waghorne, Joanne Punzo. 2004. *Diaspora of the Gods: Modern Hindu Temples in an Urban Middle-Class World*. New York: Oxford University Press.

Walsh, Andrew. 2003. "'Hot Money' and Daring Consumption in a Northern Malagasy Sapphire-Mining Town." *American Ethnologist* 30, no. 2: 290–305. doi:10.1525/ae.2003.30.2.290.

Weatherford, Jack. 1997. *The History of Money: From Sandstone to Cyberspace*. New York: Crown.

Wilk, Richard R. 2003. "Colonial Time and TV: Television and Temporality in Belize." In *Television: Critical Concepts in Media and Cultural Studies*, vol. 1, edited by Toby Miller, 94–102. London: Routledge.

Willen, Sarah S., and Don Seeman. 2012. "Introduction: Experience and Inquiétude." *Ethnos* 40, no. 1: 1–23.

Yadava, S. D. S. 2006. *Followers of Krishna: Yadavas of India*. New Delhi: Lancers.

Zarrilli, Philip B. 1987. "Where the Hand [Is] . . ." *Asian Theatre Journal* 4, no. 2: 205–14.

Zigon, Jarrett. 2008. *Morality: An Anthropological Perspective*. Oxford: Berg.

Žižek, Slavoj. 2009. *First as Tragedy, Then as Farce*. New York: Verso.

INDEX

hope, 8–9, 23; and failure, 186; and money, 106; radical, 19, 213–15; and rituals, 15, 59, 101, 114, 125, 178; and waiting, 64, 67

identity, 6, 23, 39, 67
improvisation, 54, 103, 104; and adjustment, 91; ethics and, 107; ritual, 4, 6, 15, 23, 27, 87, 118, 147, 157, 160, 169, 171; and time, 193, 198; and trust, 136; and wonder, 64; in worship, 146
inequality, 64, 104–5, 125
information technology, 138–71
information technology industry, 13–14, 97, 104, 183; and temporality, 176–77, 178
innovation, 69, 103, 107, 120, 141, 142, 149–50
ippo, 174, 178, 192–94, 196. *See also* time

Jackson, Michael, 94, 140
Jameson, Frederick, 145
Jeffrey, Craig, 67

Kannada purity movements, 46, 47
Kanu Pandige procession, 60–69, 72–89, 93, 199
karma, 114, 125; and debt, 130–31; and poverty, 125–26; and wealth, 120
Karnataka Act, 25–26, 133
Keane, Webb, 148
Keen, Sam, 19
Krishna, 123–24, 144, 151, 175
Krishna Temple, 27–30, 144–46; and caste, 126–28; gold at, 111–12; Kanu Pandige procession at, 60–69, 72–89; music in, 155–56; photos of, 61, 81, 89, 141, 149, 210; taking photographs in, 157–60

land prices, 11, 221n22
land transactions, 48–51
landscape, 37–57
Lear, Jonathan, 215
Lefebvre, Henri, 66
Levi-Strauss, Claude, 12
Levinas, Emmanuel, 17
liminality, 36, 42. *See also* thresholds
locality, 38, 41, 43, 44
Locke, Peter, 16
loss, 9–11, 37, 80, 82, 136, 173; and Kanu Pandige procession, 63, 64, 78, 79, 90; and landscape, 39; of musicians, 156; and technology, 154–55; and *Vaastu*, 52, 53, 55; and wonder, 59, 215

Mahmood, Saba, 124
Mariamman Temple, 196–98; photo, 198
materiality, 115, 140–41, 150–51, 185
Mauss, Marcel, 115
Michaels, Axel, 185
middle class, 13–14
Mines, Diane, 116
mobility, 14–15, 32, 42, 62, 64, 72, 91; moral, 69–70
modernity, 9–10, 162, 201; ethics and, 93, 94; neoliberal, 11, 32, 63, 64, 179, 191, 208, 215; and rituals, 15, 73, 209, 212; technology and, 147–48, 156; and temporality, 173, 175–78; and time, 191, 195, 201; and trust, 137; urban, 86; and *viraha*, 79; waiting and, 66, 69
Molé, Noelle, 67
money: as adornment, 100–102, 103, 106, 113–18; and aesthetics, 107; and *alankaram*, 115; black, 48–51, 133; and ritual, 103–6, 110, 114–18; and rituals, 56; soiled, 131–33; and wonder, 99–137. *See also* economics
morality, 29, 69–70, 91–92, 245n11; erosion of, 174–75, 195, 203, 215; and gold, 112; ritual and, 203; and time, 174–75, 195; of wealth, 120. *See also* ethics
Munn, Nancy, 202
music, 152–57
Muzrai Department, 25, 26

najuka, 46–48
Nandi Temple, 188–90
Narasimha (deity), 206, 208, 211, 215
Narayan, Kirin, 22–23

Obama, Barack, 215
obsolescence, 174, 175, 183–86, 199
otherness, 7, 16, 22, 31
Otto, Rudolph, 7, 72, 73

Pandian, Anand, 9, 173, 175
Park, Katharine, 7
Parvati, 75, 139, 183
patience, 64, 66, 68, 69, 82, 91
patriarchy, 88, 90, 223n38
patrons, 47, 63, 65, 163
Penkower, Linda, 27
Perumal: photos, 81, 89, 161. *See also* Kanu Pandige procession
photography: of deities, 157–64
piety, 114–28, 155, 157, 174

wealth, 119–28

Weatherford, Jack, 128

wonder, 1–33, 36, 71–72, 207–15; and aesthetics, 72–73; and ethics, 92–94; landscape and, 56–57; and money, 99–137; in processions, 94; and rituals, 57, 73–74, 80, 83–84, 92–94, 107; technologies and, 138–71; and time, 174, 178, 191, 196, 205; urban development and, 37–41; and waiting, 68

worship, 83, 114, 128, 140, 144, 187; and music, 152, 155, 156; and technology, 146, 150–51, 162–63, 167. See also *pujas*

yugas, 51, 177, 187, 203